SANTA FE, TAOS & ALBUQUERQUE

3rd Edition

Where to Stay and Eat for All Budgets

Must-See Sights and Local Secrets

Ratings You Can Trust

Excerpted from *Fodor's New Mexico*

Fodor's Travel Publications   New York, Toronto, London, Sydney, Auckland

www.fodors.com

FODOR'S SANTA FE, TAOS & ALBUQUERQUE
Editors: Eric B. Wechter, Andrew Collins

Editorial Contributors: Lynne Arany, Andrew Collins, Francesca Drago, Barbara Floria, Georgia de Katona

Production Editor: Evangelos Vasilakis
Maps & Illustrations: David Lindroth, *cartographer;* Bob Blake, Rebecca Baer, *map editors;* William Wu, *information graphics*
Design: Fabrizio La Rocca, *creative director;* Guido Caroti, Siobhan O'Hare, *art directors;* Tina Malaney, Chie Ushio, Ann McBride, Jessica Walsh, Nora Rosansky, *designers;* Melanie Marin, *senior picture editor*
Cover Photo: (Detail of a sand painting, New Mexico): Robert Harding Images/ Masterfile
Production Manager: Angela L. McLean

3rd Edition

ISBN 978-0-307-48055-2

ISSN 1095-3876

SPECIAL SALES
This book is available at special discounts for bulk purchases for sales promotions or premiums. Special editions, including personalized covers, excerpts of existing books, and corporate imprints, can be created in large quantities for special needs. For more information, write to Special Markets/Premium Sales, 1745 Broadway, MD 6-2, New York, NY 10019, or e-mail specialmarkets@randomhouse.com.

AN IMPORTANT TIP & AN INVITATION
Although all prices, opening times, and other details in this book are based on information supplied to us at press time, changes occur all the time in the travel world, and Fodor's cannot accept responsibility for facts that become outdated or for inadvertent errors or omissions. So **always confirm information when it matters,** especially if you're making a detour to visit a specific place. Your experiences—positive and negative— matter to us. If we have missed or misstated something, **please write to us.** Share your opinion instantly through our online feedback center at fodors.com/contact-us.

PRINTED IN THE UNITED STATES OF AMERICA

10 9 8 7 6 5 4 3 2 1

Eugene Fodor:
The Spy Who Loved Travel

As Fodor's celebrates our 75th anniversary, we are honoring the colorful and adventurous life of Eugene Fodor, who revolutionized guidebook publishing in 1936 with his first book, *On the Continent, the Entertaining Travel Annual*.

Eugene Fodor's life seemed to leap off the pages of a great spy novel. Born in Hungary, he spoke six languages and graduated from the Sorbonne and the London School of Economics. During World War II he joined the Office of Strategic Services, the budding spy agency for the United States. He commanded the team that went behind enemy lines to liberate Prague, and recommended to Generals Eisenhower, Bradley, and Patton that Allied troops move to the capital city. After the war, Fodor worked as a spy in Austria, posing as a U.S. diplomat.

In 1949 Eugene Fodor—with the help of the CIA—established Fodor's Modern Guides. He was passionate about travel and wanted to bring his insider's knowledge of Europe to a new generation of sophisticated Americans who wanted to explore and seek out experiences beyond their borders. Among his innovations were annual updates, consulting local experts, and including cultural and historical perspectives and an emphasis on people—not just sites. As Fodor described it, "The main interest and enjoyment of foreign travel lies not only in 'the sites,' . . . but in contact with people whose customs, habits, and general outlook are different from your own."

Eugene Fodor died in 1991, but his legacy, Fodor's Travel, continues. It is now one of the world's largest and most trusted brands in travel information, covering more than 600 destinations worldwide in guidebooks, on Fodors.com, and in ebooks and iPhone apps. Technology and the accessibility of travel may be changing, but Eugene Fodor's unique storytelling skills and reporting style are behind every word of today's Fodor's guides.

Our editors and writers continue to embrace Eugene Fodor's vision of building personal relationships through travel. We invite you to join the Fodor's community at fodors.com/community and share your experiences with like-minded travelers. Tell us when we're right. Tell us when we're wrong. And share fantastic travel secrets that aren't yet in Fodor's. Together, we will continue to deepen our understanding of our world.

Happy 75th Anniversary, Fodor's! Here's to many more.

Tim Jarrell, Publisher

CONTENTS

ABOUT THIS BOOK

Our Ratings

Sometimes you find terrific travel experiences, and sometimes they just find you. But usually the burden is on you to select the right combination of experiences. That's where our ratings come in.

As travelers we've all discovered a place so wonderful that its worthiness is obvious, a place is so unique that superlatives don't do it justice. These sights, properties, and experiences get our highest rating, **Fodor's Choice,** indicated by orange stars.

Black stars highlight sights and properties we deem **Highly Recommended,** places that our writers, editors, and readers praise for consistency and excellence.

By default, there's another category: any place we include in this book is by definition worth your time, unless we say otherwise. And we will.

Disagree with any of our choices? Care to nominate a place or suggest that we rate one more highly? Visit our feedback center at www. fodors.com/feedback.

Budget Well

Hotel and restaurant price categories from ¢ to $$$$ are defined in the opening pages of each chapter. For attractions, we always give standard adult admission fees; reductions are usually available for children, students, and senior citizens. Want to pay with plastic? **AE, D, DC, MC, V** following restaurant and hotel listings indicate whether American Express, Discover, Diners Club, MasterCard, and Visa are accepted.

Restaurants

Unless we state otherwise, restaurants are open for lunch and dinner daily. We mention dress only when there's a specific requirement and reservations only when they're essential or not accepted—it's always best to book ahead.

Hotels

Hotels have private bath, phone, TV, and air-conditioning and operate on the European Plan (EP, meaning without meals), unless we specify that they use the Continental Plan (CP, with a Continental breakfast), Breakfast Plan (BP, with a full breakfast), or Modified American Plan (MAP, with breakfast and dinner) or are all-inclusive (including all meals and most activities).

We always list facilities but not whether you'll be charged an extra fee to use them.

Many Listings

★	Fodor's Choice
★	Highly recommended
⊠	Physical address
↔	Directions or Map coordinates
⌂	Mailing address
☎	Telephone
🖷	Fax
⊕	On the Web
✍	E-mail
🎫	Admission fee
☉	Open/closed times
Ⓜ	Metro stations
⊟	Credit cards

Hotels & Restaurants

🏨	Hotel
🛏	Number of rooms
⚴	Facilities
❑	Meal plans
✕	Restaurant
✎	Reservations
🏛	Dress code
⌇	Smoking
🍸	BYOB

Outdoors

🏌	Golf
⛺	Camping

Other

♻	Family-friendly
⇨	See also
⊠	Branch address
☞	Take note

Experience Santa Fe, Taos & Albuquerque

WORD OF MOUTH

"We plan to visit historical sites, parks for hiking (definitely Bandelier National Monument) . . . rafting with Los Rios in Taos (just booked yesterday, sounds fun!), and other activities I'm sure I haven't even imagined yet. It seems the area around Sante Fe is chock-a-block with wonders."

—adventuredays

WHAT'S WHERE

Numbers correspond to chapters

2 Albuquerque. Albuquerque is the gateway to New Mexico, by far the state's largest city, and its business and education capital. Its residents—like its architecture, food, and art—reflect a confluence of Native American, Hispanic, and Anglo culture.

3 Santa Fe. On a 7,000-foot-high plateau at the base of the Sangre de Cristo Mountains, Santa Fe is one of the most visited small cities in the United States, with an abundance of museums, one-of-a-kind cultural events,

art galleries, and distinctive restaurants and shops.

4 Taos. World-famous museums and galleries, stunning views of the desert and Sangre de Cristo Mountains, and charming, cottonwood-shaded streets lined with adobe buildings are a few of this small town's attractions. Nearby, Taos Pueblo and Taos Ski Valley are major draws.

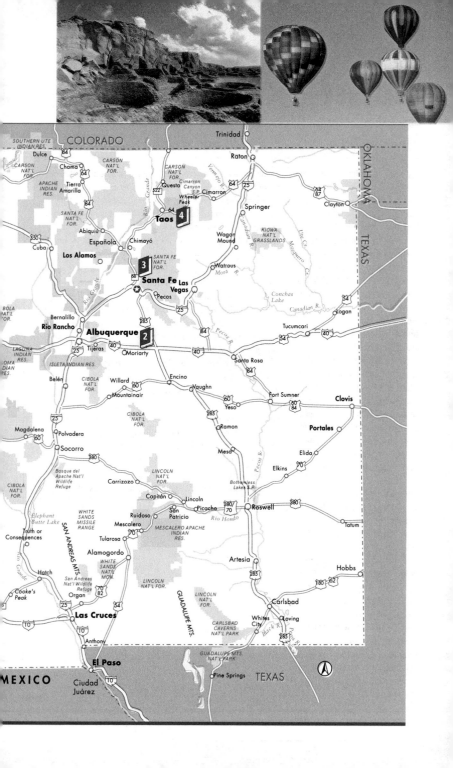

PLANNER

When to Go

The cool, dry climates of Santa Fe and Taos are as much a lure in summer as the skiing in Taos and Santa Fe is in winter. Christmas is a wonderful time to be in New Mexico because of Native American ceremonies as well as the Hispanic religious folk plays, special foods, and musical events. Santa Fe is at its most festive at this time, with incense and piñon smoke sweetening the air and the darkness of winter illuminated by thousands of *farolitos* (glowing paper-bag lanterns), which line walkways, doorways, and rooftops. Most ceremonial dances at the pueblos occur in summer, early fall, and at Christmas and Easter. Other major events—including the Santa Fe Opera, Chamber Music Festival, and Native American and Spanish markets—are geared to the heavy tourist season of July and August. The Santa Fe Fiesta and New Mexico State Fair in Albuquerque are held in September, and the Albuquerque International Balloon Fiesta in October. Hotel rates are generally highest during the peak summer season but fluctuate less than those in most major resort areas. If you plan to come in summer, be sure to make reservations in advance. Avoid the heaviest crowds by coming in spring or fall.

Flying in and Getting Around

New Mexico is easy to reach by plane but a full day's drive from major metro areas in the neighboring states of Arizona, Utah, Colorado, Oklahoma, and Texas. Unless you're a big fan of long road trips (the scenery getting here is spectacular, especially coming from Arizona, Utah, and Colorado), it generally makes the most sense to fly here.

Northern and central New Mexico's main air gateway is Albuquerque International Sunport (ABQ), which is served by virtually all of the nation's major domestic airlines as well as some smaller regional ones; there are direct flights from all major West Coast and Midwest cities and a number of big East Coast cities. From here it's an easy 60-minute drive to Santa Fe, or a 2½-hour drive to Taos (shuttle services are available). Santa Fe Municipal Airport (SAF) also has daily service on American Airlines to Dallas and Los Angeles.

A car is your best way to get around the region, whether traveling among New Mexico's main cities, or even exploring them in depth. You can see much of Downtown Santa Fe and Taos, on foot or using buses, but in Albuquerque a car is really a necessity for any serious touring and exploring.

For more flight information and ground transportation options, see the Travel Smart section at the back of this book.

WHAT'S NEW IN NEW MEXICO

Happy Anniversary

Santa Fe celebrated its 400th anniversary in 2010, and Albuquerque enjoyed its tricentennial in 2006. The entire state gets into the action in 2012, when New Mexico ushers in 100 years of statehood—it had been a territory before that, dating to when the United States took possession following the 1848 Treaty of Guadalupe Hidalgo. Many events, from museum exhibits to arts presentations, are being planned to take place throughout the year. You can learn more at ⊕ *www.nmcentennial.org.*

History in a New Light

Santa Fe's venerable **Palace of the Governors,** the oldest public building in America, is the site of the state's newest major attraction, the **New Mexico History Museum,** which opened in 2009. The sleek facility lies adjacent to and behind the palace. Exhibits here tell the rich and complex story of the state's founding through an incredible collection of artifacts that, up to this point, only made brief appearances in temporary exhibits at the Palace of the Governors. The 20,000-square-foot facility uses interactive, state-of-the-art audio and visual technology to bring New Mexico's heritage to life—a refreshing contrast to the sometimes static methods many of the state's museums employ in their exhibits (in fairness, some of the museums occupy extremely old, historic buildings).

Albuquerque's Hotel Renaissance

The Duke City's lodging landscape has been mostly dominated by predictable chains over the years, but three hip, elegant, and distinctive new properties have shaken things up considerably. Two of these hotels are historic and situated Downtown: the glamorous Andaluz is a LEED-certified, arty makeover of the historic La Posada with a swanky restaurant (Lucia), while the Hotel Parq Central, opened in late 2010 in Downtown's funky EDo section, is inside a completely reimagined 1920s hotel. The rooftop Apothecary bar is a sly nod to the building's medical legacy. A 10-minute drive south of the airport on the Isleta Pueblo, the Hard Rock Casino & Resort is an upscale, stylish addition to the growing selection of hotels that have opened on Indian pueblos around the state in recent years (Buffalo Thunder, Hyatt Regency Tamaya, Sandia, and Inn of the Mountain Gods are a few others).

New Trails to Santa Fe

Well, contrails anyway. After years of little or no commercial air service, Santa Fe Municipal Airport (SAF) has finally ushered in daily service from two of the nation's busiest airports, DFW in Dallas and LAX in Los Angeles, on American Eagle (the regional carrier of American Airlines). The service has been highly popular, making it not just easier to reach Santa Fe from many parts of the country, but also points north, such as Las Vegas and Taos, as Santa Fe's small, convenient airport is an hour closer to these areas than Albuquerque. The service comes on the heels of the expansion of **New Mexico Railrunner Express** rail service, from Albuquerque to Santa Fe's newly developed **Railyard District.** New businesses keep popping up here, including a massive branch of REI, a much-anticipated outpost of the wildly popular Flying Star restaurant-coffeehouse empire, and numerous galleries and boutiques. The district's fantastic farmers' market was named one of the nation's best by CNN in 2010.

QUINTESSENTIAL NEW MEXICO

Chile Fever

Nothing sets New Mexican food apart from other cuisines so distinctly as the chile pepper, permutations of which locals will heap upon just about any dish, from blue-corn enchiladas to turkey sandwiches. Chiles have long been a staple of both Hispanic and indigenous cuisines in the region, and they come in two varieties: red or green. Depending on the restaurant, or even the particular batch, green *or* red may be the hotter variety. Servers always ask which kind you'd prefer, and if you can't decide, try them both by answering "Christmas."

Usher in the Holidays, Santa Fe Style

Christmas in Santa Fe is perhaps the city's most festive time of year. During the 10 days of Las Posadas Novena at San Miguel Mission, the story of Mary and Joseph's journey to Bethlehem is reenacted. The Feast Day of Our Lady of Guadalupe, December 12, is grandly celebrated at the Santuario de Guadalupe, and Christmas at the Palace resounds with hours of festive music emanating from the Palace of the Governors in mid-December. The traditional Christmas Eve stroll down Canyon Road, complete with snacks and costumed carolers, is the way to celebrate the night before Christmas when in Santa Fe.

The Cradle of Creativity

New Mexico draws all kinds of vibrant spirits, both to visit and relocate, but the state is particularly a magnet for artists. Santa Fe, with its dozens of prestigious galleries and art museums, claims the third-largest art market in the nation, after New York City and Los Angeles. The much smaller town of Taos claims a similarly exciting gallery scene, and in the state's largest city, Albuquerque, galleries have popped up all over the city in recent years.

Although New Mexico's prestigious gallery scene is concentrated in its cities,

If you want to get a sense of New Mexico culture, and indulge in some of its pleasures, start by familiarizing yourself with the rituals of daily life. These are a few highlights that you can take part in with relative ease.

many of the state's most talented artists live in small, scenic villages and work out of their home studios. The best way to visit them—and also discover some of the most charming and distinctive communities in the state—is to participate in a Studio Tour Weekend. More than 40 of these events are held year-round, most of them from early fall through December. During tour weekends, the private studios in a given town open their doors to visitors—it's a great time to converse with artists, shop for their creations, and get off the beaten path. Some particularly noteworthy studio tours include those in Galisteo (late October), a funky little village near Santa Fe; and Abiquiu (mid-October), where Georgia O'Keeffe lived and some 70 artists participate.

Peak Experiences

With nearly 50 peaks towering higher than 12,000 feet, New Mexico is a wonderland for people who love the mountains. The southern spine of the Rocky Mountains range, known as the Sangre de Cristos, runs right through the center of the state, looming over Taos and Santa Fe. The stunning Sandia Mountains face the city of Albuquerque, and similarly beautiful peaks dot the landscape as far south as Cloudcroft. Much of the Land of Enchantment's high country is accessible. Hiking trails lead to some of the highest points in the state, and several first-rate ski areas have been carved out of New Mexico's mountains, including Taos Ski Valley, Angel Fire, and Ski Santa Fe to the north.

TOP ATTRACTIONS

The Santa Fe Plaza

The heart of historic Santa Fe, the Plaza has been the site of a bullring, fiestas, and fandangos. It's the center of many annual festivities and much of the town's activity. Explore the narrow streets, stroll under portals, and across ancient cobbled streets. Sip coffee on the Plaza, take in a museum or two (or three) and marvel at the cathedral. The New Mexico History Museum and Palace of the Governors are great places to start to gain a sense of the history and cultures influencing this area.

Museum of International Folk Art

A case could be made for almost any museum in Santa Fe as the most noteworthy one in New Mexico, but it's this distinct facility on Museum Hill that stands out not only for its regional exhibits but also for having one of the world's most acclaimed collections of folk art. Collections here appeal equally to kids and adults, and the two shops on-site carry an astounding array of crafts and books.

Bandelier National Monument

An easy and scenic drive from both Santa Fe and Taos, this 23,000-acre expanse of deep canyons, rushing waterfalls, and high-desert mesas contains remarkably well-preserved cliff dwellings and ceremonial kivas that trace the past millennium of the region's thriving indigenous life and culture.

Taos Art Museum and Fechin House

Northern New Mexico's reputation as an internationally renowned arts center began with the establishment of an artists' colony in Taos in 1900, and this former home of one of the movement luminaries—Nicolai Fechin—provides a rich overview of the era. More than 50 Taos masters are represented here.

Taos Pueblo

A United Nations World Heritage Site, this is the largest collection of multistory pueblo dwellings in the United States. The pueblo today appears much as it did when the first Spanish explorers arrived in New Mexico in 1540. The adobe walls glistening with mica caused the conquistadors to believe they had discovered one of the fabled Seven Cities of Gold.

National Hispanic Cultural Center

With a mix of architecturally prominent performance centers, a terrific art museum, and an excellent restaurant serving authentic regional cuisine, this comprehensive facility in a historic Albuquerque neighborhood showcases Latino arts and culture throughout the Western Hemisphere, but with a decided New Mexico emphasis.

Old Town Plaza, Albuquerque

Don Francisco Cuervo y Valdés, a provincial governor of New Mexico, laid out this small plaza in 1706. Today the plaza is tranquil, with shade trees, wrought-iron benches, and a graceful white gazebo. Roughly 200 shops, restaurants, cafés, galleries, and several cultural sites in *placitas* (small plazas) and lanes surround Old Town Plaza. During fiestas Old Town comes alive with mariachi bands and dancing señoritas.

TOP EXPERIENCES

Skiing Taos Ski Valley

Often recognized by major ski magazines for its first-rate ski school and demanding trails, Taos Ski Valley is the state's most famous winter-sports destination—it comprises a friendly, handsomely developed village of condos and restaurants. Other nearby northern New Mexico venues with great alpine and cross-country skiing, snowboarding, snowshoeing, and snowmobiling include Red River, Angel Fire, Santa Fe, and Sandia (just east of Albuquerque).

Browsing the Art Markets of Santa Fe

New Mexico's most popular destination, Santa Fe is also one of the great cultural treasures of the Southwest, packed as it is with first-rate museums. The best season for appreciating the arts is summer, when the Santa Fe Opera comes into full swing, as does the Santa Fe Chamber Music Festival. But the biggest weekends of summer are when the legendary Indian and Spanish markets come to town, and there's no more exciting time to take in Santa Fe. The Spanish Market dominates the city's historic Plaza the last weekend of July and draws more than 250 local artisans versed in the traditional regional practices of straw appliqué, hide painting, metalwork, retablo and santo carving, weaving, and furniture making. During the third weekend in August, more than 1,200 artists representing some 100 tribes throughout North America display their jewelry, textiles, paintings, and other fine works during the Santa Fe Indian Market. Additional antiques-related markets take place in mid-August, and the city hosts a smaller but still excellent Spanish Winter Market in December.

Taking the Tramway to Albuquerque's Sandia Peak

Take the aerial tramway to the top of the Sandia Mountains for an incomparable view over Albuquerque. You can ride the world's longest aerial tram (it climbs over 5,000 feet in elevation, and covers nearly 3 mi in distance) to the top, take in the soaring panoramas of the entire Rio Grande Valley from Santa Fe down toward Socorro, and enjoy drinks plus lunch or dinner at the lofty High Finance Restaurant & Tavern, which clings precipitously to the sheer edge of Sandia Peak. But if you have time, use the tram as a means to an exhilarating outdoor adventure—at the top you can access the Sandia Peak Ski Area in winter for fun in the snow, or for challenging mountain biking down these very slopes in summer. You can hike on short and easy trails or choose far more challenging ones, including the famed La Luz trail, which descends down the face of the Sandias back into Albuquerque's Northeast Heights neighborhood. You can also drive to the ski area and ranger station (and then hike or take the chairlift to the tram station)—this beautiful drive takes about 45 minutes.

IF YOU LIKE

Historic Sites

There's no state in the Union with a richer historical heritage than New Mexico, which contains not only buildings constructed by Europeans well before the Pilgrims set foot in Massachusetts but also still-inhabited pueblos that date back more than a millennium.

The entire state can feel like one massive archaeological dig, with its mystical Native American ruins and weathered adobe buildings. Stately plazas laid out as fortifications by the Spanish in the 17th century still anchor many communities, including Albuquerque, Las Cruces, Las Vegas, Santa Fe, and Taos. And side trips from these cities lead to ghost towns and deserted pueblos that have been carefully preserved by historians. Here are some of the top draws for history buffs.

One of the most well-preserved and fascinating ruin sites on the continent, the ancient **Chaco Culture National Historical Park** in Chaco Canyon was home to the forerunners of today's Pueblo Indians more than 1,000 years ago.

Santa Fe's **San Miguel Mission** is a simple, earth-hue adobe structure built in about 1625—it's the oldest church still in use in the continental United States.

A United Nations World Heritage Site, the 1,000-year-old **Taos Pueblo** has the largest collection of multistory pueblo dwellings in the United States.

The oldest public building in the United States, the Pueblo-style **Palace of the Governors** anchors Santa Fe's historic Plaza and has served as the residence for 100 Spanish, Native American, Mexican, and American governors; it's now the state history museum.

Hiking Adventures

At just about every turn in the Land of Enchantment, whether you're high in the mountains or low in a dramatic river canyon, hiking opportunities abound. Six national forests cover many thousands of acres around New Mexico, as do 34 state parks and a number of other national and state monuments and recreation areas. The ski areas make for great mountaineering during the warmer months, and the state's many Native American ruins are also laced with trails.

Hiking is a year-round activity in New Mexico, as you can virtually always find temperate weather somewhere in the state. Consider the following areas for an engaging ramble.

About midway between Santa Fe and Albuquerque, **Kasha-Katuwe Tent Rocks National Monument** is so named because its bizarre rock formations look like tepees rising over a narrow box canyon. The hike here is relatively short and only moderately challenging, offering plenty of bang for the buck.

One of the more strenuous hiking challenges in the state is **Wheeler Peak**. The 8-mi trek to New Mexico's highest point (elevation 13,161 feet) rewards visitors with stunning views of the Taos Ski Valley.

From the northeastern fringes of Albuquerque, **La Luz Trail** winds 9 mi (with an elevation gain of more than 3,000 feet) to Sandia Crest.

Burger Joints

In a state with plenty of open ranching land and an appreciation for no-nonsense, homestyle eating, it's no surprise that locals debate intensely about where to find the best burger in town.

In New Mexico, the preferred meal is a green-chile cheeseburger—a culinary delight that's available just about anyplace that serves hamburgers. Burgers served in tortillas or sopaipillas also earn kudos, and increasingly, you'll find establishments serving terrific buffalo, lamb, turkey, and even tuna and veggie burgers.

With about 75 locations throughout the state, the New Mexico chain **Blake's Lotaburger** has become a cult favorite for its juicy Angus beef burgers. Just order at the counter, take a number, and wait for your meal (which is best accompanied by a bag of seasoned fries).

A friendly and funky little roadhouse about a 15-minute drive south of Santa Fe, **Bobcat Bite** is a much-loved source of outstanding green-chile burgers. Loyalists order them rare.

Feasting on a burger at the **Mineshaft Tavern** is a big reason to stop in the tiny village of Madrid, as you drive up the fabled Turquoise Trail from Albuquerque to Santa Fe. This rollicking bar serves hefty patties.

Dramatic Photo Ops

New Mexico's spectacular landscapes and crystal-clear atmosphere can help just about any amateur with a decent camera produce professional-quality photos. Many of the common scenes around the state seem tailor-made for photography sessions: terra-cotta-hued adobe buildings against azure blue skies, souped-up lowrider automobiles cruising along wide-open highways, and rustic fruit and chile stands by the side of the road. In summer, dramatic rain clouds contrast with vermilion sunsets to create memorable images. Come fall, shoot the foliage of cottonwood and aspen trees, and in winter, snap the state's snowcapped mountains.

The **High Road to Taos,** a stunning drive from Santa Fe with a rugged alpine backdrop, encompasses rolling hillsides studded with orchards and tiny villages.

More than 1,000 balloons lift off from the **Albuquerque International Balloon Fiesta,** affording shutterbugs countless opportunities for great photos—whether from the ground or the air. And there are year-round opportunities to soar above the city.

The dizzyingly high **Rio Grande Gorge Bridge,** near Taos, stands 650 feet above the Rio Grande—the reddish rocks dotted with green scrub contrast brilliantly against the blue sky.

GREAT ITINERARIES

ALBUQUERQUE TO TAOS: NEW MEXICO MOUNTAIN HIGH

Day 1: Albuquerque

Start out by strolling through the shops of Old Town Plaza, then visit the New Mexico Museum of Natural History and Science. Also be sure to check out the Albuquerque Museum of Art and History, and try to make your way over to the Albuquerque Biological Park, which contains the aquarium, zoo, and botanic park. For lunch, try the atmospheric Church Street Café or the sophisticated St. Clair Winery and Bistro, both in Old Town.

Later in the afternoon, you'll need a car to head east a couple of miles along Central to reach the University of New Mexico's main campus and the nearby Nob Hill District. Start with a stroll around the UNM campus with its many historic adobe buildings; if you have time, pop inside either the Maxwell Museum of Anthropology or the University Art Museum. When you're finished here, walk east along Central into Nob Hill and check out the dozens of offbeat shops. If it's summer, meaning that you still have some time before the sun sets, it's worth detouring from Old Town to Far Northeast Heights (a 15-minute drive), where you can take the Sandia Peak Aerial Tramway 2.7 mi up to Sandia Peak for spectacular sunset views of the city. Either way, plan to have dinner back in Nob Hill, perhaps at Zinc or Flying Star. If you're still up for more fun, check out one of the neighborhood's lively lounges; head back Downtown for a bit of late-night barhopping.

Days 2 and 3: Santa Fe

On Day 2, head to Santa Fe early in the morning by driving up the scenic Turquoise Trail; once you arrive in town, explore the adobe charms of the Downtown central Plaza. Visit the Palace of the Governors and check out the adjacent New Mexico History Museum. At the nearby Museum of Fine Arts you can see works by Southwestern artists, and a short drive away at the Museum of International Folk Art you can see how different cultures in New Mexico and elsewhere in the world have expressed themselves artistically. Give yourself time to stroll the narrow, adobe-lined streets of this charming Downtown, and treat yourself to some authentic New Mexican cuisine in the evening, perhaps with a meal at La Choza or Maria's.

On your second day in town, plan to walk a bit. Head east from the Plaza up to Canyon Road and peruse the galleries. Have lunch at one of the restaurants midway uphill, such as Geronimo or El Farol. From here, you can either continue walking 2 mi up Canyon, and then Upper Canyon, roads to the Randall Davey Audubon Center, or you can take a cab there. If you're up for some exercise, hike the foothills—there are trails within the center's property and also from the free parking area (off Cerro Gordo Road) leading into the Dale Ball Trail Network. You might want to try one of Santa Fe's truly stellar, upscale restaurants your final night in town, either La Boca or the restaurant at the Inn of the Anasazi.

Day 4: Abiquiu

From Santa Fe, drive north up U.S. 285/84 through Española, and then take U.S. 84 from Española up to Abiquiu, the fabled community where Georgia

O'Keeffe lived and painted for much of the final five decades of her life. On your way up, before you reach Española, make the detour toward Los Alamos and spend the morning visiting Bandelier National Monument. In Abiquiu, plan to tour Georgia O'Keeffe's home.

Days 5 and 6: Taos

Begin by strolling around Taos Plaza, taking in the galleries and crafts shops. Head south two blocks to visit the Harwood Museum. Then walk north on Paseo del Pueblo to the Taos Art Museum and Fechin House. In the afternoon, drive out to the Rio Grande Gorge Bridge. Return the way you came to see the Millicent Rogers Museum on your way back to town. In the evening, stop in at the Adobe Bar at the Taos Inn and plan for dinner at Graham's Grille. On the second day, drive out to Taos Pueblo in the morning and tour the ancient village while the day is fresh. Return to town and go to the Blumenschein Home and Museum, lunching afterward at the Dragonfly Café. After lunch drive out to La Hacienda de los Martinez for a look at early life in Taos and then to Ranchos de Taos to see the San Francisco de Asís Church.

Day 7: The High Road

On your final day, drive back down toward Albuquerque and Santa Fe via the famed High Road, which twists through a series of tiny, historic villages—including Peñasco, Truchas, and Chimayó. In the latter village, be sure to stop by El Santuario de Chimayó. Have lunch at Léona's Restaurante or Rancho de Chimayó, and do a little shopping at Ortega's Weaving Shop. From here, it's a 30-minute drive to Santa Fe.

GLOSSARY OF TERMS

Menu Guide

Aguacate: Spanish for avocado, the key ingredient of guacamole.

Albóndigas: Meatballs, usually cooked with rice in a meat broth.

Bizcochitos: Buttery cookies flavored with cinnamon and anise seeds and served typically at Christmas but available throughout the year.

Burrito: A warm flour tortilla wrapped around meat, beans, and vegetables and smothered in chiles and cheese; many New Mexicans also love breakfast burritos (filled with any combination of the above, along with eggs and, typically, bacon or sausage and potatoes).

Calabacitas: Summer squash, usually served with corn, chiles, and other vegetables.

Carne adovada: Red-chile-marinated pork (or, occasionally, chicken).

Chalupa: A corn tortilla deep-fried in the shape of a bowl, filled with pinto beans (sometimes meat), and topped with cheese, guacamole, sour cream, lettuce, tomatoes, and salsa.

Chicharrones: Fried pork rinds.

Chilaquiles: Often served at breakfast, this casserole-like dish consists of small pieces of fried tortillas baked with red or green chiles, bits of chicken or cheese, and sometimes eggs.

Chile relleno: A poblano pepper peeled, stuffed with cheese or a special mixture of spicy ingredients, dipped in batter, and fried.

Chile: A stewlike dish with Texas origins that typically contains beans, beef, and red chile.

Chiles: New Mexico's infamous hot peppers, which come in an endless variety of sizes and in various degrees of hotness, from the thumb-size jalapeño to the smaller and often hotter serrano. They can be canned or fresh, dried or cut up into salsa. Most traditional New Mexican dishes are served either with green, red, or both types of chiles (ask for "Christmas" when indicating to your server that you'd like both red and green). Famous regional uses for green chile include green-chile stew (usually made with shredded pork), green-chile cheeseburgers, and green-chile-and-cheese tamales.

Chimichanga: The same as a burrito, only deep-fried and topped with a dab of sour cream or salsa. (The chimichanga was allegedly invented in Tucson, Arizona.)

Chipotle: A dried smoked jalapeño with a smoky, almost sweet, chocolaty flavor.

Chorizo: Well-spiced Spanish sausage, made with pork and red chiles.

Enchilada: A rolled or flat corn tortilla filled with meat, chicken, seafood, or cheese, an enchilada is covered with chile and baked. The ultimate enchilada is made with blue Native American corn tortillas. New Mexicans order them flat, sometimes topped with a fried egg.

Fajitas: A Tex-Mex dish of grilled beef, chicken, fish, or roasted vegetables and served with peppers, onions, and pico de gallo, served with tortillas; traditionally known as *arracheras*.

Flauta: A tortilla filled with cheese or meat and rolled into a flutelike shape ("flauta" means flute) and lightly fried.

Frijoles refritos: Refried beans, often seasoned with lard or cheese.

Frito Pie: Originally from Texas but extremely popular in New Mexican diners and short-order restaurants, this savory, humble casserole consists of Fritos snack

chips layered with chile, cheese, green onions, and pinto beans.

Guacamole: Mashed avocado, mixed with tomatoes, garlic, onions, lemon juice, and chiles, used as a dip, a side dish, or a topping.

Hatch: A small southern New Mexico town in the Mesilla Valley, known for its outstanding production and quality of both green and red chiles. The "Hatch" name often is found on canned chile food products.

Huevos rancheros: New Mexico's answer to eggs Benedict—eggs doused with chile and sometimes melted cheese, served on top of a corn tortilla (they're best with a side order of chorizo).

Nopalitos: The pads of the prickly pear cactus, typically cut up and served uncooked in salads or baked or stir-fried as a vegetable side dish. (The tangy-sweet, purplish-red fruit of the prickly pear is often used to make juice drinks and margaritas.)

Posole: Resembling popcorn soup, this is a sublime marriage of lime, hominy, pork, chiles, garlic, and spices.

Quesadilla: A folded flour tortilla filled with cheese and meat or vegetables and warmed or lightly fried so the cheese melts.

Queso: Cheese; an ingredient in many Mexican and Southwestern recipes (cheddar or Jack is used most commonly in New Mexican dishes).

Ristra: String of dried red chile peppers, often used as decoration.

Salsa: Finely chopped concoction of green and red chile peppers, mixed with onion, garlic, and other spices.

Sopaipilla: Puffy deep-fried bread that's similar to Navajo fry bread (found in Arizona and western New Mexico); it's served either as a dessert with honey drizzled over it or savory as a meal stuffed with pinto beans or meat.

Taco: A corn or flour tortilla served either soft, or baked or fried and served in a hard shell; it's then stuffed with vegetables or spicy meat and garnished with shredded lettuce, chopped tomatoes, onions, and grated cheese.

Tacos al carbón: Shredded pork cooked in a mole sauce and folded into corn tortillas.

Tamale: Ground corn made into a dough, often filled with finely ground pork and red chiles; it's steamed in a corn husk.

Tortilla: A thin pancake made of corn or wheat flour, a tortilla is used as bread, as an edible "spoon," and as a container for other foods. Locals place butter in the center of a hot tortilla, roll it up, and eat it as a scroll.

Trucha en terra-cotta: Fresh trout wrapped in corn husks and baked in clay.

Verde: Spanish for "green," as in chile verde (a green chile sauce).

Perhaps more than any other region in the United States, New Mexico has its own distinctive cuisine and architectural style, both heavily influenced by Native American, Spanish-colonial, Mexican, and American frontier traditions. The brief glossary that follows explains terms used frequently in this book.

Art and Architecture

Adobe: A brick of sun-dried earth and clay, usually stabilized with straw; a structure made of adobe.

Banco: A small bench, or banquette, often upholstered with handwoven textiles, that gracefully emerges from adobe walls.

Bulto: Folk-art figures of a santo (saint), usually carved from wood.

Camposanto: A graveyard.

Capilla: A chapel.

Casita: Literally "small house," this term is generally used to describe a separate guesthouse.

Cerquita: A spiked, wrought-iron, rectangular fence, often marking grave sites.

Coyote fence: A type of wooden fence that surrounds many New Mexico homes; it comprises branches, usually from cedar or aspen trees, arranged vertically and wired tightly together.

Farolito: Small votive candles set in paperbag lanterns, farolitos are popular at Christmastime. The term is used in northern New Mexico only. People in Albuquerque and points south call the lanterns *luminarias,* which in the north is the term for the bonfires of Christmas Eve.

Heishi: Technically the word means "shell necklace," but the common usage refers to necklaces made with rounded, thin, disc-shaped beads in various materials, such as turquoise or jet.

Hornos: Domed outdoor ovens made of plastered adobe or concrete blocks.

Kiva: A circular ceremonial room, built at least partially underground, used by Pueblo Indians of the Southwest. Entrance is gained from the roof.

Kiva fireplace: A corner fireplace whose round form resembles that of a kiva.

Nicho: A built-in shelf cut into an adobe or stucco wall.

Placita: A small plaza.

Portal: A porch or large covered area adjacent to a house.

Pueblo Revival (also informally called Pueblo style): Most homes in this style, modeled after the traditional dwellings of the Southwest Pueblo Indians, are cube or rectangle shaped. Other characteristics are flat roofs, thick adobe or stucco walls, small windows, rounded corners, and viga beams.

Retablo: Holy image painted on wood or tin.

Santero: Maker of religious images.

Terrones adobes: Adobe cut from the ground rather than formed from mud.

Viga: Horizontal roof beam made of logs, usually protruding from the side of the house.

Albuquerque

WORD OF MOUTH

"Absolutely rent a car! Public transportation is available [bus] but it isn't the easiest or most convenient for visitors wanting to go to popular sites in and around ABQ. Most of the busses are really for locals going to and from work, etc. There is a rail line that runs from ABQ to Santa Fe and would work well. But to have the most flexibility, rent a car."

—DebitNM

Updated
by Andrew
Collins

A bird's-eye view of Albuquerque reveals a typical Sun Belt city, stretching more than 100 square mi with no grand design, architectural or otherwise, to hold it together. The city's growth seems as free-spirited as the hot-air balloons that take part in the Albuquerque International Balloon Fiesta. This is true, to a degree, of the city's somewhat nebulous, suburban-looking, outer neighborhoods, especially the West Side, which continues to sprawl farther west because few natural boundaries stand in the way.

On the ground, however, you'll discover a vibrant, historic urban landscape that's been inhabited for more than 300 years. In Old Town, Nob Hill, and some of the other older neighborhoods along the Central Avenue (Historic Route 66 corridor), you'll notice a vibrant mix of Spanish, Mexican, Native American, and Anglo architectural and design influences. In these areas, you can actually park the car and walk around a bit, and you'll discover increasingly dynamic and distinctive clusters of retail, dining, and mixed-use development. Downtown has even seen a spate of higher-density condos in recent years, many in converted historic buildings.

Albuquerque is the center of New Mexico's educational institutions and financial, manufacturing, and medical industries. It's an unpretentious, practical city with a metro population of nearly 850,000. Many who live here have come from outside New Mexico, giving Albuquerque a more diverse and cosmopolitan demographic than most communities in the state. The city's rich arts scene is proudly distinct from those of Santa Fe and Taos. Significant museums and galleries draw much local support, and feed off the creative energy of the many artists, writers, poets, filmmakers, and musicians who call this area home. Albuquerque has also become increasingly popular with Hollywood filmmakers in recent years because its outlying districts seem indistinctly and generically "western U.S."—they could pass for any number of locales. Recent hit movies filmed in Albuquerque include *The Book of Eli, No Country for Old Men, Transformers, The Men Who Stare at Goats,* and *Crazy Heart.*

Outdoors enthusiasts and seekers of places off the beaten path will also find plenty to see and do both in town and a very short drive away. The city's dining scene has improved markedly over the past few years, as local farmers' markets continue to grow in popularity and several local wineries have begun earning national acclaim. And the once generic supply of hotels has been bolstered by a new spate of elegant resorts opened on Native American pueblos just beyond city limits as well as a pair of hip boutique hotels Downtown. Albuquerque's star is slowly, but very clearly, rising.

ORIENTATION AND PLANNING

GETTING ORIENTED

Albuquerque contains a relatively compact and well-defined core comprising just a handful of neighborhoods—Downtown, Old Town, the University of New Mexico (UNM) district and adjacent Nob Hill—that's encircled by a somewhat sprawling and less clearly defined region. Colorful Historic Route 66 unifies the older, central neighborhoods, cutting west to east through the center of the city. Visitors tend to spend most of their time in this corridor (from Old Town to Nob Hill), as it contains the majority of the city's notable dining, lodging, shopping, and sightseeing. The more vast outlying neighborhoods are mostly residential and lack distinct boundaries: in clockwise order: the West Side, Los Ranchos/North Valley, Northeast Heights, Uptown/East Side, Airport, and Barelas/South Valley. They include a smattering of farther-afield attractions and worthwhile restaurants and hotels.

ALBUQUERQUE NEIGBHORHOODS

Old Town. As its name suggests, this historic neighborhood contains the earliest buildings in the city. Today it's home to numerous galleries, shops, boutiques, and museums, plus a few hotels, and it's one of the key destinations for visitors. It's just west of and adjacent to Downtown.

Downtown. A handful of modern office towers loom over Downtown, which is bisected by Central Avenue, the city's most important thoroughfare. This relatively compact district has few formal attractions but is home to a number of noteworthy hotels, restaurants, and shops. It's within walking distance of Old Town, which lies just to the west. The eastern edge of Downtown contains an up-and-coming subneighborhood called EDo (East of Downtown).

Barelas/South Valley. Extending just south of Downtown and Old Town, historic Barelas is home to the acclaimed National Hispanic Cultural Center and is an otherwise mostly residential area. It gradually gives way to the broad South Valley, a somewhat downcast area with a mix of residential and light-industrial blocks.

UNM/Nob Hill. Off-campus life is focused directly to the south and east of the University of New Mexico, stretching along Central Avenue from University Boulevard east through the Nob Hill neighborhood. Low-budget eateries, specialty shops, and music and arts venues are tightly clustered within the college-named streets just to the south of Central; things get more upscale as you head farther east.

Los Ranchos/North Valley. The North Valley (along with its sister South Valley) is the agrarian heart of Albuquerque. It is here, where generations of Hispanic families have resided, that you will experience the deepest sense of tradition.

Northeast Heights. This is quite a large neighborhood, taking in the area north of Interstate 40 and rising steadily east into the foothills of the Sandias, where there's great hiking and an incredible aerial tram to

TOP REASONS TO GO

Drive up the Camino Real (North 4th Street) or south into Barelas where you'll glimpse vintage shops and taquerias with hand-painted signage in idiosyncratic script and blazing-hot colors. Be sure to pause for a bite at Red Ball, Barelas Coffee House, or Mary & Tito's.

Visit the KiMo Theatre, in the center of Downtown right on old Route 66.

Walk or bike the Paseo del Bosque along the Rio Grande. The scenery along the 16-mi trail is a menagerie of cottonwoods, migrating birds, and the ever-present river rippling quietly at your side.

Explore the National Hispanic Cultural Center, a one-of-a-kind music and arts venue.

Witness the sunset over the volcanoes in the Western desert—a brilliant pink flood that creeps over the valley, making its way east to illuminate the Sandias before disappearing. It's even better in late August when the scent of roasting green chiles fills the air.

the top of the peak. You'll mostly find houses and shopping centers in this part of town, but it's worth driving up here just for the city views.

Uptown/East Side. This eclectic part of the city, ranging from the somewhat shady neighborhoods east of Nob Hill to the upscale shopping of Uptown, is a mixed bag. There are few attractions (the new National Museum of Nuclear Science & History being one exception), but Uptown has a good selection of hotels, as well as mostly chain restaurants and shops.

Airport. The mesa-top neighborhood immediately southwest of the airport has a lot of hotels, but little to see or do. It is, however, a short drive from Downtown, UNM, and Nob Hill.

West Side. This expansive, rapidly growing section of the city is mostly residential, but it is home to the fascinating and underrated Petroglyph National Monument.

ALBUQUERQUE PLANNER

WHEN TO GO

Albuquerque is sunny and relatively pleasant year-round. Fall is by far the most popular time to visit. On just about any day in late-August through November, big balloons sail across the sharp blue sky and the scent of freshly roasting green chiles permeates the air. Balloon Fiesta brings enormous crowds for nearly two weeks in early October (book hotels at this time as far in advance as possible). But shortly after, the weather's still great and hotel prices plummet. Albuquerque's winter days (usually 10°F warmer than those in Santa Fe) are usually mild enough for golf, hiking, or simply strolling around Old Town or Nob Hill. The occasional frigid spike usually thaws by morning. Spring brings winds, though plenty of sunshine, too, and rates stay low until the summer crowds flock in. Mid-May through mid-July can be brutally hot though dry, with high temperatures often soaring into the high 90s.

This is followed by roughly six to eight weeks of cooler temperatures, a bit more humidity, and the spectacular late-afternoon cloud formations that herald the brief "monsoon" season.

GETTING HERE AND AROUND

AIR TRAVEL

The major gateway to New Mexico is **Albuquerque International Sunport** (*ABQ* ☎ *505/244-7700* ⊕ *www.cabq.gov/airport*), a well-designed and attractive facility that's just 5 mi southeast of Downtown and just 3 mi south of UNM/Nob Hill. There's a free ABQ Rapid Ride bus shuttle service (⇨ *Bus Travel, below*) on weekdays from the airport to Downtown's Alvarado Transportation Center, where you can connect with Rail Runner service (⇨ *Train Travel, below*).

BUS TRAVEL

If you're only visiting for a couple of days and not planning to explore beyond Old Town, Downtown, Nob Hill, and Uptown, the city's public bus system is a practical if somewhat slow-going option. The ABQ Rapid Ride Red Line service plies the Central Avenue corridor and runs until about 9 pm Monday through Saturday and until 6 pm Sunday. The service is extended until about 2:30 am on Friday and Saturday nights June through September. Rapid Ride also has a Blue Line that runs from UNM to the West Side, and a Green Line that can get you from Downtown into Northeast Heights. You can obtain a customized trip plan at the city's public bus service, ABQ Ride.

The Alvarado Transportation Center Downtown is Rapid Ride's central hub and offers direct connections to the NM Rail Runner train service north to Santa Fe (via Bernalillo) and to the South Valley suburbs. Buses accept bicycles, although space is limited. Service is free on the Downtown Circulator shuttle route (available only on weekdays), or if you are transferring (to any route) from the Rail Runner; otherwise, the fare is $1 (bills or coins, exact change only; 25¢ transfers may be requested on boarding). Bus stops are well marked. *See also Bus Travel in the Travel Smart chapter.*

Bus Contact: ABQ Rapid Ride (☎ *505/243-7433* ⊕ *www.cabq.gov/transit*).

CAR TRAVEL

Although the city's public bus service, ABQ Ride, provides good coverage, a car is the easiest and most convenient way to get around. Albuquerque sprawls in all directions, but getting around town is not difficult. The main highways through the city, north–south Interstate 25 and east–west Interstate 40, converge just northeast of Downtown and generally offer the quickest access to outlying neighborhoods and the airport. Rush-hour jams are common in the mornings and late afternoons, but they're still far less severe than in most big U.S. cities. All the major car-rental agencies are represented at Albuquerque's Sunport airport.

Because it's a driving city, most businesses and hotels have free or inexpensive off-street parking, and it's easy to find metered street parking in many neighborhoods as well as affordable garages Downtown. Problems usually arise only when there's a major event in town, such as a concert near the University of New Mexico or a festival Downtown or in Old Town, when you may want to arrive on the early side to get a space.

TAXI TRAVEL

Taxis are metered in Albuquerque, and service is around-the-clock. Given the considerable distances around town, cabbing it can be expensive; figure about $9 from Downtown to Nob Hill, and about $20 from the airport to an Uptown hotel. There's also a $1 airport fee.

Taxi Contacts: Albuquerque Cab (☎ 505/883–4888 ⊕ www.albuquerquecab. com). **Yellow Cab** (☎ 505/247–8888).

TRAIN TRAVEL

The New Mexico Rail Runner, a commuter-train line, provides a picturesque, hassle-free way to make a day trip to Santa Fe. These sleek bi-level trains with large windows run south for about 35 mi to the suburb of Belén (stopping in Isleta Pueblo and Los Lunas), and north about 65 mi on a scenic run right into the historic heart of Santa Fe, with stops in Bernalillo, Sandoval, and a few other spots. Albuquerque stops are Downtown, at the Alvarado Transportation Center (where ABQ Ride offers free bus service to the airport), and at the north end of town at Journal Center/Los Ranchos. On weekdays, the trains run about eight or nine times per day, from about 4 am until 6:30 pm. There are also a few trains on Saturdays and a morning and late-afternoon run on Sundays. Fares are zone-based (one-way from $2 to $8), but day passes are just $1 more; bicycles ride free. Connections to local bus service are available at most stations. *For information on Amtrak service, see Train Travel in the Travel Smart chapter.*

Train Contact: New Mexico Rail Runner Express (☎ 866/795–7245 ⊕ www. nmrailrunner.com).

VISITOR INFORMATION

The Albuquerque Convention and Visitors Bureau operates tourism information kiosks at the airport (on the baggage-claim level) and in Old Town on Plaza Don Luis, across from San Felipe de Neri church.

Albuquerque Convention and Visitors Bureau (✉ Box 2686687125 ☎ 505/842–9918 or 800/284–2282 ⊕ www.itsatrip.org).

GUIDED TOURS

Established in 2009, the **ABQ Trolley Co** (☎ 505/240–8000 ⊕ www. abqtrolley.com) whisks guests on an 18-mi, 75-minute tour of the city's top attractions and neighborhoods, using colorful open-air trolleys. These narrated rides—which are offered April through October, Tuesday through Sunday—are a great way to gain an overview of the city.

The **Albuquerque Museum of Art and History** (☎ 505/243–7255 ⊕ www. cabq.gov/museum) leads free, hour-long historical walks through Old Town, beginning at 11 am Tuesday through Sunday, mid-March through mid-December.

Backcountry and local-history expert Roch Hart, owner of **NM Jeep Tours** (☎ 505/252–0112 ⊕ http://nmjeeptours.com),offers Jeep tours and guided hikes that start from Albuquerque and go as far as time and permits allow. He can suggest an itinerary (ghost towns, rock formations, petroglyphs), or tailor one to your interests and time frame.

Tours of Old Town (☎ *505/246–8687* ⊕ *http://nmjeeptours.com*) offers guided walking strolls around Old Town. The standard tour lasts about 75 minutes and is offered Friday through Wednesday, four times daily. Longer ghost-hunting and moonlight tours are also offered on occasion—check for times.

PLANNING YOUR TIME

Although the city sprawls, it does contain a handful of neighborhoods well suited to exploring on foot. In both Downtown and Old Town, you'll find plenty of garages and parking lots, and good areas to get out of the car and explore on foot. The same is true of the adjoining Nob Hill and UNM neighborhoods. For a short visit to the city, you could focus your time on these two areas.

The rest of the city stretches pretty far, and it can take anywhere from 10 to 30 minutes to get from one part of town to the other. Notable attractions, such as those along the Rio Grande Corridor and up in the Sandia Mountains, take at least a couple of hours and as much as a full day to explore. A helpful strategy is to bunch together geographically outlying attractions that interest you, perhaps hitting Gruet Winery and the Balloon Museum the same day you head up into nearby Corrales or Bernalillo, or combining a visit to the Sandia Peak Tram with an excursion east out of town, either toward Santa Fe via the Turquoise Trail or out to the historic sites in Mountainair (*as described in the Side Trips section later in this chapter*).

Most visitors to Albuquerque combine a stay here with some explorations of the entire northern Rio Grande Valley. If you're looking for the perfect regional tour, combine the short Albuquerque itinerary below with those provided in the Side Trips section below, which covers several great areas within a 60- to 90-minute drive of Albuquerque, as well as covering Isleta Pueblo and the towns of Corrales and Bernalillo, just on the outskirts of Albuquerque.

EXPLORING ALBUQUERQUE

Albuquerque's terrain is diverse. Along the river in the North and South valleys, the elevation hovers at about 4,800 feet. East of the river, the land rises gently to the foothills of the Sandia Mountains, which rise to over 6,000 feet; the 10,378-foot summit is a grand spot from which to view the city below. West of the Rio Grande, where Albuquerque is growing most aggressively, the terrain rises abruptly in a string of mesas topped by five volcanic cones. The changes in elevation from one part of the city to another result in corresponding changes in temperature, as much as 10°F at any time. It's not uncommon for snow or rain to fall on one part of town but for it to remain dry and sunny in another, and because temperatures can rise and fall considerably throughout the day and evening, it's a good idea to bring along a couple of layers when exploring large areas or for several hours.

ALBUQUERQUE IN A DAY

One of the best places to kick off the day is the Downtown branch of Flying Star restaurant, where you can enjoy breakfast in the heart of Downtown before checking out the handful of shops and galleries on Gold and Central avenues. From here, it's a short drive or 30-minute walk west along Central to reach Old Town, where you can explore the shops and museums of the neighborhood. This isn't the prettiest stretch of road, and another option for reaching Old Town is to walk north on 11th or 12th streets and then west on Mountain Road, perhaps stopping for cookies and coffee at legendary Golden Crown Panaderia. This takes an extra 20 minutes but will take you through a historic and rather humble residential area that's seen a lot of sprucing up in recent years as increasing numbers of artists and professionals have begun moving Downtown.

Once in Old Town, check out the Albuquerque Museum of Art and History, and also try to make your way over to the Albuquerque BioPark, which contains the aquarium, zoo, and botanic park. For lunch, try the atmospheric Monica's or the sophisticated St. Clair Winery & Bistro, both near the Old Town center.

Later in the afternoon, drive or take the Red Line bus a couple of miles east along Central to reach the University of New Mexico's main campus and the nearby Nob Hill District. Start with a stroll around the UNM campus with its many historic adobe buildings; if you have time, pop inside either the Maxwell Museum of Anthropology or the UNM Art Museum. When you're finished here, walk east along Central into Nob Hill and check out the dozens of offbeat shops. If it's summer, meaning that you still have some time before the sun sets, it's worth detouring from Old Town to Far Northeast Heights (a 15-minute drive), where you can take the Sandia Peak Aerial Tramway 2.7 mi up to Sandia Peak for spectacular sunset views of the city. Either way, plan to have dinner back in Nob Hill, perhaps at Nob Hill Bar and Grill or El Patio. If you're still up for more fun, check out one of the neighborhood's lively lounges or head back Downtown for a bit of late-night barhopping.

OLD TOWN

Albuquerque's social and commercial anchor since the settlement was established in 1706. Old Town and the surrounding blocks contain the wealth of the city's top cultural attractions, including several excellent museums. The action extends from the historic Old Town Plaza for several blocks in all directions—most of the museums are north and east of the plaza. In this area you'll also find a number of restaurants and scads of shops. Some of these places are touristy and can be missed, *but the better ones are included in the Where to Eat and Shopping sections of this chapter.* The artsy Saw Mill and Wells Park/Mountain Road neighborhoods extend just east of Old Town's museum row; the Los Duranes section, where the Indian Pueblo Cultural Center commands attention, is just a bit beyond walking distance to the northeast of Old Town.

From Old Town to Albuquerque's up-and-coming Downtown, it's a rather drab (though quick) 1¼-mi bus ride, walk, or drive southeast along Central Avenue.

WHAT TO SEE

Albuquerque BioPark. The city's foremost outdoor attraction and nature center, the park comprises the restored Tingley Beach as well as three distinct attractions, Albuquerque Aquarium, Rio Grande Botanic Garden, and Rio Grande Zoo. The garden and aquarium are located together (admission gets you into both facilities); the zoo is a short drive southeast. You can also ride the scenic Rio Line vintage narrow-gauge railroad between the zoo and gardens and the aquarium complex; rides are free if you purchase a combination ticket to all of the park's facilities.

Two main components of the Albuquerque BioPark, **Albuquerque Aquarium** and **Rio Grande Botanic Garden** (✉ *2601 Central Ave. NW, west of Old Town, north of Central Ave. and just east of the Central Ave. bridge*) are a huge draw with kids but also intrigue adult visitors. At the aquarium, a spectacular shark tank with floor-to-ceiling viewing is among the most popular of the marine exhibits. The Spanish-Moorish garden is one of three walled gardens near the entrance of the 36-acre botanic garden. The exquisite Sasebo Japanese Garden joins other specialty landscapes including the Curandera Garden, exhibiting herbs used by traditional Spanish folk-medicine practitioners; Rio Grande Heritage Farm, which re-creates a '30s-era local farm and features canning, quilting, and other demonstrations; and the Children's Fantasy Garden, complete with walk-through pumpkin, a 14-foot dragon, and giant bees. As of this writing, a Bugarium, which will contain open-air displays about insects, is currently under construction and expected to open in 2011. The seasonal PNM Butterfly Pavilion is open late May through mid-October and, year-round, the glass conservatory holds desert and Mediterranean plantings. In summer, concerts are given on Thursday at the botanic garden. From late November through late December, the botanic garden comes alive each evening from 6 to 9 pm for the River of Lights festival, a walk-through display of holiday lights and decorations.

The 64-acre **Rio Grande Zoo** (✉ *903 10th St. SW*) is an oasis of waterfalls, cottonwood trees, and naturalized animal habitats. More than 250 species of wildlife from around the world live here, including giraffes, camels, polar bears, elephants, zebras, and koalas. The Tropical America exhibit offers a bit of contrast for dry Albuquerque, replicating a jungle rain forest and containing toucans, spider monkeys, and brilliant orchids and bromeliads. The zoo has established captive-breeding programs for more than a dozen endangered species. Concerts are performed on the grounds on summer Friday evenings. There's a café on the premises. The Thunderbird Express is a ¾-scale train that runs in a nonstop loop within the zoo, and during the 20-minute ride conductors talk in depth about the creatures and their habitats. Running Tuesday through Sunday, it's free with combo tickets, or $2 otherwise (buy tickets onboard or at the Africa exhibit). **Tingley Beach** (✉ *1800 Tingley Dr. SW, south of Central Ave. and just east of Central Ave. bridge*) is

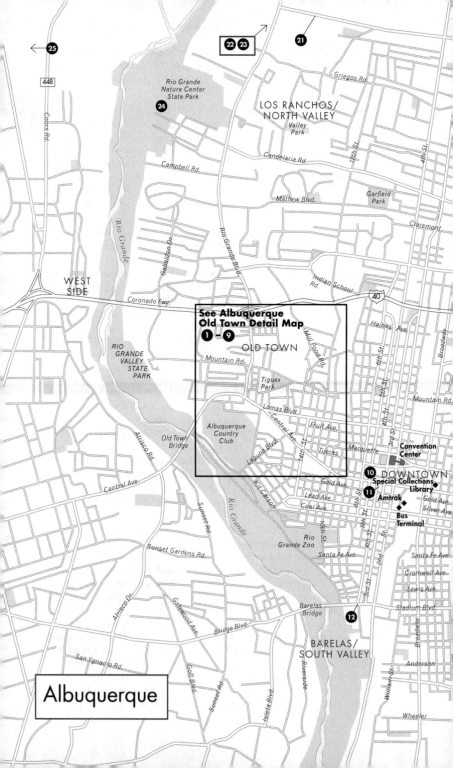

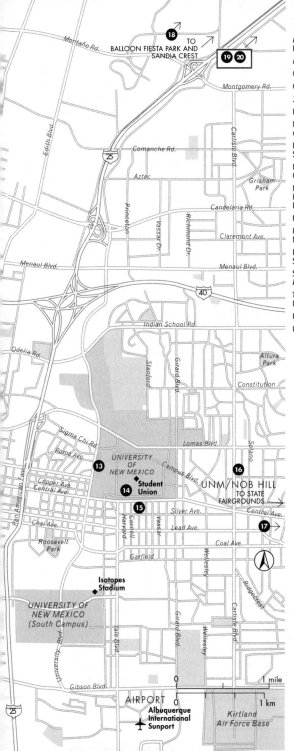

a recreational arm of the biological park that consists of three ponds, created in the 1930s by diverting water from the Rio Grande. You can rent paddleboats (or bicycles; both seasonally), fish the trout-stocked ponds (gear and fishing licenses can be purchased at the fishing-tackle shop on-site), or sail your model electric or wind-powered boats. To the west of the ponds, the cottonwood Bosque (wetlands forest) fringes the river. Ecological tours of the Bosque are given in summer. It's part of the popular 16-mi Paseo del Bosque bike path, which is open year-round. There's also a snack bar and a Rio Line station; the ¾-scale passenger trains make a stop here en route between the aquarium and garden complex and the zoo. ⊠ *903 10th St. SW, Old Town* ☎ *505/764–6200* ⊕ *www.cabq.gov/biopark* ⚑ *Tingley Beach and grounds free, Albuquerque Aquarium and Rio Grande Botanic Garden $7 (combined ticket), Rio Grande Zoo $7; combination ticket for all attractions, including unlimited rides on the Rio Line and Thunderbird Express trains $12* ☉ *Aquarium, botanic garden, and zoo Sept.–May daily 9–5; June–Aug. weekdays 9–5, weekends 9–6. Tingley Beach daily sunrise–sunset. No trains Mon.*

Fodor's Choice
★
Albuquerque Museum of Art and History. This modern structure houses the largest collection of Spanish-colonial artifacts in the nation, along with a superb photo archive and other relics of the city's birth and development. The Common Ground galleries represent an important permanent collection of primarily 20th-century paintings, all by world-renowned artists with a New Mexico connection. Changing exhibits also reveal a commitment to historically important artists and photographers of the 20th and 21st centuries. The centerpiece, *Four Centuries: A History of Albuquerque*, is a pair of life-size models of Spanish conquistadors in original chain mail and armor. Perhaps the one on horseback is Francisco Vásquez de Coronado, who, in search of gold, led a small army into New Mexico in 1540—a turning point in the region's history. A multimedia presentation chronicles the development of the city since 1875. The sculpture garden contains more than 50 contemporary works by Southwestern artists that include Glenna Goodacre, Michael Naranjo, and Luis Jiménez. Visitors may also take advantage of three 45-minute, free (with museum admission) tours. **Slate at the Museum,** a casual eatery operated by Downtown's excellent Slate Street Cafe, serves soups, salads, espresso drinks, desserts, and other tasty light fare. ⊠ *2000 Mountain Rd. NW, Old Town* ☎ *505/243–7255 museum, 505/242–0434 shop, 505/242–5316 café* ⊕ *www.cabq.gov/museum* ⚑ *$4 (free Sun. 9–1)* ☉ *Tues.–Sun. 9–5.*

☾ **American International Rattlesnake Museum.** Included in the largest collection of different species of living rattlers in the world are such rare and unusual specimens as an albino western diamondback. From the outside the museum looks for all the world like a plain old shop, but inside, the museum's exhibits, its engaging staff, and a video supply visitors with the lowdown on these venomous creatures—for instance, that they can't hear their own rattles and that the human death rate from rattlesnake bites is less than 1%. The mission here is to educate the public on the many positive benefits of rattlesnakes, and to contribute to their conservation. ⊠ *202 San Felipe St. NW, just off the southeast*

A GOOD TOUR: OLD TOWN

Soak up the history in **Old Town Plaza,** and then cross the street and visit **San Felipe de Neri Catholic Church.** Then take a five-minute (or longer if the shops or smaller museums beckon) stroll over to two of the city's grandest cultural institutions, the **Albuquerque Museum of Art and History** and the **New Mexico Museum of Natural History and Science.** Kids also enjoy **¡Explora!,** which is next door.

From here, choose one of these options (all short rides away—the first two are on primary bus routes):

1. West on Central, along a historic section of Route 66 lined with shabby vintage motels, is the **Albuquerque BioPark,** which consists of the Albuquerque Aquarium, Botanic Garden, Rio Grande Zoo, and Tingley Beach.

2. East on Central to Downtown, and a gawk at (or tour of) the **KiMo Theatre** and some neon viewing and gallery hopping. **516 Arts** is the place to start (⇨ *Art Galleries, in Shopping, below).* Detour farther east to EDo (East of Downtown) and walk by the impressive old main library

(now Special Collections Library & the Center for the Book, **but currently closed for renovations)** and its exhibits, or go directly south on 4th Street to the **National Hispanic Cultural Center.**

3. Drive east along Mountain Road and enjoy a taste of old Albuquerque neighborhoods. Stop at **Harwood Art Center,** then backtrack a few blocks turning north on 12th Street to the **Indian Pueblo Cultural Center.**

TIMING
The best time to visit Old Town is in the morning, before the stores open at 10 and the daily rush of activity begins. In the beaming morning light, the echoes of the past are almost palpable (and you might find parking). Plan to spend an hour in the plaza area, and, depending on your interests, another hour or two in the Albuquerque Museum of Art and History and the New Mexico Museum of Natural History and Science. The BioPark easily fills an afternoon by itself (allow about two hours for the gardens and aquarium; an hour or so for the zoo).

corner of the plaza, Old Town ☎ *505/242–6569* ⊕ *www.rattlesnakes. com* ✉ *$5* ☉ *June–Sept., Mon.–Sat. 10–6, Sun. 1–5; Oct.–May, weekdays 11:30–5:30, Sat. 10–6, Sun. 1–5.*

♻ **¡Explora!** This imaginatively executed science museum—its driving concept is "Ideas You Can Touch"—is right across from the New Mexico Museum of Natural History and Science. ¡Explora! bills itself as an all-ages attraction (and enthralled adults abound), but there's no question that many of the innovative hands-on exhibits such as a high-wire bicycle and a kinetic sculpture display are geared to children. They offer big fun in addition to big science (and a good dose of art as well). While its colorful Bucky dome is immediately noticeable from the street, ¡Explora! also features a playground, theater, and a freestanding staircase that appears to "float" between floors. ⊠ *1701 Mountain Rd. NW, Old Town* ☎ *505/224–8300* ⊕ *www.explora.us* ✉ *$7* ☉ *Mon.–Sat. 10–6, Sun. noon–6.*

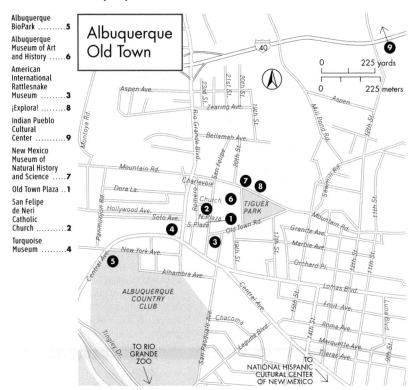

Indian Pueblo Cultural Center. The multilevel semicircular design at this museum was inspired by Pueblo Bonito, the prehistoric ruin in Chaco Canyon in northwestern New Mexico. The elegant design emphasizes the relationship between the two sites, with the museum entryway facing east, providing sacred exposure. Start by watching the museum's video about the region's Pueblo culture. Then move to the upper-level alcove, where changing exhibits feature aspects of the arts and crafts of each of the state's 19 pueblos. Lower-level exhibits trace the history of the Pueblo people. Youngsters can touch Native American pottery, jewelry, weaving, tools, and dried corn at the Hands-On Corner, draw petroglyph designs, and design pots. Paintings, sculptures, jewelry, leather crafts, rugs, souvenir items, drums, beaded necklaces, painted bowls, and fetishes are for sale. Ceremonial dances are performed on weekends at 11 and 2, and there are arts-and-crafts demonstrations each weekend. The **Pueblo Harvest Café, which is open two to three hours later than the museum,** is a great spot to try such Native American fare as blue-corn pancakes and Indian tacos, or Native Fusion items like grilled lamb "lollipops" crusted in red-chile piñons, and elk tenderloin with blackberry-sage compote. Note that technically the museum lies a bit north of Old Town, in the Los Duranes neighborhood—it's a 25-minute walk or five-minute drive. ✉ *2401 12th St. NW, Old Town*

☎ *505/843–7270 or 800/766–4405*
⊕ *www.indianpueblo.org*   ✉ *$6*
⊙ *Daily 9–5.*

ⓒ **New Mexico Museum of Natural History and Science.** The wonders at Albuquerque's most popular museum include the simulated volcano (with a river of bubbling hot lava flowing beneath the see-through glass floor), the frigid Ice Age cave, and "Dawn of the Dinosaurs." The only Triassic exhibit in North America, this permanent hall features some of the state's own rare finds. The Evolator—short for Evolution Elevator—a six-minute high-tech ride, uses video, sound, and motion to whisk you through 35 million years of New Mexico's geological history. A film in the Extreme Screen DynaTheater makes viewers feel equally involved. Arrive via the front walkway, and you'll be greeted by life-size bronze sculptures of a 21-foot-long horned Pentaceratops and a 30-foot-long carnivorous Albertosaur. Then, on the flip side of time, the Paul Allen–funded Start-Up! galleries explore the silicon age. Detailing of the birth of the PC here in the Duke City (Allen and a very young Bill Gates came here in the mid-1970s to create software for the Altair kits that Ed Roberts designed on the south end of town, and the rest, well, you know), these exhibitions are a fascinating tour through the early garage days of many such start-ups. It's also done a fair job with the Apple side of the story. Also at the museum is the LodeStar Science Center, whose state-of-the-art planetarium is home of the wildly popular First Friday Fractals show (tickets available online only). ✉ *1801 Mountain Rd. NW, Old Town* ☎ *505/841–2800* ⊕ *www.nmnaturalhistory.org* ✉ *Museum $7, DynaTheater $7, planetarium $7; combination ticket for any 2 attractions $12, for any 3 attractions $15* ⊙ *Daily 9–5.*

Fodor's Choice
★
ⓒ
Old Town Plaza. Don Francisco Cuervo y Valdés, a provincial governor of New Mexico, laid out this small plaza in 1706. No slouch when it came to political maneuvering, he named the town after the duke of Alburquerque, viceroy of New Spain. He hoped flattery would induce the duke to waive the requirement that a town have 30 families before a charter was issued—there were only 15 families living here in 1706. The duke acquiesced. (Albuquerque is nicknamed the Duke City, so he's hardly been forgotten.) Today the plaza is tranquil, with shade trees, wrought-iron benches, and a graceful white gazebo. Roughly 200 shops, restaurants, cafés, galleries, and several cultural sites in *placitas* (small plazas) and lanes surround Old Town Plaza. During fiestas Old Town comes alive with mariachi bands and dancing señoritas. ■**TIP→** **Seasonally, the Albuquerque Museum of Art and History** (⇨ *above*) **offers an excellent guided walking tour that details local history and the historic architecture that remains intact here.** Mostly dating back to the late 1800s, styles from Queen Anne to Territorial and Pueblo Revival, and even Mediterranean, are apparent in the one- and two-story (almost all adobe) structures. Event schedules and maps, which contain a list of public restrooms and many (but by no means all) Old Town shops and sights are available at the **Old Town Visitors Center** (✉ *303 Romero St.*

NW, Old Town ☎ *505/243–3215* ⊕ *www.itsatrip*.org), an outpost of the Albuquerque CVB that's somewhat hidden in the rear of Plaza Don Luis, across the street from the San Felipe de Neri Catholic Church. It is open daily, typically 9–4:30 but usually a bit later in summer.

San Felipe de Neri Catholic Church. More than two centuries after it first welcomed worshippers, this structure, erected in 1793, is still active. The building, which replaced Albuquerque's first Catholic church, has been expanded several times, but its adobe walls and other original features remain. Small gardens front and flank the church; the inside is a respite from the tourism bustle beyond its doorstep—the painting and iconography is simple, authentic, and lovely, the atmosphere hushed. Next to it is a shop and small museum that displays relics—vestments, paintings, carvings—dating from the 17th century. ■**TIP→ There's a hidden treasure behind the church: inside the gnarled tree is a statue that some speculate depicts the Virgin Mary.** ⊠ *2005 Plaza NW, Old Town* ☎ *505/243–4628* ⊕ *www.sanfelipedeneri.org* ☉ *Church open to public daily 8* am*–dusk; museum Mon.–Sat. 9:30–5.*

Turquoise Museum. Just west of the hubbub of Old Town, this museum inside a small strip mall focuses on the beauty, mythology, and physical properties of turquoise, a semiprecious but adored gemstone that many people associate with the color of New Mexico's skies. A self-guided tour, entered via a simulated mine shaft, leads to one-of-a-kind showpieces and examples from more than 65 mines on four continents. Displays show how turquoise forms, the importance of individual mines, and highlight its uses by Native Americans in prehistoric times. At the education center you can learn to distinguish the real McCoy from plastic. The museum's proprietors are a multigenerational family of longtime traders, and know whereof they speak; if you retain nothing else, do remember that only turquoise specified as "natural" is the desirable, unadulterated stuff. There is an active silversmith's shop adjacent to the display area; a small gift shop sells historic and contemporary pieces. ⊠ *2107 Central Ave. NW, Old Town* ☎ *505/247–8650* ⊕ www. turquoisemuseum.com ☜ *$4* ☉ *Weekdays 9:30–5, Sat. 9:30–4 (last entrance is one hour before closing).*

DOWNTOWN

Although Downtown doesn't have many formal attractions short of its anchor (and destination-worthy) art gallery scene, this bustling neighborhood is one of the West's developing urban-comeback stories. It's a diverting place to wander, gallery hop, shop, snack (or dine), or simply soak in some fine remnants from its Route 66–era boom years for a couple of hours. Farther east is another revitalizing section: now known as EDo (East of Downtown), which encompasses the historic Huning Highland District. This is where Albuquerque's Old Main Library—an architectural gem—and Gothic Revival high school (now condos) still stand, and several notable restaurants and shops have sprouted up.

Fodor's Choice **KiMo Theatre.** When the KiMo was built, in 1927, Route 66 was barely
★   established and running on its original alignment: north–south on 4th Street. Downtown was the center of activity, and movie palaces were

the national rage. Local merchant Oreste Bachechi saw his moment, and hired architect Carl Boller to design a theater that would reflect the local zeitgeist. And that he did. Decorated with light fixtures made from buffalo skulls (the eye sockets glow amber in the dark), Navajo symbols, and nine spectacular Western-themed wall murals by Carl Von Hassler, the KiMo represents Pueblo Deco at its apex. Luckily, it was saved from the wrecking ball in 1977, and now, fully restored, it stands—one of the few notable early-20th-century structures remaining in Downtown Albuquerque. The self-guided tour is a must (guided tours can also be arranged by appointment), or, even better, catch a live performance. ✉ *423 Central Ave. NW, at 5th St., Downtown* 🕿 *505/768–3522 theater, 505/768–3544 event info* ⊕ *www.cabq.gov/kimo* 🖾 *Free self-guided tours* ☉ *Tues.–Fri. 8:30–4:30, Sat. 11–5.*

New Mexico Holocaust & Intolerance Museum. Reestablished in a larger and more attractive Downtown space in 2009, this moving museum packs plenty of punch with its poignant exhibits that document genocide and persecution throughout history, with special emphasis placed upon the Holocaust carried out by the Nazis before and during World War II. Exhibits inside touch on child slave labor, the rescue of Bulgarian and Danish Jews, the Nuremburg Trials, and include a re-created gate from a concentration camp and many artifacts related to Holocaust survivors and the Nazis. There are also exhibits describing genocides throughout history such as the infamous Bataan Death March. ✉ *616 Central Ave. SW, Downtown* 🕿 *505/247–0606* ⊕ *www.nmholocaustmuseum. org* 🖾 *Donations accepted* ☉ *Tues.–Sat. 11–3:30.*

BARELAS/SOUTH VALLEY

The historic Barelas neighborhood, to the south of Old Town and Downtown, features the must-see National Hispanic Cultural Center. Otherwise it's mostly a residential neighborhood that gradually gives way to the broad South Valley, a rough-around-the-edges area that contains modest homes in some sections, and light industry in others.

WHAT TO SEE

Fodor's Choice
★
☺
National Hispanic Cultural Center. A showpiece for the city, and a showcase for Latino culture and genealogy in Albuquerque's old Barelas neighborhood, this exciting contemporary space contains a museum and art galleries, multiple performance venues, a 10,000-volume genealogical research center and library, a restaurant, and an education center. Exhibits include dynamic displays of photography and paintings by local artists as well as by internationally known names. The center mounts performances of flamenco dancing, bilingual theater, traditional Spanish and New Mexican music, world music, the symphony, and more. This is the largest Latino cultural center in the country, and with a $10 million programming endowment, the center provides top-notch entertainment in its stunning and acoustically superb Roy E. Disney Center for Performing Arts and smaller Albuquerque Journal Theatre, and hosts major traveling art exhibits in its first-rate museum, which also houses an esteemed permanent collection with more than 2,000 works. Architecturally, the center borrows from a variety of Spanish

cultures, from Moorish Spain (including a re-creation of a defensive tower, or Torreón; the finely detailed fresco that embellishes the interior's 45-foot-tall walls and ceiling depicts Hispanic cultural heritage through time) to Mexico and the American Southwest. There's a vintage WPA-era school that now contains the research library and **La Fonda del Bosque restaurant** ($$, no dinner), which serves tasty New Mexican fare indoors and out on the patio; Sunday brunch, live music included, draws a big family crowd. The gift shop, La Tiendita, has a well-chosen and impeccably sourced selection of books, pottery, and artwork. ⊠ *1701 4th St. SW, at Avenida César Chavez (Bridge Blvd.), Barelas* ☎ *505/246–2261 cultural center, 505/247–9480 restaurant, 505/766–6604 gift shop, 505/724–4771 box office* ⊕ *www.nhccnm. org* ⊠ *$3* ☉ *Tues.–Sun. 10–5.*

UNM/NOB HILL

Established in 1889, the University of New Mexico (UNM) is the state's leading institution of higher education, with internationally recognized programs in anthropology, biology, Latin American studies, and medicine. Its many outstanding galleries and museums are open to the public free of charge. The university's Pueblo Revival–style architecture is noteworthy, particularly the old wing of Zimmerman Library and the Alumni Chapel, both designed by John Gaw Meem, a Santa Fe–based architect whose mid-20th-century work dominates the campus.

WHAT TO SEE

Maxwell Museum of Anthropology. Many of the more than 2½ million artifacts at the Maxwell, the first public museum in Albuquerque (established in 1932), come from the Southwest. Two permanent exhibitions chronicle 4 million years of human history and the art and cultures of 11,500 years of human settlement in the Southwest. The photographic archives contain more than 250,000 images, including some of the earliest photos of Pueblo and Navajo cultures. The museum shop sells traditional and contemporary Southwestern Native American jewelry, rugs, pottery, basketry, and beadwork, along with folk art from around the world. In the children's section are inexpensive books and handmade tribal artifacts. Parking permits for adjacent UNM lots are available inside the museum. ⊠ *University of New Mexico, Redondo West Dr., west end of campus, just east of University Blvd. NE, between Las Lomas Rd. NE and Dr. Martin Luther King Blvd. NE, UNM/Nob Hill* ☎ *505/277–4405* ⊕ *www.unm.edu/~maxwell* ⊠ *Free* ☉ *Tues.–Sat. 10–4.*

Fodor's Choice ★ **Nob Hill.** The heart of Albuquerque's Route 66 culture and also its hippest, funkiest retail and entertainment district, Nob Hill is the neighborhood just east of UNM, with its commercial spine extending along Central Avenue (old Route 66). Along this stretch you'll find dozens of offbeat shops, arty cafés, and student hangouts, and on the blocks just north and south of Central Avenue, you'll see an eclectic assortment of building styles. Most of the more noteworthy businesses are along the stretch of Central between UNM and Carlisle Boulevard, but the activity is gradually moving east. Old art deco strip malls and vintage motels along this stretch are slowly being transformed into new restaurants

A GOOD WALK: DOWNTOWN

The impeccably landscaped grounds of the University of New Mexico surround a central area containing knolls, a duck pond, fountains, waterfalls, and benches. As you begin a counterclockwise route from the school's southeast corner, your first stop is for a map at the nearby Welcome Center. Then stroll north past the Student Union Building, then left into the plaza. Zimmerman Library will be on your right; stop in and take a look at the old section, yet another one of John Gaw Meem's memorable campus buildings. Directly ahead is the oasis-like Duck Pond. Loop around the pond to the west, and the Alumni Chapel comes into view. Just beyond it is the **Maxwell Museum of Anthropology**, in the Anthropology Building on the western edge of the campus. Meander southeast now to Northrup Hall and the Meteoritics Museum within. A short distance farther east you will find yourself at the Center for the Arts, just across from the parking structure where you began. Stop in at the Center, heading past Popejoy Hall to the **UNM Art Museum**, which contains the Raymond Jonson Gallery. As you exit, turn right past the UNM bookstore (Lobo gear alert!), noting

sleek and striking George Pearl Hall, which was built in 2007 to house the UNM School of Architecture and Planning, and cross Central Avenue. A half-block down on Cornell Drive is the **Tamarind Institute**. Detour nine blocks south of Central along Girard Boulevard (five blocks east of Cornell) to the **Ernie Pyle Library.** Back on Central, you're a two-minute walk from campus to the edge of **Nob Hill**, where you can shop, café hop, and admire the historic residential and commercial architecture.

TIMING
Seeing the University of New Mexico could take as little as an hour or two for the basics, and a solid half-day if you visit all the museums. If you've driven here, park the car in the Cornell Parking Structure near the southeast end of campus; it's the side adjacent to Nob Hill and is the ideal place to start—and end—a loop around the university. Spend an hour strolling the grounds, maybe catching some rays by the duck pond. Allot up to an hour for each subsequent stop. All facilities are open year-round, but some are closed from Saturday to Monday. Save Nob Hill for late afternoon or evening, when this neighborhood really comes alive.

and shops. The neighborhood was developed during the 1930s and '40s, peaked in prosperity and popularity during the 1950s, and then fell into a state of decline from the 1960s through the mid-'80s. It was at this time that a group of local business and property owners formed a neighborhood group and banded together to help turn the neighborhood around, and Nob Hill has been enjoying great cachet and popularity ever since. ⊠ *Central Ave., from University of New Mexico campus east to Washington St., UNM/Nob Hill.*

NEED A BREAK?

An airy storefront café with a few tables on the sidewalk overlooking bustling Nob Hill, cheerful Ecco Gelato & Espresso (⊠ 3409 Central Ave. NE ☎ 505/268-0070 ⊕ www.eccogelato.com) began in Santa Fe and has quickly become a huge hit in the Duke City. The artisan gelato comes in a variety of refreshing, inventive flavors—consider coconut-lime, fig-and-walnut, rhubarb-orange, and chocolate-cherry.

Ernie Pyle Library. After several visits to New Mexico, Ernie Pyle, a Pulitzer Prize–winning news reporter, built a house in 1940 that now contains the smallest branch of the Albuquerque Public Library. On display are photos, handwritten articles by Pyle, and news clippings about his career as a correspondent during World War II and his death from a sniper's bullet on April 18, 1945, on the Pacific island of Ie Shima. ⊠ *900 Girard Blvd. SE, UNM/Nob Hill* ☎ *505/256–2065* ⊕ *www.cabq. gov/library* ⊠ *Free* ⊙ *Tues. and Thurs.–Sat. 10–6, Wed. 11–7.*

Tamarind Institute. This world-famous institution played a major role in reviving the fine art of lithographic printing, which involves working with plates of traditional stone and modern metal. Tamarind certification is to a printer what a degree from Juilliard is to a musician. A small gallery within the facility exhibits prints and lithographs by well-known masters like Jim Dine, and up-and-comers in the craft as well. Guided tours (reservations essential) are conducted on the first Friday of each month at 1:30. The Tamarind moved around the corner to a spacious, contemporary space in the old UNM architecture building in summer 2010. ⊠ *2500 Central Ave. SE, UNM/Nob Hill* ☎ *505/277–3901* ⊕ *http://tamarind.unm.edu* ⊠ *Free* ⊙ *Weekdays 9–5.*

UNM Art Museum. A handsome facility inside the UNM Center for the Arts, the museum holds New Mexico's largest collection of fine art. Works of old masters share wall space with the likes of Picasso and O'Keeffe, and many photographs and prints are on display. Lectures and symposia, gallery talks, and guided tours are regularly scheduled. On the museum's lower level, the **Raymond Jonson Gallery** is dedicated to the work of Raymond Jonson (1891–1982), a pioneering modernist (and founder, in 1938, of the Transcendental Painting Group) whose paintings and drawings focus on mass and form. The gallery moved here in fall 2010, and previously occupied Jonson's former home and studio, designed by John Gaw Meem in 1950, whose impressive exterior you can still view at 1909 Las Lomas Road. Each summer the gallery mounts a major Jonson retrospective and also exhibits 21st-century works of sculpture, video, and photography, as well as maintaining an important archive on the founding artist and his contemporaries. ⊠ *University of New Mexico Center for the Arts, north of Central Ave. entrance opposite Cornell Dr. SE, UNM/Nob Hill* ☎ *505/277–4001* ⊕ *http://unmartmuseum.unm.edu* ⊠ *$5 donation suggested* ⊙ *Tues.– Fri. 10–4, weekends 1–4.*

LOS RANCHOS/NORTH VALLEY

Many attractions lie north of Downtown, Old Town, and the University of New Mexico. Quite a few, including the Anderson and Casa Rodeña wineries and the Rio Grande Nature Center, are clustered in two of the city's longest-settled areas: the more rural and lush cottonwood-lined North Valley, and Los Ranchos, along the Rio Grande. Early

Spanish settlers made their homes here, building on top of even earlier Pueblo homesteads. Historic adobe houses abound. This area is a natural gateway to the West Side. Drive across the lovely Montaño Road bridge and Petroglyph National Monument is moments away, as is the highly recommended side-trip destination, Corrales (⇨ *Side Trips from Albuquerque, below*).

> **DID YOU KNOW?**
>
> Franciscan monks first planted their grapevines in New Mexico before having more success in northern California.

WHAT TO SEE

Anderson-Abruzzo International Balloon Museum. This dramatic museum celebrates the city's legacy as the hot-air ballooning capital of the world. The dashing, massive facility is named for Maxie Anderson and Ben Abruzzo, who pioneered ballooning in Albuquerque and were part of a team of three aviators who made the first manned hot-air balloon crossing of the Atlantic Ocean in 1978. You'll understand why this museum is so large when you see the exhibits—including several historic balloons, and both large- and small-scale replicas of balloons and zeppelins. You'll also see vintage balloon baskets, china and flatware from the ill-fated *Hindenburg* and an engaging display on that tragic craft, and dynamic displays that trace the history of the sport, dating back to the first balloon ride, in 1783. Kids can design their own balloons at one creative interactive exhibit. There's a large museum shop offering just about any book or product you could imagine related to hot-air ballooning.

The museum anchors Albuquerque's Balloon Fiesta Park, home to the legendary **Albuquerque International Balloon Fiesta** (☎ *505/821–1000 or 888/422–7277* ⊕ *www.balloonfiesta.com*), which began in 1972 and runs for nearly two weeks in early October. Albuquerque's history of ballooning dates from 1882, when Professor Park A. Van Tassel, a saloon keeper, ascended in a balloon at the Territorial Fair. During the fiesta, the largest hot-air-balloon gathering anywhere, you can watch the Special Shapes Rodeo, when hundreds of unusual balloons, including depictions of the old lady who lived in the shoe, the pink pig, and dozens of other fanciful characters from fairy tales and popular culture, soar high above more than a million spectators. There are night flights, obstacle races, and many other surprising balloon events. Book your hotel far in advance if you plan to attend, and note that hotel rates also rise during the fiesta. ✉ *9201 Balloon Museum Dr. NE, off Alameda Blvd., Los Ranchos/North Valley* ☎ *505/768–6020* ⊕ *www. balloonmuseum.com* ⊠ *$4* ⊙ *Tues.–Sun. 9–5.*

Anderson Valley Vineyards. A low-key winery that was established in 1973 and enjoys a dramatic, pastoral Los Ranchos setting not far from the Rio Grande, Anderson Valley specializes in Chardonnay and Cabernet Sauvignon. The staff in the intimate tasting room is friendly and knowledgeable, and you can sip your wine while relaxing on an enchanting patio with wonderful views of the Sandia Mountains in the distance. In this agrarian, tranquil setting, it's hard to imagine that you're just a little more than 3 mi north of the bustle of Old Town and

Downtown. ⊠ *4920 Rio Grande Blvd. NW, between Montaño and Chavez Rds. NW, Los Ranchos/North Valley* ☎ *505/344–7266* ⊠ *Free* ⊙ *Wed.–Sun. noon–5.*

Fodor's Choice **Casa Rondeña Winery.** Perhaps the most architecturally stunning of New ★ Mexico's wineries, Casa Rondeña—which is technically in Los Ranchos de Albuquerque, not the Duke City proper—resembles a Tuscan villa, with its green-tile roof and verdant grounds laced with gardens and fountains. It's hard to believe that most of the structures here went up with the winery's founding in 1995. Casa Rondeña produces a superb Meritage red blend as well as a terrific Viognier. You can see a vintage oak fermentation tank and a great hall with soaring ceilings, where tastings are conducted. The winery hosts many events including a chamber music festival with wine receptions and dinners. ⊠ *733 Chavez Rd. NW, between Rio Grande Blvd. and 4th St. NW, Los Ranchos/North Valley* ☎ *505/344–5911 or 800/706–1699* ⊕ *www.casarondena.com* ⊠ *Free* ⊙ *Mon.–Sat. 10–6, Sun. noon–6.*

♺ **Rio Grande Nature Center State Park.** Along the banks of the Rio Grande, this year-round 270-acre refuge in a portion of the Bosque (about midway up on the Paseo del Bosque trail) is the nation's largest cottonwood forest. If bird-watching is your thing, you've come to the right place: this is home to all manner of birds and migratory waterfowl. Constructed half aboveground and half below the edge of a pond, the park's glass-walled interpretive center (an interesting small-scale building by noted New Mexico architect Antoine Predock) has viewing windows that provide a look at what's going on at both levels, and speakers that broadcast the sounds of the birds you're watching into the room. You may see birds, frogs, ducks, and turtles. The park has active programs for adults and children and trails for biking, walking, and jogging. ■ TIP→ **Keep your eye out for what appears to be a game of jacks abandoned by giants: these jetty jacks were built in the 1950s to protect the Rio Grande levees from flood debris.** ⊠ *2901 Candelaria Rd. NW, Los Ranchos/North Valley* ☎ *505/344–7240* ⊕ *www.rgnc.org* ⊠ *$3 per vehicle, grounds free* ⊙ *Nature center daily 10–5, park daily 8–5.*

♺ **Unser Racing Museum.** Albuquerque is home to the illustrious auto-racing family, the Unsers, whose four generations of drivers have dominated the sport since the early 20th century—the most famous members include Bobby Unser Sr. and Al Unser Sr. Exhibits at this spiffy museum include a display on Pikes Peak, Colorado, and the legendary hairpins where the Unser family first got serious about racing; a study of their legacy at the Indianapolis 500; and a good selection of vintage racers, including a few you can test-drive (virtually, that is). ⊠ *1776 Montaño Rd. NW, just east of the Rio Grande Blvd. overpass, near the Montaño Road bridge, Los Ranchos/North Valley* ☎ *505/341–1776* ⊕ *www.unserracingmuseum.com* ⊠ *$10* ⊙ *Daily 10–4.*

NORTHEAST HEIGHTS

In Northeast Heights you are in the foothills of the Sandia Mountains, in upscale neighborhoods that surprise you with the sudden appearance of piñon and ponderosa. Trips to this area can easily be combined with

2

more north-central venues like the Balloon Museum and the North Valley wineries.

Gruet Winery. It's hard to imagine a wine-tasting venue with less curb appeal. Gruet Winery sits along an ugly access road paralleling Interstate 25, sandwiched between an RV showroom and a lawn-furniture store. But behind the vaguely chaletlike exterior of this otherwise modern industrial building, you're afforded the chance to visit one of the nation's most acclaimed producers of sparkling wines (to see its actual vineyards you'll have to head south to Truth or Consequences). Gruet (pronounced *grew*-eh) had been famous in France since the 1950s for its Champagnes. In New Mexico, the Gruet family has been producing wine since 1984, and it's earned nationwide kudos for its Methode Champenoise (employing traditional Champagne-making methods for its sparkling wine), as well as for impressive Pinot Noirs, Syrahs, and Chardonnays. Most of the state's top restaurants carry Gruet vintages, as do many leading wine cellars around the country. Tastings include five wines and a souvenir glass. ⊠ *8400 Pan American Freeway (I–25) NE, on the north frontage road for I–25, between Alameda Blvd. and Paseo del Norte, Northeast Heights* ☎ *505/821–0055 or 888/857–9463* ⊕ *www.gruetwinery.com* ☒ *Winery free, 5-wine tasting $6* ☉ *Weekdays 10–5, Sat. noon–5; tours Mon.–Sat. at 2.*

Fodor's Choice ★ ☺ **Sandia Peak Aerial Tramway.** Tramway cars climb 2.7 mi up the steep western face of the Sandias, giving you a close-up view of red rocks and tall trees—it's the world's longest aerial tramway. From the observation deck at the 10,378-foot summit you can see Santa Fe to the northeast and Los Alamos to the northwest—about 11,000 square mi of spectacular scenery. Tram cars leave from the base at regular intervals for the 15-minute ride to the top. You may see birds of prey soaring above or mountain lions roaming the cliff sides. An exhibit room at the top surveys the wildlife and landscape of the mountain. Narrators point out what you're seeing below, including the barely visible remnants of a 1953 plane crash that killed all 16 passengers onboard. If you want to add a meal to the excursion, there's the upscale **High Finance Restaurant** (☎ *505/243–9742* ⊕ *www.sandiapeakrestaurants.com*) on top of the mountain, serving steaks, lobster tail, and good burgers at lunch). High Finance affords clear views from every table, making it a favorite destination for a romantic dinner—the food isn't bad, but it's more about the scenic experience here. A more casual spot, **Sandiago's** (☎ *505/856–6692* ⊕ *www.sandiapeakrestaurants.com*), is at the tram's base. ■**TIP**➔ **It's much colder and windier at the summit than at the tram's base, so pack a jacket.** You can also use the tram as a way to reach the Sandia Peak ski and mountain-biking area *(*⇨ *Sandia Park, in Side Trips from Albuquerque, below).* ⊠ *10 Tramway Loop NE, Far Northeast Heights* ☎ *505/856–7325* ⊕ *www.sandiapeak.com* ☒ *$20* ☉ *Memorial Day–Labor Day, daily 9–9; Sept.–May, Wed.–Mon. 9–8, Tues. 5 pm–8 pm.*</

UPTOWN/EAST SIDE

Just east of Nob Hill and south of Northeast Heights, Uptown and the East Side bridge the older and historic parts of Route 66 with the newer, somewhat suburban-looking parts of the city. The only attraction in these parts is the new National Museum of Nuclear Science & History. Few visitors spend time here, except to check out the shopping and dining at ABQ Uptown and Coronado Mall, which are also close to a few hotels.

Ⓒ **National Museum of Nuclear Science & History.** Renamed in 2009 following a move from its temporary former location in Old Town, this impressive museum traces the history of the atomic age and how nuclear science has dramatically influenced the course of modern history. Exhibits include replicas of Little Boy and Fat Man (the bombs dropped on Japan at the end of World War II), a compelling display about the difficult decision to drop atomic bombs, and a look at how atomic culture has dovetailed with pop culture. There are also children's programs and an exhibit about X-ray technology. This new facility also contains the 9-acre Heritage Park, which has a B-29 and other mega-airships, plus rockets, missiles, cannons, and even a nuclear sub sail. One highlight is the restored 1942 Plymouth that was used to transport the plutonium core of "the Gadget" (as that first weapon was known) down from Los Alamos to the Trinity Site for testing. ⊠ *601 Eubank Blvd. SE, a few blocks south of I–40Uptown/East Side* ☎ *505/245–2137* ⊕ *www. atomicmuseum.org* ⊠ *$8* ☉ *Daily 9–5.*

WEST SIDE

The fastest-growing part of Albuquerque lies on a broad mesa high above the Rio Grande Valley. The West Side is primarily the domain of new suburban housing developments and strip malls, some designed more attractively than others. Somewhat controversially, growth on the West Side has seemed to occur below, above, and virtually all around the archaeologically critical Petroglyph National Monument. Allow a 20-minute drive from Old Town and the North Valley to reach the monument.

Ⓒ **Petroglyph National Monument.** Beneath the stumps of five extinct volcanoes, this park encompasses more than 25,000 ancient Native American rock drawings inscribed on the 17-mi-long West Mesa escarpment overlooking the Rio Grande Valley. For centuries, Native American hunting parties camped at the base, chipping and scribbling away. Archaeologists believe most of the petroglyphs were carved on the lava formations between 1100 and 1600, but some images at the park may date back as far as 1000 BC. A paved trail at **Boca Negra Canyon** (north of the visitor center on Unser Boulevard, beyond Montaño Road) leads past several dozen petroglyphs. The trail at **Rinconado Canyon** (south of the visitor center on Unser) is unpaved. The rangers at the visitor center will supply maps and help you determine which trail is best for the time you have. ⊠ *Visitor center, 6001 Unser Blvd. NW, at Western Trail Rd., 3 mi north of I–40 Exit 154; from I–25 take Exit 228 and proceed west on Montaño Rd. across the bridge, then south on Unser*

1 mi, West Side ☎ *505/899–0205* ⊕ *www.nps.gov/petr* ✉ *$1 weekdays, $2 weekends for parking at Boca Negra Canyon; access to rest of monument is free* ☉ *Daily 8–5.*

WHERE TO EAT

The Duke City has long been a place for hearty home-style cooking in big portions, and to this day, it's easy to find great steak-and-chops houses, retro diners, and authentic New Mexican restaurants. The trick is finding them amid Albuquerque's miles of chain options and legions of dives, but if you look, you'll be rewarded with innovative food, and generally at prices much lower than in Santa Fe or other major Southwestern cities.

Albuquerque's dining scene has evolved considerably of late. In Nob Hill, Downtown, and Old Town many notable new restaurants have opened, offering swank decor and complex and artful variations on modern Southwest, Mediterranean, Asian, and other globally inspired cuisine. A significant Vietnamese population has made that cuisine a star, but Indian, Japanese, Thai, and South American traditions all have a presence, making this New Mexico's best destination for ethnic fare.

WHAT IT COSTS					
	¢	$	$$	$$$	$$$$
Restaurants	under $10	$10–$15	$16–$22	$23–$30	over $30

Prices are per person for a main course at dinner, excluding 8.25% sales tax.

Use the coordinate (✛ A2) at the end of each listing to locate a site on the corresponding map.

OLD TOWN

$$$ ✕ **Antiquity.** Within the thick adobe walls of this darkly lighted, romantic
CONTINENTAL space on the plaza in Old Town, patrons have been feasting on rich, elegantly prepared American classics for more than 50 years. This isn't the edgy, contemporary restaurant to bring an adventuresome foodie— Antiquity specializes in classics, from starters of French onion soup and escargot to main courses like Australian lobster tail with drawn butter and black angus New York strip-loin steak with horseradish sauce. But the consistently well-prepared food and charming service make it a winner. ⊠ *112 Romero St. NW, Old Town* ☎ *505/247–3545* ▤ *AE, D, MC, V* ☉ *No lunch* ✛ *B3.*

$ ✕ **Church Street Café.** Built in the early 1700s, this structure is among
NEW MEXICAN the oldest in New Mexico. Renovations have preserved the original adobe bricks to ensure that this spacious eatery remains as authentic as its menu, which features family recipes spanning four generations— with fresh, local ingredients and spirits employed to satiate streams of hungry tourists and locals. Request the courtyard for alfresco dining amid trellises of sweet grapes and flowers, and where classical and flamenco guitarist José Salazar often performs. Buttery guacamole, with

BEST BETS FOR ALBUQUERQUE DINING

With hundreds of restaurants to choose from, how will you decide where to eat? Fodor's writers and editors have selected their favorite restaurants by price and cuisine in the Best Bets lists below. Find specific details about a restaurant in the full reviews, listed below.

Fodor's Choice ★

Casa Vieja $$$, p. 85
El Patio ¢, p. 55
Farina Pizzeria & Wine Bar $, p. 52
Grove Cafe & Market ¢, p. 53
Jennifer James 101 $$$, p. 58
Range Cafe & Bakery $, p. 87

By Price

¢

Duran's Central Pharmacy, p. 49
El Patio, p. 55
Grove Cafe & Market, p. 53
Mary & Tito's, p. 57
Mineshaft Tavern, p. 90
Viet Taste, p. 58

$

Flying Star, p. 55
Farina Pizzeria & Wine Bar, p. 52
Nob Hill Bar and Grill, p. 56
Range Cafe & Bakery, p. 87

San Marcos Cafe, p. 91
Sophia's Place, p. 57

$$

Brasserie La Provence, p. 54
Seasons Rotisserie & Grill, p. 49
Slate Street Cafe, p. 53
Standard Diner, p. 54

$$$

Antiquity, p. 47
Artichoke Café, p. 52
Casa Vieja, p. 85
Jennifer James 101, p. 58
Prairie Star, p. 86
Zinc Wine Bar & Bistro, p. 56

$$$$

Bien Shur, p. 57
Corn Maiden, p. 86
Rancher's Club, p. 53

By Cuisine

AMERICAN

66 Diner ¢, p. 54
Bien Shur $$$$, p. 57

Gold Street Caffè $, p. 52
Frontier Restaurant ¢, p. 56
Mineshaft Tavern ¢, p. 90
Standard Diner $$, p. 54

CAFÉ

Flying Star $, p. 55
Golden Crown Panaderia ¢, p. 49
Grove Cafe & Market ¢, p. 53
Range Cafe & Bakery $, p. 87
San Marcos Cafe $, p. 91
Sophia's Place $, p. 57

ASIAN

Crazy Fish $, p. 55
Viet Taste ¢, p. 58

CONTEMPORARY

Casa Vieja $$$, p. 85
Jennifer James 101 $$$, p. 58
Nob Hill Bar and Grill $, p. 56
Prairie Star $$$, p. 86
Slate Street Cafe $$, p. 53

Zinc Wine Bar & Bistro $$$, p. 56

FRENCH/ITALIAN/MEDITERRANEAN

Artichoke Café $$$, p. 52
Brasserie La Provence $$, p. 54
Farina Pizzeria & Wine Bar $, p. 52
Lucia $$$, p. 53
Yanni's Mediterranean Grill $$, p. 56
Village Pizza ¢, p. 85

just a bit of bite, is the perfect appetizer to prep one's palate for tender carne asada, redolent and sumptuously spiced. Try the house specialty, chiles rellenos stuffed with beef and cheese, or a portobello-and-bell-pepper fajita. Traditional desserts and hearty breakfast choices are also offered. ✉ *2111 Church St. NW, Old Town* ☎ *505/247–8522* ⊕ *www. churchstreetcafe.com* ▭ *AE, D, MC, V* ☾ *No dinner Sun* ✛ *B3.*

¢ ✗ **Duran's Central Pharmacy.** This expanded Old Town lunch counter
NEW MEXICAN with a dozen tables and a tiny patio just might serve the best tortillas in town. A favorite of old-timers who know their way around a blue-corn enchilada, Duran's is an informal place whose patrons give their food the total attention it deserves. Be sure to leave some browsing time for the pharmacy's book section: Duran's has a good selection of not easily found history and coffee-table volumes covering the Duke City and its storied environs. ✉ *1815 Central Ave. NW, Old Town* ☎ *505/247–4141* ▭ *No credit cards* ☾ *No dinner* ✛ *B4.*

¢ ✗ **Golden Crown Panaderia.** On the eastern fringe of Old Town, in a
CAFÉ nascent arts district, this aromatic, down-home-style bakery is known for two things: the ability to custom-design and bake artful breads in the likeness of just about any person or place, and hearty green-chile bread (made with tomatoes, cilantro, Parmesan, green chile, and onions). You can order hot cocoa, cappuccino, *bizcochito* (the official state cookie, also known as New Mexican wedding cookies), pumpkin-filled empanadas, plenty of other sweets and sandwiches (ask what bread is fresh and hot), and wonderfully spicy and aromatic pizzas made with green-chile crusts. There's seating on a small patio. ✉ *1103 Mountain Rd. NW, Old Town* ☎ *505/243–2424 or 877/382–2924* ⊕ *www. goldencrown.biz* ▭ *MC, V* ☾ *Closed Mon* ✛ *C3.*

$ ✗ **Monica's El Portal.** Locals in the know favor this rambling, authentic
NEW MEXICAN New Mexican restaurant on the west side of Old Town over the more famous, though less reliable, standbys around Old Town Plaza. Monica's has a prosaic dining room plus a cute tiled patio, and the service is friendly and unhurried. If you've never had *chicharrones* (fried pork skins), try them here with beans stuffed inside a flaky sopaipilla. Or consider the traditional blue-corn chicken or beef enchiladas, and the savory green-chile stew. This is honest, home-style food, and lunch here may just fill you up for the rest of the day. ✉ *321 Rio Grande Blvd. NW, Old Town* ☎ *505/247–9625* ▭ *AE, D, MC, V* ☾ *Closed Mon. No dinner weekends* ✛ *B3*

$$ ✗ **Seasons Rotisserie & Grill.** Upbeat yet elegant, this Old Town eatery
CONTEMPORARY is an easy place to have a business lunch or a dinner date, and oenophiles will revel in its well-chosen cellar. The kitchen serves innovative grills and pastas, such as wood-roasted duck breast with Gorgonzola–sweet-potato gratin and grilled Colorado lamb with Moroccan couscous, sautéed haricots verts, and cherry-mint demi-glace; great starters include pan-seared crab cakes with cilantro-lime aioli, and sweet-corn griddle cakes with marsala-fig chutney and almond-pepper tapenade. The rooftop patio and bar provides evening cocktails and lighter meals. ✉ *2031 Mountain Rd. NW, Old Town* ☎ *505/766–5100* ⊕ *www.seasonsonthenet.com* ▭ *AE, D, DC, MC, V* ☾ *No lunch weekends* ✛ *B3.*

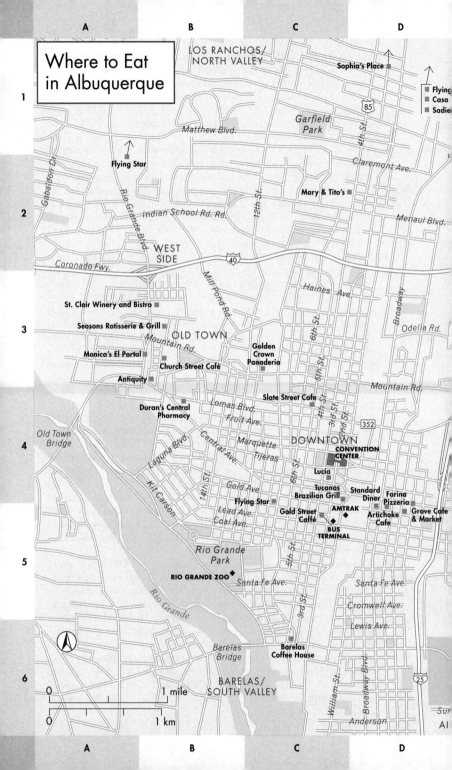

Where to Eat in Albuquerque

LOS RANCHOS/
NORTH VALLEY

Sophia's Place

Flying
Casa
Sadie

Garfield
Park

Matthew Blvd.

Claremont Ave.

Flying Star

Mary & Tito's

Indian School Rd. Rd.

Menaul Blvd.

WEST
SIDE

Coronado Fwy.

St. Clair Winery and Bistro

Haines Ave.

Seasons Rotisserie & Grill

OLD TOWN

Odelia Rd.

Mountain Rd.

Golden
Crown
Panaderia

Monica's El Portal

Church Street Café

Mountain Rd.

Antiquity

Slate Street Cafe

Lomas Blvd.

Duran's Central
Pharmacy

Fruit Ave.

Old Town
Bridge

Marquette

DOWNTOWN

Tijeras

CONVENTION
CENTER

Lucia

Tucanos
Brazilian Grill

Standard
Diner

Farina
Pizzeria

Flying Star

Gold Ave.

Grove Cafe
& Market

Gold Street
Caffé

AMTRAK

Artichoke
Cafe

Lead Ave.

Coal Ave.

BUS
TERMINAL

Rio Grande
Park

RIO GRANDE ZOO

Santa Fe Ave.

Santa Fe Ave.

Cromwell Ave.

Lewis Ave.

Barelas
Bridge

Barelas
Coffee House

BARELAS/
SOUTH VALLEY

Anderson

0   1 mile

0   1 km

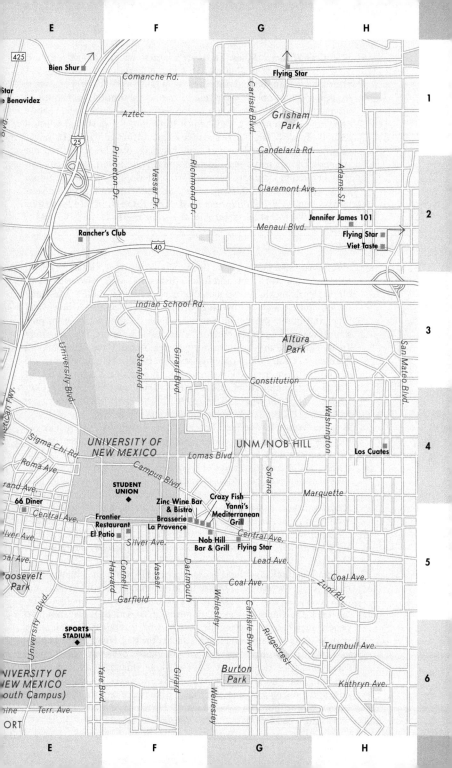

$ ✗**St. Clair Winery & Bistro.** The state's largest winery, in the southern
CONTINENTAL   New Mexico town of Deming, St. Clair Winery has a charming and
affordable restaurant and tasting room in Old Town. It's part of a small
shopping center on the west side of the neighborhood, just south of
Interstate 40. You enter a shop with a bar for wine tasting and shelves
of wines and gourmet goods, which leads into the dark and warmly
lighted dining room. There's also a large, attractive patio. At lunch,
sample the panini sandwich of New Mexico goat cheese and roasted
peppers. Dinner treats include crab-and-artichoke dip, garlic chicken
slow-cooked in Chardonnay, and pork tenderloin cooked in Nebbiolo
wine with raspberry-chipotle sauce. St. Clair serves a popular Sunday brunch. ⊠ *901 Rio Grande Blvd., Old Town* ☎ *505/243–9916 or*
888/870–9916 ⊕ *www.stclairvineyards.com* ▭ *AE, D, MC, V* ✛ *B3.*

DOWNTOWN

$$$ ✗**Artichoke Café.** Locals praise the Artichoke for its service and French,
CONTEMPORARY   contemporary American, and Italian dishes prepared, whenever possi-
ble, with organically grown ingredients. Specialties include house-made
ravioli stuffed with ricotta and butternut squash with a white wine,
sage, and butter sauce; and pan-seared sea scallops wrapped in pro-
sciutto with red potatoes, haricots verts, and wax beans. The appetizers
are so tasty you may want to make a meal out of them. The building
is about a century old, in the historic Huning Highland district in the
emerging EDo section of Downtown, but the decor is Uptown modern.
The two-tier dining room spills out into a small courtyard. ⊠ *424 Cen-*
tral Ave. SE, Downtown ☎ *505/243–0200* ⊕ *www.artichokecafe.com*
▭ *AE, D, DC, MC, V* ☽ *No lunch weekends* ✛ *D5.*

$ ✗**Farina Pizzeria & Wine Bar.** The team at the Artichoke Café, just across
PIZZA   the street, has opened this stellar pizza lounge inside an ancient former
Fodor's Choice   grocery store with hardwood floors, exposed-brick walls, pressed-tin
★   ceiling, and a couple of rows of wooden tables along with a long bar.
This noisy, spirited place doles out exceptionally tasty pizzas with blis-
tering-hot crusts and imaginative toppings; the Salsiccia, with sweet-
fennel sausage, roasted onions, and mozzarella, has plenty of fans.
Finish with rich butterscotch *budino* (Italian pudding), and take note of
the extensive, fair-priced list of wines by the glass. ⊠ *510 Central Ave.*
SE, Downtown ☎ *505/243–0130* ⊕ *www.farinapizzeria.com* ▭ *AE, D,*
DC, MC, V ☽ *No lunch weekends* ✛ *D4.*

$ ✗**Gold Street Caffè.** A culinary cornerstone of Downtown Albuquerque's
CAFÉ   renaissance, this dapper storefront café with exposed-brick walls and
high ceilings serves breakfast fare that is a cut above, plus equally satisfy-
ing lunch and dinner entrées. In the morning, go with Eggs Eleganza (two
poached eggs atop a green-chile brioche with local goat cheese), along
with a side of chile-glazed bacon. Later in the day, consider the Dunge-
ness crab cakes with almond-crusted goat cheese, or seared-beef chopped
salad with fried rice noodles and chile-lime vinaigrette. You can also
just hang out among the hipsters and office workers, sipping a caramel
latte and munching on one of the tasty desserts, or enjoy a glass of wine
from the short but well-selected list. ⊠ *218 Gold Ave. SW, Downtown*
☎ *505/765–1633* ▭ *MC, V* ☽ *No dinner Sun. and Mon* ✛ *C5.*

¢
CAFÉ
Fodor's Choice
★

✕ **Grove Cafe & Market.** On the east side of Downtown in the historic Huning Highland district (an area now commonly called EDo), this airy, modern establishment is a local favorite that features locally grown, seasonal specials at reasonable prices. Enjoy such fresh, quality treats as Grove Pancakes with fresh fruit, crème fraîche, local honey, and real maple syrup; a Farmers Salad with roasted golden beets, Marcona almonds, goat cheese, and lemon-basil vinaigrette; or an aged Genoa salami sandwich with olive tapenade, arugula, and provolone on an artisanal sourdough bread. You can dine on the arbored patio. Or come by for a loose-leaf tea or latte with a cupcake. The market sells an impressive mix of chocolates, cheeses, and gourmet foods. ⊠ *600 Central Ave. SE, Downtown* ☎ *505/248–9800* ⊕ *www.thegrovecafemarket. com* 🖃 *AE, D, MC, V* ☺ *Closed Mon. No dinner* ✛ *D5.*

$$$
MEDITERRANEAN

✕ **Lucia.** Lucia provides Albuquerque with a much-needed dose of style. The angular, spare dining room with mod overhanging lights and contemporary furnishings is downright edgy and unexpected for a dining venue inside the historic Hotel Andaluz. The menu pushes the envelope, too, with pricey (by local standards) and creative Mediterranean fare with nary a hint of green chiles. You might start with grilled baby artichokes with caper-saffron butter, followed by Catalonian-herb-crusted rack of lamb with oil-poached tomatoes, chickpea compote, and roasted-garlic asparagus. There are no weak links on this ambitious menu. Breakfast and lunch are served, too. The patio area is dog-friendly. ⊠ *Hotel Andaluz, 125 2nd St. NW, Downtown* ☎ *505/923–9080* ⊕ *www.hotelandaluz.com/lucia* 🖃 *AE, D, DC, MC, V* ✛ *C4.*

$$$$
STEAK

✕ **Rancher's Club.** Few hotel restaurants in Albuquerque merit serious culinary consideration, but this clubby, old-world steak house in the Albuquerque Hilton earns raves among deep-pocketed carnivores for its delicious aged steaks and ribs. The dining room is hung with saddles, mounted bison heads, and ranching-related art. If you want to impress a date or clients, order the fillet of Wagyu Kobe beef with creamed spinach, lobster-mashed potatoes, and morel-mushroom jus. Other standouts include elk chops, Alaskan wild salmon, and porterhouse steak. ⊠ *Albuquerque Hilton, 1901 University Blvd. NE, Downtown* ☎ *505/889–8071* ⊕ *http://theranchersclubofnm.com* 🖃 *AE, D, DC, MC, V* ☺ *No lunch* ✛ *E2*

$$
ECLECTIC

✕ **Slate Street Cafe.** A high-energy, high-ceiling dining room with a semi-circular, central wine bar and modern lighting, this stylish restaurant sits amid pawn shops and bail-bond outposts on a quiet, unprepossessing side street Downtown. But once inside, you'll find a sophisticated, colorful space serving memorable, modern renditions of classic American fare, such as fried chicken and meat loaf. The starters are notable, including grilled sesame-crusted ahi with wasabi cream, and bruschetta topped with honey-cured ham and Brie. Banana-stuffed brioche French toast is a favorite at breakfast and weekend brunch. More than 25 wines by the glass are served. ⊠ *515 Slate St. NW, Downtown* ☎ *505/243–2210* ⊕ *www.slatestreetcafe.com* 🖃 *AE, D, MC, V* ☺ *No dinner Sun.* ✛ *C4.*

$$ ✕ **Standard Diner.** In the historic Huning Highlands district, aka EDo (for
CONTEMPORARY   East of Downtown), the Standard occupies a 1930s Texaco station with
high ceilings, massive plate-glass windows, and rich tile floors—it's at
once elegant yet casual, serving upscale yet affordable takes on tradi-
tional diner standbys. The extensive menu dabbles in meal-size salads
(try the tempura-lobster Caesar salad), burgers (including a terrific one
topped with bourbon butter), sandwiches, and traditional diner entrées
given nouvelle flourishes (fish tacos with fresh bay scallops, bacon-
wrapped meat loaf with red-wine gravy). Kick everything up with a
side of truffle-pecorino french fries, and save room for the fancy milk
shakes in novel flavors such as apricot–crème brûlée and espresso Guin-
ness. ⊠ *320 Central Ave. SE, Downtown* ☎ *505/243–1440* ⊕ *www.
standarddiner.com* ▭ *AE, D, MC, V* ✛ *D4.*

$$ ✕ **Tucanos Brazilian Grill.** There isn't much point in going to Tucanos if
BRAZILIAN   you don't love meat. Sure, they serve some vegetables, but the real focus
is on *churrasco,* South American–style grilled skewers of beef, chicken,
pork, and turkey that parade endlessly out of the open kitchen on the
arms of enthusiastic waiters. Carnivore-centrism aside, one unexpected
treat, if it's available, is the grilled pineapple. The noisy, high-ceiling
spot next to the Century 14 Downtown movie theater is a good place
to go for drinks, too, and if you're looking for either a stand-alone
cooler or a liquid partner for your hearty fare, look no further than a
bracing *caipirinha,* the lime-steeped national cocktail of Brazil. ⊠ *110
Central Ave. SW, Downtown* ☎ *505/246–9900* ⊕ *www.tucanos.com*
▭ *AE, D, MC, V* ✛ *C4.*

BARELAS/SOUTH VALLEY

¢   ✕ **Barelas Coffee House.** Barelas may look like a set in search of a script,
NEW MEXICAN   but it's the real deal: diners come from all over the city to sup in this
old-fashioned chile parlor in the Hispanic Historic Route 66 neighborhood south of Downtown. You may notice looks of quiet contentment
on the faces of the many dedicated chile eaters as they dive into their
bowls of Barelas's potent red. There's also tasty breakfast fare. The staff
treats everybody like an old friend—indeed, many of the regulars who
come here have been fans of Barelas for decades. ⊠ *1502 4th St. SW,
Barelas/South Valley* ☎ *505/843–7577* ⌾ *Reservations not accepted*
▭ *D, MC, V* ⊗ *Closed Sun. No dinner* ✛ *C6.*

UNM/NOB HILL

¢   ✕ **66 Diner.** Dining at this '50s-style art deco diner is a must for fans of
AMERICAN   Route 66 nostalgia, and the upbeat decor and friendly service also make
it a hit with families. The specialties here are many: chicken-fried steak,
burgers, malted milk shakes, enchiladas. Plenty of breakfast treats are
available, too. ⊠ *1405 Central Ave. NE, UNM/Nob Hill* ☎ *505/247–
1421* ⊕ *www.66diner.com* ▭ *AE, D, MC, V* ✛ *E4.*

$$ ✕ **Brasserie La Provence.** You'll find classic French bistro dishes—*moules
FRENCH   frites,* couscous *merguez* (spicy lamb sausage), and *croque madame*
(grilled ham, egg, and cheese sandwich)—and a nice wine list in this ami-
able corner spot on the west edge of Nob Hill, steps from UNM campus.

2

Service is good, and the food—which is very good—is improved by the congenial atmosphere. Try the patio when the weather is fair, or the lemon-colored back room when it's not. There are specials each day, and the less-expected menu items such as *Poulet du Midi* (seared chicken breast stuffed with chèvre and figs) are palate- and budget-pleasing as well. ⊠ *3001 Central Ave. NE, UNM/Nob Hill* ☎ *505/254–7644* ⊕ *www.laprovencenobhill.com* ▭ *AE, D, MC, V* ✢ *F5.*

$
JAPANESE

✕**Crazy Fish.** A good bet for relatively straightforward sushi and sashimi, Crazy Fish is an attractive, upbeat storefront space with minimal fuss and gimmickry—just clean lines and a black-and-gray color scheme. Friendly young servers whisk out plates of fresh food to a mix of students and yuppies. In addition to sushi, the kitchen prepares such favorites as crispy chicken, garlic-peppered beef, and seared-albacore salad with a ginger-soy dressing. Tempura-fried bananas with chocolate ice cream make for a sweet ending. ⊠ *3015 Central Ave. NE, UNM/ Nob Hill* ☎ *505/232–3474* ⊕ *www.crazyfishabq.com* ▭ *AE, D, MC, V* ☽ *Closed Mon. No lunch weekends* ✢ *F5.*

¢
NEW MEXICAN
Fodor's Choice
★

✕**El Patio.** A university-area hangout, this sentimental favorite serves consistently exemplary New Mexican food on a funky patio and inside a cozy dining room. The service is sometimes pokey, but always friendly. Go for the green-chile-chicken enchiladas or any of the heart-healthy and vegetarian selections. But watch out for the fiery green chiles served at harvesttime—this is spicy food even by local standards. Note that liquor isn't served, but beer and wine are—you can get decent-tasting "margaritas" made with wine. ⊠ *142 Harvard St. NE, UNM/Nob Hill* ☎ *505/268–4245* ⊕ *www.elpatiodealbuquerque.com* ⊰ *Reservations not accepted* ▭ *MC, V* ✢ *F5.*

$
★
CAFÉ

✕**Flying Star.** Flying Star has become a staple and miniphenom here, and although it's a chain, it's locally owned and—just as at its Satellite Coffee spots around town—each outpost offers something a little different. The cavernous Downtown branch is a favorite for its striking setting inside the historic Southern Union Gas Co. building and its unexpected modernist motif; the newer Corrales and Bernalillo locales are notable for their shaded outdoor patio and indoor fireplaces. At the original Nob Hill space, the crowd is youthful and bohemian, and the space tighter. The concept works on many levels: it's a newsstand, late-night coffeehouse (there's free Wi-Fi), and an order-at-the-counter restaurant serving a mix of creative Asian, American, and New Mexican dishes (plus several types of wine and beer). Options include Greek pasta with shrimp, green-chile cheeseburgers, Thai-style tofu salad with tangy lime dressing, turkey-and-Jack-cheese-melt sandwiches, and an egg- and chile-packed "graburrito." Desserts change often, but count on a tantalizing array. For a winning pick-me-up, employ some strong hot coffee to wash down a tall slice of the fantastic coconut cream pie. We list a few of our favorite locations. ⊠ *3416 Central Ave. SE, UNM/Nob Hill* ☎ *505/255–6633* ⊠ *723 Silver Ave., Downtown* ☎ *505/244–8099* ⊠ *10700 Corrales Rd., Corrales* ☎ *505/938–4717* ⊠ *200 S. Camino del Pueblo, Bernalillo* ☎ *505/404–2100* ⊕ *www.flyingstarcafe.com* ▭ *AE, D, MC, V.* ✢ *A2; C4; D1; G5; G1; H2.*

¢   ✕**Frontier Restaurant.** This definitive student hangout across from UNM
CAFÉ   is open daily until late 1 am for inexpensive diner-style American and
New Mexican chow. A notch up from a fast-food joint, it's open later
than most such spots in town, and the breakfast burritos are terrific.
Featured along with the John Wayne and Elvis artwork in this sprawl-
ing '70s spot are oversize cinnamon buns. We won't fault you if you
cave and order one. ✉ *2400 Central Ave. SE, at Cornell Dr. SE,UNM/
Nob Hill* ☎ *505/266–0550* ⊕ *www.frontierrestaurant.com* ▭ *AE, D,
MC, V* ✛ *F5.*

$ ✕**Nob Hill Bar and Grill.** This elegant, centrally situated space in Nob Hill
NEW AMERICAN   has been the site of two failed yet very good restaurants in recent years,
but the latest occupant—the dapper and nearly always packed Nob Hill
Bar and Grill—appears to be succeeding. The staff's youthful and energetic personality, and the dining room and bar's swanky yet still unfussy
decor are big plusses, as are the consistently delicious modern takes
on American classics. Tuck into a plate of applewood-smoked chicken
wings with Coca-Cola barbecue sauce, or nachos topped with ahi tuna,
before feasting on hearty mains like steak-frites with garlic-parsley fries,
and a terrific veggie burger fashioned out of *edamame* (green soy beans)
and wild mushrooms, and served with ginger-lime mayo. ✉ *3128 Central Ave. SE, UNM/Nob Hill* ☎ *505/266–4455* ⊕ *www.upscalejoint.
com* ▭ *AE, D, MC, V* ☾ *Closed Mon* ✛ *F5*

$$ ✕**Yanni's Mediterranean Grill.** Yanni's is a convivial place where the food
GREEK   can run second to its refreshing azure-tiled ambience. Serving mari-
nated grilled lamb chops with lemon and oregano, grilled yellowfin
sole encrusted with Parmesan, *pastitsio* (a Greek version of mac and
cheese), and spinach, feta, and roasted garlic pizzas, Yanni's also offers
a vegetarian plate with good meatless moussaka, tabbouleh, spanako-
pita, and stuffed grape leaves. There's a huge patio off the main dining
room, and next door you can sip cocktails and mingle with locals at
Opa Bar. ✉ *3109 Central Ave. NE, UNM/Nob Hill* ☎ *505/268–9250*
⊕ *www.yannisandopabar.com* ▭ *AE, D, MC, V* ✛ *F5.*

$$$ ✕**Zinc Wine Bar & Bistro.** A snazzy spot in lower Nob Hill, fairly close
CONTEMPORARY   to UNM, Zinc captures the essence of a San Francisco neighborhood
bistro with its high ceilings, hardwood floors, and white tablecloths and
dark-wood straight-back café chairs. You can sample wine from the
long list or listen to live music downstairs in the Cellar Bar. Consider
the starter of crispy duck-confit eggrolls with curry-chile-lime dipping
sauce; or the main dish of seared scallops with wild-rice–cranberry pilaf
and a tarragon-crayfish beurre blanc. The kitchen uses organic ingredients whenever available. Don't miss the exceptional weekend brunch.
✉ *3009 Central Ave. NE, UNM/Nob Hill* ☎ *505/254–9462* ⊕ *www.
zincabq.com* ▭ *AE, D, MC, V* ✛ *G5*

LOS RANCHOS/NORTH VALLEY

$ ✕**Casa de Benavidez.** The fajitas at this sprawling local favorite with a
NEW MEXICAN   romantic patio are among the best in town, and the *carne adovada* is
faultless; the burger wrapped inside a sopaipilla is another specialty, as
are the chimichangas packed with beef. The charming restaurant occupies a late-19th-century Territorial-style house. ✉ *8032 4th St. NW, Los*

Ranchos/North Valley ☎ *505/898–3311* ⊕ *www.casadebenavidez.com*
⊟ *AE, D, MC, V* ☯ *No dinner Sun* ✛ *D1.*

¢ ✕ **Mary & Tito's.** Locals do go on about who's got the best chile, red or
NEW MEXICAN green. What they don't dispute is that Mary & Tito's—an institution
for decades, and run by the same family since it opened—is as tasty
as it comes. It's casual, friendly, and the real deal. Grab a booth and
try the rellenos or the enchiladas. A bonus: the chile is vegetarian,
and the red is always sm-o-o-o-th. Although open for dinner nightly,
the kitchen closes at 6 pm Monday through Thursday. ✉ *2711 4th St.
NW, 2 blocks north of Menaul Blvd. NW, Los Ranchos/North Valley* ☎ *505/344–6266* ⚌ *Reservations not accepted* ⊟ *AE, D, MC, V*
☯ *Closed Sun* ✛ *D2*

$ ✕ **Sadie's.** One of the city's longtime favorites for simple-but-spicy,
NEW MEXICAN no-nonsense, New Mexican fare, Sadie's—remembered fondly by old-
timers for the era when it made its home in the Lucky 66 bowling alley
next door—now occupies a long, fortresslike adobe building. Specialties include carne adovada, spicy beef burritos, and chiles rellenos.
The service is always prompt, though sometimes there's a wait for a
table. While you're waiting, try one of the excellent margaritas. Sadie's
salsa is locally renowned and available by the jar for takeout. ✉ *6230
4th St. NW, Los Ranchos/North Valley* ☎ *505/345–5339* ⊕ *www.
sadiesofnewmexico.com* ⊟ *AE, D, MC, V* ✛ *D1*

$ ✕ **Sophia's Place.** Devotees can't get enough of the *muy buenos* berry
NEW MEXICAN pancakes with real maple syrup, breakfast burritos (with the *papas*—
or potatoes—inside, so ask if you'd like them out instead), enchiladas
sprinkled with *cotija* (a mild, crumbly cow's milk cheese), and just about
anything the kitchen whips up. Dishes range from creative and generous
salads and chipotle-chile bacon cheeseburgers to udon noodles and fish
tacos. In Los Ranchos de Albuquerque, in the heart of the North Valley,
Sophia's (named after the Alice Waters–trained chef-owner's daughter)
is a simple neighborhood spot, yet one that people drive out of their
way for—especially for the weekend brunch. Everything is fresh, often
organic, prettily presented, and always made-to-order. ✉ *6313 4th St.
NW, Los Ranchos/North Valley* ☎ *505/345–3935* ⚌ *Reservations not
accepted* ⊟ *AE, D, MC, V* ☯ *No dinner Sun.* ✛ *D1.*

NORTHEAST HEIGHTS

$$$$ ✕ **Bien Shur.** The panoramic city and mountain views are an essential
AMERICAN part of this quietly refined restaurant on the ninth floor of the Sandia Casino complex, but Bien Shur also aspires to be one of the most
sophisticated restaurants in the city. Alas, the service can be uneven at
times, and although the food is usually on the mark, it's quite pricey for
Albuquerque. You might start with a panfried crab cake with cilantro
oil, saffron aioli, and tomato salsa. Among the several stellar entrées,
skip the seafood and go right for the steaks and chops, such as buffalo
tenderloin, or the prodigious 20-ounce porterhouse steak. ✉ *Sandia
Resort & Casino, Tramway Rd. NE, east of I–25, Northeast Heights*
☎ *505/798–3700* ⊕ *www.sandiacasino.com* ⊟ *AE, D, MC, V* ☯ *Closed
Sun. and Mon. No lunch* ✛ *E1.*

UPTOWN/EAST SIDE

$$$
ECLECTIC
Fodor's Choice
★

✕ **Jennifer James 101.** Helmed by and named for one of New Mexico's most respected chefs, this small Uptown eatery is known mostly by foodies, locals, and fans of Jennifer James' previous restaurants around town. The menu is limited, and reservations are a must, but once you take your seat in the simple, high-ceilinged dining room in an unassuming shopping center, you're in for a treat. The menu changes often and focuses on seasonal ingredients; perhaps an appetizer of salt-cured foie gras with mâche and a balsamic-pomegranate reduction, or a main dish featuring wild boar braised with red wine and rosemary and served with polenta, grilled radicchio, and Gorgonzola. There's also a carefully considered wine list that includes several surprisingly affordable, good bottles. ⊠ *4615 Menaul Blvd. NE, Uptown/East Side* ☏ *505/884–3860* ⊕ *http://web.me.com/jenniferjames101* ⌲ *Reservations essential* ⊟ *AE, MC, V* ⊘ *No lunch Sun. and Mon.* ✛ *H2.*

¢
NEW MEXICAN

✕ **Los Cuates.** A short drive northeast of Nob Hill and UNM, Los Cuates (a three-location local minichain) doesn't get as much attention as some of the city's more touristy New Mexican restaurants, but the food here is reliable, and prepared with pure vegetable oil rather than lard, which is one reason it's never as greasy as at some competitors. The green-chile stew is vegetarian (unless you request meat). All the usual favorites are served here, but top picks include the roast-beef burrito covered with melted cheese, and the tostada *compuesta* (a corn tortilla stuffed with beef, beans, rice, potatoes, carne adovada, and *chile con queso*—chile cheese sauce). ⊠ *4901 Lomas Blvd. NE, Uptown/East Side* ☏ *505/255–5079* ⊕ *www.loscuatesrestaurants.com* ⌲ *Reservations not accepted* ⊟ *AE, D, MC, V* ✛ *H4.*

¢
VIETNAMESE

✕ **Viet Taste.** Come here for another side of spicy hot. Excellent, authentic Vietnamese food is served up in this compact, modern, bamboo-accented restaurant. Ignore the fact that it's within one of Albuquerque's ubiquitous strip malls. Consider the popular *pho* (noodle soup) variations, order the tofu (or chicken or shrimp) spring rolls with tangy peanut sauce, dig into the spicy lemongrass with chicken, and all will be well. ⊠ *5721 Menaul Blvd. NE, Uptown/East Side* ☏ *505/888–0101* ⊟ *AE, D, MC, V* ✛ *H2.*

WHERE TO STAY

With a few exceptions, Albuquerque's lodging options fall into two categories: modern chain hotels and motels, and distinctive and typically historic inns and B&Bs. You won't find many larger hotels that are independently owned, historic, or rife with personality, although Central Avenue—all across the city—is lined with fascinating old motor courts and motels from the 1930s through the '50s, many with original neon signs and quirky roadside architecture. Alas, nearly all of these are run-down and substandard; they should be avoided unless you're extremely adventurous and can't resist the super-low rates (often as little as $18 a night).

If you're seeking charm and history, try one of the many excellent inns and B&Bs, or the Andaluz and Parq Central hotels, which are both Downtown and quite new, but set inside distinctive historic buildings. Although the chain hotels may appear interchangeable, there are several that stand out, and many of these are described below. Two parts of the city with an excellent variety of economical, plain-Jane, franchise hotels (Hampton Inn, Comfort Inn, Courtyard Marriott, etc.) are the airport area and the north Interstate 25 corridor. Albuquerque's airport is convenient to attractions and Downtown, and the north Interstate 25 corridor offers easy access to sightseeing, dining, and Balloon Fiesta Park. Wherever you stay in Albuquerque, you can generally count on finding rates considerably lower than the national average, and much cheaper than those in Santa Fe.

WHAT IT COSTS				
¢	$	$$	$$$	$$$$

	¢	$	$$	$$$	$$$$
Hotels	under $70	$70–$120	$121–$175	$176–$250	over $250

Prices are for two people in a standard double room in high season, excluding 12%–13% tax.

Use the coordinate (✛ A2) at the end of each listing to locate a site on the corresponding map.

OLD TOWN

$
HOTEL
Best Western Rio Grande Inn. Although part of the Best Western chain, this contemporary four-story low-rise just off Interstate 40—a 10-minute walk from Old Town's plaza—has an attractive Southwestern design and furnishings, plus such modern touches as free Wi-Fi. The heavy, handcrafted wood furniture, tin sconces, and artwork in the rooms come from local suppliers and artisans. The quite decent Albuquerque Grill serves three meals daily. It's a good value. **Pros:** free shuttle to airport and around town within 1-mi radius; excellent value. **Cons:** it's a hike from the rear rooms to the front desk; a bit close to the interstate. ⊠ *1015 Rio Grande Blvd. NW, Old Town* ☎ *505/843–9500 or 800/959–4726* ⊕ *www.riograndeinn.com* ➽ *173 rooms* ☖ *In-room: a/c, refrigerator, Wi-Fi. In-hotel: restaurant, room service, bar, pool, gym, laundry facilities, parking (free), some pets allowed* ⊟ *AE, D, DC, MC, V* ✛ *F4*

$$
BED & BREAKFAST
Böttger Mansion of Old Town. Charles Böttger, a German immigrant, built this pink two-story mansion in 1912. The lacy, richly appointed rooms vary greatly in size and decor; some have four-poster beds, slate floors, claw-foot tubs, or pressed-tin ceilings. All have down comforters, fluffy pillows, and terry robes—and a few are said to be haunted by a friendly ghost or two. The Wine Cellar Suite, in the basement, can accommodate up to six guests and has a kitchenette. A grassy courtyard fronted by a patio provides an escape from the Old Town crowds. Breakfast might consist of stuffed French toast or perhaps burritos smothered in green chile, which you can also enjoy in your room. **Pros:** balloon, golf, and tour packages are available; very handy location to dining and

BEST BETS FOR ALBUQUERQUE LODGING

Fodor's offers a selective listing of quality lodging experiences in every price range, from the city's best budget beds to its most sophisticated luxury hotels. Here, we've compiled our top recommendations by price and experience. The very best properties—in other words, those that provide a particularly remarkable experience in their price range—are designated in the listings with the Fodor's Choice logo.

Fodor's Choice ★

Andaluz $$$, p. 61
Downtown Historic Bed & Breakfasts of Albuquerque $$, p. 64
Hyatt Regency Tamaya $$$, p. 87
Los Poblanos Inn $$$, p. 67
Mauger Estate B&B Inn $$, p. 66

By Price

$

Chocolate Turtle B&B, p. 85
Cinnamon Morning B&B, p. 66
Holiday Inn Hotel & Suites Albuquerque Airport, p. 69
Hotel Blue, p. 65
Nativo Lodge Hotel, p. 67
Shaffer Hotel, p. 84

$$

Casas de Sueños, p. 61
Downtown Historic Bed & Breakfasts of Albuquerque, p. 64
Embassy Suites Hotel Albuquerque, p. 64
Hard Rock Hotel & Casino, p. 82
Hotel Albuquerque at Old Town, p. 61
Mauger Estate B&B Inn, p. 66

$$$

Andaluz, p. 61
High Feather Ranch, p. 92
Hotel Parq Central, p. 65
Hyatt Regency Tamaya, p. 87
Los Poblanos Inn, p. 67
Sandia Resort & Casino, p. 68

By Experience

BEST FOR KIDS

Best Western Rio Grande Inn, p. 59
Embassy Suites Hotel Albuquerque, p. 64
Hard Rock Hotel & Casino, p. 82
Hyatt Regency Tamaya, p. 87
Shaffer Hotel, p. 84

ROMANTIC

Andaluz $$$, p. 61
Downtown Historic Bed & Breakfasts of Albuquerque, p. 64
High Feather Ranch, p. 92
Hyatt Regency Tamaya, p. 87
Los Poblanos Inn, p. 67
Mauger Estate B&B Inn, p. 66

BEST SERVICE

Chocolate Turtle B&B, p. 85
Cinnamon Morning B&B, p. 66
Hyatt Regency Tamaya, p. 87

Los Poblanos Inn, p. 67
Sandia Resort & Casino, p. 68

HISTORIC SIGNIFICANCE

Andaluz, p. 61
Hotel Parq Central, p. 65
Böttger Mansion of Old Town, p. 59
Mauger Estate B&B Inn, p. 66
Shaffer Hotel, p. 84

SCENIC VIEWS

Albuquerque Marriott, p. 68
Elaine's, A Bed and Breakfast, p. 89
High Feather Ranch, p. 92
Hyatt Regency Albuquerque, p. 65
Hyatt Regency Tamaya, p. 87
Sandia Resort & Casino, p. 68

BEST-KEPT SECRET

Casas de Sueños, p. 61
High Feather Ranch, p. 92
Hotel Parq Central, p. 65
Mauger Estate B&B Inn, p. 66
Nativo Lodge Hotel, p. 67
Shaffer Hotel, p. 84

attractions. **Cons:** not for the floral-and-frilly phobic. ⊠ *110 San Felipe St. NW, Old Town* ☏ *505/243–3639 or 800/758–3639* ⊕ *www.bottger. com* ⇆ *7 rooms, 1 2-bedroom suite* ♿ *In-room: a/c, kitchen (some), Wi-Fi. In-hotel: parking (paid)* ▤ *AE, MC, V* ⍾ *BP* ⧓ *F5.*

$$ ⊡ **Casas de Sueños.** This historic compound of 1930s- and '40s-era
BED & BREAKFAST adobe casitas is perfect if you're seeking seclusion and quiet, yet seek proximity to museums, restaurants, and shops. Casas de Sueños (*sueños* means dreams in Spanish) is a few blocks south of Old Town Plaza, but on a peaceful residential street fringing the lush grounds of Albuquerque Country Club. The individually decorated units, which open onto a warren of courtyards and gardens, come in a variety of shapes and con-figurations. Typical features include Saltillo-tile floors, wood-burning kiva-style fireplaces, leather or upholstered armchairs, skylights, and contemporary Southwestern furnishings. Many rooms have large flat-screen TVs with DVD players and CD stereos, and some sleep as many as four adults. The full breakfast is served outside in the garden when the weather permits, and inside a lovely artists' studio at other times. **Pros:** charming and tucked away; some private patios. **Cons:** rooms vary greatly in amenities and configuration—some are more enchanting than others. ⊠ *310 Rio Grande Blvd. SW, on the south side of Central Ave., Old Town* ☏ *505/247–4560 or 800/665–7002* ⊕ *www.casasdesuenos. com* ⇆ *21 casitas* ♿ *In-room: a/c, kitchen (some), DVD (some), Wi-Fi. In-hotel: parking (free)* ▤ *AE, MC, V* ⍾ *BP* ⧓ *F5.*

$$ ⊡ **Hotel Albuquerque at Old Town.** This 11-story Southwestern-style hotel
HOTEL rises distinctly above Old Town's ancient structures. The large rooms have elegant, contemporary desert-color appointments, hand-wrought furnishings, and tile bathrooms; most rooms have a small balcony with no patio furniture but nice views. Cristobal's serves commendable Spanish-style steaks and seafood; Café Plazuela & Cantina offers more casual American and New Mexican food; and a fine flamenco guitarist entertains in the Q-Bar & Gallery Lounge. Spa treatments and facials are available. **Pros:** the high-ceiling, rustically furnished, Territorial-style lobby is a comfy place to hang out; hotel employs many eco-friendly practices. **Cons:** rather unattractive from the outside. ⊠ *800 Rio Grande Blvd. NW, Old Town* ☏ *505/843–6300 or 877/901–7666* ⊕ *www.hhandr.com/albuquerque* ⇆ *168 rooms, 20 suites* ♿ *In-room: a/c, refrigerator (some), Wi-Fi. In-hotel: 2 restaurants, room service, bar, pool, gym, spa, parking (free)* ▤ *AE, D, DC, MC, V* ⧓ *F4.*

DOWNTOWN

$$$ ⊡ **Andaluz.** Opened in 1939 by Conrad Hilton (who honeymooned here
HOTEL with Zsa Zsa Gabor), this glamorous 10-story hotel on the National
Fodor's Choice Register of Historic Places was known as La Posada de Albuquerque
★ until it was reinvented (and completely redone inside)—at a cost of $30 million—as a high-end boutique hotel in 2009. Its new name, Anda-luz, and its stunning decor reflect the Moroccan and Spanish-colonial influences of the original Hilton design. Its pursuit of Silver LEED cer-tification reflects the hotel's commitment to eco-friendly practices. The restaurant's beautiful two-story lobby is a wonderful spot to soak up the building's rich ambience, perhaps before grabbing cocktails in the

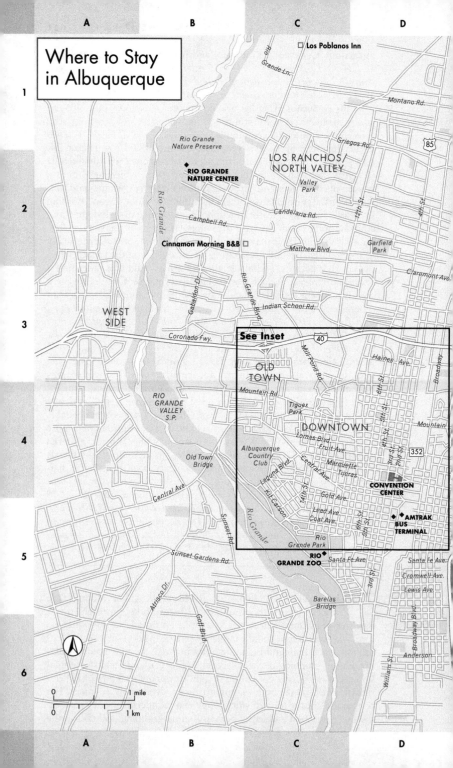

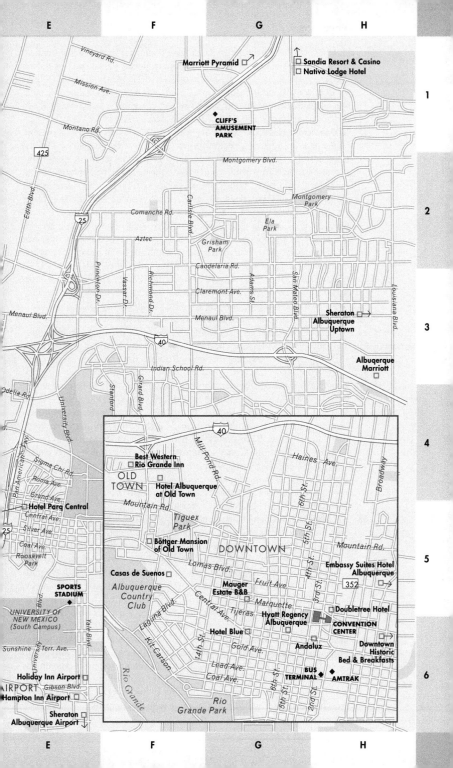

swank Ibiza bar or dinner in acclaimed Lucia restaurant. **Pros:** historic cachet aesthetic but with plenty of modern perks. **Cons:** priciest rooms in town. ⊠ *125 2nd St. NW, Downtown* ☎ *505/242–9090 or 800/777–5732* ⊕ *www.hotelandaluz.com* ⊳ *107 rooms, 7 suites* ⟁ *In-room: a/c, Wi-Fi. In-hotel: restaurant, room service, bar, laundry service, Wi-Fi hotspot, parking (paid)* ⊟ *AE, D, DC, MC, V* ⊕ *H6*

$$
HOTEL

Doubletree Hotel. A two-story waterfall splashes down a marble backdrop in the sleek, contemporary lobby of this 15-story Downtown hotel, with attractive, pale-gold rooms that contain mid-20th-century-inspired furnishings and art—larger units have wet bars, sitting areas, and sofa beds. Popular with business travelers, the hotel offers some very attractive rates on weekends, when occupancy is often a bit higher. The restaurant at the foot of the waterfall is called, appropriately, La Cascada (The Cascade). **Pros:** Old Town shuttle service available; nicely updated rooms and amenities; free Wi-Fi. **Cons:** not all rooms have mountain views; not enough spaces in parking lot when hotel is full. ⊠ *201 Marquette Ave. NW, Downtown* ☎ *505/247–3344 or 800/222–8733* ⊕ *www.doubletree.com* ⊳ *295 rooms* ⟁ *In-room: a/c, Internet. In-hotel: restaurant, room service, bar, pool, gym, laundry service, Wi-Fi hotspot, parking (paid)* ⊟ *AE, D, DC, MC, V* ⊕ *H5.*

$$
BED & BREAKFAST
Fodor's Choice
★

Downtown Historic Bed & Breakfasts of Albuquerque. Comprising a pair of grand early-20th-century homes as well as a private carriage house and one other cottage in the Huning Highland Historic District, this stunning property exudes romance. Rooms come in many shapes and sizes, from cozier and less-pricey units to spacious cottages with full kitchens and private exterior entrances. Antiques fill the rooms, which have hardwood floors, bathrobes, modern bathrooms, and free Wi-Fi. A lavish full breakfast is included, and the accommodations open onto neatly tended gardens. **Pros:** exquisite furnishings; intimate property but where guests have plenty of privacy and independence; central Downtown location. **Cons:** some my find the decor to be excessively antique. ⊠ *207 High St., Downtown* ☎ *505/842–0223 or 888/342–0223* ⊕ *www.albuquerquebedandbreakfasts.com* ⊳ *8 rooms, 2 cottages* ⟁ *In-room: a/c, kitchen (some), refrigerator, Wi-Fi. In-hotel: parking (free)* ⊟ *AE, D, MC, V* ⊕ *H6.*

$$
HOTEL

Embassy Suites Hotel Albuquerque. This all-suites high-rise with a striking contemporary design sits on a bluff alongside Interstate 25, affording guests fabulous views of the Downtown skyline and vast desert mesas to the west, and the verdant Sandia Mountains to the east. Rooms are large and done in soothing Tuscan colors; the living areas have pull-out sleeper sofas, refrigerators, dining and work areas, microwaves, and coffeemakers. You'll also find two phones and two TVs in each suite. Included in the rates is a nightly reception with hors d'oeuvres and cocktails, and a full breakfast each morning. With so much living and sleeping space and a great location accessible to Downtown, Nob Hill, and the airport, this is a great option if you're staying in town for a while or traveling with a family. **Pros:** quiet but convenient location adjacent to Interstate 25 and just south of Interstate 40; congenial staff. **Cons:** suites attract families in addition to business travelers; the occasional child run rampant may not appeal to all. ⊠ *1000*

Woodward Pl. NE, Downtown ☎ 505/245–7100 or 800/362–2779 ⊕ www.embassysuitesalbuquerque.com ⤴ 261 suites ⚷ In-room: a/c, refrigerator, Wi-Fi. In-hotel: restaurant, bar, gym, spa, parking (free) ▤ AE, D, MC, V ⦿ BP ⊹ H5.

$ ☷ **Hotel Blue.** The reasonable rates here draw a party crowd, and the
HOTEL art deco–inspired rooms can pick up street noise as well; based on the (fairly basic) services alone it would be a stretch to call this place hip or boutique. Still, people rave about the beds and 40-inch flat-screen TVs, and it is ideally located, especially for those with business Downtown. It overlooks a small park, is a short stroll from Downtown's music clubs and restaurants, and it's a short drive, bus ride, or 15-minute walk from Old Town. In summer, a lively Saturday growers' market (including arts vendors, music, and more) sets up in Robinson Park next door. **Pros:** comfortable Tempur-Pedic beds; complimentary shuttle to the airport, convention center, and Old Town from 7 am until 10 pm. **Cons:** this part of Downtown can feel a little unsettling and desolate at night. ✉ 717 Central Ave. NW, Downtown ☎ 505/924–2400 or 877/878–4868 ⊕ www.thehotelblue.com ⤴ 125 rooms, 10 suites ⚷ In-room: a/c, refrigerators, Internet. In-hotel: bar, pool, gym, parking (free) ▤ AE, D, MC, V ⦿ CP ⊹ G6.

$$$ ☷ **Hotel Parq Central.** One of the more imaginative—and handsomely
HOTEL executed—adaptations of a disused building into a fine hotel, the Parq Central opened in late 2010 inside a striking three-story former hospital that dates to 1926. In the up-and-coming EDo neighborhood, the hotel is just off I–25, a short drive west of UNM and Nob Hill. The designers had fun with this project, creating the Apothecary rooftop bar in which vintage 1920s cocktails are served, and utilizing many of the building's original features, from clay tiles to original windows. The spacious rooms have high-quality Fretté linens, terry robes, 37-inch LCD flat-screen TVs, iPod consoles, and free Wi-Fi. In-room massage services can be arranged by the solicitous staff. **Pros:** wonderfully historic building; beautifully designed rooms; hip clientele. **Cons:** within earshot of busy I–25; the building's medical past may creep some people out. ✉ 806 Central Ave. SE, Downtown ☎ 505/242–0040 ⊕ www.hotelparqcentral.com ⤴ 56 rooms, 18 suites ⚷ In-room: a/c, safe, refrigerator, Wi-Fi. In-hotel: restaurant, bar, gym, laundry service, parking (free), some pets allowed ▤ AE, D, MC, V ⊹ E5.

$$$ ☷ **Hyatt Regency Albuquerque.** Adjacent to the Albuquerque Convention
HOTEL Center, this upscale high-rise comprises a pair of soaring, desert-color towers that figure prominently in the city's skyline. The gleaming art deco–inspired interior is refined and not overbearing. The contemporary rooms, done in mauve, burgundy, and tan, combine Southwestern style with all the amenities you'd expect of a high-caliber business-oriented hotel, including Wi-Fi, iPod docking stations, flat-screen TVs, plush pillow-top mattresses, and fluffy bathrobes. McGrath's Bar and Grill serves steaks, chops, chicken, and seafood (and breakfast to the power crowd), and there's also a Starbucks on-site. Bigwigs of all stripes stay in the penthouse. **Pros:** easy walking distance from the KiMo Theatre and Downtown's art galleries and restaurants, and a quick cab (or bus) ride elsewhere; the views, lap pool, and well-equipped 24/7

fitness center. **Cons:** until you get your bearings the layout can seem somewhat mazelike; no views on lower floors. ⊠ *330 Tijeras Ave. NW, Downtown* ☎ *505/842–1234 or 800/233–1234* ⊕ *www.albuquerque. hyatt.com* ➪ *395 rooms, 14 suites* ⌂ *In-room: a/c, Wi-Fi. In-hotel: restaurant, bar, pool, gym, laundry service, parking (paid)* ⊟ *AE, D, DC, MC, V* ⊹ *G6.*

$$
BED & BREAKFAST
Fodor's Choice
★

🛏 **Mauger Estate B&B Inn.** This 1897 Queen Anne–style mansion—on the National Register of Historic Places—was the first home in Albuquerque to have electricity. While the mercantile Mauger (pronounced *major*) family is long gone (and the electricity long since upgraded, along with a detailed restoration throughout), this well-run B&B has retained many of the building's original architectural elements, including oval windows with beveled and "feather-pattern" glass, hardwood floors, high ceilings, a redbrick exterior, and a front veranda. Rooms—clean and contemporary with a restrained Victorian touch (seen best in the dark woods)—have refrigerators and baskets stocked with munchies, triple-sheeted beds with soft feather duvets, irons and boards, and fresh flowers. There's also a two-bedroom, two-bathroom town house next door. Guests have access to a full-service health club a few blocks away. **Pros:** pleasant common room, with a library and a late-afternoon cookies-and-wine spread; responsive and informed innkeeper; good breakfasts, which they will pack to go on request. **Cons:** at night, on the western fringe of Downtown, it can feel a bit sketchy for walking, but parking is secure. ⊠ *701 Roma Ave. NW, Downtown* ☎ *505/242–8755 or 800/719–9189* ⊕ *www.maugerbb.com* ➪ *8 rooms, 1 2-bedroom town house* ⌂ *In-room: a/c, refrigerator, Wi-Fi. In-hotel: parking (free), some pets allowed* ⊟ *AE, D, MC, V* � *BP* ⊹ *G5.*

LOS RANCHOS/NORTH VALLEY

$
BED & BREAKFAST

🛏 **Cinnamon Morning B&B.** A private, beautifully maintained, pet-friendly compound set back from the road and a 10-minute drive north of Old Town, Cinnamon Morning is just south of Rio Grande Nature Center State Park and a perfect roost if you want to be close to the city's wineries and the launching areas used by most hot-air-ballooning companies. Three rooms are in the main house, a richly furnished adobe home with colorful decorations and a lush garden patio. There's also a secluded two-bedroom guesthouse with a bath, full kitchen, private entrance, living room, and fireplace; and a colorfully painted one-bedroom casita with a private patio, Mexican-style furnishings, a viga ceiling, and a living room with a sleeper sofa. The full breakfasts here are filling and delicious, served by a roaring fire in winter or in the courtyard in summer. **Pros:** hosts will gladly help with travel ideas and planning. **Cons:** cancellations must be made 14 days ahead; you need a car to get around town from here. ⊠ *2700 Rio Grande Blvd. NW, Los Ranchos/North Valley* ☎ *505/345–3541 or 800/214–9481* ⊕ *www.cinnamonmorning. com* ➪ *3 rooms, 1 casita, 1 guesthouse* ⌂ *In-room: kitchen (some), Wi-Fi. In-hotel: parking (free), some pets allowed* ⊟ *AE, D, MC, V* 101 *BP* ⊹ *C2.*

$$$
INN
Fodor's Choice
★

☷ **Los Poblanos Inn.** Designed by acclaimed architect John Gaw Meem, this rambling, historic inn lies outside of Albuquerque's sprawl, on 25 acres of organic farm fields, lavender plantings, and gardens in Los Ranchos on the town's north side, near the Rio Grande and just across the street from Anderson Valley Vineyards—with all the greenery and the quiet pace of life here, you'd never know you're in the desert, or in the middle of a large city. You reach the inn via a spectacular tree-lined lane. Accommodations, including 12 new rooms added in 2010, contain folk paintings, painted viga ceilings, and high-quality linens. Rooms also contain bath products made on-site, including lavender soap and oils; all have kiva fireplaces, too. The property also includes the 15,000-square-foot La Quinta Cultural Center, with dramatic fresco by Peter Hurd. There's also a library with beautiful artwork and a farm shop selling gifts and gourmet goods, and rates include a stellar breakfast using organic eggs and produce (also available to nonguests by reservation). **Pros:** pastoral setting amid lovely lavender fields; superb breakfast. **Cons:** 10-minute drive from Old Town and Downtown. ⊠ *4803 Rio Grande Blvd. NW, Los Ranchos/North Valley* ☎ *505/344–9297 or 866/344–9297* ⊕ *www.lospoblanos.com* ➭ *12 rooms, 8 suites, 2 guesthouses* ⚐ *In-room: a/c, kitchen (some), refrigerator (some), DVD (some), Wi-Fi. In-hotel: gym, pool, parking (free)* ☰ *AE, MC, V* ⲓⵙⵍ *BP* ✛ *C1.*

NORTHEAST HEIGHTS

$$
HOTEL

☷ **Marriott Pyramid.** This curious ziggurat-shaped 10-story building fits in nicely with the other examples of postmodern architecture that have sprung up in northern Albuquerque. It's among the more upscale chain hotels in the north Interstate 25 corridor, and it's an excellent base for exploring Northeast Heights and the North Valley—plus it's a bit closer to Santa Fe than Downtown or airport hotels. Rooms have sponge-painted walls, dapper country-French decor, large flat-screen TVs, and open onto a soaring atrium lobby. Perks include evening turndown service and newspapers delivered to the room each morning. **Pros:** easy access to Interstate 25. **Cons:** the lobby layout is a bit confusing; setting is by a busy interstate with a fairly bland view; a bit of a drive from Downtown. ⊠ *5151 San Francisco Rd. NE, Northeast Heights* ☎ *505/821–3333 or 800/466–8356* ⊕ *www.albuquerquemarriottnorth.com* ➭ *248 rooms, 54 suites* ⚐ *In-room: a/c, refrigerator, Wi-Fi. In-hotel: restaurant, room service, bar, pool, gym, laundry facilities, laundry service, parking (free)* ☰ *AE, D, DC, MC, V* ✛ *G1.*

$
HOTEL

☷ **Nativo Lodge Hotel.** Although it's priced similarly to a number of generic midrange chain properties on the north side, this five-story property has more character than most, especially in the expansive public areas, bar, and restaurant, which have an attractive Southwestern motif that includes hand-carved panels depicting symbols from Native American lore and river-rock walls. Rooms at this eco-conscious property have wing chairs, work desks, Wi-Fi, and dual-line phones. The hotel is just off Interstate 25, but set back far enough to avoid highway noise; several movie theaters and a bounty of mostly chain restaurants are nearby. **Pros:** personable service; relaxing atmosphere. **Cons:**

if your primary business is Downtown, this is a bit far north. ⊠ *6000 Pan American Freeway NE, Northeast Heights* ☎ *505/798–4300 or 888/628–4861* ⊕ *www.hhandr.com/nativo.php* ⬍ *146 rooms, 2 suites* ⬧ *In-room: a/c, refrigerator (some), Wi-Fi. In-hotel: restaurant, room service, bar, pool, gym, laundry facilities, parking (free), some pets allowed* ⊟ *AE, D, DC, MC, V* ⊹ *H1.*

$$$
RESORT

⛶ Sandia Resort & Casino. On a bluff with sweeping views of the Sandia Mountains and Rio Grande Valley, this seven-story casino-resort sets a standard for luxury in Albuquerque; unfortunately the service here doesn't always quite match the promise. Nevertheless, appointments like 32-inch plasma TVs, handcrafted wooden furniture, louvered wooden blinds, and muted, natural-color palettes lend elegance to the spacious rooms. The 700-acre grounds, which are in the Far Northeast Heights, just across Interstate 25 from Balloon Fiesta Park, ensure privacy and quiet and include a superb golf course and an amphitheater that hosts top-of-the-line music and comedy acts. The Green Reed Spa offers a wide range of treatments, many using local clay and plants. One of the city's best restaurants, Bien Shur, occupies the casino's top floor, and there are three other places to eat on-site. The casino is open 24 hours. **Pros:** 24/7 room service; lots to see and do on the grounds. **Cons:** smoking is allowed on premises; pool not open year-round. ⊠ *Tramway Rd. NE, just east of I–25 Northeast Heights* ☎ *505/796–7500 or 800/526–9366* ⊕ *www.sandiacasino.com* ⬍ *198 rooms, 30 suites* ⬧ *In-room: Wi-Fi. In-hotel: 4 restaurants, room service, bars, golf course, pool, gym, spa, laundry service, parking (free)* ⊟ *AE, D, DC, MC, V* ⊹ *H1.*

UPTOWN/EAST SIDE

$$
HOTEL

⛶ Albuquerque Marriott. This 17-story, upscale, Uptown property draws a mix of business and leisure travelers; it's close to three shopping malls and not too far from Nob Hill. Kachina dolls, Native American pottery, and other regional artworks decorate the elegant public areas. The rooms are traditional American, with walk-in closets, 32-inch LCD TVs, armoires, and crystal lamps, and a few Southwestern accents. Rooms—which have floor-to-ceiling windows—enjoy staggering views (the higher the floor the better), either of Sandias to the east or the vast mesas to the west. Cielo Sandia specializes in steaks and contemporary New Mexican fare. **Pros:** cozy lobby lounge; close to upscale shopping and dining. **Cons:** a little far from Downtown; a large property that can feel a bit impersonal. ⊠ *2101 Louisiana Blvd. NE, Uptown/East Side* ☎ *505/881–6800 or 800/228–9290* ⊕ *www.marriott.com/abqnm* ⬍ *405 rooms, 6 suites* ⬧ *In-room: a/c, refrigerator, Internet. In-hotel: restaurant, room service, bar, pool, gym, laundry facilities, laundry service, parking (free)* ⊟ *AE, D, DC, MC, V* ⊹ *H3*

$$
HOTEL

⛶ Sheraton Albuquerque Uptown. Within walking distance of two noted shopping malls, this 2008-renovated property meets the consistent Sheraton standard with a pleasant lobby with a cozy bar area. Earthy and muted reds, oranges, and sand-shaded colors accent the lobby and functional but ample rooms, whose nicer touches include a second sink outside the bathroom, 37-inch LCD TVs, comfy mattresses, and bathrobes. **Pros:** close to Northeast Heights attractions and with easy interstate (and shopping) access. **Cons:** at a busy intersection; a bit far from Downtown. ⊠ *2600 Louisiana Blvd. NE, Uptown* ☎ *505/881–0000 or 866/716–8134* ⊕ *www.sheratonabq.com* ➴ *295 rooms* ⏦ *In-room: a/c, refrigerator, Wi-Fi. In-hotel: 2 restaurants, room service, bar, pool, gym, parking (free)* ▤ *AE, D, DC, MC, V* ⊹ *H3.*

CAMPING

¢ 𝒜 **Albuquerque Central KOA.** At town's edge, in the foothills of the Sandia Mountains, this well-equipped campground has expansive views, a dog run, and Wi-Fi, but only a few trees. Reservations are essential during Balloon Fiesta in October. ⊠ *12400 Skyline NE, Exit 166 off I-40, Uptown/East Side* ☎ *505/296–2729 or 800/562–7781* ⊕ *www.koakampgrounds.com* ⏦ *Flush toilets, full hookups, partial hookups (electric and water), dump station, drinking water, guest laundry, showers, fire grates, grills, picnic tables, electricity, public telephone, general store, service station, play area, swimming (pool)* ➴ *206 sites, 100 with full hookups* ▤ *AE, D, MC, V.*

AIRPORT

$ 📺 **Hampton Inn Airport.** One of the better midprice options near the air-
HOTEL port, the Hampton Inn can be counted on for clean, updated rooms with plenty of perks (free Wi-Fi, a pool, on-the-run breakfast bags to take with you to the airport or wherever you're off to that day). **Pros:** easy in, easy out. **Cons:** though convenient, neighborhood isn't especially scenic or pleasant. ⊠ *2231 Yale Blvd. SE, Airport* ☎ *505/246–2255 or 800/426–7866* ⊕ *www.hamptoninn.com* ➴ *62 rooms, 9 suites* ⏦ *In-room: a/c, Wi-Fi. In-hotel: restaurant, bar, pool, gym, laundry facilities, parking (free)* ▤ *AE, D, DC, MC, V* ⊹ *E6.*

$ 📺 **Holiday Inn Hotel & Suites Albuquerque Airport.** Just west of the airport,
HOTEL this upscale, four-story hotel sits high on a bluff, affording nice views of Downtown and the western mesa as well as the Sandia Mountains. Some suites have whirlpool tubs. The indoor pool and a small, 24/7 fitness room, along with a 24-hour business center, make this a favorite with business travelers. **Pros:** work areas are well lit, a plus for the business traveler. **Cons:** bland neighborhood—you'll need to drive or take cab to get to Downtown or Nob Hill. ⊠ *1501 Sunport Pl. SE, Airport* ☎ *505/944–2255 or 800/465–4329* ⊕ *www.holidayinnabq.com* ➴ *110 rooms, 20 suites* ⏦ *In-room: a/c, Wi-Fi. In-hotel: a/c, restaurant, room service, bar, pool, gym, laundry facilities, parking (free)* ▤ *AE, D, DC, MC, V* ⊹ *E6.*

$$ 📺 **Sheraton Albuquerque Airport Hotel.** Only 350 yards from the airport,
HOTEL this 2010-renovated 15-story hotel sits up high on a mesa with vast views of the Sandia Mountains to the east and Downtown Albuquerque to the northwest. It's handy being so close to the terminal, and the Southwest-accented rooms have cushy Sheraton Sweet Sleeper beds, large work desks, Wi-Fi, and coffeemakers. Rojo Grill ranks among the better hotel restaurants in town. Ask for a room on an upper floor for the best view. **Pros:** short walk from airport; sleek, contemporary room decor. **Cons:** bland neighborhood—you'll need to drive or take

cab to get Downtown or to Nob Hill. ⊠ *2910 Yale Blvd. SE, Airport* ☎ *505/843–7000 or 800/325–3535* ⊕ *www.starwoodhotels.com* ➪*276 rooms, 2 suites* ♨ *In-room: a/c, Wi-Fi. In-hotel: restaurant, room service, bar, pool, gym, parking (free), some pets allowed (paid)* ▤ *AE, D, DC, MC, V* ✛ *E6.*

NIGHTLIFE AND THE ARTS

For the 411 on arts and nightlife, consult the "Venue" section of the Sunday edition of the *Albuquerque Journal* (⊕ *www.abqjournal.com*), the freebie weekly *Alibi* (⊕ *www.alibi.com*), and the Arts Alliance's inclusive Arts & Cultural Calendar (⊕ *www.abqarts.org*). For highlights on some of the best music programming in town, go to ⊕ *http:// ampconcerts.org.*

NIGHTLIFE

BARS AND LOUNGES

Atomic Cantina (⊠ *315 Gold Ave. SW, Downtown* ☎ *505/242–2200* ⊕ *www.atomiccantina.com*), a funky-hip Downtown lounge popular for its cool juke box and extensive happy hours, draws a mix of students, yuppies, and music fans. Many nights there's live music, from punk to rockabilly to trance.

Like its neighbor, Atomic Cantina, **Burt's Tiki Lounge** (⊠ *313 Gold Ave. SW, Downtown* ☎ *505/247–2878* ⊕ *www.burtstikilounge.com*) is a place to mingle with unpretentious locals.

With more than 20 beers on tap and an airy patio out back, **Copper Lounge** (⊠ *1504 Central Ave. SE, UNM/Nob Hill* ☎ *505/242–7490* ⊕ *www.thecopperlounge.com*) is a friendly neighborhood bar near UNM. It's a favorite of students, artists, and workers from nearby Downtown looking to relax after work.

Albuquerque's sizable gay and lesbian community rejoiced with the 2010 opening of **Effex** (⊠ *100 5th St. NW, UNM/Nob Hill* ☎ *505/842– 8870*) an impressive, centrally located, two-level nightclub with a huge rooftop bar and an even larger downstairs dance floor.

Graham Central Station (⊠ *4770 Montgomery Blvd. NE, Northeast Heights* ☎ *505/883–3041* ⊕ *www.grahamcentralstationalbuquerque. com*), part of a rowdy regional chain of massive nightclubs, consists of four distinct bars under one roof: country-western, rock, dance, and Latin. It's open Wednesday through Saturday.

Fodor's Choice ★   Distinctive craft brews like hoppy Imperial Red and rich Oatmeal Stout draw fans of artisan beer to Downtown's **Marble Brewery** (⊠ *111 Marble Ave. NW, Downtown* ☎ *505/243–2739* ⊕ *www.marblebrewery.com*). The elegant tasting room and pub, with an expansive outdoor patio, contains a beautiful 40-foot bar and serves tasty apps and sandwiches— there's live music some evenings, and the owners have opened a taproom on the Plaza in Santa Fe, too.

O'Niell's Pub (⊠ *4310 Central Ave. SE, UNM/Nob Hill* ☎ *505/256– 0564*) occupies a handsome space on the eastern edge of Nob Hill, where it serves good Mexican and American comfort food and presents jazz, bebop, and other music. The expansive patio is perfect for afternoon beer and snacks.

CASINOS

If you love to gamble, the area surrounding Albuquerque has a surfeit of options, including Santa Ana, San Felipe, Isleta, Laguna, and Acoma pueblos. Sandia is the one resort that's right within city limits.

Sandia Resort & Casino (✉ *Tramway Rd. NE at I–25, Northeast Heights* ☎ *505/796–7500 or 800/526–9366* ⊕ *www.sandiacasino.com*) is a light, open, airy resort with an enormous gaming area brightened by soaring ceilings and big windows. In addition to 2,100 slot machines, you'll find craps, blackjack, mini baccarat, and several versions of poker. The 4,200-seat casino amphitheater hosts rock-circuit stalwarts such as the B-52s, and has hosted B.B. King, Kenny Rogers, Chicago, the occasional big-name comedian, and other acts.

LIVE MUSIC

For a city its size, Albuquerque has a rich and varied music scene—and at reasonable prices to boot. You can find world-class world-music festivals like ¡Globalquerque! and the NM Jazz Festival, Norteño roots music, heartstring-tearing country, blues, folk, and the latest rock permutations—and all manner of venues in which to hear (or dance to) them. There's even room for the big-arena warhorses, who mostly play the casinos these days.

¡Globalquerque! (⊕ *www.globalquerque.com*), a two-day world-music festival held at the National Hispanic Cultural Center, has been running annually in late September since 2005, and the acts and auxiliary programming just keep getting better. Festival producer AMP Concerts is also the organization that lures acts like David Byrne and the Cowboy Junkies to intimate Downtown venues.

The 15,000-seat **Hard Rock Pavilion** (✉ *5601 University Blvd. SE, Airport* ☎ *505/452–5100* ⊕ *www.hardrockpavilion.com*) amphitheater attracts big-name acts such as Green Day, Nine Inch Nails, Cher, and Rhianna. Formerly known as Journal Pavilion, the venue was expanded and rebranded in 2010 by the new Hard Rock Resort, 7 mi south on Isleta Pueblo.

Outpost Performance Space (✉ *210 Yale Blvd. SE, UNM/Nob Hill* ☎ *505/268–0044* ⊕ *www.outpostspace.org*) programs an inspired, eclectic slate, from local *nuevo*-folk to techno, jazz, and traveling East Indian ethnic. Some big names—especially in the jazz world—show up at this special small venue.

THE ARTS

Albuquerque has a remarkable wealth of local talent, but it also draws a surprising number of world-class stage performers from just about every discipline imaginable. Check the listings mentioned at the introduction to this section for everything from poetry readings, impromptu chamber music recitals, folk, jazz, and blues festivals, and formal symphony performances to film festivals, Flamenco Internacional, and theater.

MUSIC

The well-respected **New Mexico Symphony Orchestra** (☎ *505/881–8999 or 800/251–6676* ⊕ *www.nmso.org*) plays pops, Beethoven, and, at Christmas, Handel's *Messiah*. Most performances are at 2,000-seat Popejoy Hall.

Popejoy Hall (✉ *University of New Mexico Center for the Arts, North of Central Ave. entrance opposite Cornell Dr. SE, UNM/Nob Hill* ☎ *505/925–5858 or 877/664–8661* ⊕ *www.popejoyhall.com*) presents concerts, from rock and pop to classical, plus comedy acts, lectures, and national tours of Broadway shows. UNM's Keller Hall, also in the Center for the Arts, is a small venue with fine acoustics, a perfect home for the university's excellent chamber music program.

THEATER

Albuquerque Little Theatre (✉ *224 San Pasquale Ave. SW, Old Town* ☎ *505/242–4750* ⊕ *www.albuquerquelittletheatre.org*) is a nonprofit community troupe that's been going strong since 1930. Its staff of professionals teams up with local volunteer talent to produce comedies, dramas, musicals, and mysteries. The company theater, across the street from Old Town, was built in 1936 and designed by John Gaw Meem. It contains an art gallery, a large lobby, and a cocktail lounge.

Fodor's Choice
★
The stunning **KiMo Theatre** (✉ *423 Central Ave. NW, Downtown* ☎ *505/768–3544* ⊕ *www.cabq.gov/kimo*), an extravagantly ornamented 650-seat Pueblo Deco movie palace, is one of the best places in town to see anything. Jazz, dance—everything from traveling road shows to local song-and-dance acts—might turn up here. Former Albuquerque resident Vivian Vance of *I Love Lucy* fame once performed on the stage; today you're more likely to see Wilco or a film-festival screening.

While Popejoy Hall draws them in with huge Broadway touring shows, UNM's **Rodey Theater** (✉ *North of Central Ave. entrance opposite Cornell Dr. SE, UNM/Nob Hill* ☎ *505//925–5858 or 877/664–8661* ⊕ *www.unmtickets.com*), a smaller, 400-seat house in the same complex, stages experimental and niche works throughout the year, including student and professional plays and dance performances such as the acclaimed annual Summerfest Festival of New Plays during July and the June Flamenco Festival.

The **Teatro Nuevo México** (✉ *107 Bryn Mawr Dr. SE, UNM/Nob Hill* ☎ *505/362–6567* ⊕ *www.teatronuevomexico.com*) is dedicated to presenting works created by Latino artists. In addition to plays by the likes of Federico García Lorca and Nilo Cruz, notable in their production roster is a revival of the Spanish operetta form known as zarzuela. These crowd-pleasing pieces may be comedies or drama, and are presented in collaboration with NHCC and the New Mexico Symphony Orchestra.

In January and February, theater fans of the fresh and new flock to the Revolutions International Theatre Festival, presented by the **Tricklock Company** (✉ *1705 Mesa Vista Dr. NE, UNM/Nob Hill* ☎ *505/254–8393* ⊕ *www.tricklock.com*). Recognized internationally, Tricklock's productions tour regularly and emphasize works that take it—and the audience—to the edge of theatrical possibility.

SHOPPING

Albuquerque's shopping strengths include a handful of cool retail districts, such as Nob Hill, Old Town, and the rapidly gentrifying Downtown. These are good neighborhoods for galleries, antiques, and home-furnishing shops, bookstores, and offbeat gift shops. Otherwise, the city is mostly the domain of both strip and indoor malls, mostly filled with ubiquitous chain shops, although you can find some worthwhile independent shops even there.

SHOPPING NEIGHBORHOODS AND MALLS

The **Uptown** (⊠ *Louisiana Blvd. NE, between I–40 and Menaul Blvd. NE, Uptown/East Side*) neighborhood is Albuquerque's hub of chains and mall shopping. The older traditional mall is Coronado (at Louisiana Blvd. NE and Menaul Blvd. NE), which has a big Barnes & Noble and a new Sephora. New and upscale ABQ Uptown is an attractive outdoor village containing an Apple Store, Borders, Coldwater Creek, Lucky Brand Jeans, and Williams-Sonoma.

On the far northwest outskirts of town, **Cottonwood Mall** (⊠ *10000 Coors Blvd. NW at Coors Bypass, West Side* ☎ *505/899–7467* ⊕ *www.simon.com/mall/?id=214*) is anchored by Dillard's, Macy's, JCPenney, and Sears, and has about 135 midrange to upscale shops, including Williams-Sonoma, Aveda, Cache, and Abercrombie & Fitch. There are a dozen restaurants and food stalls, plus a 14-screen theater.

Albuquerque's **Downtown** (⊠ *Central and Gold Aves. from 1st to 10th Sts., Downtown*) has had its highs and lows, but local developers are only renting to independent businesses in an effort to keep Downtown from turning into a collection of chain outlets. Stroll along Central and Gold avenues (and neighboring blocks) to admire avant-garde galleries, cool cafés, and curious boutiques.

Fodor's Choice Funky **Nob Hill** (⊠ *Central Ave. from Girard Blvd. to Washington St., UNM/Nob Hill*), just east of the University of New Mexico and anchored by old Route 66, pulses with colorful storefronts and kitschy signs. At night, neon-lighted boutiques, galleries, and performing-arts spaces encourage foot traffic. Many of the best shops are clustered inside or on the blocks near Nob Hill Business Center, an art deco structure containing several intriguing businesses and La Montañita Natural Foods Co-op, an excellent spot for a snack. There are also branches of the popular clothing chains Urban Outfitters and Buffalo Exchange.

Old Town (⊠ *Central Ave. and Rio Grande Blvd., Old Town*) has the city's largest concentration of one-of-a-kind retail shops, selling clothing, home accessories, Native American art, and Mexican imports—and the predictable schlock targeted at tourists.

ART GALLERIES

In addition to Tamarind Institute and Jonson Gallery, both at UNM (⇨ *UNM/Nob Hill section in Exploring Albuquerque, above*), Albuquerque has a solid and growing gallery scene. For comprehensive gallery listings, pick up a copy of the free annual *Collector's Guide* (⊕ *www.collectorsguide.com*); for current shows and ArtsCrawl schedules, look up the Arts & Cultural Calendar online (⊕ *www.abqarts.org*).

516 Arts (✉ *516 Central Ave. SW, Downtown* ☎ *505/242–1445* ⊕ *www.516arts.org*) holds a special place in the Duke City's art world. They offer world-class contemporary art in changing shows that often cross media boundaries. Exhibits mine the work of local and national artists, and are as likely to speak to issues as they are to offer a powerfully appealing visual presence.

DSG (✉ *510 14th St. SW, Old Town* ☎ *505/266–7751 or 800/474–7751* ⊕ *www.dsg-art.com*), owned by John Cacciatore, handles works of paint, tapestry, sculpture, and photography by leading regional artists, including Frank McCulloch, Carol Hoy, Leo Neufeld, Larry Bell, Angus Macpherson, Jim Bagley, Nancy Kozikowski, and photographer Nathan Small.

Harwood Art Center (✉ *1114 7th St. NW, off Mountain Rd., Old Town* ☎ *505/242–6367* ⊕ *www.harwoodartcenter.org*), on the fringe of Downtown and Old Town in the Sawmill/Wells Park neighborhood, is a remarkable resource for its huge roster of community-oriented art classes, and a gallery in its own right. Shows—predominantly of New Mexico–based artists working in nontraditional forms—take place in their historic brick school building and change monthly.

Mariposa Gallery (✉ *3500 Central Ave. SE, UNM/Nob Hill* ☎ *505/268–6828* ⊕ *www.mariposa-gallery.com*) sells contemporary fine crafts, including jewelry, sculptural glass, works in mixed media and clay, and fiber arts. The changing exhibits focus on upcoming artists; its buyer's sharp eyes can result in real finds for the serious browser.

A 2,000-square-foot space specializing in works by some of the state's most acclaimed current artists, **Matrix Fine Art** (✉ *3812 Central Ave. SE, UNM/Nob Hill* ☎ *505/268–8952* ⊕ *www.matrixfineart.com*) carries an impressive collection of paintings and photography.

★ **Weyrich Gallery** (✉ *2935–D Louisiana Blvd. NE, Uptown/East Side* ☎ *505/883–7410* ⊕ *www.weyrichgallery.com*) carries distinctive jewelry, fine art, Japanese tea bowls, woodblocks, hand-colored photography, and other largely Asian-inspired pieces.

SPECIALTY STORES

ANTIQUES

Classic Century Square Antique Mall (✉ *4516 Central Ave. SE, UNM/Nob Hill* ☎ *505/265–3161*) is a three-story emporium of collectibles and antiques. The emphasis is on memorabilia from the early 1880s to the 1950s. (When the set designers for the television miniseries *Lonesome Dove* needed props, they came here.) Items for sale include art deco and art nouveau objects, retro-cool '50s designs, Depression-era glass, Native American goods, quilts and linens, vintage clothes, and Western memorabilia.

Cowboys & Indians (✉ *4000 Central Ave. SE, UNM/Nob Hill* ☎ *505/255–4054* ⊕ *www.cowboysandindiansnm.com*) carries Native American and cowboy art and artifacts.

BOOKS

One of the last of the great independents, **Bookworks** (✉ *4022 Rio Grande Blvd. NW, Los Ranchos/North Valley* ☎ *505/344–8139* ⊕ *www.bkwrks.com*), maintains an eclectic stock of regional coffee-table books, a well-culled selection of modern fiction and nonfiction, architecture and design titles, and a (small) playground's worth of kids' books. Regular signings and readings draw some very big guns to this tiny treasure.

Massive **Page One** (✉ *11018 Montgomery Blvd. NE, Northeast Heights* ☎ *505/294–2026* ⊕ *www.page1book.com*), arguably the best bookstore in Albuquerque, specializes in technical and professional titles, maps, globes, children's titles, and 150 out-of-state and foreign newspapers. Book signings, poetry readings, and children's events are frequently scheduled.

GIFTS, FOOD, AND TOYS

Beeps (✉ *Nob Hill Shopping Center, 3500 Central Ave. SE, UNM/Nob Hill* ☎ *505/262–1900*), a Nob Hill favorite, carries cards, T-shirts, and amusing, if bawdy, novelties.

Candy Lady (✉ *Mountain Rd. at Rio Grande Blvd., Old Town* ☎ *505/224–9837 or 800/214–7731* ⊕ *www.thecandylady.com*) is known as much for its scandalous adult novelty candies as for its tasty red- and green-chile brittle, plus the usual fudge, chocolates, piñon caramels, and candies. A small room, to the right as you enter, displays the "adult" candy.

La Casita de Kaleidoscopes (✉ *Poco A Poco Patio, 326–D San Felipe St. NW, Old Town* ☎ *505/247–4242* ⊕ *www.casitascopes.com*) carries both contemporary and vintage kaleidoscopes of all styles, by more than 80 top artists in the field.

Fodor'sChoice
★ **Los Poblanos Farm Shop** (*4803 Rio Grande Blvd. NW, Los Ranchos/North Valley* ☎ *505/344–9297 or 866/344–9297* ⊕ *www.lospoblanos.com*), beside the beautiful country inn of the same name, carries books, culinary gadgets, organic house-made lavender products, and a considerable variety of artisan jams, vinegars, sauces, and gourmet goodies. It overlooks a fragrant lavender field.

Theobroma Chocolatier (✉ *12611 Montgomery Blvd. NE, Northeast Heights* ☎ *505/293–6545,* ⊕ *www.theobromachocolatier.com*) carries beautiful, handcrafted, high-quality chocolates, truffles, and candies (most of them made on premises), as well as Taos Cow ice cream.

HISPANIC IMPORTS AND TRADITIONS

An Old Town stalwart since the late 1970s, **Casa Talavera** (✉ *621 Rio Grande Blvd., Old Town* ☎ *505/243–2413* ⊕ *www.casatalavera.com*) is just outside the plaza area, across Rio Grande Boulevard. Do go peruse the wide selection of hand-painted Mexican Talavera tiles. Prices are reasonable, making the colorful geometrics, florals, mural patterns, and solids, close to irresistible. Tin lighting fixtures as well as ceramic sink and cabinet knobs fill in the rest of the space in this DIY-inspiring shop.

Hispaniae (✉ *410 Romero St. NW, Old Town* ☎ *505/244–1533* ⊕ *www. hispaniae.com*) is like the Jackalope of yore, and then some. Sure it has every permutation of Our Lady of Guadalupe imaginable (on switch plates, tin tokens, etc.), but Nuestra Señora is just the tip of it. This long narrow space is packed with finds of the Latino craft kind, from inexpensive cake toppers in the shape of sweet little pigs to painted tin Christmas ornaments and hand-carved hardwood furnishings.

La Piñata (✉ *No. 2 Patio Market, 206 San Felipe St. NW, Old Town* ☎ *505/242–2400*) specializes in piñatas and papier-mâché products, plus Native American jewelry and leather goods.

Saints & Martyrs (✉ *404A San Felipe NW, Old Town* ☎ *505/224–9323* ⊕ *www.saints-martyrs.com*) has almost a gallery feel. The hand-painted *retablos* and other saintly images are displayed so well that it's easy to imagine how one might look in your house. There's also a high-quality selection of sterling-silver *milagros*.

HOME FURNISHINGS

Fodor's Choice ★ **A** (✉ *3500 Central Ave. SE, UNM/Nob Hill* ☎ *505/266–2222* ⊕ *www. theastore.com*) is a Nob Hill stop for housewares, soaps, candles, body-care products, and jewelry.

A branch of a popular regional chain, **El Paso Import Co.** (✉ *3500 Central Ave. SE, UNM/Nob Hill* ☎ *505/265–1160* ⊕ *www.elpasoimportco. com*) carries distressed and "peely-paint" antique-looking chests and tables loaded with character. If you love the shabby-chic look, head to this Nob Hill furniture shop.

Hey Jhonny (✉ *3418 Central Ave. SE, UNM/Nob Hill* ☎ *505/256–9244* ⊕ *www.heyjhonny.com*) is an aromatic store full of exquisite candles, soaps, pillows, fountains, and other soothing items for the home; there's also a branch that carries more furniture and larger pieces around the corner, at 118 Tulane Street.

Objects of Desire (✉ *3225 Central Ave. NE, UNM/Nob Hill* ☎ *505/232–3088* ⊕ *www.objectsofdesireabq.com*) is the place to find that special lamp or table from a whimsical and worldly collection of furnishings.

Qué Chula del Corazón (✉ *3410 Central Ave. NE, UNM/Nob Hill* ☎ *505/255–0515* ⊕ *www.quechulastyle.com*) imports brightly colored (and displayed) folk art, glassware, tooled leather bags, *equipale* furniture, textiles, and pottery from throughout Mexico.

Peacecraft (✉ *3215 Central Ave. NE, UNM/Nob Hill* ☎ *505/255–5229* ⊕ *www.peacecraft.org*) supports fair trade and stocks handmade folk art and crafts from around the world—wooden boxes from Kenya, clothing from Guatemala, hats from Honduras. The store employs university students in work-study programs.

NATIVE AMERICAN ARTS AND CRAFTS

Andrews Pueblo Pottery (✉ *303 Romero St. NW, Suite 116, Old Town* ☎ *505/243–0414 or 877/606–0543* ⊕ *www.andrewspp.com*) carries a terrific selection of Pueblo pottery, fetishes, kachina dolls, and baskets for the beginning and seasoned collector.

Bien Mur Indian Market Center (✉ *100 Bien Mur Dr. NE, off Tramway Rd. NE east of I–25, Northeast Heights* ☎ *505/821–5400 or 800/365–5400* ⊕ *www.sandiapueblo.nsn.us/bienmur.html*) in Sandia Pueblo showcases the best of the best in regional Native American rugs, jewelry, and crafts of all kinds. You can feel very secure about what you purchase at this trading post, and prices are fair.

Gertrude Zachary (✉ *1501 Lomas Blvd. NW, Old Town* ☎ *505/247–4442* ✉ *3300 Central Ave. SE, UNM/Nob Hill* ☎ *505/766–4700* ⊕ *www.gertrudezachary.com*) dazzles with its selection of Native American jewelry. Don't let the screaming billboards around town deter you—this may be the best place to get a bargain on a good bracelet or ring. Locals buy here, too.

To understand what it takes to make Native American jewelry (or if you want to learn the craft yourself), a stop at the fascinating **Indian Jewelers Supply** (✉ *2105 San Mateo Blvd. NE, 1 block south of Indian School Rd. NE, at Haines Ave. NE, Uptown/East Side* ☎ *505/265–3701* ⊕ *www.ijsinc.com*) is a must. Trays of gemstones (finished and not), silver sold by weight, findings, and the tools to work them with, fill this large space. It's open 8 to 5 (closed Sunday)—go midmorning to avoid the early rush.

Margaret Moses Gallery (✉ *326 San Felipe St. NW, Old Town* ☎ *505/842–1808 or 888/842–1808* ⊕ *www.margaretmoses.com*) stocks Pueblo pottery, including the black earthenware pottery of San Ildefonso, as well as the work of potters from Acoma, Santa Clara, Isleta, and Zía. Rare Zuni and Navajo jewelry is on display, as are Navajo weavings from 1900 to the present.

SPORTS AND THE OUTDOORS

Albuquerque is blessed with an exceptional setting for outdoor sports, backed by a favorable, if unpredictable, climate. Usually 10°F warmer than Santa Fe's, Albuquerque's winter days are often mild enough for most outdoor activities. The Sandias tempt you with challenging mountain adventures *(see Sandia Park in the Side Trips from Albuquerque section, below, for details on mountain biking and skiing in the Sandia Mountains above Albuquerque)*; the Rio Grande and its cottonwood forest, the Bosque, provide settings for additional outdoors pursuits.

PARTICIPANT SPORTS

The **City of Albuquerque** (☎ *505/768–5300* ⊕ *www.cabq.gov/living.html*) maintains diverse cultural and recreational programs. Among the city's assets are more than 20,000 acres of open space, four golf courses, 200 parks, more than 400 mi of tracks for biking and jogging, as well as swimming pools, tennis courts, ball fields, playgrounds, and a shooting range.

AMUSEMENT PARK

Drive down San Mateo Northeast in summer and you may see a roller coaster smack in the middle of the city. **Cliff's Amusement Park** (⊠ *4800 Osuna Rd. NE, off I–25 at San Mateo Blvd. NE, Northeast Heights* ☎ *505/881–9373* ⊕ *www.cliffsamusementpark.com*) is a clean, well-run attraction for everyone from two-year-olds on up. It features a wooden-track roller coaster as well as rides for all ages and state-fair-type games of chance. The park also has a large water-play area. Cliff's is open early April through September, but days and hours vary, so call first.

BALLOONING

Albuquerque's high altitude, mild climate, and steady but manageable winds, make it an ideal destination for ballooning. A wind pattern known as the Albuquerque Box, created by the city's location against the Sandia Mountains, makes Albuquerque a great place to fly.

If you've never been ballooning, you may picture a bumpy ride, where changes in altitude produce the queasy feeling you get in a tiny propeller plane. But the experience is far calmer than that. The balloons are flown by licensed pilots (don't call them operators) who deftly turn propane-fueled flames on and off, climbing and descending to find winds blowing the way they want to go—there's no real steering involved, which makes the pilots' control that much more admirable. Pilots generally land balloons where the wind dictates, so chase vehicles pick you up and return you to your departure point, but particularly skilled pilots can use conditions created by the Box to land precisely where you started. Even without door-to-door service, many visitors rank a balloon ride over the Rio Grande Valley as their most memorable experience.

Several reliable companies around Albuquerque offer tours. A ride costs about $160 to $180 per person.

Fodor's Choice One of the best balloon tours is with **Rainbow Ryders** (☎ *505/823–1111* ★ *or 800/725–2477* ⊕ *www.rainbowryders.com*), an official ride conces-sion for the Albuquerque International Balloon Fiesta. As part of the fun, you get to help inflate and pack away the balloon. In case you missed breakfast prior to your flight, a Continental breakfast and glass of champagne await your return.

BICYCLING

With the creation of many lanes, trails, and dedicated bike paths, Albuquerque's city leaders are recognized for their bike-friendly efforts—a serious challenge given the committed car culture of its residents. The city's public works department produces a detailed **bike map,** which can be obtained free by calling ☎ *505/768–3550* or downloaded from ⊕ *www.cabq.gov/bike*.

Albuquerque has miles of bike lanes and trails through and around the city as well as great mountain-biking trails at Sandia Peak Ski Area (⇨ *Sandia Park, in Side Trips from Albuquerque, below*).

Although mountain bikes may be rented in the Sandias, bike-rental sources are scarce around town. **Northeast Cyclery** (⊠ *8305 Menaul Blvd. NE, Northeast Heights* ☎ *505/299–1210*) has a good range of road and mountain bikes for rent. Most are unisex styles, and they carry kid sizes as well.

Seasonally, at **Tingley Beach** (⊕ *www.cabq.gov*) balloon-tire and mountain bikes are available by the hour *(⇨ Albuquerque BioPark, in Exploring Albuquerque, above)*.

★ The **Paseo del Bosque Bike Trail** (⊕ *www.cabq.gov*) runs right through Tingley. It's flat for most of its 16-mi run, and it's one of the loveliest rides in town.

BIRD-WATCHING

The Rio Grande Valley, one of the continent's major flyways, attracts many migratory bird species. Good bird-viewing locales include the **Rio Grande Nature Center State Park** (✉ *2901 Candelaria Rd. NW, Los Ranchos/North Valley* ☎ *505/344–7240* ⊕ *www.nmparks.com*).

GOLF

Most of the better courses in the region—and there are some outstanding ones—are just outside town *(⇨ Side Trips from Albuquerque, below, for details)*. The four courses operated by the city of Albuquerque have their charms, and the rates are reasonable. Each course has a clubhouse and pro shop, where clubs and other equipment can be rented. Weekday play is first-come, first-served, but reservations are taken for weekends. Contact the **Golf Management Office** (☎ *505/888–8115* ⊕ *www.cabq.gov/golf*) for details. Of the four city courses, **Arroyo del Oso** (✉ *7001 Osuna Rd. NE, Northeast Heights* ☎ *505/884–7505*) earns high marks for its undulating 27-hole layout; greens fees are $22 to $29 for 18 holes. The 18-hole **Los Altos Golf Course** (✉ *9717 Copper Ave. NE, Northeast Heights* ☎ *505/298–1897*), one of the region's most popular facilities, has $22 to $29 greens fees. There's also a short, par-3, 9-hole executive course.

Sandia Golf Club (✉ *Tramway Rd. NE just east of I–25, Northeast Heights* ☎ *505/798–3990* ⊕ *www.sandiagolf.com*), at the swanky Sandia Resort & Casino, offers 18 holes set amid lush hilly fairways, cascading waterfalls, and desert brush. Greens fees are $53 to $65.

The University of New Mexico has two superb courses. Both are open daily and have full-service pro shops, instruction, and snack bars. Greens fees for out-of-staters run about $35 to $45 without a cart. **UNM North** (✉ *2201 Tucker Rd. NE, at Yale Blvd., UNM/Nob Hill* ☎ *505/277–4146*) is a first-class 9-hole, par-36 course on the north side of campus. The 18-hole facility at **UNM South** (✉ *3601 University Blvd., just west of airport off I–25, Airport* ☎ *505/277–4546* ⊕ *www.unmgolf.com*) has garnered countless awards from major golf magazines and hosted PGA and LPGA qualifying events; there's also a short par-3 9-hole course.

HIKING

Fodor's Choice In the foothills in Albuquerque's Northeast Heights, you'll find great
★ hiking in **Cibola National Forest**, which can be accessed from Tramway Road Northeast, about 4 mi east of Interstate 25 or 2 mi north of Paseo del Norte. Just follow the road into the hillside, and you'll find several parking areas (there's a daily parking fee of $3). This is where you'll find the trailhead for the steep and challenging **La Luz Trail**, which rises some 9 mi (an elevation gain of more than 3,000 feet) to the top of Sandia Crest. You can take the Sandia Peak Aerial Tram *(⇨ Exploring*

Albuquerque, above) to the top and then hike down the trail, or vice versa (keep in mind that it can take up to six hours to hike up the trail, and four to five hours to hike down). Spectacular views of Albuquerque and many miles of desert and mountain beyond that are had from the trail. You can also enjoy a hike here without going the whole way—if your energy and time are limited, just hike a mile or two and back. No matter how far you hike, however, pack plenty of water.

SPECTATOR SPORTS

BASEBALL

The city hosts Triple A minor league baseball's **Albuquerque Isotopes** (⊠ *1601 Avenida César Chavez SE, UNM/Nob Hill* ☎ *505/924–2255* ⊕ *www.albuquerquebaseball.com*), the farm club of the major league Los Angeles Dodgers; the season runs April through August.

BASKETBALL

It's hard to beat the excitement of home basketball games of the **University of New Mexico Lobos** (⊠ *University Ave., at Avenida César Chavez, UNM/Nob Hill* ☎ *505/925–5858 or 877/664–8661* ⊕ *www.golobos. com*), when 18,000 rabid fans crowd into the school's arena, "the Pit," from November to March. Both the women's and men's teams have enjoyed huge success in past years.

FOOTBALL

The competitively ranked **University of New Mexico Lobos** (⊠ *University Ave., at Avenida César Chavez, UNM/Nob Hill* ☎ *505/925–5858 or 877/664–8661* ⊕ *www.golobos.com*) play at the 40,000-seat University Stadium in the fall.

SIDE TRIPS FROM ALBUQUERQUE

It takes only a few minutes of driving in any direction to leave urban Albuquerque behind and experience some of New Mexico's natural and small-town beauty. Rivers, valleys, canyons, and peaks are just outside the city's limits, and amid them are many villages worth a stop. If you're headed up to Santa Fe, definitely consider traveling there by way of the rambling and tortuous Turquoise Trail, a charming alternative to speedy Interstate 25.

SOUTH OF ALBUQUERQUE

When Francisco Vásquez de Coronado arrived in what is now New Mexico in 1540, he found a dozen or so villages along the Rio Grande in the ancient province of Tiguex, between what is now Bernalillo to the north of Albuquerque and Isleta to the south. Of those, only Sandia and Isleta survive today. The Salinas Pueblo Missions ruins, about 65 mi southeast of Albuquerque, remain a striking example of the Spanish penchant for building churches on sites inhabited by native people.

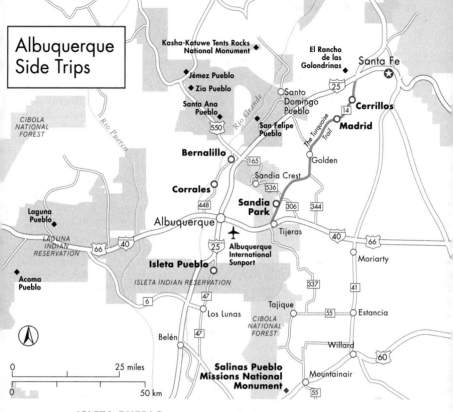

Albuquerque Side Trips

Kasha-Katuwe Tents Rocks National Monument

Jémez Pueblo

Zia Pueblo

Santa Ana Pueblo

CIBOLA NATIONAL FOREST

Rio Puerco

Rio Grande

550

El Rancho de las Golondrinas

Santa Fe

Santo Domingo Pueblo

25

Cerrillos

14

Madrid

The Turquoise Trail

San Felipe Pueblo

Bernalillo

165

Golden

Corrales

448

Sandia Crest

536

Sandia Park

306   344

Albuquerque

Laguna Pueblo

LAGUNA INDIAN RESERVATION

66   40   40

Tijeras

40   66

Moriarty

Albuquerque International Sunport

25

Acoma Pueblo

Isleta Pueblo

ISLETA INDIAN RESERVATION

6   47

Los Lunas

337   41

Tajique

55   Estancia

CIBOLA NATIONAL FOREST

Belén   47

Willard

60

0   25 miles

0   50 km

Salinas Pueblo Missions National Monument

Mountainair

55

ISLETA PUEBLO

13 mi south of Albuquerque, via I–25 (Exit 213) and NM 47.

Of the pueblos in New Mexico when the Spanish first arrived, Isleta Pueblo is one of two Tiwa-speaking communities left in the middle of the Rio Grande Valley. It was also one of a handful of pueblos that didn't participate in the Pueblo Revolt of 1680, during which Isleta was abandoned. Some of the residents fled New Mexico with the Spanish to El Paso, where their descendants live to this day on a reservation called Ysleta del Sur. Other members went to live with the Hopi of Arizona but eventually returned and rebuilt the pueblo.

Facing the quiet plaza is Isleta's church, **St. Augustine,** built in 1629. One of the oldest churches in New Mexico, it has thick adobe walls, a viga-crossed ceiling, and an austere interior. Legend has it that the ground beneath the floor has the odd propensity to push church and community figures buried under the floor back up out of the ground; bodies have been reburied several times, only to emerge again.

Polychrome pottery with red and black designs on a white background is a specialty here. The pueblo celebrates its feast days on August 28 and September 4, both in honor of St. Augustine. The tribal government maintains picnicking and camping facilities, several fishing ponds, and a renowned 18-hole golf course. It also runs the **Hard Rock Casino &**

Resort (✉ *11000 Broadway SE [NM 47]* ☎ *505/724–3800 or 877/475–3827* ⊕ *www.hardrockcasinoabq.com*), which ranks among the state's most popular gaming facilities. It was known as Isleta Casino up until summer 2010, when the tribe formed a branding agreement with the popular Hard Rock hospitality brand and reopened the entire resort with a sleek new look. It's a large and handsome space with more than 1,600 slots and myriad gaming tables; the concert hall hosts a mix of oldies, pop stars, and country-and-western acts—past numbers have included Tom Jones, Vince Gill, and Tony Bennett. There's also boxing held throughout the year, and local bands as well as comedy acts often perform at the resort's two nightspots, Fusion and Lucha. Additionally, Hard Rock operates Albuquerque's largest rock-concert venue, the Hard Rock Pavilion (⇨ *Nightlife and the Arts, above*). The resort also includes a snazzy, 201-room Hard Rock Hotel, with a full-service spa, making Isleta more competitive with other high-profile Native American resorts in the region (i.e., Sandia Resort & Casino; Santa Ana Pueblo, with its Hyatt Regency Tamaya; and Pojoaque, with Buffalo Thunder Resort). Although Isleta is wonderfully picturesque—beehive ovens stand beside adobe homes bedecked with crimson chiles—camera use is restricted here. Only the church may be photographed. ✉ *Tribal Rd. 40* ☎ *505/869–3111* ⊕ *www.isletapueblo.com.*

WHERE TO STAY

$$ ⊞ **Hard Rock Hotel & Casino.** Opened in 2010 as one of the newest proper-
RESORT ties in the gaming-driven Hard Rock hotel chain, this full-service resort is a bit more reasonably priced than others in the region and is also a bit more kid-friendly, with a huge pool and a family-fun center with a bowling alley, billiards, Laser Tag, an arcade. Rooms come in a wide range of configurations, some with sitting areas, wet bars, whirlpool tubs, and balconies overlooking the high-desert scenery. All have large flat-screen TVs, iPod docking stations, and good-size bathrooms with soaking tubs and rain showerheads. Adults will find plenty of keep them occupied here, too, from an extensive full-service spa to a slew of casual bars, restaurants, and gaming areas. **Pros:** sleek and attractive rooms with cushy furnishing; closer to airport than other casino resorts in the area; a bit less pricy than other Albuquerque casino resorts. **Cons:** somewhat isolated from Albuquerque and not much to see or do in area; few places to eat nearby. ✉ *11000 Broadway SE (NM 47)* ☎ *505/724–3800 or 877/475–3827* ⊕ *www.hardrockcasinoabq.com* ⇆ *201 rooms* ⟁ *In-room: a/c, Wi-Fi. In-hotel: 5 restaurants, room service, bars, golf course, pool, gym, spa, parking (free)* ▭ *AE, D, DC, MC, V.*

SPORTS AND THE OUTDOORS

One of the most esteemed facilities in the state, **Isleta Eagle Golf Course** (✉ *4001 NM 47 SE* ☎ *505/848–1900 or 866/475–3822* ⊕ *www. hardrockcasinoabq.com*) consists of three 9-hole layouts set around three lakes; greens fees are $50 to $65 for 18 holes.

SALINAS PUEBLO MISSIONS NATIONAL MONUMENT

58 mi (to Punta Agua/Quarai) from Albuquerque, east on I–40 (to Tijeras Exit), south on NM 337 and NM 55; 23 mi from Punta Agua to Abó, south on NM 55, west (at Mountainair) on U.S. 60, and north on NM 513; 34 mi from Punta Agua to Gran Quivira, south on NM 55.

Salinas Pueblo Missions National Monument is made up of three sites—**Quarai, Abó, and Gran Quivira**—each with the ruins of a 17th-century Spanish-colonial Franciscan missionary church and an associated pueblo. The sites represent the convergence of two Native American peoples, the Anasazi and the Mogollon, who lived here for centuries before the Spanish arrived. Quarai, the nearest to Albuquerque, was a flourishing Tiwa pueblo whose inhabitants' pottery, weaving, and basket-making techniques were quite refined. On the fringe of the Great Plains, all three of the Salinas pueblos were vulnerable to raids by nomadic Plains Indians. Quarai was abandoned about 50 years after its mission church, **San Purísima Concepción de Cuarac,** was built in 1630. If you can arrange it, arrive in time for the late-afternoon light—the church's red sandstone walls still rise 40 feet out of the earth, and are a powerful sight. At Abó are the remains of the three-story church of San Gregorio and a large unexcavated pueblo. (The masonry style at Abó, also built of red stone, bore some similarity to that at Chaco Canyon, which has led some archaeologists to speculate that the pueblo was built by people who left the Chaco Canyon area.) Gran Quivira contains two churches and some excavated Native American structures. There are walking trails and small interpretive centers at each of the pueblos, and expanded exhibits at the monument headquarters in the old cow town cum arts center of Mountainair. You'll come to Quarai first via this route, and this is the loveliest of the three; Abó—which you can swing by easily enough if you loop back to Albuquerque via U.S.60 west (through Mountainair), then north on either NM 47 (for the scenic back route through Isleta) or Interstate 25—is a close second. Gran Quivira is more a detour, and you might find yourself wanting to take a little time to stroll down Mountainair's quaint main street then getting a bite at Pop Shaffer's Café *(⇨ below)* instead. ⊠ *N. Ripley Ave., at W. Broadway (U.S. 60), Mountainair* ☎ *505/847–2585* ⊕ *www.nps. gov/sapu* ⊠ *Free* ⊙ *Late May–early Sept., daily 9–6; early Sept.–late May, daily 9–5.*

WHERE TO STAY

$ 🖼 **Casa Manzano.** Tucked about a mile up a dirt-and-gravel forest road,
INN Casa Manzano rewards its guests with intimate views of the Manzano Mountains, and accommodations that warrant its reputation as a retreat. Designed by cohost Bert Herrman, this thoughtfully laid-out modern property is beautifully detailed with red-tile roofs, Saltillo-tile floors, courtyard garden with a hot tub, hand-plastered *nichos*, hand-crafted woodwork, and finely impressed tinwork. And it's as environmentally up-to-date as can be. A case study of solar-powered elegance, the property contains two wings, each with two separate guest rooms and one bathroom (both rooms in each wing are ever only rented to families or friends traveling together, and who don't mind sharing a bath). **Pros:** breakfast is sumptuous—and often includes offerings from

the lovingly tended garden. **Cons:** other meals require a drive, either into town or down to Mountainair. ⊠ *103 Forest Rd. 321, 29 mi south from Tijeras on NM 337 and NM 55, Tajique* ☎ *505/384–9767* ⊕ *www. home.earthlink.net/~casa.manzano* ➷ *4 rooms with shared bath* ♿ *In-room: no a/c, no TV, Internet. In-hotel: gym, some pets allowed* ➱ *MC, V* ⫾○⫾ *BP* ☺ *Closed Dec.–Apr.*

$ ⚏ **Shaffer Hotel.** One of the nation's few remaining structures built in
HOTEL the Pueblo Deco style, the Shaffer was restored and reopened as a hotel in 2005 after many years of neglect. The 1923 building, in the heart of historic—if modest—Downtown Mountainair, offers a wide range of accommodations. The simple "cowboy rooms" share a community bathroom but have rates starting at just $28—all others have private baths, some with original claw-foot tubs. All are done with 1920s and '30s deco antiques and tile bathrooms; they're not fancy, but they are comfortable. Try for a side room facing the park—you'll still hear the freight trains rumbling by much of the night, but it's worse in the back. The lobby's a tin-ceiling period gem (original owner Pop Shaffer himself did all the woodwork), and from it you can step right into **Pop Shaffer's Café** ($). The homemade pie (pecan, mmm), breakfast burritos, and bizcochito cookies are all highly commendable, as is the hand-painted true-to-era Native American–inspired decor. **Pros:** rife with history, this place is a real slice. **Cons:** service can be a bit spotty and the rooms a bit sterile. ⊠ *103 W. Main St., Mountainair* ☎ *505/847–2888 or 888/595–2888* ⊕ *www.shafferhotel.com* ➷ *11 rooms, 9 with bath; 8 suites* ♿ *In-room: no a/c, Internet. In-hotel: restaurant, gym, Wi-Fi hotspot* ➱ *AE, D, MC, V.*

NORTH OF ALBUQUERQUE

CORRALES

2 mi north of Albuquerque. Take Paseo Del Norte (NM 423) or Alameda Blvd. (NM 528) west from I–25 and head north on Corrales Rd. (NM 448).

This sweet village just north of Albuquerque is a little bit cooler, a little bit greener, and a lot more pastoral than the city. Drive slowly through Bernalillo and Corrales, and you're bound to see lots of horses, cows, and llamas.

Serene Corrales is an ancient agricultural community now inhabited by artists, craftspeople, and the affluent—plus a few descendants of the old families. Small galleries, shops, and places to eat dot the town, and in fall, roadside fruit and vegetable stands open. Bordered by Albuquerque and Rio Rancho, Corrales makes a pleasant escape to winding dirt roads, fields of corn, and apple orchards. On summer weekends visit the Corrales Farmers' Market; in October, the village holds a Harvest Festival. The village's main drag, NM 448, is one of New Mexico's official scenic byways, lined with grand estates and haciendas and shaded by cottonwoods. Just off the byway, you can break for a stroll through Corrales Bosque Preserve, a shaded sanctuary abutting the Rio Grande that's a favorite spot for bird-watching—some 180 species pass through here throughout the year. You can also catch a glimpse of historic hacienda life when you take a tour of the exquisitely restored 19th-century adobe compound of **Casa San Ysidro** (✉ *973 Old Church Rd.* ☎ *505/898–3915* ⊕ *www.cabq.gov* ✎ *$4* ⊙ *Wed.–Sun., call for times*).

WHERE TO EAT AND STAY

$$$

ECLECTIC

Fodor's Choice

★

✕ **Casa Vieja.** Set in a rambling early-18th-century compound along the Corrales Scenic Byway, this purportedly haunted hacienda had bounced among a couple of different owners in recent years before falling into the very capable hands of talented chef and slow-food proponent Josh Gerwin. The atmospheric restaurant, with a large patio that's ideal in warm weather, earns raves for its creatively prepared, sustainable cuisine, which mixes local ingredients with global preparations, and top-notch wine list. You might start with a duck-confit tamale cooked in mole and served with a cilantro-chive-crème-fraîche sauce, before tucking into cast-iron-seared scallops with garlic-potato-and-scallion croquettes, cauliflower soup, and sorrel puree. The chipotle-buttermilk flan makes for a terrific ending. ✉ *4541 Corrales Rd.* ☎ *505/898–7489* ⊕ *www.casaviejanm.com* ▭ *AE, D, MC, V* ⊙ *No lunch weekdays.*

¢

PIZZA

✕ **Village Pizza.** A Chicago native with a knack for baking runs this ordinarily named joint that serves extraordinarily good pizza. Crusts come in different styles (including Chicago-style deep dish), and a wide range of toppings is offered, including such gourmet fixings as artichoke hearts and smoked oysters. In back is an adobe-walled courtyard with a couple of big leafy trees and lots of seating. There's a bargain-priced all-you-can-eat pizza buffet at lunchtime and on Monday and Tuesday nights, and you get a 10% discount if you ride in on horseback. ✉ *4266 Corrales Rd.* ☎ *505/898–0045* ⊕ *www.villagepizzacorrales.com* ▭ *AE, D, MC, V.*

$

BED & BREAKFAST

⬚ **Chocolate Turtle B&B.** Hosts Nancy and Dallas Renner run this light-filled four-room hideaway in a quiet neighborhood in West Corrales. It's a short drive from Rio Rancho and 20 minutes from Downtown Albuquerque, but the setting is as peaceful as can be. This Territorial-style home's large windows and neatly landscaped grounds afford sweeping views of the Sandia Mountains. Fresh flowers further brighten the colorfully painted Southwestern-themed rooms, which range from a cozy single to three more substantial doubles, the most desirable with its own private terrace. **Pros:** friendly and knowledgeable hosts. **Cons:** no TVs or phones in room; it's a 20-minute walk to the nearest restaurants. ✉ *1098 W. Meadowlark La.* ☎ *505/898–1800 or 877/298–1800* ⊕ *www.chocolateturtlebb.com* ⬚ *4 rooms* ♿ *In-room: a/c, no phone, no TV, Wi-Fi. In-hotel: Internet terminal.* ▭ *AE, D, MC, V* ⦿ *BP.*

BERNALILLO

17 mi north of Albuquerque via I–25, 8 mi north of Corrales via NM 448 to NM 528.

Once a rather tranquil Hispanic village, Bernalillo is today one of New Mexico's fastest-growing towns—it's increasingly absorbing the suburban growth northward from Albuquerque. The town holds a Wine Festival each Labor Day weekend, but the most memorable annual event is the Fiesta of San Lorenzo, which has honored the town's patron saint for nearly 400 years. On August 10, San Lorenzo Day, the entire town takes to the streets to participate in the traditional masked *matachine* dance. Matachines, of Moorish origin, were brought to this hemisphere by the Spanish. In New Mexico various versions are danced to haunting fiddle music, in both Native American pueblos and old Spanish villages at different holidays. Though interpretations of the matachines are inexact, one general theme is that of conquest. One dancer, wearing a devil's mask and wielding a whip, presides over the others. A young girl, dressed in white, is also present.

WHAT TO SEE

The town's leading attraction, **Coronado State Monument,** is named in honor of Francisco Vásquez de Coronado, the leader of the first organized Spanish expedition into the Southwest, from 1540 to 1542. The prehistoric **Kuaua Pueblo,** on a bluff overlooking the Rio Grande, is believed to have been the headquarters of Coronado and his army, who were caught unprepared by severe winter weather during their search for the legendary Seven Cities of Gold. A worthy stop, the monument has a museum in a restored kiva, with copies of magnificent frescoes done in black, yellow, red, blue, green, and white. The frescoes depict fertility rites, rain dances, and hunting rituals. The original artworks are preserved in the small visitor center. Adjacent to the monument is **Coronado State Park,** which has campsites and picnic grounds, both open year-round. In autumn the views at the monument and park are especially breathtaking, with the trees turning russet and gold. There's also overnight camping at the adjacent Coronado Campground (☎ *505/980–8256).* ⊠ *485 Kuaua Rd., off NM 44/U.S. 550* ☎ *505/867–5351* ⊕ *www.nmstatemonuments.org* ᗌ *$3* ☺ *Wed.–Mon. 8:30–5.*

WHERE TO EAT AND STAY

$$$$
ECLECTIC
✕ **Corn Maiden.** The upscale dining option at the posh Hyatt Regency Tamaya resort, this art-filled dining room with large windows taking in views of the Sandias is also one of the great special-occasion venues in greater Albuquerque (albeit with lofty prices). Many seats view the bustle of the open kitchen, where a talented culinary team mix Native American, Mexican, and global ingredients to lavish effect. Share-worthy starts include crostini topped with grilled buffalo and poached quail eggs, and jicama-wrapped lobster ravioli with tomato relish. The specialty among main dishes is a mixed grill of chorizo, organic chicken, and chile-rubbed beef rib-eye. Friends may consider splitting the decadent sampler of four luscious desserts. ⊠ *Hyatt Regency Tamaya, 1300 Tuyuna Trail, Santa Ana Pueblo* ☎ *505/771–6037* ⊕ *www.tamaya. hyatt.com* ᗌ *Reservations essential* ▤ *AE, D, DC, MC, V* ☺ *Closed Sun. and Mon. No lunch.*

$$$
ECLECTIC
★
✕ **Prairie Star.** Residents from as far as Santa Fe have been known to make the drive to this 1920s Pueblo Revival hacienda, renowned for the sunset views from its patio. The menu combines contemporary American, Southwestern, and Asian cuisine, including duck-confit crepes with red-chile-infused blueberries, lemon chèvre, mint, and pistachios, and coriander-rubbed ahi tuna with ginger-jasmine rice cakes and seaweed slaw. The lamb chops, from Chama Valley, are also delicious. The culinary quality has become consistently outstanding over

2

the years, the wine list is among the best in the state, and the setting is gorgeous. Prairie Star is on the Santa Ana reservation, overlooking the acclaimed Santa Ana Golf Course. ⊠ *288 Prairie Star Rd., Santa Ana Pueblo* ☎ *505/867–3327* ⊕ *www.santaanagolf.com* ▭ *AE, D, DC, MC, V* ☉ *Closed Mon. No lunch.*

$

ECLECTIC

Fodor'sChoice

★

✕ **Range Cafe & Bakery.** Banana pancakes, giant cinnamon rolls, Asian spinach salad, grilled portobello burgers, homemade meat loaf with garlic mashed potatoes, steak-and-enchilada platters, and the signature dessert, Death by Lemon, are among the highlights at this quirky spot known for down-home fare with creative touches. All the above, plus a full complement of rich, decadent Taos Cow ice cream, is served in a refurbished mercantile building with a dead-center view of the Sandia Mountains. You can order breakfast fare until 3 pm. There are also two newer branches in Albuquerque (the one near Downtown is nicest), but the original has the best ambience. ⊠ *925 Camino del Pueblo* ☎ *505/867–1700* ⊠ *2200 Menaul Blvd. NE, Downtown* ☎ *505/888–1660* ⊠ *4401 Wyoming Blvd. NE, Northeast Heights* ☎ *505/293–2633* ⊕ *www.rangecafe.com* ≜ *Reservations not accepted* ▭ *AE, D, MC, V.*

$$$

RESORT

Fodor'sChoice

★

⊡ **Hyatt Regency Tamaya.** This spectacular large-scale resort, on 500 acres on the Santa Ana Pueblo, includes a top-rated golf course, state-of-the-art spa, and cultural museum and learning center. Most rooms, swathed in natural stone, wood, and adobe and filled with pueblo-inspired textiles and pottery, overlook the Sandia Mountains or cottonwood groves; many have balconies or patios. Cultural events include bread-baking demonstrations (in traditional adobe ovens), storytelling, and live tribal dance and music performances. Other amenities include waterslides over two of the outdoor pools, atmospheric bars, guided nature walks, and hot-air ballooning nearby. Three restaurants all serve consistently excellent food. The Santa Ana Star Casino is a free shuttle ride away. And if you're looking for an exceptional horseback ride, arrange one with the Tamaya stables. As you drink in eyefuls of the spectacular pueblo backcountry and weave among trees and plantings, you'll wonder why you ever settled for the dull nose-to-butt riding experiences of yesteryear. **Pros:** this is *the* place to come to get away; it's in the direction of Santa Fe, making it a good base for day trips to that area. **Cons:** it's way out there—factor in a 15-minute drive even into Downtown Bernalillo. ⊠ *1300 Tuyuna Trail, Santa Ana Pueblo* ☎ *505/867–1234 or 800/633–7313* ⊕ *www.tamaya.hyatt.com* ➴ *331 rooms, 19 suites* ⚑ *In-room: a/c, refrigerator, Wi-Fi. In-hotel: 3 restaurants, room service, bars, golf course, tennis courts, pools, gym, spa, children's programs (ages 2–14)* ▭ *AE, D, DC, MC, V.*

THE TURQUOISE TRAIL

Fodor'sChoice

★

Etched out in the early 1970s and still well traveled is the scenic Turquoise Trail (or more prosaically, NM 14), a National Scenic Byway which follows an old route between Albuquerque and Santa Fe that's dotted with ghost towns now being restored by writers, artists, and other urban refugees. This 70 mi of piñon-studded mountain back road along the eastern flank of the sacred Sandia Mountains is a gentle roller coaster that also affords panoramic views of the Ortiz, Jémez, and Sangre de Cristo mountains. It's believed that 2,000 years ago Native Americans mined turquoise in these hills. The Spanish took up turquoise mining in the 16th century, and the practice continued into the early 20th century, with Tiffany & Co. removing a fair share of the semiprecious stone. In addition, gold, silver, tin, lead, and coal have been mined here. There's plenty of opportunity for picture taking and picnicking along the way. The pace is slow, the talk is about the weather, and Albuquerque might as well be on another planet. The entire loop of this trip takes a day, the drive up the Sandia Crest a half day. Two Web sites offer good information: ⊕ *www.turquoisetrail.org* and ⊕ *www.byways.org.*

SANDIA PARK

7 mi north of Tijeras. From Tijeras, take I–40 east and exit north on the Turquoise Trail (NM 14); proceed 6 mi and turn left onto NM 536.

Driving east from Albuquerque, before you head up the Turquoise Trail, drop down south from Interstate 40 first, and stop at the **Sandia Ranger Station** for a bit of orientation on the Cibola National Forest and the mountains you're about to drive through. Pick up pamphlets and trail maps, and—if there are enough kids in the audience—witness a fire-prevention program with a Smokey the Bear motif. From here you can also embark on a short self-guided tour to the nearby **fire lookout tower** and **Tijeras Pueblo ruins,** and head out on the trails throughout the forest. ✉ *11776 NM 337, Tijeras, south of I–40, off Exit 175* ☎ *505/281–3304* ⊕ *www.fs.fed.us/r3/cibola/districts/sandia.shtml* ✉ *Ranger station free, parking in Cibola National Forest $3* ☉ *Mon.–Sat. 8–4:30.*

In Cedar Crest, just off NM 14 a couple of miles south of Sandia Park, the modest but nicely laid-out **Museum of Archaeology & Material Culture** chronicles archaeological finds and contains artifacts dating from the Ice Age to the Battle of Wounded Knee. Exhibits shed light on prehistoric man, buffalo hunting, a history of turquoise mining in north-central New Mexico, and the 1930s excavations of Sandia Cave (about 15 mi away) that offered evidence of some of the earliest human life in North America. ✉ *22 Calvary Rd.; turn west 5 mi north of I–40 Exit 175 in Cedar Crest* ☎ *505/281–2005* ✉ *$3* ☉ *May–Oct., daily noon–7.*

☺ Fodor's Choice ★ It may take months for this odyssey of a place to completely sink in: quirky and utterly fascinating, **Tinkertown Museum** contains a world of miniature carved-wood characters. The museum's late founder, Ross Ward, spent more than 40 years carving and collecting the hundreds of figures that populate this cheerfully bizarre museum, including an animated miniature Western village, a Boot Hill cemetery, and a 1940s circus exhibit. Ragtime piano music, a 40-foot sailboat, and a life-size general store are other highlights. The walls surrounding this 22-room museum have been fashioned out of more than 50,000 glass bottles pressed into cement. This homage to folk art, found art, and eccentric kitsch tends to strike a chord with people of all ages. As you might expect, the gift shop offers plenty of fun oddities. ✉ *121 Sandia Crest Rd. (NM 536); take Cedar Crest Exit 175 north off I–40 east and follow signs on NM 14 to Sandia Crest turnoff* ☎ *505/281–5233* ⊕ *www.tinkertown.com* ✉ *$3* ☉ *Apr.–Oct., daily 9–6.*

2

For awesome views of Albuquerque and half of New Mexico, take NM 536 up the back side of the Sandia Mountains through Cibola National Forest to **Sandia Crest.** At the 10,378-foot summit, explore the foot trails along the rim (particularly in summer) and take in the breathtaking views of Albuquerque down below, and of the so-called Steel Forest—the nearby cluster of radio and television towers. Always bring an extra layer of clothing, even in summer—the temperature at the crest can be anywhere from 15 to 25 degrees cooler than down in Albuquerque. If you're in need of refreshments or are searching for some inexpensive souvenirs, visit the **Sandia Crest House Gift Shop and Restaurant** (☎ 505/243–0605), on the rim of the crest.

As you continue north up NM 14 from Sandia Park, after about 12 mi you pass through the sleepy village of **Golden,** the site of the first gold rush (in 1825) west of the Mississippi. It has a rock shop and a mercantile store. The rustic adobe church and graveyard are popular with photographers. Be aware that locals are very protective of this area and aren't known to warm up to strangers.

WHERE TO STAY

$$

BED & BREAKFAST

Elaine's, A Bed and Breakfast. This antique-filled three-story log-and-stone home is set in the evergreen folds of the Sandia Mountain foothills. Four acres of wooded grounds beckon outside the back door. The top two floors have rooms with balconies and big picture windows that bring the lush mountain views indoors. The third-floor room also has cathedral ceilings and a brass bed; some rooms have fireplaces, and one has its own outside entrance. Breakfast, served in a plant-filled room or outside on a patio with a fountain, often includes fresh fruit, pancakes, or waffles with sausage. ⊠ *Snowline Estate, 72 Snowline Rd.* ⊕ *Box 444, Cedar Crest 87008* ☎ *505/281–2467 or 800/821–3092* ⊕ *www. elainesbnb.com* ⊃ *5 rooms* ☖ *In-room: no a/c, no phone, no TV, Wi-Fi* ⊟ *AE, D, MC, V* ⊚ *BP.*

CAMPING

¢

Turquoise Trail Campground and RV Park. Pine and cedar trees dot this 14-acre park in the Sandias, which has hiking trails with access to the Cibola National Forest. Adjacent to the premises is the Museum of Archaeology & Material Culture. Campsite rates are calculated per person; you will need reservations in October when spots fill up quickly. ⊠ *22 Calvary Rd., 5 mi north of I–40 Exit 175 in Cedar Crest* ☎ *505/281–2005* ⊕ *www.turquoisetrailcampground.com* ☖ *Flush toilets, full hookups, partial hookups (electric and water), dump station, drinking water, guest laundry, showers, fire grates, fire pits, grills, picnic tables, electricity, public telephone, general store, play area* ⊃ *57 sites, 45 with hookups* ⊟ *AE, D, MC, V.*

SPORTS AND THE OUTDOORS

Fodor's Choice

★

The 18-hole **Paa-Ko Ridge Golf Course** (⊠ *1 Club House Dr.* ☎ *505/281– 6000 or 866/898–5987* ⊕ *www.paakoridge.com*) has been voted New Mexico's best place to play golf by *Golf Digest.* Golfers enjoy vistas of the mesas and the Sandia Mountains from any of five tee placements on each hole. Greens fees are $89 to $114, and tee-time reservations may be made a month ahead. The course is just off NM 14, 3½ mi north of the turnoff for Sandia Crest (NM 536).

Although less extensive and challenging than the ski areas farther north in the Sangre de Cristos, **Sandia Peak** (✉ *NM 536* ☎ *505/242–9052 ski area, 505/857–8977 snow conditions* ⊕ *www.sandiapeak.com*) is extremely popular with locals from Albuquerque and offers a nice range of novice, intermediate, and expert downhill trails; there's also a ski school. Snowboarding is welcome on all trails, and there's cross-country terrain as well, whenever snow is available. Snowfall can be sporadic, so call ahead to check for cross-country; Sandia has snowmaking capacity for about 30 of its 200 acres of downhill skiing. The season runs from mid-December to mid-March, and lift tickets cost $43. Keep in mind that you can also access the ski area year-round via the Sandia Peak Aerial Tramway (⇨ *Exploring Albuquerque, above*), which is faster from Albuquerque than driving all the way around. In summer, the ski area converts into a fantastic mountain-biking and hiking terrain. The ski area offers a number of packages with bike and helmet rentals and lift tickets. Other summer activities at Sandia Peak include sand volleyball, horseshoes, and picnicking.

MADRID

37 mi northeast of Albuquerque, 12 mi north of Golden on NM 14.

Totally abandoned when its coal mine closed in the 1950s, Madrid (locals put the emphasis on the first syllable: *mah*-drid) has gradually been rebuilt and is now—to the dismay of some longtime locals—on the verge of trendiness (some would say it's already there). The entire town was offered for sale for $250,000 back then, but there were no takers. Finally, in the early 1970s, a few artists fleeing big cities settled in and began restoration. Weathered houses and old company stores have been repaired and turned into boutiques and galleries, some of them selling high-quality furniture, paintings, and crafts. Big events here include Old Timers Days on July 4th weekend, and the Christmas open house, held weekends in December, when galleries and studios are open and the famous Madrid Christmas lights twinkle brightly.

OFF THE BEATEN PATH

Aged hippies, youthful hipsters, and everyone in between congregate at **Java Junction** (✉ *2855 NM 14* ☎ *505/438–2772 or 877/308–8884* ⊕ *www.java-junction.com*) for lattes, chai, sandwiches, breakfast burritos, pastries, and other toothsome treats. You can also pick up a number of house-made gourmet goods, from hot sauces to jalapeño-raspberry preserves. Upstairs there's a pleasantly decorated room for rent that can sleep up to three guests.

WHERE TO EAT

¢

CAFÉ

✗ **Mineshaft Tavern.** A rollicking old bar and restaurant adjacent to the Old Coal Mine Museum, this boisterous place—there's live music many nights—was a miners' commissary back in the day. Today it serves what many people consider the best green-chile cheeseburger (available with beef or buffalo) in New Mexico, along with 12 ice-cold beers on tap and a selection of other pub favorites and comfort foods—the Cobb salad, for one, is excellent. Although open daily, the kitchen closes around 7:30 pm on weekdays. ⊠ *2846 NM 14* ☎ *505/473–0743* ⊕ *www.themineshafttavern.com* ▤ *D, MC, V.*

SHOPPING

The town of Madrid has only one street, so the three-dozen-or-so shops and galleries are easy to find.

You can watch live glassblowing demonstrations at **Al Leedom Studio** (☎ *505/473–2054* ⊕ *www.alleedom.com*) ; his vibrant vases and bowls are sold alongside the beautiful handcrafted jewelry of wife Barbara Leedom. The Leedoms' friendly cat and dancing dog are also big crowd pleasers. In a pale blue cottage in the center of town, the **Ghost Town Trading Post** (☎ *505/471–7605* ⊕ *www.wildhogsmadridnm.com*) is a great bet for fine Western jewelry fashioned out of local gemstones (not just turquoise, but opal, amber, and onyx). **Johnsons of Madrid** (☎ *505/471– 1054*) ranks among the most prestigious galleries in town, showing painting, photography, sculpture, and textiles created by some of the region's leading artists. You could spend hours browsing the fine rugs and furnishings at **Seppanen & Daughters Fine Textiles** (☎ *505/424–7470* ⊕ *www.finetextiles.com*), which stocks custom Zapotec textiles from Oaxaca, Navajo weavings, Tibetan carpets, and fine Arts and Crafts tables, sofas, and chairs.

CERRILLOS

3 mi northeast of Madrid on NM 14.

Cerrillos was a boomtown in the 1880s—its mines brimmed with gold, silver, and turquoise, and eight newspapers, four hotels, and 21 taverns flourished. When the mines went dry the town went bust. Since then, Cerrillos has served as the backdrop for feature-film and television Westerns, among them *Young Guns* and *The Hi-Lo Country.* Today, it might easily be mistaken for a ghost town, which it's been well on the way to becoming for decades. Time has left its streets dry, dusty, and almost deserted, although it is home to a number of artists, and the occasional Amtrak roars through to remind you what century you're in.

Casa Grande (⊠ *17 Waldo St.* ☎ *505/438–3008* ⊕ *www.casagrande tradingpost.com*), a 28-room adobe (several rooms of which are part of a shop), has a small museum ($2) with a display of early mining exhibits. There's also a clean and neat, but oddly out-of-place petting zoo ($2) with about 20 animals, and a genuinely scenic overlook. Casa Grande is open daily 8 am–sunset.

Pack rats and browsers alike ought not to miss the **What-Not Shop** (⊠ *15B 1st St.* ☎ *505/471–2744*), a venerable secondhand-antiques shop of a half-century's standing packed floor to ceiling with Native American pottery, cut glass, rocks, political buttons, old postcards, clocks, and who knows what else.

WHERE TO EAT AND STAY

$ ✗ **San Marcos Cafe.** In Lone Butte, about 6 mi north of Cerrillos (and
CAFÉ actually quite a lot closer to Santa Fe than to Albuquerque but nevertheless a fixture on the Turquoise Trail), this restaurant is known for its creative fare and nontraditional setting—an actual feed store, with roosters, turkeys, and peacocks running about outside. In one of the two

bric-a-brac–filled dining rooms, sample rich cinnamon rolls and such delectables as burritos stuffed with roast beef and potatoes and topped with green chile, and the classic eggs San Marcos: tortillas stuffed with scrambled eggs and topped with guacamole, pinto beans, melted Jack cheese, and red chile. Hot apple pie à la mode with rum sauce is a favorite. Expect a wait on weekends unless you make a reservation. ✉ *3877 NM 14* ☎ *505/471–9298* ▭ *MC, V* ☻ *No dinner.*

$$$
BED & BREAKFAST

⊡ **High Feather Ranch.** A grand adobe homestead and B&B, plush High Feather Ranch anchors 130 wide-open acres with breathtaking mountain views. It feels completely removed from civilization but is, in fact, within an hour's drive of both Santa Fe and Albuquerque. Although built in the late 1990s, the sprawling inn contains reclaimed 19th-century timber, antique gates, and fine vintage furnishings. Rooms have high ceilings and plenty of windows, and you're never far from a portal or patio; one room has an outdoor shower in a private courtyard. Rates include an impressive full breakfast. **Pros:** between Madrid and Cerrillos, you're alone with the scenery and certain to leave relaxed and well fed. **Cons:** there's a 1-mi stretch of dirt road to get to the door, but it's nothing to fret about. ✉ *29 High Feather Ranch; 2 mi north of Madrid, turn right onto CR 55/Gold Mine Rd.* ☎ *505/424–1333 or 800/757–4410* ⊕ *www.highfeatherranch.com* ⬎ *2 rooms, 1 suite* ♨ *In-room: no a/c, no phone, no TV, Wi-Fi. In-hotel: some pets allowed* ▭ *AE, D, MC, V* �ⓘ⦀ *BP.*

SPORTS AND THE OUTDOORS

Fodor's Choice
★

Rides with **Broken Saddle Riding Co.** (✉ *Off NM 14, Cerrillos* ☎ *505/424–7774* ⊕ *www.brokensaddle.com*) take you around the old turquoise and silver mines the Cerrillos area is noted for. On a Tennessee Walker or a Missouri Fox Trotter you can explore the Cerrillos hills and canyons, 23 mi southeast of Santa Fe. This is not the usual nose-to-tail trail ride.

Santa Fe

"Lunch at Tia Sophia's (good and simple), and then a little more shopping. Then back to the lower part of Canyon Road for more galleries. So much art, so little time! We spent our last evening polishing off the leftovers from our wonderful Thursday night dinner before our early departure on Sunday. All in all we had a great time; Santa Fe is a wonderful place for a girl's get-a-way."

—PaigeS

Updated by
Georgia de
Katona

On a plateau at the base of the Sangre de Cristo Mountains—at an elevation of 7,000 feet—Santa Fe is brimming with reminders of nearly four centuries of Spanish and Mexican rule, and of the Pueblo cultures that have been here for hundreds more.

The town's placid central Plaza, which dates from the early 17th century, has been the site of bullfights, gunfights, political rallies, promenades, and public markets over the years. A one-of-a-kind destination, Santa Fe is fabled for its rows of chic art galleries, superb restaurants, and diverse shops selling everything from Southwestern furnishings and cowboy gear, to Tibetan textiles and Moroccan jewelry.

La Villa Real de la Santa Fe de San Francisco de Asísi (the Royal City of the Holy Faith of St. Francis of Assisi) was founded in the early 1600s by Don Pedro de Peralta, who planted his banner in the name of Spain. During its formative years, Santa Fe was maintained primarily for the purpose of bringing the Catholic faith to New Mexico's Pueblo Indians. In 1680, however, the Indians rose in revolt and the Spanish colonists were driven out of New Mexico. The tide turned 12 years later, when General Don Diego de Vargas returned with a new army from El Paso and recaptured Santa Fe. To commemorate de Vargas's recapture of the town in 1692, Las Fiestas de Santa Fe have been held annually since 1712. The nation's oldest community celebration takes place on the weekend after Labor Day, with parades, mariachi bands, pageants, and the burning of Zozóbra—a must-see extravaganza held in Fort Marcy Park just blocks north of the Plaza.

Following de Vargas's defeat of the Pueblos, the then-grand Camino Real (Royal Road), stretching from Mexico City to Santa Fe, brought an army of conquistadors, clergymen, and settlers to the northernmost reaches of Spain's New World conquests. In 1820 the Santa Fe Trail—a prime artery of U.S. westward expansion—spilled a flood of covered wagons from Missouri onto the Plaza. A booming trade with the United States was born. After Mexico achieved independence from Spain in 1821, its subsequent rule of New Mexico further increased this commerce.

The Santa Fe Trail's heyday ended with the arrival of the Atchison, Topeka & Santa Fe Railway in 1880. The trains, and later the nation's first highways, brought a new type of settler to Santa Fe—artists who fell in love with its cultural diversity, history, and magical color and light. They were especially drawn to the area because eccentricity was embraced not discouraged, as it often was in the social confines of the East Coast. Their presence attracted tourists, who quickly became a primary source of income for the proud, but largely poor, populace.

Cosmopolitan visitors from around the world are consistently surprised by the city's rich and varied cultural offerings despite its relatively small size. Often referred to as the "City Different," Santa Fe became the first

TOP REASONS TO GO

A winter stroll on Canyon Road. There are few experiences to match walking this ancient street on Christmas Eve when it's covered with snow, scented by piñon fires burning in luminarias along the road, and echoing with the voices of carolers and happy families.

A culinary adventure. Start with rellenos for breakfast and try tapas for dinner. Enjoy some strawberry habanero gelato or sip an Aztec Warrior Chocolate Elixir. Take a cooking lesson. Santa Fe is an exceptional dining town, the perfect place to push the frontiers of your palate.

Into the wild. Follow the lead of locals and take any one of the many easy-access points into the incredible, and surprisingly lush, mountains that rise out of Santa Fe. Raft the Rio Grande, snowboard, snowshoe, or try mountain biking.

Market mashup. Summer offers the phenomenal International Folk Art Market, the famed Indian Market, and the two-for-one weekend of Traditional Spanish Market and Contemporary Hispanic Market. The offerings are breathtaking and the community involvement yet another aspect of Santa Fe to fall in love with.

American city to be designated a UNESCO Creative City, acknowledging its place in the global community as a leader in art, crafts, design, and lifestyle.

ORIENTATION AND PLANNING

GETTING ORIENTED

Humorist Will Rogers said on his first visit to Santa Fe, "Whoever designed this town did so while riding on a jackass, backwards, and drunk." The maze of narrow streets and alleyways confounds motorists; however, pedestrians delight in the vast array of shops, restaurants, flowered courtyards, and eye-catching galleries at nearly every turn. Park your car, grab a map, and explore the town on foot.

Interstate 25 cuts just south of Santa Fe, which is 62 mi northeast of Albuquerque. U.S. 285/84 runs north–south through the city. The NM 599 bypass, also called the Santa Fe Relief Route, cuts around the west side of the city from Interstate 25's Exit 276, southwest of the city, to U.S. 285/84, north of the city; it's a great shortcut if you're heading from Albuquerque to Española, Abiquiu, Taos, or other points north of Santa Fe. The modest flow of water called the Santa Fe River runs west, parallel to Alameda Street, from the Sangre de Cristo Mountains to the open prairie southwest of town, where it disappears into a narrow canyon before joining the Rio Grande. There's a *dicho*, or saying, in New Mexico: "*agua es vida*"—water is life—and every little trickle counts.

SANTA FE NEIGHBORHOODS

The Plaza. The heart of historic Santa Fe, the Plaza has been the site of a bullring, fiestas, and fandangos. Despite the buildup of tourist shops, the Plaza retains its old-world feel and is still the center of many annual festivities and much of the town's activity.

East Side and Canyon Road. One of the city's oldest streets, Canyon Road is lined with galleries, shops, and restaurants housed in adobe compounds, with thick walls, and lush courtyard gardens. The architectural influence of Old Mexico and Spain, and the indigenous Pueblo cultures, makes this street as historic as it is artistic.

Old Santa Fe Trail and South Capitol. In the 1800s wagon trains from Missouri rolled into town from the Old Santa Fe Trail, opening trade into what had been a very insular Spanish colony and forever changing Santa Fe's destiny. This street joins the Plaza on the south side after passing the state capitol and some of the area's oldest neighborhoods.

Museum Hill. What used to be the outskirts of town became the site of gracious, neo-Pueblo style homes in the mid-20th century, many of them designed by the famed architect John Gaw Meem. Old Santa Fe Trail takes you to Camino Lejo, aka Museum Hill, where you'll find four excellent museums and a café.

The Railyard District. This bustling area, also known as the Guadalupe District, has undergone a major transformation in the last decade. The new Railyard Park is a model for urban green space and is across the street from a permanent new home for the vibrant farmers' market. The redevelopment along Guadalupe Street has added dozens of shops, galleries, and restaurants to the town's already rich assortment.

SANTA FE PLANNER

WHEN TO GO

The city's population, an estimated 72,000, swells by many thousands in summer. In winter, skiers and snowboarders arrive, lured by the challenging slopes and fluffy, powdery snow of Ski Santa Fe and—within a two-hour drive—Angel Fire and Taos Ski Valley (⇨ *chapter 4*). Prices are highest June through August. Between September and November and in April and May they're lower, and (except for the major holidays) from December to March they're the lowest.

Santa Fe has four distinct seasons, though the sun shines nearly every day of the year. June through August temperatures are high 80s to low 90s during the day, 50s at night, with afternoon rain showers—monsoons—cooling the air. During this season it's advisable to keep a lightweight, waterproof jacket with you. The monsoons come suddenly and can quickly drench you. September and October bring beautiful weather and a marked reduction in crowds. Temperatures—and prices—drop significantly after Halloween. December through March is ski season. Spring comes late at this elevation. April and May are blustery, with daily warm weather (70s and above) finally arriving in May. ■TIP➔ **The high elevation here catches people unawares and altitude sickness** can utterly ruin a day of fun. Drink water, drink more water, and then have a little more.

GETTING HERE AND AROUND

AIR TRAVEL

Among the smallest state capitals in the country, Santa Fe has only a small airport. Albuquerque's is the nearest major one, about an hour away. Tiny Santa Fe Municipal Airport is served by one commercial airline, American Eagle, with daily flights to Dallas (DFW) and Los Angeles (LAX). The airport is 9 mi southwest of Downtown.

Airport Contacts: Albuquerque International Sunport (*ABQ* ☎ *505/244–7700* ⊕ *www.cabq.gov/airport*). **Santa Fe Municipal Airport** (*SAF* ✉ *Airport Rd. and NM 599* ☎ *505/473–4118*).

BUS TRAVEL

The city's bus system, Santa Fe Trails, covers 10 major routes through town and is useful for getting from the Plaza to some of the outlying attractions. Route M is most useful for visitors, as it runs from Downtown to the museums on Old Santa Fe Trail south of town, and Route 2 is useful if you're staying at one of the motels out on Cerrillos Road and need to get into town (if time is a factor for your visit, a car is a much more practical way to get around). Individual rides cost $1, and a daily pass costs $2. Buses run about every 30 minutes on weekdays, every hour on weekends. Service begins at 6 am and continues until 11 pm on weekdays, 8 to 8 on Saturday, and 10 to 7 (limited routes) on Sunday.

Bus Contacts. Santa Fe Trails (☎ *505/955–2001* ⊕ *www.santafenm.gov*).

CAR TRAVEL

Santa Fe is served by several national rental car agencies, including Avis, Budget, and Hertz. Additional agencies with locations in Santa Fe include Advantage, Enterprise, Sears, and Thrifty. *See Car Travel in the Travel Smart chapter for national rental agency phone numbers.*

Car Rental Contacts. Advantage (☎ *505/983–9470* ⊕ *www.advantage.com*). **Enterprise** (☎ *505/473–3600* ⊕ *www.enterprise.com*). **Sears** (☎ *505/984–8038* ⊕ *www.sears.avis.com*). **Thrifty** (☎ *505/474–3365 or 800/367–2277* ⊕ *www. thrifty.com*).

TAXI TRAVEL

Capital City Cab Company controls all the cabs in Santa Fe. The taxis aren't metered; you pay a flat fee based on how far you're going, usually $6 to $10 within the Downtown area. There are no cabstands; you must phone to arrange a ride.

Taxi Contact: Capital City Cab (☎ *505/438–0000*).

TRAIN TRAVEL

Amtrak's Southwest Chief stops in Lamy, a short drive south of Santa Fe, on its route from Chicago to Los Angeles via Kansas City; other New Mexico stops include Raton, Las Vegas, Albuquerque, and Gallup daily. In 2006, the state's first-ever commuter train line, the New Mexico Rail Runner Express, began serving the north-central part of the state. Service is from Belén, south of Albuquerque, to Santa Fe, with numerous stops in between. The Rail Runner offers a scenic, efficient alternative to reaching Santa Fe from the airport in Albuquerque (a shuttle bus operates between Albuquerque's Downtown train station and the airport).

Train Contacts: Amtrak (☎ 800/872–7245 ⊕ www.amtrak.com). **New Mexico Rail Runner Express** (☎ 866/795–7245 ⊕ www.nmrailrunner.com).

GUIDED TOURS
GENERAL INTEREST
Custom Tours by Clarice (☎ 505/438–7116 ⊕ www.santafecustomtours. com) are guided open-air tram excursions that run four times a day from the corner of Lincoln Avenue and West Palace Avenue. These 90-minute tours don't require reservations and offer a nice overview of Downtown; the company also gives bus and shuttle tours of Bandelier and Taos, and shuttle services from town to the Santa Fe Opera (reservations required).

> **PEDICABS**
>
> **Santa Fe Pedicabs** offer a great alternative to getting around the heart of town, especially if your restaurant is a ways from your hotel. Friendly drivers can regale you with all sorts of information and trivia about Santa Fe as they whisk you along in bicycle carriages. Sit back and enjoy watching the crowds and the sights go by. Cost is $1 per minute. ⊠ Santa Fe Plaza, Canyon Rd., Railyard District ☎ 505/577–5056 ⊕ www. santafepedicabs.com.

Great Southwest Adventures (☎ 505/455–2700 ⊕ www.swadventures. com) conducts guided tours in 7- to 35-passenger van and bus excursions to Bandelier, O'Keeffe country, the High Road and Taos, and elsewhere in the region.Guides are avid outdoors enthusiasts; in addition to their regular tour offerings, the company arranges eye-opening single- and multiday custom hikes and photography trips.

Rojo Tours (☎ 505/474–8333 ⊕ www.rojotours.com) designs specialized trips—to view wildflowers, pueblo ruins and cliff dwellings, galleries and studios, Native American arts and crafts, and private homes—as well as adventure activity tours.

Santa Fe Detours (☎ 505/983–6565 or 800/338–6877 ⊕ www.sfdetours. com) offers a more limited selection of tours, by reservation only.

Santa Fe Guides (☎ 505/466–4877 ⊕ www.santafeguides.org) is an organization of about 15 respected independent tour guides—its Web site lists each member and his or her specialties.

MAKING THE MOST OF YOUR TIME
It's best to explore Santa Fe one neighborhood at a time and arrange your activities within each. If you've got more than two days, be sure to explore the northern Rio Grande Valley. For the best tour, combine your adventures in Santa Fe with some from the Side Trips section (⇨ *below*), which highlights several trips within a 60- to 90-minute drive of town.

Plan on spending a full day wandering around Santa Fe Plaza, strolling down narrow streets, under portals, and across ancient cobbled streets. Sip coffee on the Plaza, take in a museum or two (or three) and marvel at the cathedral. The **New Mexico History Museum** and **Palace of the Governors** are great places to start to gain a sense of the history and cultures influencing this area. ■**TIP➡** Take one of the docent-led tours offered by

the museums. Almost without exception the docents are engaging and passionate about their subjects. You gain invaluable insight into the collections and their context by taking these free tours. Inquire at the front desk of the museums for more information.

On a stretch called Museum Hill, you'll find four world-class museums, all quite different and all highly relevant to the culture of Santa Fe and northern New Mexico. Start at the intimate gem, the **Museum of Spanish Colonial Art,** where you'll gain a real sense of the Spanish empire's influence on the world beyond Spain. The **Museum of International Folk Art** is thoroughly engaging for both young and old. If you have the stamina to keep going, have lunch at the tasty Museum Café and then visit the **Museum of Indian Arts and Culture** and then move on to the **Wheelwright Museum of the American Indian.** There is a path linking all these museums together, and the walk is easy. The museum shops at these four museums are outstanding—if you're a shopper you could easily spend an entire day in the shops alone.

An easy walk from any of the Downtown lodgings, Canyon Road should definitely be explored on foot. Take any of the side streets and stroll amongst historical homes and ancient *acequias* (irrigation ditches). If you really enjoy walking, keep going up Canyon Road past Cristo Rey Church, where the street gets even narrower and is lined with residential compounds. At the top is the **Randall Davey Audubon Center,** where bird-watching abounds.

Another enjoyable day can be spent exploring the hip Railyard District, which is bursting with energy and development from the new Railyard Park and the various businesses surrounding it. The **Santuario de Guadalupe** is a great place to start. Head south from there and enjoy shops, cafés, art galleries, the farmers' market, and the fun new Railyard Park. If you enjoy ceramics, don't miss a stop at **Santa Fe Clay,** an amazing gallery, supply store, and studio where dozens of artists are busy at work. The venerable **SITE Santa Fe** is also here, with its cutting-edge modern art installations.

There are more galleries and shops in Downtown Santa Fe than can be handled in one day. If you've got the time, or if you don't want to spend hours in multiple museums, take a look at our shopping recommendations *(⇨ Shopping, below)* and go from there.

VISITOR INFORMATION

New Mexico Department of Tourism visitor center (✉ *Lamy Building, 491 Old Santa Fe Trail* ☎ *505/827–7400* ⊕ *www.newmexico.org).* **Santa Fe Convention and Visitors Bureau** (✉ *201 W. Marcy St.* ☎ *505/955–6200 or 800/777–2489* ⊕ *www.santafe.org).*

EXPLORING SANTA FE

Five Santa Fe museums participate in the Museum of New Mexico pass (four state museums and the privately run Museum of Spanish Colonial Art) and it is by far the most economical way to visit them all. The four-day pass costs $20 and is sold at all five museums, which include the New Mexico History Museum/Palace of the Governors, Museum of Fine Arts, Museum of Indian Arts and Culture, Museum of International Folk Art, and Museum of Spanish Colonial Art.

THE PLAZA

Much of the history of Santa Fe, New Mexico, the Southwest, and even the West has some association with Santa Fe's central Plaza, which New Mexico governor Don Pedro de Peralta laid out in 1607. The Plaza was already well established by the time of the Pueblo revolt in 1680. Freight wagons unloaded here after completing their arduous journey across the Santa Fe Trail. The American flag was raised over the Plaza in 1846, during the Mexican War, which resulted in Mexico's loss of all its territories in the present southwestern United States. For a time the Plaza was a tree-shaded park with a white picket fence. In the 1890s it was an expanse of lawn where uniformed bands played in an ornate gazebo. Particularly festive times on the Plaza are the weekend after Labor Day, during Las Fiestas de Santa Fe, and at Christmas, when all the trees are filled with lights, and rooftops are outlined with *farolitos,* votive candles lit within paper-bag lanterns.

TOP ATTRACTIONS

★ **Georgia O'Keeffe Museum.** One of many East Coast artists who visited New Mexico in the first half of the 20th century, O'Keeffe returned to live and paint here, eventually emerging as the demigoddess of Southwestern art. O'Keeffe's innovative view of the landscape is captured in *From the Plains,* inspired by her memory of the Texas plains, and *Jimson Weed,* a study of one of her favorite plants. Special exhibitions with O'Keeffe's modernist peers are on view throughout the year—many of these are exceptional, sometimes even more interesting than the permanent collection. ⊠ *217 Johnson St.* ☎ *505/946–1000* ⊕ *www. okeeffemuseum.org* ✉ *$8, free 5–8 pm first Fri. of the month* ☽ *Mon.– Thur. and Sat.–Sun. 10–5; Fri. 10–7.*

☾ **The New Mexico History Museum.** The new museum is the anchor of a campus that encompasses the **Palace of the Governors,** the **Museum of New Mexico Press,** the **Fray Angélico Chávez History Library,** and **Photo Archives** (an assemblage of more than 750,000 images dating from the 1850s). Behind the palace on Lincoln Avenue, the museum thoroughly encompasses the early history of indigenous people, Spanish colonization, the Mexican Period, and travel and commerce on the legendary Santa Fe Trail. Opened in May 2009, the museum has permanent and changing exhibits, such as "Jewish Pioneers of New Mexico," which explores the vital role Jewish immigrants played during the late 19th and early 20th centuries in the state's civic, economic, and cultural development. With advance permission, students and researchers have access to the comprehensive Fray Angélico Chávez Library and its rare maps, manuscripts, and photographs (more than 120,000 prints and negatives). The Museum of New Mexico Press, which prints books, pamphlets, and cards on antique presses, also hosts bookbinding demonstrations, lectures, and slide shows. The Palace of the Governors is a humble one-story neo-Pueblo adobe on the north side of the Plaza, and is the oldest public building in the United States. Its rooms contain

Fodor's Choice
★

period furnishings and exhibits illustrating the building's many functions over the past four centuries. Built at the same time as the Plaza, circa 1610 (scholars debate the exact year), it was the seat of four regional governments—those of Spain, Mexico, the Confederacy, and the U.S. territory that preceded New Mexico's statehood, which was achieved in 1912. The building was abandoned in 1680, following the Pueblo Revolt, but resumed its role as government headquarters when Don Diego de Vargas successfully returned in 1692. It served as the residence for 100 Spanish, Mexican, and American governors, including Governor Lew Wallace, who wrote his epic *Ben Hur* in its then drafty rooms, all the while complaining of the dust and mud that fell from its earthen ceiling.

Dozens of Native American vendors gather daily under the portal of the Palace of the Governors to display and sell pottery, jewelry, bread, and other goods. With few exceptions, the more than 500 artists and craftspeople registered to sell here are Pueblo or Navajo Indians. The merchandise for sale is required to meet strict standards: all items are handmade or hand-strung in Native American households; silver jewelry is either sterling (92.5% pure) or coin (90% pure) silver; all metal jewelry bears the maker's mark, which is registered with the Museum of New Mexico. Prices tend to reflect the high quality of the merchandise but are often significantly less that what you'd pay in a shop. Please remember not to take photographs without permission.

There's an outstanding gift shop and bookstore with many high-quality, New Mexico–produced items. ⊠ *Palace Ave., north side of Plaza, Lincoln Ave., west of the Palace* ☎ *505/476–5100* ⊕ *www. nmhistorymuseum.org* ⊠ *$9, 4-day pass $20 (good at all 4 state museums and Museum of Spanish Colonial Art), free Fri. 5–8* ☉ *Tues.–Thurs. and weekends 10–5, Fri. 10–8 (also Mon. 10–5 June–early Sept.)*

★ **St. Francis Cathedral Basilica.** The iconic cathedral, a block east of the Plaza, is one of the rare significant departures from the city's nearly ubiquitous Pueblo architecture. Construction was begun in 1869 by Jean Baptiste Lamy, Santa Fe's first archbishop, who worked with French architects and Italian stonemasons. The Romanesque style was popular in Lamy's native home in southwest France. The circuit-riding cleric was sent by the Catholic Church to the Southwest to change the religious practices of its native population (to "civilize" them, as one period document puts it) and is buried in the crypt beneath the church's high altar. He was the inspiration behind Willa Cather's novel *Death Comes for the Archbishop* (1927). In 2005 Pope Benedict XVI declared St. Francis the "cradle of Catholicism" in the Southwestern United States, and upgraded the status of the building from mere cathedral to cathedral basilica—it's one of just 36 in the country.

Just south of the cathedral, where the parking lot meets Paseo de Peralta, is the **Archdiocese of Santa Fe Museum** (☎ *505/983–3811*), a small museum where many of the area's historic, liturgical artifacts are on view. ⊠ *231 Cathedral Pl.* ☎ *505/982–5619* ☉ *Mon.–Sat. 6–6, Sun. 7–7, except during Mass. Mass Mon.–Sat. at 7 am and 5:15 pm and Sun. at 8 am, 10 am, noon, and 7 pm. Museum weekdays 8:30–4:30.*

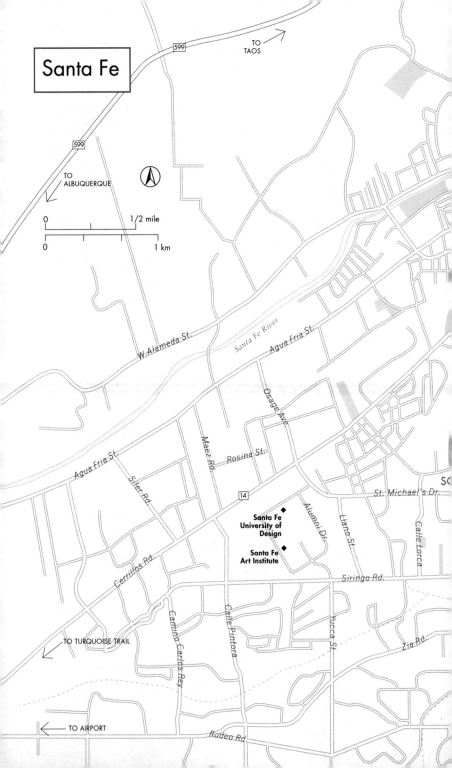

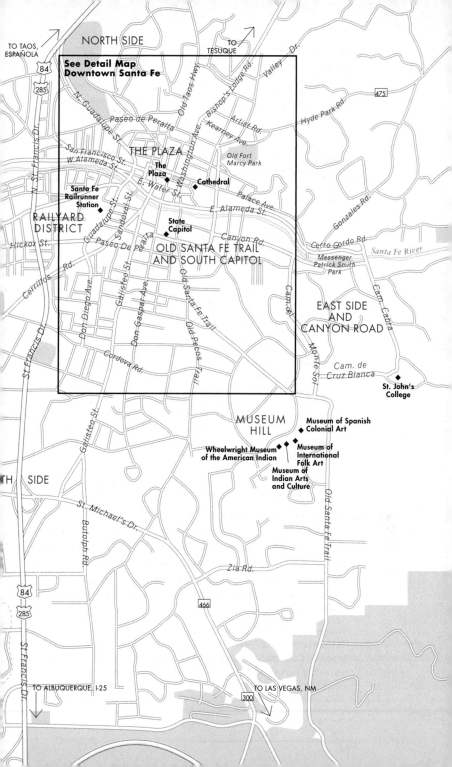

WORTH NOTING

Institute of American Indian Arts (IAIA) Museum. This fascinating museum just a block from the Plaza contains the largest collection of contemporary Native American art in the United States. The collection of paintings, photography, sculptures, prints, and traditional crafts was created by past and present students and teachers. In the 1960s and 1970s it blossomed into the nation's premier center for Native American arts and its alumni represent almost 600 tribes around the country. The museum continues to showcase the cultural and artistic vibrancy of indigenous people and expands what is still an often limited public perception of what "Indian" art is and can be. Artist Fritz Scholder taught here, as did sculptor Allan Houser. Among their disciples was the painter T. C. Cannon. ✉ *108 Cathedral Pl.* ☎ *505/983–1777* ⊕ *www.iaia.edu* ⌚ *$5* ☉ *June–Oct., Mon.–Sat. 10–5, Sun. noon–5; Nov.–May, Wed.–Sat. and Mon. 10–5, Sun. noon–5.*

> **FLAME ON!**
>
> Every weekend after Labor Day thousands gather to watch a groaning, flailing, 50-foot bogey-man-puppet known as Zozóbra go up in flames amidst an incredible display of fireworks—taking troubles of the past year with him. It's wildly pagan and utterly Santa Fe.

La Fonda. A *fonda* (inn) has stood on this site, southeast of the Plaza, for centuries. Architect Isaac Hamilton Rapp, who put Santa Fe style on the map, built this area landmark in 1922. Remodeled in 1926 by architect John Gaw Meem, the hotel was sold to the Santa Fe Railway in 1926 and remained a Harvey House hotel until 1968. Because of its proximity to the Plaza and its history as a gathering place for everyone from cowboys to movie stars (Errol Flynn stayed here), it's referred to as "The Inn at the End of the Trail." Step inside to browse the shops on the main floor or to eat at one of the restaurants (La Plazuela or the French Bakery). The dark, cozy bar draws both locals and tourists and has live music many nights. For a real treat: Have a drink at the fifth-floor Bell Tower Bar (open late spring–early fall), which offers tremendous sunset views. ✉ *E. San Francisco St., at Old Santa Fe Trail* ☎ *505/982–5511.*

NEED A BREAK?

Ecco Gelato (✉ *105 E. Marcy St.* ☎ *505/986–9778*) is a clean, contemporary café across from the Downtown public library with large plate-glass windows, and brushed-metal tables inside and out on the sidewalk under the portal. Try the delicious and creative gelato flavors (strawberry-habanero, saffron-honey, minty white grape, chocolate-banana) or some of the espressos and coffees, pastries, and sandwiches (roast beef and blue cheese, tuna with dill, cucumber, and sprouts).

New Mexico Museum of Art *(Museum of Fine Arts).* Designed by Isaac Hamilton Rapp in 1917, the museum contains one of America's finest regional collections. It's also one of Santa Fe's earliest Pueblo Revival structures, inspired by the adobe structures at Acoma Pueblo. Split-cedar *latillas* (branches set in a crosshatch pattern) and hand-hewn vigas form the ceilings. The 8,000-piece permanent collection, of which

A GOOD WALK: THE PLAZA

To get started, drop by the information booth at the Plaza's northwest corner, across the street from the clock, where Palace Street meets Lincoln Street (in front of the bank) to pick up a free map. From there, begin your walk around the Plaza. You can get an overview of the history of Santa Fe and New Mexico at the **Palace of the Governors** on the campus of the just-opened **New Mexico History Museum**, which borders the northern side of the Plaza on Palace Avenue. Outside, under the palace portal, dozens of Native American artisans sell handcrafted wares. From the palace, round the corner to Lincoln Street to the **New Mexico Museum of Art**, where the works of regional masters are on display. The **Georgia O'Keeffe Museum**, on nearby Johnson Street, exhibits the works of its namesake, New Mexico's best-known painter.

From the O'Keeffe Museum, return to the Plaza and cut across to its southeast corner to Old Santa Fe Trail, where you can find the town's oldest hotel, **La Fonda**, a good place to soak up a little of bygone Santa Fe. One block east on Cathedral Place looms the imposing facade of **St. Francis Cathedral Basilica**. Across from the cathedral is the **Institute of American Indian Arts**, with its wonderful museum of contemporary Native art. A stone's throw from the museum is cool, quiet Sena Plaza, accessible through two doorways on Palace Avenue.

TIMING

It's possible to zoom through this compact area in about five hours—two hours exploring the Plaza and the Palace of the Governors, two hours seeing the Museum of Fine Arts and the Museum of the Institute of American Indian Arts, and an hour visiting the other sites.

only a fraction is exhibited at any given time, emphasizes the work of regional and nationally renowned artists, including the early modernist Georgia O'Keeffe; realist Robert Henri; the Cinco Pintores (five painters) of Santa Fe (including Fremont Elis and Will Shuster, the creative mind behind Zozóbra); members of the Taos Society of Artists (Ernest L. Blumenschein, Bert G. Phillips, Joseph H. Sharp, and E. Irving Couse, among others); and the works of noted 20th-century photographers of the Southwest, including Laura Gilpin, Ansel Adams, and Dorothea Lange. Rotating exhibits are staged throughout the year. Many excellent examples of Spanish-colonial-style furniture are on display. An interior *placita* (small plaza) with fountains, WPA murals, and sculpture, and the St. Francis Auditorium, where concerts and lectures are often held, are other highlights. ⊠ *107 W. Palace Ave.* ☎ *505/476–5072* ⊕ *www. mfasantafe.org* ✉ *$9, 4-day pass $20 (good at 4 state museums and the Museum of Spanish Colonial Art), free Fri. 5–8 pm* ☉ *Tues.–Thurs and weekends 10–5, Fri. 10–8 (also Mon. 10–5 June–early Sept.).*

Sena Plaza. Two-story buildings enclose this courtyard, which can be entered only through two small doorways on Palace Avenue or the shops facing Palace Avenue. Surrounding the oasis of flowering fruit trees, a fountain, and inviting benches are a variety of locally owned

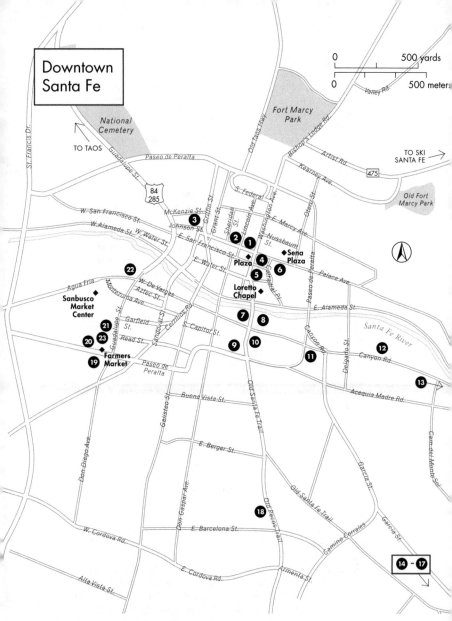

Downtown Santa Fe

CLOSE UP

Art & Architecture: Glossary of Terms

Perhaps more than any other region in the United States, New Mexico has its own distinctive cuisine and architectural style, both heavily influenced by Native American, Spanish-colonial, Mexican, and American frontier traditions. The brief glossary that follows explains terms used frequently in this book.

ART AND ARCHITECTURE

Adobe: A brick of sun-dried earth and clay, usually stabilized with straw; a structure made of adobe.

Banco: A small bench, or banquette, often upholstered with handwoven textiles, that gracefully emerges from adobe walls.

Bulto: Folk-art figures of a santo (saint), usually carved from wood.

Camposanto: A graveyard.

Capilla: A chapel.

Casita: Literally "small house," this term is generally used to describe a separate guesthouse.

Cerquita: A spiked, wrought-iron, rectangular fence, often marking grave sites.

Coyote fence: A type of wooden fence that surrounds many New Mexico homes; it comprises branches, usually from cedar or aspen trees, arranged vertically and wired tightly together.

Farolito: Small votive candles set in paper-bag lanterns, farolitos are popular at Christmastime. The term is used in northern New Mexico only. People in Albuquerque and points south call the lanterns *luminarias,* which in the north is the term for the bonfires of Christmas Eve.

Heishi: Technically the word means "shell necklace," but the common usage refers to necklaces made with rounded, thin, disc-shaped beads in various materials, such as turquoise or jet.

Hornos: Domed outdoor ovens made of plastered adobe or concrete blocks.

Kiva: A circular ceremonial room, built at least partially underground, used by Pueblo Indians of the Southwest. Entrance is gained from the roof.

Kiva fireplace: A corner fireplace whose round form resembles that of a kiva.

Nicho: A built-in shelf cut into an adobe or stucco wall.

Placita: A small plaza.

Portal: A porch or large covered area adjacent to a house.

Pueblo Revival (also informally called Pueblo style): Most homes in this style, modeled after the traditional dwellings of the Southwest Pueblo Indians, are cube or rectangle shaped. Other characteristics are flat roofs, thick adobe or stucco walls, small windows, rounded corners, and viga beams.

Retablo: Holy image painted on wood or tin.

Santero: Maker of religious images.

Terrones adobes: Adobe cut from the ground rather than formed from mud.

Viga: Horizontal roof beam made of logs, usually protruding from the side of the house.

3

A GOOD WALK: CANYON ROAD

Begin on Paseo de Peralta at the **Gerald Peters Gallery**, which has an enormous collection. Continue a half block north to Canyon Road. Turn right (east) and follow the road, which unfolds in shadows of undulating adobe walls. Street parking is at a premium, but there's a city-owned pay lot at the corner of Camino del Monte Sol, a few blocks up. Between visits to galleries and shops, take a break at one of the courtyards or fine restaurants. Be sure to stop by the beautiful gardens outside **El Zaguan**. At the intersection of Upper Canyon and Cristo Rey, you'll find the massive **Cristo Rey**

Church. Wear good walking shoes and watch out for the irregular sidewalks, which can get icy in winter.

TIMING

A tour of Canyon Road could take a whole day or as little as a few hours. If art is more than a curiosity to you, you may want to view the Gerald Peters Gallery apart from your Canyon Road tour. There's so much to see there that visual overload could hit before you get halfway up the road. Even on a cold day the walk is a pleasure, with massive, glistening icicles hanging off roofs and a silence shrouding the side streets.

shops. The quiet courtyard is a good place for repose or to have lunch at La Casa Sena. The buildings, erected in the 1700s as a single-family residence, had quarters for blacksmiths, bakers, farmers, and all manner of help. ⊠ *125 E. Palace Ave.*

EAST SIDE AND CANYON ROAD

Once a trail used by indigenous people to access water and the lush forest in the foothills east of town, then a route for Hispanic woodcutters and their burros, and for most of the 20th century a prosaic residential street with only a gas station and a general store, Canyon Road is now lined with upscale art galleries, shops, and restaurants. The narrow road begins at the eastern curve of Paseo de Peralta and stretches for about 2 mi at a moderate incline toward the base of the mountains. Lower Canyon Road is where you'll find the galleries, shops, and restaurants. Upper Canyon Road (above East Alameda) is narrow and residential, with access to hiking and biking trails along the way, and the Randall Davey Audubon Center at the very top.

Most establishments are in authentic, old adobe homes with thick, undulating walls that appear to have been carved out of the earth. Within those walls is art ranging from cutting-edge contemporary to traditional and even ancient works. Some artists are internationally renowned, like Fernando Botero, others' identities have been lost with time, like the weavers of magnificent Navajo rugs.

There are few places as festive as Canyon Road on Christmas Eve, when thousands of farolitos illuminate walkways, walls, roofs, and even trees. In May the scent of lilacs wafts over the adobe walls, and in August red hollyhocks enhance the surreal color of the blue sky on a dry summer day.

Cristo Rey Church. Built in 1940 and designed by legendary Santa Fe architect John Gaw Meem to commemorate the 400th anniversary of Francisco Vásquez de Coronado's exploration of the Southwest, this church is the largest Spanish adobe structure in the United States and is considered by many the finest example of Pueblo-style architecture anywhere. The church was constructed in the old-fashioned way by parishioners, who mixed the more than 200,000 mud-and-straw adobe bricks and hauled them into place. The 225-ton stone reredos (altar screen) is magnificent. ⊠ *1120 Canyon Rd., at Cristo Rey* ☎ *505/983–8528* ☉ *Daily 8–5.*

3

NEED A BREAK?

Kakawa (⊠ *1050 Paseo de Peralta, across the street from Gerald Peters Gallery* ☎ *505/982-0388* ⊕ *www.kakawachocolates.com*) is the place to go if chocolate—very good chocolate—is an essential part of your day. Proprietor Mark Sciscenti is a self-described chocolate historian and chocolate alchemist, and you're unlikely to ever have tasted anything like the divine, agave-sweetened, artisanal creations that emerge from his kitchen. Historically accurate chocolate drinks, like the Aztec Warrior Chocolate Elixir, divine caramels, and agave-sweetened, gluten-free chocolate baked goods are served in this cozy, welcoming shop that's as much a taste experience as an educational one.

El Zaguan. Headquarters of the **Historic Santa Fe Foundation (HSFF)**, this 19th-century Territorial-style house has a small exhibit on Santa Fe architecture and preservation, but the real draw is the small but stunning garden abundant with lavender, roses, and 160-year-old trees. You can relax on a wrought-iron bench and take in the fine views of the hills northeast of town. An HSFF horticulturist often gives free tours and lectures in the garden on Thursday at 1 in summer (call to confirm). Tours are available of many of the foundation's properties on Mother's Day. ⊠ *545 Canyon Rd.* ☎ *505/983–2567* ⊕ *www.historicsantafe.org* ▧ *Free* ☉ *Foundation office weekdays 9–noon and 1:30–5; gardens Mon.–Sat. 9–5.*

Gerald Peters Gallery. While under construction, this 32,000-square-foot building was dubbed the "ninth northern pueblo," its scale supposedly rivaling that of the eight northern pueblos around Santa Fe. The suavely designed Pueblo-style gallery is Santa Fe's premier showcase for American and European art from the 19th century to the present. It feels like a museum, but all the works are for sale. Pablo Picasso, Georgia O'Keeffe, Charles M. Russell, Deborah Butterfield, George Rickey, and members of the Taos Society are among the artists represented, along with nationally renowned contemporary ones. ⊠ *1011 Paseo de Peralta* ☎ *505/954–5700* ⊕ *www.gpgallery.com* ▧ *Free* ☉ *Mon.–Sat. 10–5.*

NEED A BREAK?

Locals congregate in the courtyard or on the front portal of **Downtown Subscription** (⊠ *376 Garcia St.* ☎ *505/983–3085*), a block east of Canyon Road. A great, friendly spot to people-watch, this café-newsstand sells coffees, snacks, and pastries, plus one of the largest assortments of newspapers and magazines in New Mexico. It has lovely outdoor spaces to sit and sip during warm weather. A delightful spot toward the end of gallery row on Canyon Road, right at the intersection with East Palace Avenue, the **Teahouse** (⊠ *821 Canyon Rd.* ☎ *505/992–0972*) has several bright dining rooms throughout the converted adobe home, and a tranquil outdoor seating area in a rock garden. In addition to fine teas from all over the world, you can find extremely well-prepared breakfast and lunch fare. The service tends to be leisurely but friendly.

OLD SANTA FE TRAIL AND SOUTH CAPITOL

It was along the Old Santa Fe Trail that wagon trains from Missouri rolled into town in the 1800s, forever changing Santa Fe's destiny. This street, off the south corner of the Plaza, is one of Santa Fe's most historic and is dotted with houses, shops, markets and the state capitol several blocks down.

TOP ATTRACTIONS

★ **New Mexico State Capitol.** The symbol of the Zía Pueblo, which represents the Circle of Life, was the inspiration for the capitol, also known as the Roundhouse. Doorways at opposing sides of this 1966 structure symbolize the four winds, the four directions, and the four seasons. Throughout the building are artworks from the outstanding collection of the Capitol Art Foundation, historical and cultural displays, and handcrafted furniture—it's a superb and somewhat overlooked array of fine art. The **Governor's Gallery** hosts temporary exhibits. Six acres of imaginatively landscaped gardens shelter outstanding sculptures. ⊠ *Old Santa Fe Trail at Paseo de Peralta* ☎ *505/986–4589* ⊕ *www.newmexico. gov* ☞ *Free* ☉ *Weekdays 7–6; tours weekdays by appt.*

Fodor's Choice **San Miguel Mission.** The oldest church still in use in the United States, this ★ simple earth-hue adobe structure was built in the early 17th century by the Tlaxcalan Indians of Mexico, who came to New Mexico as servants of the Spanish. Badly damaged in the 1680 Pueblo Revolt, the structure was restored and enlarged in 1710. On display in the chapel are priceless statues and paintings and the San José Bell, weighing nearly 800 pounds, which is believed to have been cast in Spain in 1356. In winter the church sometimes closes before its official closing hour. Mass is held on Sunday at 5 pm. Next door in the back of the Territorial-style dormitories of the old St. Michael's High School, a **Visitor Information Center** can help you find your way around northern New Mexico. ⊠ *401 Old Santa Fe Trail* ☎ *505/983–3974* ☞ *$1* ☉ *Mon.–Sat. 9–4:30, Sun. 10–4.*

WORTH NOTING

Barrio de Analco. Along the south bank of the Santa Fe River, the barrio—its name means "District on the Other Side of the Water"—is one of America's oldest neighborhoods, settled in the early 1600s by the Tlaxcalan Indians (who were forbidden to live with the Spanish near the Plaza) and in the 1690s by soldiers who had helped recapture New Mexico after the Pueblo Revolt. Plaques on houses on East De Vargas Street will help you locate some of the important structures. Check the

A GOOD TOUR: MUSEUM HILL

This museum tour begins 2 mi southeast of the Plaza, an area known as Museum Hill that's best reached by car or via one of the city buses that leaves hourly from near the Plaza. Begin at the **Museum of Indian Arts and Culture,** which is set around Milner Plaza, an attractively landscaped courtyard and gardens with outdoor art installations. On some summer days the Plaza hosts Native American dances, jewelry-making demonstrations, kids' activities, and other interactive events; there's also the Museum Hill Cafe, which is open for lunch (and Sunday brunch) and serves delicious and reasonably priced salads, quiche, burgers, sandwiches and wraps, ice cream, and other light fare. To get here from Downtown, drive uphill on Old Santa Fe Trail to Camino Lejo. Across Milner Plaza is the **Museum of International Folk Art (MOIFA).** From Milner Plaza, a pedestrian path leads a short way to the **Museum of Spanish Colonial Art.** Return to Milner Plaza, from which a different pedestrian path leads west a short way to the **Wheelwright Museum of the American Indian.** To reach the **Santa Fe Children's Museum,** you need to drive back down the hill or ask the bus driver to let you off near it.

TIMING

Set aside a full day to see all the museums on the Upper Santa Fe Trail/Museum Hill. Kids usually have to be dragged from the Children's Museum, even after an hour or two.

performance schedule at the **Santa Fe Playhouse** on De Vargas Street, founded by writer Mary Austin and other Santa Feans in the 1920s.

Loretto Chapel. A delicate Gothic church modeled after Sainte-Chapelle in Paris, Loretto was built in 1873 by the same French architects and Italian stonemasons who built St. Francis Cathedral. The chapel is known for the "Miraculous Staircase" that leads to the choir loft. Legend has it that the chapel was almost complete when it became obvious that there wasn't room to build a staircase to the choir loft. In answer to the prayers of the cathedral's nuns, a mysterious carpenter arrived on a donkey, built a 20-foot staircase—using only a square, a saw, and a tub of water to season the wood—and then disappeared as quickly as he came. Many of the faithful believed it was St. Joseph himself. The staircase contains two complete 360-degree turns with no central support; no nails were used in its construction. The chapel closes for services and special events. Adjoining the chapel are a small museum and gift shop. ✉ 207 Old Santa Fe Trail ☎ 505/982–0092 ⊕ www.lorettochapel.com ⌨ Donations accepted ☉ Mon.–Sat. 9–6, Sun. 10:30–5.

The Oldest House. More than 800 years ago, Pueblo people built this structure out of "puddled" adobe (liquid mud poured between upright wooden frames). This house, which contains a gift shop, is said to be the oldest in the United States. ✉ 215 E. De Vargas St.

MUSEUM HILL

TOP ATTRACTIONS

★ **Museum of Indian Arts and Culture.** An interactive, multimedia exhibition tells the story of Native American history in the Southwest, merging contemporary Native American experience with historical accounts and artifacts. The collection has some of New Mexico's oldest works of art: pottery vessels, fine stone and silver jewelry, intricate textiles, and other arts and crafts created by Pueblo, Navajo, and Apache artisans. Changing exhibitions feature arts and traditions of historic and contemporary Native Americans. You can also see art demonstrations and a video about the life and work of Pueblo potter Maria Martinez. ⊠ *710 Camino Lejo* ☎ *505/476–1250 or 505/476-1269* ⊕ *www.indianartsandculture.org* ⊠ *$9, 4-day pass $20, good at all 4 state museums and the Museum of Spanish Colonial Art* ☉ *Tues.–Sun. 10–5 (also Mon. 10–5 June–early Sept.).*

Fodor's Choice **Museum of International Folk Art** (MOIFA). A delight for adults and chil-
★ dren alike, this museum is the premier institution of its kind in the
☾ world. In the Girard Wing you'll find thousands of amazingly inventive handmade objects—a tin Madonna, a devil made from bread dough, dolls from around the world, and miniature village scenes galore. The Hispanic Heritage Wing contains art dating from the Spanish-colonial period (in New Mexico, 1598–1821) to the present. The 5,000-piece exhibit includes religious works—particularly *bultos* (carved wooden statues of saints) and retablos, as well as textiles and furniture. The exhibits in the Neutrogena Wing rotate, showing subjects ranging from outsider art to the magnificent quilts of Gee's Bend. Lloyd's Treasure Chest, the wing's innovative basement section, provides a behind-the-scenes look at this collection. You can rummage through storage drawers, peer into microscopes, and, on occasion, speak with conservators and other museum personnel. Check the Web site or call to see if any of the excellent children's activities are scheduled for the time of your visit. Allow time to visit the incredible gift shop and bookstore. ⊠ *706 Camino Lejo* ☎ *505/476–1200* ⊕ *www.moifa.org* ⊠ *$9, 4-day pass $20, good at all 4 state museums and the Museum of Spanish Colonial Art* ☉ *Tues.–Sun. 10–5 (also Mon. 10–5 June–early Sept.).*

Fodor's Choice **Museum of Spanish Colonial Art.** This 5,000-square-foot adobe museum
★ occupies a classically Southwestern former home designed in 1930 by acclaimed regional architect John Gaw Meem. The Spanish Colonial Art Society formed in Santa Fe in 1925 to preserve traditional Spanish-colonial art and culture, and the museum, which sits next to the Museum of International Folk Art and the Museum of Indian Arts and Culture complex, displays the fruits of the society's labor—one of the most comprehensive collections of Spanish-colonial art in the world. Objects here, dating from the 16th century to the present, include *retablos* (holy images painted on wood or tin), elaborate santos, tinwork, straw appliqué, furniture, ceramics, and ironwork. The contemporary collection of works by New Mexico Hispanic artists of the 20th century helps put all this history into regional context. ⊠ *750 Camino Lejo* ☎ *505/982–2226* ⊕ *www.spanishcolonial.org* ⊠ *$6, 4-day pass $20,*

good at all 4 state museums and the Museum of Spanish Colonial Art ۞ *Tues.–Sun. 10–5 (also Mon. 10–5 June–Sept.).*

WORTH NOTING

Santa Fe Children's Museum. Stimulating hands-on exhibits, a solar greenhouse, oversize geometric forms, and an 18-foot indoor rock-climbing wall all contribute to this museum's popularity with kids. Outdoor gardens with climbing structures, forts, and hands-on activities are great for whiling away the time in the shade of big trees. Puppeteers and storytellers perform often. ⊠ *1050 Old Pecos Trail* ☎ *505/989–8359* ⊕ *www. santafechildrensmuseum.org* 💲 *$9* ۞ *Sept.–May, Wed.–Sat. 10–5, Sun. noon–5; June–Aug., Tues.–Sat. 10–5, Sun. noon–5.*

> **IFAM**
>
> The **International Folk Art Market** (☎ *505/476–1197* ⊕ *www. folkartmarket.org*), held the second full weekend in July on Milner, is *a truly remarkable* art gathering. Master folk artists from every corner of the planet come together to sell their work amidst a festive array of huge tents, colorful banners, music, food, and delighted crowds. There is a feeling of fellowship and celebration here that enhances the satisfaction of buying wonderful folk art.

Wheelwright Museum of the American Indian. A private institution in a building shaped like a traditional octagonal Navajo hogan, the Wheelwright opened in 1937. Founded by Boston scholar Mary Cabot Wheelwright and Navajo medicine man Hastiin Klah, the museum originated as a place to house ceremonial materials. Those items were returned to the Navajo in 1977, but what remains is an incredible collection of 19th- and 20th-century baskets, pottery, sculpture, weavings, metalwork, photography, paintings, including contemporary works by Native American artists, and typically fascinating changing exhibits. The Case Trading Post on the lower level is modeled after the trading posts that dotted the southwestern frontier more than 100 years ago. It carries an extensive selection of books and contemporary Native American jewelry, kachina dolls, weaving, and pottery. ⊠ *704 Camino Lejo* ☎ *505/982–4636 or 800/607–4636* ⊕ *www.wheelwright.org* 💲 *Free* ۞ *Mon.–Sat. 10–5, Sun. 1–5; gallery tours weekdays at 2, Sat. at 1.*

RAILYARD DISTRICT

The most significant development in Santa Fe in recent years has taken place in the Railyard District, a neighborhood just south of the Plaza that was for years called the Guadalupe District (and occasionally still known as that). Comprising a few easily walked blocks along Guadalupe Street between Agua Fria and Paseo de Peralta, the district has been revitalized with a snazzy new park and outdoor performance space, a shopping complex, a new permanent indoor-outdoor home for the farmers' market, and several new restaurants and galleries.

This historic warehouse and rail district endured several decades of neglect after the demise of the train route through town. But rather than tearing the buildings down (this is a city where 200-year-old mud-brick

A GOOD TOUR: THE RAILYARD DISTRICT

From the Plaza, head west on San Francisco Street, and then take a left onto Guadalupe Street toward **Santuario de Guadalupe,** two blocks up on your right. After you visit the Santuario, take your time browsing through the shops and eating lunch in one of the restaurants lining Guadalupe Street or around the corner, to the right on Montezuma Street, at the Sanbusco Market Center, a massive, converted warehouse full of boutiques and a Borders bookstore. Check out the great shops and the photographic history on the walls near the market's main entrance. Back on Guadalupe, head south to the historic Gross Kelly Warehouse, one of the earliest Santa Fe–style buildings. Note Santa Fe's two train depots—one is now the site of popular, but touristy, Tomasita's Restaurant; the other, set farther back, is the Santa Fe Depot, where the **Santa Fe Southern Railway** trains and the New Mexico Rail Runner depart. Continue a short distance south on Guadalupe until you reach **SITE Santa Fe** gallery and performance space, set inside a former bottling warehouse. Across the street, spend some time wandering the aisles, or picking up

picnic supplies, at the friendly, bustling **Santa Fe Farmers' Market.** It's amazing both the amount of produce and goods coming from this high desert region and the huge crowds that pack the market. Just beyond the Farmers' Market is the Railyard Park, where you can stroll, or lounge, and enjoy your edible goodies amidst green grass, lovely trees, and great stonework. Catercorner from SITE Santa Fe, **El Museo Cultural de Santa Fe** is one of the state's more unusual museums, a combination performance space, classroom, gallery, and event venue that promotes Hispanic culture and education in the City Different. Be sure to visit the gallery at Santa Fe Clay, next door to El Museo, where you'll find world-class ceramic sculpture and working studios.

TIMING

A visit to the Santuario de Guadalupe can take 15 minutes to an hour, depending on whether or not there's an art show in progress. If you like shopping and visiting art galleries, and decide to eat in this area, you might spend hours in this diverse and exciting neighborhood.

buildings sell at a premium, after all), developers gradually converted the low-lying warehouses into artists' studios, antiques shops, bookstores, indie shops, and restaurants. The restored scenic train to Lamy and the Rail Runner commuter train to Albuquerque have put the rail tracks as well as the vintage mission-style depot back into use.

A central feature of the district's redevelopment is the Railyard Park, at the corner of Cerrillos Road and Guadalupe Street, which was designed to highlight native plants and provide citizens with a lush, urban space. The adjoining buildings contain the vibrant Santa Fe Farmers' Market, the teen-oriented community art center Warehouse21, SITE Santa Fe museum, art galleries, shops, restaurants, and live-work spaces for artists. This dramatic development reveals the fascinating way Santa Feans have worked to meet the needs of an expanding city while paying strict attention to the city's historic relevance.

WHAT TO SEE

El Museo Cultural de Santa Fe. More an arts, educational, and community gathering space than a museum, El Museo celebrates Santa Fe's—and New Mexico's—rich Hispanic heritage by presenting a wide range of events, from children's theater, to musical concerts, to a great Dia de Los Muertos celebration at the beginning of November. The facility sponsors the Contemporary Hispanic Market just off the Plaza each July (held the same time as Spanish Market), and the Contemporary Hispanic Artists Winter Market, held at the center in late November. There's a small gallery showing contemporary art by Hispanic artists. A great resource to visitors who plan ahead are the many classes and workshops, which touch on everything from guitar and Mexican folkloric dance to children's theater and art. ✉ *1615 Paseo de Peralta* ☎ *505/992–0591* ⊕ *www.elmuseocultural.org* ▣ *Free; prices vary for events and shows* ☉ *Tues.–Fri. 1–5, Sat. 10–5.*

Santa Fe Southern Railway. For a leisurely tour across the Santa Fe plateau and into the vast Galisteo Basin, where panoramic views extend for up to 120 mi, take a nostalgic ride on the antique cars of the Santa Fe Southern Railway. The train once served as a spur of the Atchison, Topeka & Santa Fe Railway. Today the train takes visitors on 36-mi round-trip scenic trips to Lamy, a sleepy village with the region's only Amtrak service, offering picnics under the cottonwoods (bring your own or buy one from the caterer that meets the train) at the quaint rail station. Aside from day trips, the railway offers special events such as a Friday-night "High Desert High Ball" cash bar with appetizers and a Saturday Night Barbecue Train ($58). Trains depart from the Santa Fe Depot, rebuilt in 1909 after the original was destroyed in a fire. Reservations are essential. ✉ *410 S. Guadalupe St. 888/989–8600* ⊕ *www.sfsr.com* ▣ *Day trips from $32* ☉ *Call for schedule.*

Santuario de Guadalupe. A massive-walled adobe structure built by Franciscan missionaries between 1776 and 1795, this is the oldest shrine in the United States to Our Lady of Guadalupe, Mexico's patron saint. The church's adobe walls are nearly 3 feet thick, and among the sanctuary's religious art and artifacts is a beloved image of Nuestra Virgen de Guadalupe, painted by Mexican master Jose de Alzibar in 1783. Highlights are the traditional New Mexican carved and painted altar screen called a reredo, an authentic 19th-century sacristy, a pictorial-history archive, a library devoted to Archbishop Jean Baptiste Lamy that is furnished with many of his belongings, and a garden with plants from the Holy Land. ✉ *100 Guadalupe St.* ☎ *505/988–2027* ▣ *Donations accepted* ☉ *May–Oct., Mon.–Sat. 9–4; Nov.–Apr., weekdays 9–4.*

★ **SITE Santa Fe.** The events at this nexus of international contemporary art include lectures, concerts, author readings, performance art, and gallery shows. The facility hosts a biennial exhibition every even-numbered year. Exhibitions are often provocative, and the immense, open space is ideal for taking in the many larger-than-life installations. ✉ *1606 Paseo de Peralta* ☎ *505/989–1199* ⊕ *www.sitesantafe.org* ▣ *$10, free Fri., free Sat. 10–noon during Santa Fe Farmers' Market* ☉ *Wed., Thurs., and Sat. 10–5, Fri. 10–7, Sun. noon–5.*

WHERE TO EAT

Eating out is a major pastime in Santa Fe and it's well worth coming here with a mind to join in on the fun. Restaurants with high-profile chefs stand beside low-key joints, many offering unique and intriguing variations on regional and international cuisine. You'll find restaurants full of locals and tourists alike all over the Downtown and surrounding areas. Although Santa Fe does have some high-end restaurants where dinner for two can easily exceed $200, the city also has plenty of reasonably priced dining options.

Waits for tables are very common during the busy summer season, so it's a good idea to call ahead even when reservations aren't accepted, if only to get a sense of the waiting time. Reservations for dinner at the better restaurants are a must in summer and on weekends the rest of the year.

So-called Santa Fe–style cuisine has so many influences that the term is virtually meaningless. Traditional, old-style Santa Fe restaurants serve New Mexican fare, which combines both Native American and Hispanic traditions and is quite different from Americanized or even authentic Mexican cooking. Many of the better restaurants in town serve a contemporary regional style of cooking that blends New Mexican ingredients and preparations with those of interior and coastal Mexico, Latin America, the Mediterranean, East Asia, and varied parts of the United States.

For a city this small, there is a delightful array of cuisines available aside from the delicious and spicy food of northern New Mexico: Middle Eastern, Spanish, Japanese, Italian, East Indian, and French, to name just a few. More and more restaurants, from casual lunch joints to the finest dining establishments, are focusing on using local and regional ingredients, from meats, to cheeses, to produce. Smoking was recently banned in all bars and restaurants in the city, infuriating some and thrilling many.

WHAT IT COSTS					
	¢	$	$$	$$$	$$$$
Restaurants	under $10	$10–$17	$18–$24	$25–$30	over $30

Prices are per person for a main course at dinner, excluding 8.25% sales tax.

THE PLAZA

Use the coordinate (✛ A1) at the end of each listing to locate a site on the corresponding map.

¢   ✗ **Atomic Grill.** Burgers, salads, pizzas, sandwiches, and other light fare
AMERICAN   are served at this tiny café a block off the Plaza. The food is decent but the service can be brusque. The best attributes are the comfy patio overlooking pedestrian-heavy Water Street, the huge list of imported beers, and the late hours (it's open until 3 most nights)—an extreme rarity in Santa Fe. You'll be glad this place exists when the bars let

BEST BETS FOR SANTA FE DINING

With hundreds of restaurants to choose from, how will you decide where to eat? Fodor's writers and editors have selected their favorite restaurants by price, cuisine, and experience in the Best Bets lists below. Find specific details about a restaurant in the full reviews, listed alphabetically in the chapter.

3

Aqua Santa $$, p. 126
Cafe Pasqual's $$$, p. 119
Restaurant Martin $$$, p. 126
Ristra $$$, p. 128

ITALIAN

Andiamo $, p. 126
Il Piatto $, p. 120

NEW MEXICAN

La Choza ¢, p. 128
Tia Sophia's ¢, p. 123
The Shed $, p. 122

Fodor's Choice ★

Aqua Santa $$, p. 126
Aztec Cafe ¢, p. 127
Bert's Burger Bowl ¢, p. 129
Bobcat Bite ¢, p. 132
Bumble Bee's Baja Grill ¢, p. 129
Cafe Pasqual's $$$, p. 119
The Compound $$$$, p. 123
Galisteo Bistro $$, p. 120
Geronimo $$$$, p. 124
Harry's Roadhouse $, p. 132
Il Piatto $, p. 120
Inn of the Anasazi $$$$, p. 120
La Boca $$, p. 121
La Choza ¢, p. 128
The Shed $, p. 122

By Price

¢

Aztec Cafe, p. 127
Bobcat Bite, p. 132

Bumble Bee's Baja Grill, p. 129
Clafoutis, p. 129
La Choza, p. 128

$

Andiamo, p. 126
Harry's Roadhouse, p. 132
Il Piatto, p. 120
Jambo, p. 130
Pyramid Cafe, p. 125
The Shed, p. 122
Tune Up, p. 131
Zia Diner, p. 128

$$

Aqua Santa, p. 126
Galisteo Bistro, p. 120
La Boca, p. 121
The Shed, p. 122

$$$

315 Restaurant and Wine Bar, p. 124
Cafe Pasqual's, p. 119
El Mesón & Chispa Tapas Bar, p. 119
Ristra, p. 128
Shohko, p. 123

Restaurant Martin, p. 126

$$$$

The Compound, p. 123
Inn of the Anasazi, p. 120
Fuego, p. 120
Geronimo, p. 124

By Cuisine

AMERICAN

Bobcat Bite ¢, p. 132
Railyard Restaurant & Saloon $, p. 128
Zia Diner $, p. 128

CAFÉ

Aztec Cafe ¢, p. 127
Chocolate Maven $, p. 130
Clafoutis ¢, p. 129

ASIAN

Mu Du Noodles $$, p. 131
Shohko $$$, p. 123

CONTEMPORARY

315 Restaurant & Wine Bar $$$, p. 124

By Experience

BAR MENU

El Farol $$$, p. 124
El Mesón & Chispa Tapas Bar $$$, p. 119
Railyard Restaurant & Saloon $, p. 128
Zia Diner $, p. 128

BEST BURGER

Bobcat Bite ¢, p. 132
The Compound $$$$, p. 123
Ristra $$$, p. 128
Tune Up $, p. 131

BREAKFAST

Cafe Pasqual's $$$, p. 119
Harry's Roadhouse $, p. 132
Tecolote Cafe ¢, p. 131
Tia Sophia's ¢, p. 123

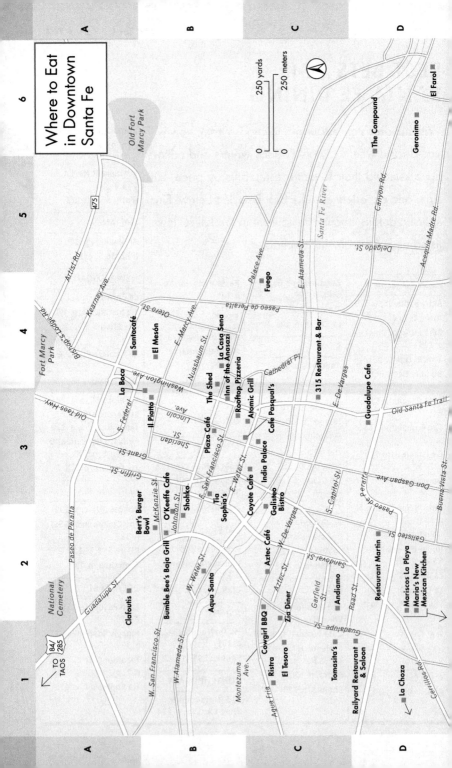

out and you're famished. ✉ *103 Water St.* ☎ *505/820–2866* ⊕ *http:// theatomicgrill.com* ▤ *MC, V* ✛ *C3.*

$$$

CONTEMPORARY

Fodor's Choice

★

✕ **Cafe Pasqual's.** A perennial favorite, this cheerful cubbyhole dishes up Southwestern and Nuevo Latino specialties for breakfast, lunch, and dinner. Don't be discouraged by lines out front—it's worth the wait. The culinary muse behind it all is Katharine Kagel, who championed organic, local ingredients, and whose expert kitchen staff produces mouthwatering breakfast and lunch specialties like the breakfast relleno (a big, cheese-stuffed chile with eggs and a smoky tomato salsa served with beans and tortillas), huevos motuleños (eggs in a tangy tomatillo salsa with black beans and fried bananas), and the sublime grilled free-range chicken sandwich. Dinner is a more formal, though still friendly and easygoing, affair: char-grilled lamb with pomegranate-molasses glaze, steamed sugar snap peas, and pan-seared potato cakes is a pleasure; the kicky starter of the Thai mint salad with chicken is a revelation. Mexican folk art, colorful tiles, and murals by Oaxacan artist Leovigildo Martinez create a festive atmosphere. Try the chummy communal table, or go late morning or after 1:30 pm to (hopefully) avoid the crush. ✉ *121 Don Gaspar Ave.* ☎ *505/983–9340* ⊕ *www.pasquals. com* ▤ *AE, MC, V* ⬧ *No reservations for breakfast and lunch* ✛ *C3.*

$$$$

CONTEMPORARY

✕ **Coyote Cafe.** In 2007 Eric DiStefano took over Coyote Cafe with three other local industry veterans and the results have been mixed. Adding to—or detracting from, depending on who you ask—the challenges at Coyote is the fact that DiStefano has also resumed the position as executive chef at Geronimo—with many of the same items appearing on both menus. Coyote Cafe is reliable for taste variations on the beloved green chile, but the menu has evolved to include the flavors of French and Asian cuisine. Menu offerings include griddled buttermilk corn cakes with chipotle prawns, DiStefano's signature dish; a peppery elk tenderloin; and the five-spice rotisserie rock hen with green-chile "mac 'n' cheese." Service and food quality vary widely—not an encouraging trend considering the high cost of dining here. Your best bet may be to head to the adjacent Rooftop Cantina (open April through October), a fun outdoor gathering spot with a loud and lively social scene where you can enjoy cool cocktails and flavorful under-$15 fare like burgers and Mexico-inspired fish tacos. ✉ *132 W. Water St.* ☎ *505/983–1615* ⊕ *www.coyotecafe.com* ▤ *AE, D, DC, MC, V* ⊗ *No lunch at Coyote Cafe (Rooftop Cantina only)* ✛ *C3.*

$$$

SPANISH

✕ **El Mesón & Chispa Tapas Bar.** This place is as fun for having drinks and tapas or catching live music (from tango nights to Sephardic music) as for enjoying a full meal. The dining room has an old-world feel with simple dark-wood tables and chairs, creamy plastered walls, and a wood-beam ceiling—unpretentious yet elegant. The Chispa bar is livelier and feels like a Spanish *taberna*. The delicious tapas menu includes dishes like Serrano ham and fried artichoke hearts stuffed with Spanish goat cheese over *romesco* sauce. Among the more substantial entrées are a stellar paella as well as cannelloni stuffed with veal, smothered with béchamel sauce, and topped with Manchego au gratin. ✉ *213 Washington Ave.* ☎ *505/983–6756* ▤ *AE, MC, V* ⊕ *http://elmeson-santafe. com* ⊗ *Closed Sun. and Mon. No lunch* ✛ *B4.*

$$$$ ✕**Fuego.** An elegant yet comfortable dining room inside the oasis of La
CONTEMPORARY Posada resort, Fuego has become a local favorite for fantastic, inventive
food and flawless service. It is one of Santa Fe's top culinary secrets,
albeit with sky-high prices. You might start with seared foie gras with
apple pie au poivre before trying free-range *poussin* (young chicken)
over a nest of braised leeks and salsify, or roast rack of Colorado elk
with parsnip dumplings and a dried-cherry mole. Perhaps the most
astounding offering is the artisanal cheese plate—Fuego has one of the
largest selections of cheeses west of Manhattan. The wine list is similarly
impressive and the helpful sommelier is always on hand to advise. Le
Menu Découverte allows you to sample a five-course meal of chef's specialties for $125 (additional $65 for wine pairing). The spectacular Sunday Rancher's Brunch, at $45 per person, is a bargain. ⊠ *La Posada de
Santa Fe Resort and Spa, 330 E. Palace Ave.* ☎ *505/986–0000* ⊕ *www.
laposadadesantafe.com* ☰ *AE, D, DC, MC, V* ✛ *C4.*

$$ ✕**Galisteo Bistro.** Walk into this inviting space a few blocks from the
ECLECTIC Plaza—with its open kitchen, stacked stone walls, and high ceiling—and
Fodor's Choice you'll likely hope that the food tastes as good as the room feels. Thank-
★ fully, it does. The crab cakes are stellar; leading entrées include chicken
saltimbocca, grass-fed beef cooked á la béarnaise or Roberto-style (with
sautéed marsala mushrooms and roasted green chiles), and manda-
rin mango pasta with pan-roasted chicken, fresh vegetables, and cur-
ried orange-mango sauce over semolina penne. The beautiful desserts
often favor chocolate. There's a nice selection of wines, plus a limited
offering of locally brewed beers. ⊠ *227 Galisteo St.* ☎ *505/982–3700*
⊕ *www.galisteobistro.com* ☰ *AE, D, MC, V* ⊗ *Closed Mon. and Tues.
No lunch* ✛ *C3.*

$ ✕**Il Piatto.** Chef Matt Yohalem continues to charm the legions of local
ITALIAN fans and lucky visitors who dine at his place with creative pasta dishes
Fodor's Choice like *pappardelle* with braised duckling, caramelized onions, sun-dried
★ tomatoes, and mascarpone-duck au jus or homemade pumpkin ravioli
with pine nuts and sage brown butter. Entrées include grilled salmon
with spinach risotto and tomato-caper sauce, and a superb pancetta-
wrapped trout with rosemary, wild mushrooms, and polenta. The menu
changes seasonally and emphasizes locally sourced ingredients. It's a
crowded but enjoyable trattoria with informal ambience, reasonable
prices, and a snug bar. For about $30, the prix-fixe dinner, with an appe-
tizer, main dish, and dessert, is a steal. Add a glass of wine from the rep-
utable list of Italians and both your stomach and your wallet will leave
happy. ⊠ *95 W. Marcy St.* ☎ *505/984–1091* ⊕ *www.ilpiattosantafe.com*
☰ *AE, D, MC, V* ⊗ *No lunch weekends* ✛ *B3.*

$ ✕**India Palace.** The kitchen prepares fairly traditional recipes—tandoori
INDIAN chicken, lamb vindaloo, *saag paneer* (spinach with farmer cheese),
shrimp *biryani* (tossed with cashews, raisins, almonds, and saffron
rice)—but the presentation is always flawless and the ingredients fresh.
Meals are cooked as hot or mild as requested. Try the Indian buffet at
lunch. ⊠ *227 Don Gaspar Ave., enter from parking lot on Water St.*
☎ *505/986–5859* ⊕ *www.indiapalace.com* ☰ *AE, MC, V* ✛ *C3.*

$$$$ ✕**Inn of the Anasazi.** Executive chef Oliver Ridgeway takes a global
CONTEMPORARY approach and uses locally and seasonally available ingredients in
Fodor's Choice
★

3

creating dishes like mole-glazed veal medallions with white and green asparagus, Oregon morels, and elephant garlic or Hawaiian tuna with wasabi-nut crust. Fare served on the patio (open in summer) and the bar is lighter and just as interesting—the ahi tuna gyro and the fennel salad with kalamata tapenade are terrific. The romantic, 90-seat restaurant with hardwood floors, soft lighting, smooth-plastered walls, and beam ceilings feels slightly less formal than the other big-ticket dining rooms in town. The patio makes for fun street-side people-watching and the bar is a cozy, convivial nook. Sunday brunch is superb. ⊠ *113 Washington Ave.* ☎ *505/988–3030* ⊕ *www.innoftheanasazi.com* ▤ *AE, D, DC, MC, V* ♣ *B3.*

$$
SPANISH
Fodor's Choice
★

✕ **La Boca.** This little restaurant, a clean, bright room within an old adobe building, earns rave reviews and has become a local favorite for its intriguingly prepared Spanish food and excellent wine list. Chef James Campbell Caruso has created a menu just right for Santa Fe's eating style; a wide, changing array of delectable tapas and an edited selection of classic entrées, like the paella. The friendly, efficient staff is happy to advise on wine and food selections. The chef's tasting menu for $55 per person (additional $25 for wine or sherry pairings) is a fun way to experience Caruso's well-honed approach to his food. Desserts, like the rich chocolate pot-au-feu, are sumptuous. The room tends to be loud and can get stuffy during winter when the Dutch door and windows are closed, but crowds are friendly and you never know who you'll end up next to in this town of low-key luminaries and celebrities. Half-price tapas, during Tapas en la Tarde, from 3 to 5 during the week, make a perfect and economical late lunch. ⊠ *72 W. Marcy St., The Plaza* ☎ *505/982–3433* ⊕ *www.labocasf.com* ▤ *AE, D, DC, MC, V* ⊗ *No lunch Sun.* ♣ *B3.*

$$$
ECLECTIC

✕ **La Casa Sena.** The Southwestern-accented and Continental fare served at La Casa Sena is beautifully presented if not consistently as delicious as it appears. Weather permitting, get a table on the patio surrounded by hollyhocks, flowering shrubs, and centuries-old adobe walls. A favorite entrée is the braised Colorado lamb shank with chipotle-*huitlacoche* demi-glace, roasted purple- and Yukon-gold potatoes, braised *cipollini* onions, and orange *gremolata*. There's a knockout lavender crème brûlée as well as a tantalizingly spicy-sweet chocolate–red chile soup served with strawberries, whipped cream, and honey-sugared piñons on the dessert menu. For a musical meal (evenings only), sit in the restaurant's adjacent, less-pricey Cantina ($$), where the talented and perky staff belt out Broadway show tunes. An on-site wine shop sells many of the estimable vintages offered on the restaurant's wine list. ⊠ *Sena Plaza, 125 E. Palace Ave.* ☎ *505/988–9232* ⊕ *www.lacasasena.com* ▤ *AE, D, DC, MC, V* ♣ *B4.*

$$$$
CONTEMPORARY

✕ **O'Keeffe Cafe.** This swanky but low-key restaurant next to the Georgia O'Keeffe Museum turns out some delicious and creative fare with generous influences from Basque and French traditions. This is much more than a typical museum café, although the lunches do make a great, if expensive, break following a jaunt through the galleries. Dinner is the main event, however, showcasing such tempting and tasty selections as sweetbreads with shallots and cherry demi-glace; cashew-encrusted mahimahi over garlic-mashed potatoes with a mango–citrus butter sauce; and Colorado lamb chops with red chile–honey glaze and mint-infused couscous. Chef Leo Varos's prix-fixe dinner menu, when offered, is a fantastic deal at around $35. The wine selection is incredibly extensive, with a number of highly prized international offerings. Patios shaded by leafy trees are great dining spots during warm weather. Free, validated parking is available at the Eldorado Hotel. ⊠ *217 Johnson St.* ☎ *505/946–1065* ⊕ *www.okeeffecafe.com* ⊟ *AE, D, MC, V* ✛ *B2.*

$
ECLECTIC
★
✕ **Plaza Café.** Run with homespun care by the Razatos family since 1947, this café has been a fixture on the Plaza since 1918. The decor—red leather banquettes, black Formica tables, tile floors, a coffered tin ceiling, and a 1940s-style service counter—hasn't changed much in the past half century. The food runs the gamut, from cashew mole enchiladas to New Mexico meat loaf to chile-smothered burritos to a handful of Greek favorites, but the ingredients tend toward Southwestern. You'll be hard put to find a better tortilla soup. You can cool it off with an old-fashioned ice-cream treat from the soda fountain or a slice of one of the delicious, homemade pies. It's a good, tasty stop for breakfast, lunch, or dinner. ⊠ *54 Lincoln Ave.* ☎ *505/982–1664* ⊕ *http://thefamousplazacafe.com* ⌦ *Reservations not accepted* ⊟ *AE, D, MC, V* ✛ *B3.*

$
PIZZA
★
✕ **Rooftop Pizzeria.** For sophisticated pizza, head to this slick indoor-outdoor restaurant atop the Santa Fe Arcade. The kitchen here scores high marks for its rich and imaginative pizza toppings: consider the one topped with lobster, shrimp, mushrooms, apple-smoked bacon, caramelized leeks, truffle oil, Alfredo sauce, and four cheeses on a blue-corn crust. Antipasti and salads are impressive, too, as there's a wonderful smoked-duck-confit-and-peppercorn spread, or the smoked-salmon Caesar salad. There's also an extensive beer and wine list. Although the Santa Fe Arcade's main entrance is on the Plaza, it's easier to access the restaurant from the arcade's Water Street entrance, a few doors up from Don Gaspar Avenue. ⊠ *60 E. San Francisco St.* ☎ *505/984–0008* ⊕ *www.rooftoppizzeria.com* ⊟ *AE, D, MC, V* ✛ *B3.*

$$$
CONTEMPORARY
★
✕ **Santacafé.** Southwest minimalist elegance marks the interior of Santacafé, one of Santa Fe's vanguard "food as art" restaurants, two blocks north of the Plaza in the historic Padre Gallegos House. Seasonal ingredients are used in the inventive dishes, which might include Alaskan halibut with English peas, saffron couscous, capers, and preserved lemon. Shiitake-and-cactus spring rolls with ponzu sauce make a terrific starter, as does the sublime crispy-fried calamari with a snappy lime-chile dipping sauce. The latter is big—add a salad for a few dollars and you've got a meal. The shady patio is a joy in summer, and the bar is a snazzy spot to meet friends for drinks just about any time of year. If you're on a tight budget, consider the reasonably priced and equally delicious lunch menu. Sunday brunch is a favorite among locals. ⊠ *231 Washington Ave.* ☎ *505/984–1788* ⊕ *www.santacafe.com* ⊟ *AE, MC, V* ✛ *A4.*

$
NEW MEXICAN
Fodor's Choice
★
✕ **The Shed.** The lines at lunch attest to the status of this Downtown New Mexican eatery. The rambling, low-doored, and atmospheric adobe dating from 1692 is decorated with folk art, and service is downright

neighborly. Even if you're a devoted green-chile sauce fan, you must try the locally grown red chile the place is famous for; it is rich and perfectly spicy. Specialties include red-chile enchiladas, green-chile stew with potatoes and pork, comforting posole, and their charbroiled Shed-burgers. The mushroom bisque is a surprising and delicious offering. Homemade desserts, like the mocha cake, are a yummy way to smooth out the spice. There's a full bar, too. ⊠ *113½ E. Palace Ave.* ☎ *505/982–9030* ⊕ *www.sfshed.com* ▤ *AE, DC, MC, V* ☺ *Closed Sun.* ✛ *B4.*

\$\$\$
JAPANESE
★
✕ **Shohko.** After a brief hiatus Shohko and her family have returned and once again this is the place for the freshest, best-prepared sushi and sashimi in town. On any given night there are two-dozen or more varieties of fresh fish available. The soft-shell crab tempura is feather-light, and the Kobe beef with Japanese salsa is tender and delicious. Sit at the sushi bar and watch the expert chefs, including Shohko, work their magic, or at one of the tables in this old adobe with whitewashed walls, dark-wood vigas, and Japanese decorative details. Table service is friendly, but can be slow. ⊠ *321 Johnson St., The Plaza* ☎ *505/982–9708* ⊕ *www.shohkocafe.com* ▤ *AE, D, DC, MC, V* ☺ *No lunch weekends* ✛ *B2.*

¢
NEW MEXICAN
★
✕ **Tia Sophia's.** This Downtown joint serves strictly New Mexican breakfasts and lunches (open until 2 pm). You're as likely to be seated next to a family from a remote village in the mountains as you are to a legislator or lobbyist from the nearby state capitol. Tia's ("Auntie's") delicious homemade chorizo disappears fast on Saturdays; if you're an aficionado, get there early. Order anything and expect a true taste of local tradition, including perfectly flaky, light sopaipillas. Mammoth chile-smothered breakfast burritos will hold you over for hours on the powdery ski slopes during winter. Be warned, though: the red and green chiles are spicy and you're expected to understand this elemental fact of local cuisine. Alcohol is not served here. ⊠ *210 W. San Francisco St.* ☎ *505/983–9880* ▤ *MC, V* ☺ *No dinner. Closed Sun.* ✛ *B3.*

EAST SIDE AND CANYON ROAD

Use the coordinate (✛ A1) at the end of each listing to locate a site on the corresponding map.

\$\$\$\$
CONTEMPORARY
Fodor's Choice
★
✕ **The Compound.** Chef Mark Kiffin has transformed this gracious, folk-art-filled old restaurant into one of the state's culinary darlings. No longer white-glove formal, it's still a fancy place, thanks to decor by famed designer Alexander Girard and a highly attentive staff, but it maintains an easygoing, distinctly Santa Fe feel. From chef Kiffin's oft-changing menu, devoted to ingredients based on those introduced to the area by the Spanish, consider a starter of warm flan of summer sweet corn, with lobster succotash and radish sprouts. Memorable entrées include Alaskan halibut with orange lentils, summer squash, and *piquillo* peppers in a smoked ham hock broth; and buttermilk roast chicken with creamed fresh spinach and foie gras pan gravy. The extensive and carefully chosen wine list will please the most discerning oenophile. Lunch is as delightful as dinner, while considerably less expensive—about \$14 per person. ⊠ *653 Canyon Rd.* ☎ *505/982–4353*

3

⊕ *www.compoundrestaurant.com* ▤ *AE, D, DC, MC, V* ⊗ *No lunch weekends* ✛ *D6.*

$$$
SPANISH

✗ **El Farol.** In this crossover-cuisine town, owner David Salazar sums up his food in one word: "Spanish." Order a classic entrée like paella or make a meal from the nearly 30 different tapas—from tiny fried squid to wild mushrooms. Dining is indoors and out. Touted as the oldest continuously operated restaurant in Santa Fe, El Farol (built in 1835) has a relaxed ambience, a unique blend of the Western frontier and contemporary Santa Fe. People push back the chairs and start dancing at around 9:30. The restaurant books live entertainment seven nights a week, from blues and Latin to rock, and there's a festive flamenco performance on Wednesday. End a long day of sightseeing by grabbing a table on the porch in the late afternoon and sipping a refreshing margaritas. ⊠ *808 Canyon Rd.* ☎ *505/983–9912* ⊕ *www.elfarolsf.com* ▤ *AE, D, MC, V* ✛ *D6.*

$$$$
CONTEMPORARY
Fodor's Choice
★

✗ **Geronimo.** At this bastion of high cuisine, the complex dishes range from pan-roasted Kurobuta pork tenderloin with spicy soy apricot glaze and scallion black pepper risotto, to fiery sweet-chile-and-honey-grilled Mexican sweet prawns with jasmine-almond rice cakes, frisée-and-red-onion salad, and *yuzu* (Japanese citrus fruit)-and-basil aioli. Chef Eric Di Stefano's peppery elk tenderloin remains a perennial favorite. Desserts are artful and rich, and the Sunday brunch is well regarded. Located in the Borrego House, a massive-walled adobe dating from 1756, the intimate, white dining rooms have beamed ceilings, wood floors, fireplaces, and cushioned *bancos* (banquettes). The restaurant is renowned for both its cuisine and its highly refined service. In summer you can dine under the front portal; in winter the bar with fireplace is inviting. For a less formal experience, dine in the dark, seductive bar—the cocktails are excellent. ⊠ *724 Canyon Rd.* ☎ *505/982–1500* ⊕ *www. geronimorestaurant.com* ▤ *AE, MC, V* ⊗ *No lunch Mon.* ✛ *D6.*

OLD SANTA FE TRAIL AND SOUTH CAPITOL

Use the coordinate (✛ A1) at the end of each listing to locate a site on the corresponding map.

$$$
CONTEMPORARY
★

✗ **315 Restaurant & Wine Bar.** As if it were on a thoroughfare in Paris rather than on Old Santa Fe Trail, 315 has a Continental, white-tablecloth sophistication, but the offbeat wall art gives it a contemporary feel. Chef-owner Louis Moskow, who also owns the popular Railyard Restaurant *(⇨ below)*, uses traditional techniques to prepare innovative yet simple fare using organic vegetables and locally raised meats. Daily specialties on the ever-evolving menu might include squash-blossom beignets with local goat cheese, basil-wrapped shrimp with apricot chutney and curry sauce, or grilled boneless lamb loin with crispy polenta, spring vegetables, and green peppercorn sauce. The garden patio opens onto the street scene. There's also a wine bar with an exceptional list of vintages; ask for Moskow's pairing advice. ⊠ *315 Old Santa Fe Trail* ☎ *505/986–9190* ⊕ *www.315santafe.com* ▤ *AE, MC, V* ⊗ *Closed Sun. No lunch Mon* ✛ *C3.*

3

¢ ✕ **Body Cafe.** There is a world of things to do inside the contemporary,
CAFÉ   Asian-inspired Body. At this holistically minded center five minutes
from Downtown, you'll find a spa offering a full range of treatments,
a yoga studio (with a good range of classes open to visitors), a child-
care center, and a boutique selling a wide range of beauty, health, and
lifestyle products, plus jewelry, clothing, music, tarot cards, and all
sorts of interesting gifts. The café uses mostly organic, local ingredients and serves three meals a day, with an emphasis on vegan and raw
food. The breakfast smoothies and homemade granola are delicious.
At lunch try soba noodles with peanuts and ginger-soy vinaigrette, or
the raw enchiladas (really!), and at dinner there's an unbelievably good
raw vegan lasagna layered with basil-sunflower pesto, portobello mushrooms, spinach, squash, tomatoes, nut cheese, and marinara sauce. Beer
and wine are served. ⊠ *333 W. Cordova Rd.* ☎ *505/986–0362* ⊕ *www.
bodyofsantafe.com* ▭ *AE, D, MC, V* ✛ *E4.*

$ ✕ **Guadalupe Cafe.** Come to this informal café for hefty servings of New
NEW MEXICAN   Mexican favorites like enchiladas—vegetarian options are delicious—
and quesadillas, or burritos smothered in green or red chile, topped off
with sopaipilla and honey. The seasonal raspberry pancakes are one
of many breakfast favorites as are eggs Benedict with green-chile hollandaise sauce. Service is hit-or-miss and the wait for a table considerable—but the spicy food keeps 'em coming back for more. ⊠ *422 Old
Santa Fe Trail* ☎ *505/982–9762* ⌂ *Reservations not accepted* ▭ *DC,
MC, V* ⊗ *Closed Mon. No dinner Sun.* ✛ *D3.*

$ ✕ **Maria's New Mexican Kitchen.** Creaky wood floors and dark-wood vigas
NEW MEXICAN   set the scene for some quite good local cuisine. Serving more than 100
★   kinds of margaritas is but one of this rustic restaurant's claims to fame.
The house margarita is one of the best in town (and you may have sur-
mised that we take our margaritas seriously here). Get the SilverCoin if
you want to go top-shelf and leave the rest of the super tequilas to sip
on without intrusion of other flavors. The place holds its own as a reliable, supertasty source of authentic New Mexican fare, including chiles
rellenos, blue-corn enchiladas, and green-chile tamales. The Galisteo
chicken, parboiled and covered in red chiles, is simple and satisfying.
Don't be surprised to have to wait for a table, and don't worry, the
line moves quickly. ⊠ *555 W. Cordova Rd.* ☎ *505/983–7929* ⊕ *www.
marias-santafe.com* ▭ *AE, D, DC, MC, V* ✛ *E4.*

$ ✕ **Mariscos la Playa.** Yes, even in landlocked Santa Fe it's possible to find
SEAFOOD   incredibly fresh and well-prepared seafood served in big portions. This
★   cheery, colorful Mexican restaurant surrounded by strip malls is just a
short hop south of Downtown. Favorite dishes include the absolutely
delicious shrimp wrapped in bacon with Mexican cheese and *caldo
vuelve a la vida* ("come back to life"), a hearty soup of shrimp, octo-
pus, scallops, clams, crab, and calamari. There's also shrimp soup in
a tomato broth, fresh oysters on the half shell, and *pescado a la plan-
cha,* super-tender trout cooked with butter and paprika. The staff and
service are delightful. ⊠ *537 W. Cordova Rd.* ☎ *505/982–2790* ▭ *AE,
DC, MC, V* ✛ *E4.*

$ ✕ **Pyramid Cafe.** Tucked into a strip mall five minutes south of the Plaza,
MIDDLE EASTERN   this casual restaurant—with photos of Tunisia, kilim rugs, and North

African textiles on the walls—delights locals with flavors not available anywhere else in town. The Tunisian owner and his staff are adept at preparing classic dishes with the Mediterranean flavors of Lebanon and Greece, but when they turn their attention to home flavors, and those of neighboring Morocco, your taste buds will sing. Try the specials, like the Moroccan *tajin,* with chicken, prunes, raisins, and spices served with rice in a domed terra-cotta dish. The *brik a l'oeuf,* a turnover-like Tunisian specialty in phyllo dough with an egg and creamy herbed mashed potatoes tucked inside, is as wonderful as it is unusual. The Tunisian Plate, a sampler, is incredible. Local, organic ingredients are used, and there are excellent vegetarian options. The lunch buffet is fresh and satisfying. ⊠ *505 W. Cordova Rd.* ☎ *505/989–1378* ▭ *AE, MC, V* ✛ *E4.*

$$$ ✕ **Restaurant Martin.** After cooking at some of the best restaurants in

CONTEMPORARY   town (Geronimo, the Old House, Anasazi), acclaimed chef Martin Rios is finally flexing his culinary muscles in his own place. Martin and his savvy wife, Jennifer, took a ramshackle old building on a big lot behind the capitol and have created a simple, elegant restaurant with a gorgeous patio. Martin prepares progressive American cuisine, which is heavily influenced by his French culinary training. Lunch favorites include his superb Caesar salad, and a deftly prepared Atlantic salmon BLT sandwich. The crispy coconut-chicken-and-glass-noodle salad is both hot and tangy. Dinner entrées include a delicious vegetarian tasting plate with spring pea ravioli, sweet potato puree, asparagus, carrots, and goat cheese and a grilled Kurobuta pork striploin with *guajillo* chile–and–plum glaze with sweet potato and crispy young vegetables. The brunch menu on the weekends includes classic huevos rancheros prepared with typical Martin flair, and crispy Alaskan halibut Baja fish tacos. ⊠ *526 Galisteo St.* ☎ *505/820–0919* ⊕ *www.restaurantmartinsantafe.com* ▭ *AE, MC, V* ☉ *Closed Mon* ✛ *D2.*

RAILYARD DISTRICT

Use the coordinate (✛ A1) at the end of each listing to locate a site on the corresponding map.

$ ✕ **Andiamo.** A longtime locals' favorite, Andiamo scores high marks for

ITALIAN   its friendly staff, consistently good food, and comfortable dining room.

★   Produce from the farmers' market down the street adds to the seasonal surprises of this intimate northern Italian restaurant set inside a sweet cottage in the Railyard District. Start with the addictively delectable crispy polenta with rosemary and Gorgonzola sauce; move on to the white pizza with roasted garlic, fontina, grilled radicchio, pancetta, and rosemary; and consider such hearty entrées as crispy duck legs with grilled polenta, roasted turnips, and sautéed spinach; or linguine with spicy grilled shrimp and olives in a white wine tomato cream sauce. There's a super wine list with varied prices. Save room for the chocolate *pot de crème.* ⊠ *322 Garfield St.* ☎ *505/995–9595* ⊕ *www. andiamoonline.com* ▭ *AE, DC, MC, V* ☉ *No lunch weekends* ✛ *C2.*

$$ ✕ **Aqua Santa.** Brian Knox, the charming, gregarious chef at the helm

CONTEMPORARY   of this locals' favorite, is a devotee of the Slow Food philosophy. His

Fodor's Choice   love and appreciation of food is palpable; some of the finest, simplest,

★

3

yet most sophisticated dishes in town come from the open kitchen in this tiny, one-room gem of a restaurant. The creamy plastered walls of the intimate dining room are hung with art from local artists, and the ramada-covered patio open in summer feels like dining at a chic friend's house. Diners enjoy dishes like the fabulously tangy Caesar salad, pan-fried oysters with bitter honey and a balsamic reduction, Tuscan bean soup with white-truffle oil, and braised organic New Mexico lamb with olives and summer squash. Brian can be spotted shopping around town for fresh, local ingredients, and the menu changes regularly based on his gastronomic discoveries. Save room for dessert; the silky *panna cotta* (Italian custard) may be the best on the continent. There's an extensive, reasonable wine list, too; ask the friendly staff for their current favorites. ⊠ *451 W. Alameda St. (entrance off Water St.)* ☏ *505/982–6297* ▭ *MC, V* ⊙ *Closed Sun. and Mon. No lunch Tues. or Sat.* ✛ *B2*.

¢ ✕ **Aztec Cafe.** If a cup of really tasty, locally roasted, noncorporate coffee
CAFÉ in a funky, creaky-wood-floored old adobe sounds like nirvana to you,
Fodor's Choice then this is the place. Cozy, colorful rooms inside are lined with local
★ art (and artists), the staff is laid-back and friendly, and the shady patio outside is a busy meeting ground for locals. Food is homemade, healthy, and flavorful. The menu includes sandwiches such as the Martin-roast turkey, green apples, and Swiss cheese; fabulous, fluffy quiches; soups, breakfast burritos, and superyummy homemade ice cream in the warm season. Brunch happens on the weekends. It's open until 7 (6 pm Sundays) in case you get late-afternoon munchies. There's free Wi-Fi and a public computer with Internet access, and beer and wine are available. ⊠ *317 Aztec St., Railyard District* ☏ *505/820–0025* ⊕ *www.azteccafe. com* ⌦ *Reservations not accepted* ▭ *AE, MC, V* ✛ *C2*.

$ ✕ **Cowgirl BBQ.** A rollicking, popular bar and grill with several rooms
AMERICAN overflowing with Old West memorabilia, Cowgirl has reasonably priced
ⓒ Southwestern, Tex-Mex, barbecue, and Southern fare. Highlights include barbecue, buffalo burgers, chiles rellenos, and salmon tacos with tomatillo salsa. A real treat for parents is the outdoor-but-enclosed Kiddie Corral where kids have swings, a climbing structure, and various games to entertain themselves. If you catch one of the nightly music acts—usually rock or blues—you're likely to leave smiling. When the weather is good, grab a seat on the spacious patio out front, order a delicious margarita and some green-chile cheese fries, and settle in for great people-watching. The attached pool hall has a great jukebox to keep toes tapping. Alas, service can be spotty. ⊠ *319 S. Guadalupe St.* ☏ *505/982–2565* ⊕ *www.cowgirlsantafe.com* ▭ *AE, D, MC, V* ✛ *C1*.

¢ ✕ **El Tesoro.** One of the Railyard District's better-kept secrets, this small
LATIN café occupies a spot in the high-ceilinged center of the Sanbusco Center, steps from several chic boutiques. The tiny kitchen turns out a mix of Central American, New Mexican, and American dishes, all of them reliable. Grilled tuna tacos with *salsa fresca*, black beans, and rice; and Salvadorian chicken tamales wrapped in banana leaves are among the tastiest treats. El Tesoro also serves pastries, gelato, lemon bars, hot cocoa, and other snacks, making it a perfect break from shopping. ⊠ *Sanbusco Market Center, 500 Montezuma Ave.* ☏ *505/988–3886* ▭ *MC, V* ⊙ *No dinner* ✛ *C1*.

¢　✕**La Choza.** The harder-to-find, and less expensive sister to the Shed, La
NEW MEXICAN　Choza (which means "the shed" in Spanish), serves supertasty, super-
☺　traditional New Mexican fare. It's hard to go wrong here: chicken
Fodor's Choice　or pork *carne adovada* (marinated in red chile and slow-cooked until
★　tender) burritos, white clam chowder spiced with green chiles, and the
classic huevos rancheros are exceptional. The dining rooms are dark
and cozy, with vigas across the ceiling and local art on the walls. The
staff is friendly and competent, and the addition of a full liquor license
has been a boon for dedicated regulars who formerly rued the absence
of margaritas. ✉ *905 Alarid St., near Cerrillos Rd. at St. Francis Dr.,*
around the corner from the Railyard Park ☎ *505/982–0909* ▤ *AE, DC,*
MC, V ☺ *Closed Sun.* ✛ *D1.*

$　✕**Railyard Restaurant & Saloon.** Set inside a bustling, handsome ware-
AMERICAN　house in the Railyard District, this trendy spot operated by the same
owner of 315 Restaurant & Wine Bar serves American favorites that
have been given nouvelle twists. Good bets include steamed black mus-
sels in fresh tomato-and-basil broth, fried buttermilk-chicken strips with
Creole rémoulade dipping sauce, sesame-and-panko-crusted tuna with
a soy-honey sauce, and barbecued baby back ribs. If the softshell crab
is available, order it. Many patrons sit in the casual bar, where both the
full and bar menus are available, and sip on pomegranate margaritas or
well-chosen wines by the glass. The patio out front, with breathtaking
views of the Sangre de Cristo Mountains, is a great spot to sit in the
summer. Lunch prices average about $10. Service and food quality have
been an issue in recent years. ✉ *530 S. Guadalupe St.* ☎ *505/989–3300*
⊕ *www.railyardrestaurantandsaloon.com* ▤ *AE, D, MC, V* ☺ *No lunch*
Sun. ✛ *D1.*

$$$　✕**Ristra.** This unprepossessing restaurant, set in an old house on the edge
CONTEMPORARY　of the trendy Railyard District, presents a first-rate menu of Southwest-
ern-influenced modern French cooking. You might start with chorizo-
stuffed calamari with watercress and smoked-tomato sauce; roasted rack
of lamb with couscous, minted tomatoes, preserved lemon, and Niçoise
olives is a tempting main dish. Top off your meal with an almond-
butter cake served with warm spiced apples and a mascarpone-caramel
sauce. The wines are well selected, and the service is generally good.
There's a hip, stylish cocktail bar with its own menu of lighter dishes,
including a great burger. ✉ *548 Agua Fria St.* ☎ *505/982–8608* ⊕ *www.*
ristrarestaurant.com ▤ *AE, MC, V* ☺ *No lunch Sun. and Mon.* ✛ *C1.*

¢　✕**Tomasita's.** Open for years and almost always crowded, this cavernous
NEW MEXICAN　place serves up reliable—if unspectacular—and spicy, New Mexican
food and margaritas. Located in one of the old railroad depots, the
interior is nondescript, with vinyl-seated booths and tables packed in—
though the yellow-glass windows cast a strange light over the place. The
full bar is an interesting place to watch a local, not-for-tourists, scene
unfold. ✉ *500 S. Guadalupe St., Railyard District* ☎ *505/983–5721*
⚇ *Reservations not accepted* ▤ *AE, D, DC, MC, V* ✛ *C1.*

$　✕**Zia Diner.** Located in a renovated coal warehouse from the 1880s, this
AMERICAN　slick diner with a low-key, art-deco-style interior serves comfort food
with a twist (green-chile-piñon meat loaf, for example). Stop in for a
full meal or just snack on their classic banana split with homemade

hot fudge sauce. Zia's Cobb salad is one of the best in town, and the amazingly fluffy corn, green chile, and Asiago pie served with a mixed green salad is hard to match. Service is friendly, and the food is fresh with lots of local ingredients. There's a small patio and a friendly bar known for its tasty mixed drinks and personable bartenders. Breakfast here is great start to the day: try the Nutty New Mexican, a take on eggs Benedict with green-chile corned beef hash, poached eggs, and hollandaise sauce. Yum! ⊠ *326 S. Guadalupe St.* ☎ *505/988–7008* ⊕ *www. ziadiner.com* ⊟ *AE, MC, V* ✢ *C2.*

WEST OF PLAZA

Use the coordinate (✢ A1) at the end of each listing to locate a site on the corresponding map.

¢
AMERICAN
☙
Fodor's Choice
★
✗**Bert's Burger Bowl.** This unassuming, old-fashioned burger stand has brought fans back year after year for the past 55 years with favorites like their flame-broiled green-chile cheeseburgers (veggie burgers are available, too), crispy onion rings, and hand-mixed cherry-lime Cokes. More recently, they've added higher-end burger options like Kobe beef, organic local lamb, and buffalo (these all come with specific toppings). French fries, tacos, and breakfast burritos are also served. The T-shirts here proudly proclaim: "one location worldwide." ⊠ *235 N. Guadalupe St.* ☎ *505/982–0215* ⊟ *MC, V* ✢ *B2.*

¢
MEXICAN
Fodor's Choice
★
✗**Bumble Bee's Baja Grill.** A bright, vibrantly colored restaurant with closely spaced tables, piñatas, and ceiling fans wafting overhead, Bumble Bee's (it's the nickname of the ebullient owner, Bob) delights locals with its super-fresh Cal Mex–style food. If you like fish tacos, the mahimahi ones with creamy, nondairy slaw are outstanding; try them with a side of salad instead of beans and rice—and *hijole!* (wow!) What a meal! Mammoth burritos with a wide range of fillings (including asparagus—yum!), roasted chicken with cilantro-lime rice, char-grilled trout platters, and a wide variety of vegetarian options keep folks pouring through the doors. You order at the counter, grab some chips and any one of a number of freshly made salsas from the bar, and wait for your number to come up. Beer, wine, and Mexican soft drinks are served. Try a homemade Mexican chocolate brownie for dessert. There's live jazz on Saturday nights. ⊠ *301 Jefferson St.* ☎ *505/820–2862* ⊕ *www.bumblebeesbajagrill.com* ⊠ *3701 Cerrillos Rd.* ☎ *505/988–3278* ⊟ *AE, D, MC, V* ✢ *B2.*

¢
CAFÉ
★
✗**Clafoutis.** Undeniably French, this bustling café serves authentic, delicious food. Walk through the door of this bright, open space and you'll almost certainly be greeted with a cheery *"bonjour"* from Anne-Laure, who owns it with her husband, Philippe. Start your day with a crepe, one of their fluffy omelets, or *les gauffres* (large house waffles). Lunch offers quiches with perfectly flaky crusts, an enticing selection of large salads (the *salade de la maison* has pears, pine nuts, blue cheese, Spanish chorizo, tomatoes, and cucumbers atop mixed greens), and savory sandwiches, like the classic *croque madame* (grilled ham, egg, and cheese) on homemade bread. The classic onion soup is amazingly comforting on a cold day. The café's namesake dessert, clafoutis, is

SANTA FE COOKING

If you'd like to bring the flavors of the Southwest to your own kitchen, consider taking one or more of the wildly popular and fun cooking classes at the **Santa Fe School of Cooking** (✉ 116 W. San Francisco St., The Plaza ☎ 505/983–4511 ⊕ www.santafeschoolofcooking.com) Regular classes are taught during days and evenings, and more elaborate courses include the Insider's Culinary Adventure, a meeting-and-eating tour with some of Santa Fe's most notable chefs, or the multiday New Mexico Culture & Cuisine Tour that introduces participants to the chefs, restaurants, and farmers whose passionate devotion to food has made Santa Fe the culinary hot spot that it is. It offers courses that are kid-friendly, too. Reservations are a must.

worth saving room for. Their baguettes and pastries are perfectly prepared—no small feat at this elevation. ✉ 402 N. Guadalupe St., near The Plaza ☎ 505/988–1809 ⌔ Reservations not accepted ▤ AE, MC, V ⊗ No dinner. Closed Sun. ✛ A2.

SOUTH SIDE

Use the coordinate (✛ A1) at the end of each listing to locate a site on the corresponding map.

$ ✗ **Chocolate Maven.** Although the name of this cheery bakery suggests
CAFÉ sweets, and it does sweets especially well, Chocolate Maven produces
★ impressive savory breakfast and lunch fare. Dinner is "farmers' market–inspired" and features seasonal dishes. Favorite treats include wild-mushroom-and-goat-cheese focaccia sandwiches, eggs ménage à trois (one each of eggs Benedict, Florentine, and Madison—the latter consisting of smoked salmon and poached egg), and Caprese salad of fresh mozzarella, basil, and tomatoes. Pizzas are thin-crusted and delicate. Some of the top desserts include Belgian chocolate fudge brownies, mocha-buttercream torte with chocolate-covered strawberries, and French lemon-raspberry cake. Don't let the industrial building put you off; the interior is light, bright, and cozy. Try the Mayan Mocha, espresso mixed with steamed milk and a delicious combo of chocolate, cinnamon, and red chiles—heavenly! ✉ 821 W. San Mateo St. ☎ 505/984–1980 ⊕ www.chocolatemaven.com ▤ AE, D, MC, V ✛ D5.

$ ✗ **Jambo.** In a town where self-professed foodies discuss restaurants and
AFRICAN dishes ardently, it really says something when a newcomer like Jambo instantly becomes a hot topic. Ahmed Obo, the Kenyan-born owner, who's been in Santa Fe for years, applies great skill and enthusiasm to the food he loves. Afro-Caribbean flavors of coconut, peanuts, and curry influence everything from shrimp to goat stew. Vegetarian choices like the coconut lentil stew are rich and comforting. The restaurant is in a strip mall, but don't let that throw you. Venture inside this casual, homey eatery and enjoy the world-beat music, African art, and the friendly waiters who will happily mention their favorite dishes. ✉ 2010

Cerrillos Rd. ☎ 505/473–1269 ⊕ www.jambocafe.net ▤ AE, MC, V ⊙ Closed Sun. ⊹ B5.

$$

ASIAN

✗**Mu Du Noodles.** This warm and cozy eatery on a busy stretch of Cerrillos Road excels both in its friendly and helpful staff and its interesting pan-Asian fare. Book ahead on weekends—this place fills up fast. Dinner specials are always good, though if you're fond of spicy food be sure to ask for "hot" as their food tends to the mild. Sample sweet-and-sour rockfish with water chestnuts, smoked bacon, and jasmine rice; Vietnamese spring rolls with peanut-hoisin sauce; or stir-fried tenderloin beef with whole scallions, sweet peppers, bean sprouts, and fat rice noodles. The Malaysian *loksa* (a spicy noodle soup) is especially good. Mu, the proprietor, is a strong advocate of cooking with local, organic ingredients. On Sundays, only a light tapas-style menu is served. ✉ 1494 Cerrillos Rd. ☎ 505/988–1411 ⊕ www.mudunoodles.com ▤ AE, MC, V ⊙ Closed Mon. No lunch ⊹ C4.

¢

ECLECTIC

✗**Tecolote Cafe.** The mantra here is "no toast," and you won't miss it. Since 1980, the bellies of locals and tourists alike have been satisfied with delicious breakfasts and lunches founded primarily on northern New Mexican cuisine. The simple rooms and comfortable seating allow you to focus on such dishes as the Sheepherder's Breakfast (red potatoes browned with jalapeños and topped with red and green chiles and two eggs), delicious carne adovada (lean pork slow-cooked in their homemade red chile), and a green-chile stew that locals swear by to cure colds. French toast is prepared with homemade breads. When the server asks if you'd like a tortilla or the bakery basket, go for the basket—it's full of warm, fresh muffins and biscuits that are out of this world. ✉ 1203 Cerrillos Rd. ☎ 505/988–1362 ⊕ www.tecolotecafe.com ⌂ Reservations not accepted ▤ AE, D, DC, MC, V ⊙ No dinner ⊹ D4.

$

ECLECTIC

✗**Tune Up.** The local favorite formerly known as Dave's Not Here is a cozy spot with colorful walls and wood details, booths, a few tables, and a community table. The shaded patio out front is a great summertime spot to enjoy the toothsome breakfasts and lunches served. Start the day with savory, and surprisingly delicate, breakfast rellenos, fluffy buttermilk pancakes, or the *huevos salvadoreños* (eggs scrambled with scallions and tomatoes, served with refried beans, panfried bananas, and a tortilla). Lunch offerings include the super-juicy Dave Was Here burger served with crispy home-cut fries, a ginger-chicken sandwich on ciabatta bread, and Salvadoran treats called *pupusas,* which are most like griddled, flattened, soft tamales—delicious! Dinner offers Yucatecan fish tacos, the succulent Salvadoran combo (with a tamale and a pupusa with roasted tomato salsa and *curtido*—cabbage salad), or an organic flatiron steak. Homemade baked goods include a peanut-butter-cookie sandwich filled with Nutella, and a variety of pies. The staff is friendly and efficient and the care taken by the owners, Chuy and Charlotte Rivera, is evident. ✉ 115 Hickox St. ☎ 505/983–7060 ⊕ www.tuneupcafe.com ⌂ Reservations not accepted ▤ AE, MC, V ⊹ D3.

OLD LAS VEGAS HIGHWAY

Use the coordinate (✛ A1) at the end of each listing to locate a site on the corresponding map.

¢

AMERICAN

Fodor's Choice

★

✕ **Bobcat Bite.** It'll take you 15 easy minutes from Downtown to drive to this tiny roadhouse southeast of town—and it's worth it. Folks drive a lot farther for Bobcat Bite's steaks and chops ($17) but come especially for one thing: the juiciest burgers in the area. Locals prefer them topped with cheese and green chiles. Only early dinners are available (and no dessert is served), as the place closes by 8 most nights; you'll want to arrive early to get a seat. ⊠ *Old Las Vegas Hwy., 4½ mi south of Old Pecos Trail exit off I–25* ☎ *505/983–5319* ⊕ *www.bobcatbite. com* ⚄ *Reservations not accepted* ⊟ *No credit cards* ⊘ *Closed Sun. and Mon. (also closed Tues. in winter)* ✛ *F6.*

$

ECLECTIC

☾

Fodor's Choice

★

✕ **Harry's Roadhouse.** This busy, friendly, art-filled compound just southeast of town consists of several inviting rooms, from a diner-style space with counter seating to a cozier nook with a fireplace—there's also an enchanting courtyard out back with juniper trees and flower gardens. The varied menu of contemporary diner favorites, pizzas, New Mexican fare, and bountiful salads is supplemented by a long list of daily specials—which often include delicious ethnic dishes. Favorites include smoked-chicken quesadillas and grilled-salmon tacos with tomatillo salsa and black beans. Breakfast is fantastic. On weekends, if you're there early, you might just get a chance at one of owner–pastry chef Peyton's phenomenal cinnamon rolls. Desserts here are homey favorites, from the chocolate pudding to the blueberry cobbler. Many gluten-free and veggie options are available, and Harry's is also known for stellar margaritas. The owners are committed to recycling and sustainable business practices. ⊠ *96-B Old Las Vegas Hwy., 1 mi east of Old Pecos Trail exit off I–25* ☎ *505/989–4629* ⊕ *www.harrysroadhousesantafe. com* ⊟ *AE, D, MC, V* ✛ *F6.*

WHERE TO STAY

In Santa Fe you can ensconce yourself in quintessential Southwestern style or anonymous hotel-chain decor, depending on how much you want to spend—the city has costlier accommodations than anywhere in the Southwest. Cheaper options are available on Cerrillos (pronounced sir-*ee*-yos) Road, the rather unattractive business thoroughfare southwest of Downtown. Quality varies greatly on Cerrillos, but some of the best-managed, most attractive properties are (from most to least expensive) the Holiday Inn, the Courtyard Marriott, and the Motel 6. You generally pay more as you get closer to the Plaza, but for many visitors it's worth it to be within walking distance of many attractions. Some of the best deals are offered by bed-and-breakfasts—many of those near the Plaza offer much better values than the big, touristy hotels. Rates drop, often from 30% to 50%, from November to April (excluding Thanksgiving and Christmas).

In addition to the usual array of inns and hotels here, Santa Fe has a wide range of **long- and short-term vacation rentals**, some of them available through the **Management Group** (☎ 866/982–2823 ⊕ *www. santaferentals.com*). Rates generally range from $100 to $300 per night for double-occupancy units, with better values at some of the two- to four-bedroom properties. Many have fully stocked kitchens. Another route is to rent a furnished condo or casita at one of several compounds geared to travelers seeking longer stays. The best of these is the luxurious **Campanilla Compound** (☎ 505/988–7585 or 800/828–9700 ⊕ *www.campanillacompound.com*), on a hill just north of Downtown; rates run from about $1,400 to $1,800 per week in summer. Another good, similarly priced bet is **Fort Marcy Suites** (☎ 888/570–2775 ⊕ *www.allseasonsresortlodging.com/santa_fe/fortmarcy*), on a bluff just northeast of the Plaza with great views. The individually furnished units accommodate two to six guests and come with full kitchens, wood fireplaces, VCRs, and CD stereos—these can be rented nightly or weekly.

WHAT IT COSTS					
	¢	$	$$	$$$	$$$$
Hotels	under $70	$70–$130	$131–$190	$191–$260	over $260

Prices are for a standard double room in room in high season, excluding 13.5%–14.5% tax.

THE PLAZA

Use the coordinate (✛ A1) at the end of each listing to locate a site on the corresponding map.

$$$ ⬚**Eldorado Hotel & Spa.** Because it's the closest thing Santa Fe has to a
HOTEL   convention hotel, the Eldorado sometimes gets a bad rap, but it's actually quite inviting, with individually decorated rooms and stunning mountain views. Rooms are stylishly furnished with carved Southwestern-style desks and chairs, large upholstered club chairs, and art prints; many have terraces or kiva-style fireplaces. The rooftop pool and gym are great fun, and there's music nightly, from classical Spanish guitar to piano, in the comfortable lobby lounge. A full slate of treatments, from Vichy rain showers to High Mesa salt scrubs, is offered by the hotel's luxe Nidah Spa. The Old House restaurant has been a solid contender in the local restaurant scene for years. **Pros:** serviceable accommodations three blocks from Santa Fe Plaza. **Cons:** staff's attention to service varies considerably. ⊠ *309 W. San Francisco St.* ☎ *505/988–4455 or 800/955–4455* ⊕ *www.eldoradohotel.com* ⇗ *213 rooms* ⌂ *In-room: a/c, kitchen (some), Wi-Fi. In-hotel: restaurant, room service, bar, pool, gym, spa, laundry service, parking (paid)* ⊟ *AE, D, DC, MC, V* ✛ *B3.*

$$$ ⬚**Hotel St. Francis.** Listed on the National Register of Historic Places,
HOTEL   this three-story building, parts of which were constructed in 1923, has walkways lined with turn-of-the-20th-century lampposts and is one block south of the Plaza. The hotel recently underwent a dramatic renovation and is now reminiscent of a Tuscan monastery, with expansive stone floors, plaster walls, and spare furnishings lit by massive pillar candles at night. The simple, elegant rooms with high ceilings, and casement windows have rustic Mexican furnishings and beautiful,

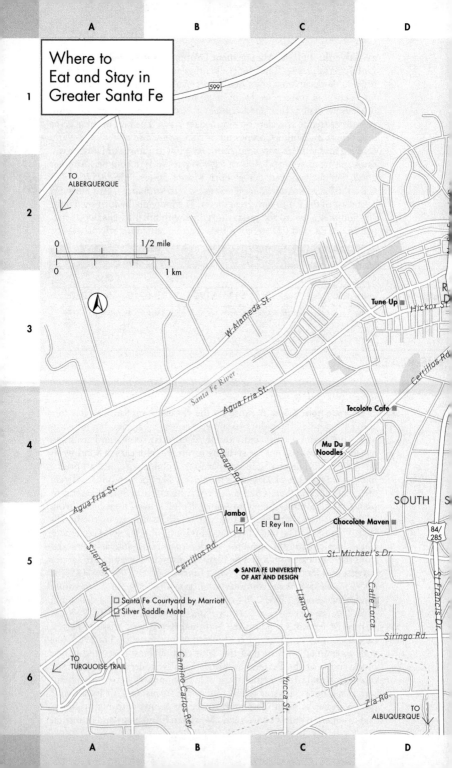

Where to Eat and Stay in Greater Santa Fe

599

TO ALBERQUERQUE

0   1/2 mile

0   1 km

W. Alameda St.

Tune Up

Hickox St.

R

Santa Fe River

Agua Fria St.

Cerrillos Rd.

Tecolote Cafe

Mu Du Noodles

Agua Fria St.

Osage Rd.

SOUTH   S

Jambo

14

El Rey Inn

Chocolate Maven

84/ 285

St. Michael's Dr.

Cerrillos Rd.

Siler Rd.

◆ SANTA FE UNIVERSITY OF ART AND DESIGN

Llano St.

Catle Lorca

St. Francis Dr.

□ Santa Fe Courtyard by Marriott
□ Silver Saddle Motel

Siringo Rd.

TO TURQUOISE TRAIL

Camino Carlos Rey

Yucca St.

Zia Rd.

TO ALBUQUERQUE

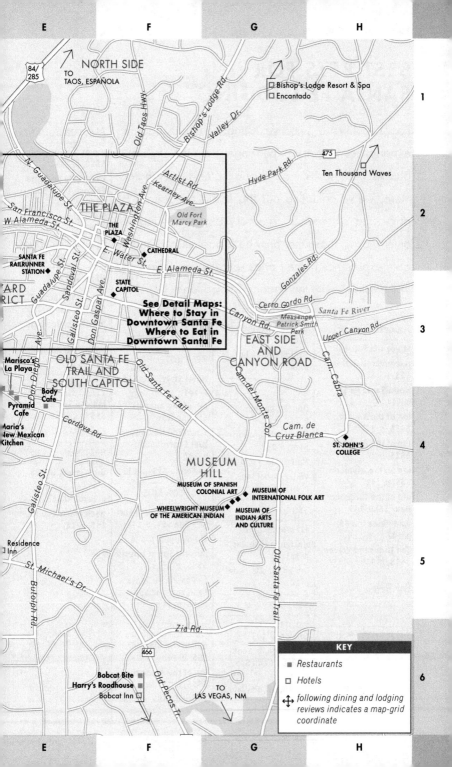

BEST BETS FOR SANTA FE LODGING

Fodor's offers a selective listing of quality lodging experiences in every price range, from the city's best budget beds to its most sophisticated luxury hotels. Here, we've compiled our top recommendations by price and experience. The very best properties—in other words, those that provide a particularly remarkable experience in their price range—are designated in the listings with the Fodor's Choice logo.

custom linens. The modern New Mexican restaurant, Tabla de Los Santos ($$$), has popular local chef Esteban Garcia at the helm. **Pros:** highly distinct ambience; two blocks from the Plaza and near many shops. **Cons:** service can be spotty; many of the rooms (and especially bathrooms) are quite small. ⊠ *210 Don Gaspar Ave.* ☎ *505/983–5700 or 800/529–5700* ⊕ *www.hotelstfrancis.com* ⌂ *80 rooms, 2 suites* ⌂ *In-room: a/c, refrigerator, Wi-Fi. In-hotel: restaurant, room service, bar, gym, laundry service, parking (paid)* ═ *AE, D, DC, MC, V* ✢ *B3.*

$$$$
HOTEL
Fodor'sChoice
★

☷ Inn of the Anasazi. Unassuming from the outside, this first-rate boutique hotel is one of Santa Fe's finest, with superb architectural detail. The prestigious Rosewood Hotel manages the property and has steadily and carefully upgraded the already sumptuous linens and furnishings over the years. Each room has a beamed viga-and-latilla ceiling, kiva-style gas fireplace, antique Navajo rugs, handwoven fabrics, and organic toiletries (including sunblock). Other amenities include full concierge services, twice-daily maid service, exercise bikes upon request, and a library. Especially nice touches in this desert town are the humidifiers in each guest room. A few deluxe rooms have balconies. The restaurant and bar are excellent. **Pros:** staff is thorough, gracious, and highly professional. **Cons:** standard rooms tend to be small for the price; few rooms have balconies; no hot tub or pool. ⊠ *113 Washington Ave.* ☎ *505/988–3030 or 800/688–8100* ⊕ *www.innoftheanasazi.com* ⌂ *58 rooms* ⌂ *In-room: a/c, safe, Wi-Fi. In-hotel: restaurant, bar, parking (paid), some pets allowed* ═ *AE, D, DC, MC, V* ✢ *B4.*

$$$
HOTEL
★

☷ Inn of the Governors. This rambling hotel by the Santa Fe River is staffed by a polite, enthusiastic bunch. Rooms have a Mexican theme, with bright colors, hand-painted folk art, feather pillows, Southwestern fabrics, and handmade furnishings; deluxe rooms also have balconies and fireplaces. Perks include a complimentary tea-and-sherry social each afternoon and a quite extensive breakfast buffet along with free Wi-Fi and newspapers. New Mexican dishes and lighter fare like wood-oven pizzas are served in the very popular and very reasonably priced bar-restaurant, Del Charro (¢). **Pros:** close to Plaza; friendly, helpful staff. **Cons:** standard rooms are a bit small and cramped. ⊠ *101 W. Alameda St.* ☎ *505/982–4333 or 800/234–4534* ⊕ *www.innofthegovernors.com* ⌂ *100 rooms* ⌂ *In-room: a/c, refrigerator, Wi-Fi. In-hotel: restaurant, room service, bar, pool, parking (free)* ═ *AE, D, DC, MC, V* �ⓘ◐ *CP* ✢ *C3.*

$$$$
HOTEL
☾

☷ Inn and Spa at Loretto. This plush, oft-photographed, pueblo-inspired property attracts a loyal clientele, many of whom swear by the friendly staff and high decorating standards. The lobby opens up to the gardens and large pool, and leather couches and high-end architectural details make the hotel a pleasure to relax in. Rooms are among the largest of any Downtown property and contain vibrantly upholstered, hand-crafted furnishings and sumptuous slate-floor bathrooms—many have large balconies overlooking Downtown. Other nice touches include an iPod dock and a complimentary newspaper each day. The restaurant, Luminaria, serves creative Southwestern fare and the lounge, the Living Room, offers a number of specialty cocktails in a sophisticated but relaxed room. The spa offers a wide range of Balinese and Thai-style

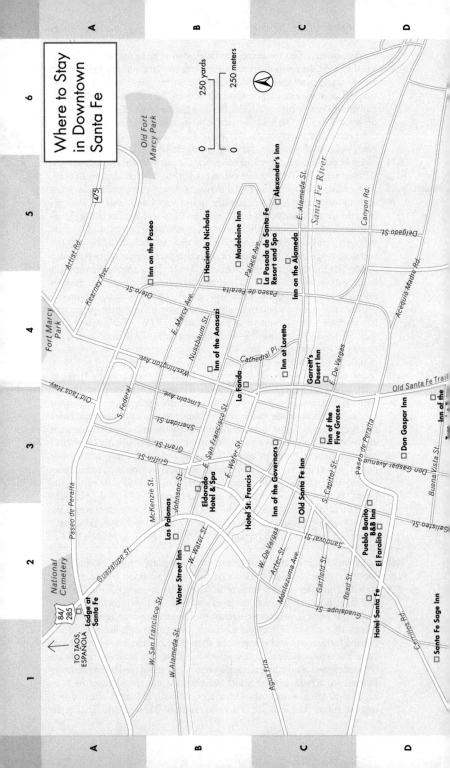

Where to Stay in Downtown Santa Fe

0   250 yards

0   250 meters

TO TAOS, ESPAÑOLA

National Cemetery

Fort Marcy Park

Old Fort Marcy Park

Lodge at Santa Fe

Water Street Inn

Las Palomas

Eldorado Hotel & Spa

Hotel St. Francis

Inn of the Governors

Old Santa Fe Inn

Pueblo Bonito B&B Inn

El Farolito

Hotel Santa Fe

Santa Fe Sage Inn

Inn of the Five Graces

Inn of the Anasazi

La Fonda

Inn at Loretto

Garrett's Desert Inn

Don Gaspar Inn

Inn of the

Inn on the Paseo

Hacienda Nicholas

Madeleine Inn

La Posada de Santa Fe Resort and Spa

Inn on the Alameda

Alexander's Inn

Santa Fe River

Paseo de Peralta

Guadalupe St.

Agua Fria

W. Alameda St.

W. San Francisco St.

Old Taos Hwy.

S. Federal

Kearney Ave.

Artist Rd.

Otero St.

E. Marcy Ave.

Nussbaum St.

Washington Ave.

Lincoln Ave.

Sheridan St.

Grant St.

Griffin St.

McKenzie St.

Johnson St.

W. Water St.

E. San Francisco St.

E. Water St.

W. De Vargas

Aztec St.

Sandoval St.

Montezuma Ave.

Garfield St.

Read St.

S. Capitol St.

Cathedral Pl.

Palace Ave.

Paseo de Peralta

E. De Vargas

Old Santa Fe Trail

Don Gaspar Avenue

Paseo de Peralta

Buena Vista St.

Salisteo St.

Cerrillos Rd.

Guadalupe St.

E. Alameda St.

Canyon Rd.

Delgado St.

Acequia Madre Rd.

475

84/285

treatments and services. **Pros:** the location, two blocks from the Plaza, is ideal; gorgeous grounds. **Cons:** expensive parking and resort fees; rooms tend to be dark. ✉ *211 Old Santa Fe Trail* ☎ *505/988–5531 or 800/727–5531* ⊕ *www.hotelloretto.com* ⤢ *134 rooms, 5 suites* ⚒ *In-room: a/c, Wi-Fi, refrigerator. In-hotel: restaurant, bar, gym, spa, parking (paid)* ⊟ *AE, D, DC, MC, V* ✛ *C4.*

$ ⚏ **Inn on the Paseo.** This inn is on a busy road, but at least this stretch
INN   of Paseo de Peralta is two lanes wide and is in a semiresidential neighborhood a short walk from the Plaza. Rooms are fairly simple, and can be small, but clean and light, some with hardwood floors and all with pleasing Southwestern furnishings and color schemes—some have fireplaces and private patios. The staff is laid-back and friendly. The two historic main buildings are joined by a modern lobby with a pitched ceiling, where the Continental breakfast is served—in warm weather you can dine on the sundeck. **Pros:** just a few blocks from the Plaza. **Cons:** you need a room away from the road to avoid traffic noise. ✉ *630 Paseo de Peralta* ☎ *505/984–8200 or 800/457–9045* ⊕ *www.innonthepaseo. com* ⤢ *16 rooms, 2 suites* ⚒ *In-room: a/c, Internet. In-hotel: parking (free), no kids under 8* ⊟ *MC, V* ⍥ *CP* ✛ *B4.*

$$$ ⚏ **La Fonda.** History and charm are more prevalent in this sole Plaza-
HOTEL   front hotel than first-class service and amenities. Though there has been an inn on this corner for centuries, the pueblo-inspired structure you see today was redesigned in 1922 by famed regional architect John Gaw Meem and has since been enlarged many times. Antiques and Native American art decorate the tiled lobby, and each room has hand-decorated wood furniture, wrought-iron light fixtures, beamed ceilings, and high-speed wireless. Some suites have fireplaces. The 14 rooftop suites are the most luxurious and include Continental breakfast and private concierge services; there's also an exercise room, garden, and outdoor hot tub there. La Plazuela Restaurant, with its hand-painted glass tiles, serves good and creative Southwestern food. Folk and R&B bands rotate nightly in the bar. **Pros:** great building and location; steeped in history. **Cons:** for the price, facilities don't stand up to comparison with other Downtown properties. ✉ *100 E. San Francisco St.* ☎ *505/982–5511 or 800/523–5002* ⊕ *www.lafondasantafe.com* ⤢ *143 rooms, 14 suites* ⚒ *In-room: a/c, Wi-Fi. In-hotel: restaurant, bars, pool, gym, laundry service, parking (paid)* ⊟ *AE, D, DC, MC, V* ✛ *B4.*

EAST SIDE AND CANYON ROAD

Use the coordinate (✛ A1) at the end of each listing to locate a site on the corresponding map.

$$$ ⚏ **Alexander's Inn.** Once a bed-and-breakfast, Alexander's now rents two
COTTAGES   two-story cottages. It remains an excellent lodging option. Located just
★   a few blocks from the Plaza and Canyon Road, it exudes the charm of old Santa Fe. Cottages are cozy, with Southwest- and American country–style furnishings, ethnic heirlooms, skylights, tall windows, and fireplaces. Each has a kitchen, fireplace, full bathroom, and private bedroom upstairs. The grounds are dotted with tulips, hyacinths, lilac, and apricot trees. Guests receive discounts at the nearby Absolute Nirvana

Santa Fe: Spa Mecca of the Southwest

Santa Fe has established itself as a major spa destination. From day spas to resorts where you can spend days ensconced in beautiful surroundings with endless treatment options, there is a spa and a specialty for everyone in this town. There are spas at most of the better hotel resorts, but the spas listed here stand out for their highly trained therapists, specialized treatments, and overall experience.

Absolute Nirvana lives up to its name with its lush, peaceful Indo-Asian setting and the sumptuous treatments it offers. Master-level massage therapists use all-organic, delectable food-grade ingredients. Most treatments finish with home-made snacks and a rose-petal bath in a massive stone tub. Eco-friendly Nirvana is certified by the non-profit Green Spa Network. ⊠ Madeleine Inn, 106 Faithway St., The Plaza ☎ 505/983–7942 ⊕ www.absolutenirvana.com.

Body is a day spa just south of the Guadalupe District offering Thai, Swedish, and Japanese massage in addition to Rolfing, Reiki, and prenatal massage. Facials focus on rehydrating skin. A café, boutique, and child-care are on the premises. ⊠ 333 Cordova Rd. ☎ 505/986–0362 ⊕ www.bodyofsantafe.com.

La Posada Resort & Spa offers a wide range of treatments, many with regional ingredients, in this historic Downtown resort. Hair and nail services and a fitness center are also in the spa complex. ⊠ 330 E. Palace Ave., The Plaza ☎ 505/986–0000 ⊕ www.laposadadesantafe.com.

Spa Samadhi at Sunrise Springs Resort offers art-strewn walls and waterfalls, fruit and tea, and a profusion of treatments to move one's chi. Earthy cedar sauna and outdoor hot tubs are at your disposal. Transformative sessions, such as holographic and polarity therapies, sound healing, nutritional counseling, and lymphatic release are also available. This ecoresort unfolds over 70 green and serene acres, 15 mi southwest of Downtown Santa Fe. ⊠ 242 Los Piños Rd. ☎ 505/471–3600 ⊕ www.sunrisesprings.com.

Ten Thousand Waves is a renowned Japanese-style spa with outstanding facilities and treatments, 10 minutes north of Santa Fe toward the ski basin. Primarily a day spa—the hot tubs are a popular option—it has a limited number of suites available for longer stays. ⊠ 3451 Hyde Park Rd. ☎ 505/992–5025 ⊕ www.tenthousandwaves.com.

Spa (⇨ *"Santa Fe: Spa Mecca of the Southwest" box, above*) and full access to El Gancho Health Club, a 10-minute drive away. You'll find a generous welcome basket with wine and snacks, and attentive service. **Pros:** private, homey retreat in the heart of historic Santa Fe; an excellent value. **Cons:** shares open yard with private home. ⊠ 529 E. Palace Ave. ☎ 505/986–1431 or 888/321–5123 ⊕ www.alexanders-inn.com ⇱ 2 cottages ⚬ In-room: kitchen. In-hotel: Wi-Fi hotspot, parking (free), some pets allowed ⊟ D, MC, V ¦◯¦ CP ⊹ CS.

$$$
INN
Fodor's Choice
★

Hacienda Nicholas. It is rare to find classic Santa Fe accommodations—this actually *is* an old hacienda—blocks from the Plaza for reasonable prices. This is one such place. The thick adobe walls surrounding the building create a peace and solitude that belies its central location. Southwest decor mixes with French country and Mexican details to create an ambience perfectly suited to this city. Homemade, organic breakfasts are deluxe; afternoon snacks will leave you begging for the recipes (which they'll cheerfully provide). The rooms are extremely comfortable and quiet, with details like plush comforters and sheets, and cozy robes. Several rooms open on to the interior courtyard, which has a kiva fireplace and offers a perfect respite after a long day of exploring. This is a real find. **Pros:** rates are significantly lower than one would expect for the level of service and amenities here; the inn is one of the most eco-friendly in town. **Cons:** no hot tub or pool, though guests have privileges at El Gancho Health & Fitness Club 15 minutes away. ⊠ *320 E. Marcy St., The Plaza* ☎ *505/986–1431 or 888/284–3170* ⊕ *www.haciendanicholas.com* ⇆ *7 rooms* ♿ *In-rooms: Wi-Fi. In-hotel: Wi-Fi hotspot, parking (free)* ☱ *AE, D, MC, V* ✛ *B4.*

$$$
HOTEL
Fodor's Choice
★

Inn on the Alameda. Near the Plaza and Canyon Road is one of the Southwest's best small hotels. *Alameda* means "tree-lined lane," and this one perfectly complements the inn's location by the gurgling Santa Fe River. The adobe architecture and enclosed courtyards strewn with climbing rose vines combine a relaxed New Mexico country atmosphere with the luxury and amenities of a top-notch hotel, from afternoon wine and cheese to free local and toll-free calls to triple-sheeted beds with luxurious Egyptian cotton bedding. Rooms have a Southwestern color scheme, handmade armoires and headboards, and ceramic lamps and tiles—many have patios and kiva fireplaces. **Pros:** the solicitous staff is first-rate; excellent, expansive breakfast buffet with lots of extras. **Cons:** rooms closest to Alameda can be noisy; no pool. ⊠ *303 E. Alameda St.* ☎ *505/984–2121 or 888/984–2121* ⊕ *www.innonthealameda.com* ⇆ *59 rooms, 10 suites* ♿ *In-room: a/c, refrigerator (some), Wi-Fi. In-hotel: bar, gym, laundry facilities, parking (free), some pets allowed* ☱ *AE, D, DC, MC, V* ¡◎¡ *CP* ✛ *C5.*

$$$$
HOTEL
☾

La Posada de Santa Fe Resort and Spa. Rooms on the beautiful, quiet grounds of this hotel vary, but extensive renovations have enhanced all rooms to a level of luxury befitting the steep rates. Many have fireplaces, all have flat-screen TVs, CD players, leather couches, marble bathrooms, and Navajo-inspired rugs. The main building contains a handful of luxurious, high-ceiling Victorian rooms. The property boasts excellent bar, spa, and common areas, including the fantastic contemporary restaurant Fuego *(⇨ Where to Eat, above)*, the casual Viga restaurant (which has indoor and outdoor seating), and the Staab House Lounge. Guests are offered numerous complimentary events throughout the week, like Margarita Monday, wine-and-cheese pairings on Wednesday, and chef's receptions on Friday. **Pros:** numerous amenities; two blocks from Plaza and similarly close to Canyon Road. **Cons:** resort can sometimes feel overrun with tour-bus crowds; $30 daily resort fee. ⊠ *330 E. Palace Ave.* ☎ *505/986–0000 or 866/331–7625* ⊕ *www.laposadadesantafe.com* ⇆ *120 rooms, 39 suites* ♿ *In-room: a/c, Wi-Fi.*

In-hotel: restaurant, bar, pool, gym, spa, parking (paid) ⊟ *AE, D, DC, MC, V* ⊕ *C4.*

$$ 🏨 **Madeleine Inn.** Santa Fe hasn't always been a town of pseudopueblo
INN buildings and this lovely Queen Anne Victorian is living proof. Built by
Fodor's Choice a railroad tycoon in 1886, this beautifully maintained B&B is nestled
★ amongst mature trees and gardens just four blocks from the Plaza.
Plush beds, lovely antiques and art adorn the rooms. Fireplaces grace
four rooms and the smells of freshly baked goodies welcome you in the
afternoon. Homemade organic breakfasts with too many options to list
here are worth sticking around for, and the staff is professional and gra-
cious. The amazing Absolute Nirvana spa is on the premises. Guests
have privileges to El Gancho Health & Tennis Club 15 minutes away.
Pros: excellent value; great service; eco-friendly. **Cons:** steep stairs; no
elevators in this three-story Victorian. ⊠ *106 Faithway St., The Plaza*
☎ *505/982–3465 or 888/877–7622* ⊕ *www.madeleineinn.com* ↘*7
rooms* ⚑ *In-hotel: Wi-Fi hotspot, parking (free)* ⊟ *AE, D, MC, V* ⊕ *B5.*

OLD SANTA FE AND SOUTH CAPITOL

*Use the coordinate (⊕ A1) at the end of each listing to locate a site on
the corresponding map.*

$$ 🏨 **Don Gaspar Inn.** One of the city's best-kept secrets, this exquisitely
INN landscaped and attractively decorated compound is on a pretty resi-
dential street a few blocks south of the Plaza. Its three historic houses
have three distinct architectural styles: Arts and Crafts, Pueblo Revival,
and Territorial. Floral gardens and aspen and cottonwood trees shade
the tranquil paths and terraces, and both Southwest and Native American paintings and handmade furnishings enliven the sunny rooms and
suites. The Arts and Crafts main house has two fireplaces, two bedrooms, and a fully equipped kitchen. Staff is attentive without hovering.
Considering the setting and amenities, it's a great value. **Pros:** beautiful
decor; delicious and generous breakfasts; lush gardens. **Cons:** some
rooms close to elementary school can be noisy in the morning when
school is in. ⊠ *623 Don Gaspar Ave.* ☎ *505/986–8664 or 888/986–
8664* ⊕ *www.dongaspar.com* ↘*4 rooms, 3 suites, 2 casitas, 1 house*
⚑ *In-room: kitchen (some), refrigerator, Wi-Fi. In-hotel: parking (free)*
⊟ *MC, V* ⊙*BP* ⊕ *D3.*

$$$ 🏨 **El Farolito.** All the beautiful Southwestern and Mexican furniture in
INN this small, upscale compound is custom-made, and all the art and pho-
tography original. Rooms are spacious and pleasant with fireplaces and
separate entrances; some are in their own little buildings. El Farolito has
a peaceful Downtown location, just steps from the capitol and a few
blocks from the Plaza. The same owners run the smaller Four Kachinas
inn, which is close by and has one handicapped-accessible room (rare
among smaller Santa Fe properties). The breakfast here is a real treat,
featuring a tempting range of delicious baked goods. **Pros:** attentive ser-
vice; special dietary requests accommodated. **Cons:** no on-site pool or
hot tub. ⊠ *514 Galisteo St.* ☎ *505/988–1631 or 888/634–8782* ⊕ *www.
farolito.com* ↘*7 rooms, 1 suite* ⚑ *In-room: a/c, Wi-Fi. In-hotel: park-
ing (free)* ⊟ *AE, D, MC, V* ⊙*BP* ⊕ *D2.*

$ ⛣**Garrett's Desert Inn.** This sprawling, U-shaped motel may surround a
MOTEL parking lot and offer relatively little in the way of ambience, but it's
fairly well maintained and you can't beat its location just a few blocks
from the Plaza, smack in the middle of historic Barrio de Analco. The
clean, no-frills rooms are done in earthy tones with a smattering of
Southwest touches, and there's a pleasant pool and patio as well. **Pros:**
The restaurant, Ze French Bistro, offers delicious French food with chef
Laurent Rea at the helm. **Cons:** $8 per night parking fee; not much curb
appeal. ⊠ *311 Old Santa Fe Trail* ☎ *505/982–1851 or 800/888–2145*
⊕ *www.garrettsdesertinn.com* ↪ *83 rooms* ⚬ *In-room: a/c, Wi-Fi. In-
hotel: restaurant, pool, gym, laundry facilities, parking (paid)* ▤ *AE,
D, MC, V* ✛ *C4.*

$$$$ ⛣**Inn of the Five Graces.** There isn't another property in Santa Fe to
HOTEL compare to this sumptuous yet relaxed inn with an unmistakable East-
Fodor'sChoice meets-West feel. The management and staff at this Relais & Chateaux
★ hotel have created a property that fits right in with the kind of memorable properties you hear about in Morocco and Bali. The decor differs
from the cliché Santa Fe style, yet locals would tell you that this melding
of styles is what true Santa Fe style is all about. The suites have Asian
and Latin American antiques and art, kilim rugs, jewel-tone throw pillows, and mosaic-tile bathrooms; most have fireplaces, and many have
soaking tubs or walk-in steam showers. The personal service stands out:
treats are left on your pillow, refrigerators are stocked, and afternoon
margarita and wine-and-cheese spreads, an exquisite breakfast, and
even daily walking tours are all available. A new spa treatment room
has been added with several luxe treatments to salve the skin from
the high, dry mountain climate. Management continues to improve
the gardens and outdoor areas, with more lush, flowering plants, gurgling fountains and cozy nooks to relax into. **Pros:** tucked into a quiet,
ancient neighborhood; the Plaza is only minutes away; fantastic staff,
attentive but not overbearing. **Cons:** very steep rates. ⊠ *150 E. DeVargas St.* ☎ *505/992–0957 or 866/992–0957* ⊕ *www.fivegraces.com* ↪ *22
suites 1 house* ⚬ *In-room: kitchen (some), refrigerator, Wi-Fi. In-hotel:
parking (free), some pets allowed* ▤ *AE, D, MC, V* ⎮◉⎮ *BP* ✛ *C3.*

$$ ⛣**Inn of the Turquoise Bear.** In the 1920s, poet Witter Bynner played host
INN to an eccentric circle of artists and intellectuals, as well as some wild
Fodor'sChoice parties in his mid-19th-century Spanish–Pueblo Revival home, which
★ is now a bed-and-breakfast. Rooms are simple, traditional Southwest-
ern style with heavy wood furniture and plush linens. The inn's style
preserves the building's historic integrity, starting with the ranchlike
lobby and extending throughout the rambling ambience-thick public
rooms. You might sleep in the room where D.H. Lawrence or Willa
Cather slept, or perhaps in Robert Oppenheimer's room. The lush, ter-
raced flower gardens provide plenty of places to repose away from the
traffic on Old Santa Fe Trail, which borders the property. This is the
quintessential Santa Fe inn. **Pros:** gorgeous grounds and a house steeped
in local history; gracious, knowledgeable staff; generous Continental
breakfasts. **Cons:** no pool or hot tub on-site; quirky layout of some
rooms isn't for everyone. ⊠ *342 E. Buena Vista* ☎ *505/983–0798 or
800/396–4104* ⊕ *www.turquoisebear.com* ↪ *8 rooms, 2 with shared*

bath; 3 suites ♿ *In-room: Wi-Fi. In-hotel: parking (free), some pets allowed* ▤ *AE, D, MC, V* ⦿ *CP* ⊹ *D3.*

$$ 🏠 **Pueblo Bonito B&B Inn.** Rooms in this 1873 adobe compound have

BED AND handmade and hand-painted furnishings, Navajo weavings, brick and

BREAKFAST hardwood floors, sand paintings and pottery, locally carved santos (Catholic saints), and Western art. All have kiva fireplaces and private entrances, and many have kitchens. A breakfast buffet is served in the convivial main dining room with lots of fresh fruits and yogurt, baked goods, cereals, coffee and teas. Afternoon tea also offers complimentary margaritas. The Plaza is a five-minute walk away. **Pros:** intimate, cozy inn on peaceful grounds; hot tub. **Cons:** bathrooms tend to be small; breakfast is Continental. ✉ *138 W. Manhattan Ave.* ☎ *505/984–8001 or 800/461–4599* ⊕ *www.pueblobonitoinn.com* ⤵ *13 rooms, 5 suites* ♿ *In-room: kitchen (some), refrigerator (some), Wi-Fi. In-hotel: restaurant, laundry facilities, parking (free)* ▤ *AE, DC, MC, V* ⦿ *CP* ⊹ *D3.*

RAILYARD DISTRICT

Use the coordinate (⊹ A1) at the end of each listing to locate a site on the corresponding map.

$$ 🏨 **Hotel Santa Fe.** Picurís Pueblo has controlling interest in this hand-

HOTEL some Pueblo-style three-story hotel on the Railyard District's edge and

Fodor's Choice a short walk from the Plaza. The light, airy rooms and suites are tradi-

★ tional Southwestern, with locally handmade furniture, wooden blinds, and Pueblo paintings; many have balconies. The hotel gift shop, Santa Fe's only tribally owned store, has lower prices than many nearby retail stores. The 35 rooms and suites in the posh Hacienda wing have corner fireplaces and the use of a London-trained butler. Amaya is one of the better hotel restaurants in town. Informal talks about Native American history and culture are held in the lobby, and Native American dances take place May through October. **Pros:** professional, helpful staff; lots of amenities. **Cons:** standard rooms are fairly small. ✉ *1501 Paseo de Peralta* ☎ *505/982–1200 or 800/825–9876* ⊕ *www.hotelsantafe.com* ⤵ *40 rooms, 91 suites* ♿ *In-room: a/c, Wi-Fi. In-hotel: restaurant, bar, pool, laundry service, parking (free)* ▤ *AE, D, DC, MC, V* ⊹ *D2.*

$$ 🏨 **Old Santa Fe Inn.** This contemporary motor-court-style inn looks like

HOTEL an attractive, if fairly ordinary, adobe motel, but it has stunning and

★ spotless rooms with elegant Southwestern furnishings. Tile baths, high-quality linens, and upscale furnishings fill every room, along with two phone lines and CD stereos; many have kiva fireplaces, or balconies and patios. A small business center and gym are open 24 hours. Most rooms open onto a gravel courtyard parking lot, although chile *ristras* hanging outside each unit brighten things up. The make-your-own-breakfast-burrito buffet is a nice touch. **Pros:** rooms are more inviting than several more-expensive Downtown hotels and it's a short walk to the Plaza; some rooms have Jacuzzi tubs. **Cons:** minimal, though friendly and professional, staffing. ✉ *320 Galisteo St.* ☎ *505/995–0800 or 800/745–9910* ⊕ *www.oldsantafeinn.com* ⤵ *34 rooms, 9 suites* ♿ *In-room: a/c, refrigerator (some), Wi-Fi. In-hotel: gym, parking (free)* ▤ *AE, D, DC, MC, V* ⦿ *CP* ⊹ *C2.*

$ 🏨 **Santa Fe Sage Inn.** On the southern edge of the Railyard District,
MOTEL this smartly renovated motel offers affordable comfort and surprisingly
☺ attractive (given the low rates) Southwestern decor within walking dis-
★ tance of the Plaza (six blocks). Special packages are available for three-
and four-day stays during peak-season events. Get a room upstairs and
in one of the rear buildings for the most privacy and quiet. Continental
breakfast is included. **Pros:** comfortable; affordable; close to Plaza and
train station. **Cons:** rooms on corner of Cerrillos and Don Diego can be
noisy. ⊠ *725 Cerrillos Rd.* ☎ *505/982–5952 or 866/433–0335* ⊕ *www.
santafesageinn.com* ⤴ *156 rooms* ☖ *In-room: a/c, Wi-Fi. In-hotel: gym,
pool, laundry facilities, parking (free), some pets allowed* ⊟ *AE, DC,
MC, V* ⦿ *CP* ⊹ *D1.*

WEST OF PLAZA

*Use the coordinate (⊹ A1) at the end of each listing to locate a site on
the corresponding map.*

$$$ 🏨 **Las Palomas.** It's a pleasant 10-minute walk west of the Plaza to reach
VACATION this group of properties, consisting of two historic, luxurious com-
COTTAGES pounds, one of them Spanish Pueblo–style adobe, the other done in the
Territorial style, with a Victorian ambience, as well as the 15 rooms in
the recently acquired La Tienda & Duran House compound. A network
of brick paths shaded by mature trees leads past the casitas, connect-
ing them with secluded courtyards and flower gardens. Each casita has
a bedroom, full kitchen, living room with pull-out sofa, and fireplace,
and each opens onto a terrace or patio. Locally handcrafted wood-and-
leather sofas, desks, and tables fill these spacious accommodations,
along with Native American artwork and sculptures. It's an elegant
alternative to the city's upscale full-service hotels, affording guests a
bit more privacy and the feel of a private cottage rental—though it is
managed by the Hotel Santa Fe. **Pros:** kid-friendly, with swings and a
play yard; on-site fitness center. **Cons:** big variation in accommodations;
no hot tub or pool on-site (guests may use pool at the Hotel Santa Fe).
⊠ *460 W. San Francisco St.* ☎ *505/982–5560 or 877/982–5560* ⊕ *www.
laspalomas.com* ⤴ *38 units* ☖ *In-room: kitchen, Wi-Fi. In-hotel: gym,
parking (free)* ⊟ *AE, D, DC, MC, V* ⦿ *CP* ⊹ *B2.*

$$ 🏨 **Water Street Inn.** The large rooms in this restored adobe 2½ blocks
INN from the Plaza are decorated with reed shutters, antique pine beds,
viga-beam ceilings, hand-stenciled artwork, and a blend of cowboy, Hispanic, and Native American art and artifacts. Most have fireplaces, and
all have flat-screen TVs with DVD players and CD stereos. Afternoon
hors d'oeuvres are served in the living room; breakfasts are ample and
tasty. A patio deck is available for relaxing. Many of the guests here
return year after year. **Pros:** elegant décor; gracious, noteworthy staff.
Cons: grounds are restricted—the inn overlooks a parking lot. ⊠ *427 W.
Water St.* ☎ *505/984–1193 or 800/646–6752* ⊕ *www.waterstreetinn.
com* ⤴ *8 rooms, 4 suites* ☖ *In-room: a/c, DVD, Wi-Fi. In-hotel: parking (free)* ⊟ *AE, DC, MC, V* ⦿ *BP* ⊹ *B2.*

SOUTH SIDE

Use the coordinate (✛ A1) at the end of each listing to locate a site on the corresponding map.

$ ⊞ **El Rey Inn.** The kind of place where Lucy and Ricky might have stayed
HOTEL   during one of their cross-country adventures, the El Rey was built in
Fodor's Choice   1936 but has been brought gracefully into the 21st century, its rooms
★   and bathrooms handsomely updated without losing any period charm.
☾   Rooms are individually decorated and might include antique television armoires, beamed ceilings, upholstered wing chairs and sofas; some have kitchenettes. Each unit has a small covered front patio with wrought-iron chairs. Beautifully landscaped grounds are covered with flowers in the summer and towering trees shade the parking lot. There's a landscaped courtyard with tables and chairs by the pool. **Pros:** excellent price for a distinctive, charming property. **Cons:** rooms closest to Cerrillos can be noisy; some rooms are quite dark. ✉ *1862 Cerrillos Rd.* ☎ *505/982–1931 or 800/521–1349* ⊕ *www.elreyinnsantafe.com* ⇆ *86 rooms* ⚷ *In-room: a/c, kitchen (some), Wi-Fi. In-hotel: pool, gym, laundry facilities, parking (free)* ▭ *AE, DC, MC, V* ⏣|*CP* ✛ *C5.*

$$$ ⊞ **Residence Inn.** This compound consists of clusters of three-story adobe
TOWN HOUSES   town houses with pitched roofs and tall chimneys. Best bets for families or up to four adults traveling together are the one-room suites, which each have a loft bedroom and a separate sitting area (with a curtain divider) that has a Murphy bed. All units have wood-burning fireplaces. It's right off a major intersection about 3 mi south of the Plaza, but it's set back far enough so that there's no traffic noise. Ask for one of the second-floor end units for the best mountain views. **Pros:** complimentary full breakfast; evening socials; grocery-shopping service. **Cons:** not within easy walking distance of many restaurants or attractions. ✉ *1698 Galisteo St.* ☎ *505/988–7300 or 800/331–3131* ⊕ *www.marriott.com/ safnm* ⇆ *120 suites* ⚷ *In-room: a/c, kitchen, Internet. In-hotel: pool, gym, laundry facilities, Wi-Fi hotspot, parking (free)* ▭ *AE, D, DC, MC, V* ⏣|*BP* ✛ *E5.*

$$ ⊞ **Santa Fe Courtyard by Marriott.** Of the dozens of chain properties along
HOTEL   prosaic Cerrillos Road, this is the only bona fide gem, even though it looks like all the others: clad in faux adobe and surrounded by parking lots and strip malls. Don't fret—it's easy to forget about the nondescript setting once inside this polished miniature resort, which comprises several buildings set around a warren of lushly landscaped interior courtyards. Aesthetically, the rooms look Southwestern, with chunky carved-wood armoires, desks, and headboards reminiscent of a Spanish-colonial hacienda. **Pros:** rooms have the usual upscale-chain doodads: mini-refrigerators, coffeemakers, hair dryers, and clock radios. **Cons:** hotel lacks character; Cerrillos Road is unattractive; a 10-minute drive from Plaza. ✉ *3347 Cerrillos Rd.* ☎ *505/473–2800 or 800/777–3347* ⊕ *www.santafecourtyard.com* ⇆ *209 rooms* ⚷ *In-room: a/c, refrigerator, Wi-Fi. In-hotel: restaurant, room service, bar, pool, gym, laundry facilities, parking (free)* ▭ *AE, D, DC, MC, V* ✛ *A5.*

¢   ⊞ **Silver Saddle Motel.** This low-slung adobe property transcends the gen-
MOTEL   erally sketchy quality of the several other budget motels along Cerrillos
★   Road, thanks to the tireless efforts of a new owner. There's a kitschy,

Western aspect to the place—rooms are named for icons of the West (Annie Oakley, Wyatt Earp) and contain related plaques with colorful biographies and local cowboy art. Furnishings are decidedly Southwest: Mexican-tile bathrooms, serape tapestries, built-in bancos, and *equipale* chairs ("seat of the gods" made of woven wood and leather) are present in most. Recent improvements include new carpets, mattresses, a breakfast patio, and a big dose of general TLC. The popular home-furnishings and gift emporium, Jackalope, is next door. The motel is across the street from the town's one strip club, which could be either a pro or a con. **Pros:** superaffordable; good-sized rooms, some with refrigerators; friendly, helpful staff. **Cons:** rooms toward the front get noise from Cerrillos Boulevard; fairly basic. ✉ *2810 Cerrillos Rd.* ☎ *505/471–7663* ⊕ *www.santafesilversaddlemotel.com* ⤴ *27 rooms* ⚬ *In-room: a/c, kitchen (some), Wi-fi. In-hotel: parking (free)* ▭ *D, MC, V* ⍥ *CP* ✛ *A5.*

OLD LAS VEGAS HIGHWAY

Use the coordinate (✛ A1) at the end of each listing to locate a site on the corresponding map.

$ 🏨 **Bobcat Inn.** A delightful, affordable, country hacienda that's a 15-minute drive southeast of the Plaza, this adobe bed-and-breakfast sits amid 10 secluded acres of piñon and ponderosa pine, with grand views of the Ortiz Mountains and the area's high-desert mesas. John and Amy Bobrick run this low-key retreat and prepare expansive full breakfasts as well as high tea on Saturday during the summer high season (these are by reservation only). Arts and Crafts furniture and Southwest pottery fill the common room, in which breakfast is served and guests can relax throughout the day. The individually decorated rooms are brightened by Talavera tiles, folk art, and colorful blankets and rugs; some have kiva fireplaces. The Lodge Room is outfitted with handcrafted Adirondack furniture, and its bathroom has a whirlpool tub. Guests have access to El Gancho Health & Fitness center (fee) nearby. **Pros:** gracious, secluded inn; wonderful hosts. **Cons:** located outside town, and a drive is required for all activities except eating at Bobcat Bite, which is right next door; no pets; no children under age six. ✉ *442 Old Las Vegas Hwy.* ☎ *505/988–9239* ⊕ *www.nm-inn.com* ⤴ *5 rooms* ⚬ *In-room: no TV, Wi-fi. In-hotel: parking (free), no kids under 6* ▭ *D, MC, V* ⍥ *BP* ✛ *F6.*

INN
★

NORTH SIDE

Use the coordinate (✛ A1) at the end of each listing to locate a site on the corresponding map.

$$$ 🏨 **Bishop's Lodge Resort and Spa.** Although this historic resort is just a five-minute drive from the Plaza, its setting in a bucolic valley at the foot of the Sangre de Cristo Mountains makes it feel worlds apart. Outdoor activities abound including hiking, horseback riding, skeet shooting, tennis (professional lessons available) and trapshooting. History runs deep here with the nearly 150-year-old chapel built by Archbishop

RESORT
☾

Jean Baptiste Lamy—a figure lionized by writer Willa Cather—at the resort's center. Rooms have antique and reproduction Southwestern furnishings—shipping chests, Mexican tinwork, and Native American and Western art. Many offer balconies or patios with spectacular mountain vistas. The Las Fuentes Restaurant & Bar specializes in inventive Nuevo Latino fare, and the kitchen uses produce and herbs from the property's heritage garden. Recently, they've replanted the vineyard with vines descended from those brought to America by Bishop Lamy and intend soon to produce wine. Locals often descend on the excellent Sunday brunch. The tranquil ShàNah Spa and the beautiful grounds make this place a special getaway only minutes from Downtown. **Pros:** staff is friendly and well-trained. **Cons:** resort is spread out over 700 acres and some rooms seem rather far-flung. ⊠ *Bishop's Lodge Rd., 2½ mi north of Downtown* ☎ *505/983–6377 or 800/419–0492* ⊕ *www. bishopslodge.com* ⟿ *91 rooms, 12 suites 7 villas* ⟲ *In-room: a/c, refrigerator, Internet. In-hotel: 2 restaurants (one open in summer only), bar, tennis courts, pool, gym, spa, children's programs (ages 5–13), parking (free)* ⊟ *AE, D, MC, V* ⊹ *G1.*

$$$$
RESORT

⌖ **Encantado.** Sister to California's famed Auberge du Soleil and Cabo's Esperanza Resort, Encantado provides over-the-top luxury while respecting the region's distinct architectural style. Taking advantage of Santa Fe's endless supply of sunshine, villa-style casitas are contemporary, airy, and earthy. Kitted with adobe fireplaces, deep soaking tubs, heated bathroom floors and spacious dressing areas, rooms exemplify comfortable cushiness. Local products in the minibar (Cap Rock Organic Grape Vodka and C. G. Higgins Caramel Corn) are a thoughtful touch. Detox at the spa with regionally inspired treatments like Mountain Spirit Purification, or take a Pilates class in the movement studio before enjoying a sunset cocktail at the bar and a sumptuous globe-spanning culinary adventure at the restaurant, Terra. Complimentary shuttles run regularly into town and guests have access to Encantado's Downtown concierge center. **Pros:** freestanding couples spa suites; complimentary minibar (nonalcoholic beverages only); stunning rooms. **Cons:** several of the private terraces overlook parking lots; service, though friendly and eager, doesn't always live up to expectation; remote location. ⊠ *198 NM 592* ☎ *877/262–4666* ⊕ *www.encantadoresort. com* ⟿ *65 rooms* ⟲ *In-room: a/c, safe, refrigerator, DVD, Wi-Fi. In-hotel: restaurant, room service, bar, pool, gym, spa, laundry service, Wi-Fi hotspot, parking (free), some pets allowed* ⊟ *AE, MC, V* ⊹ *G1.*

$$
HOTEL

⌖ **Lodge at Santa Fe.** Rooms at this midprice property have pleasant Southwestern furnishings and earth-tone fabrics, though some of the furnishings and facilities are showing wear. The hilltop location offers spectacular views east toward the Sangre de Cristo Mountains and south toward the Sandias—but only from certain rooms, so ask when reserving. The Plaza is a five-minute drive (they offer free shuttle service), the Santa Fe Opera just a bit farther. Las Mañanitas restaurant serves decent Spanish and Southwestern fare, and the adjacent cabaret is home in summer to flamenco dancer Maria Benitez's troupe. **Pros:** guests have free access to the Santa Fe Spa health club next door, away from the crowds and noise of the Plaza. **Cons:** service is sometimes lackluster; no restaurants or attractions within walking distance. ✉ *750 N. St. Francis Dr.* ☎ *505/992–5800 or 888/563–4373* ⊕ *www.hhandr. com* ➯ *103 rooms, 25 suites* ⅃ *In-room: a/c, Wi-Fi. In-hotel: restaurant, room service, bar, pool, parking (free)* ☲ *AE, D, DC, MC, V* ✛ *A1.*

$$$
COTTAGES
Fodor'sChoice
★

🖭 **Ten Thousand Waves.** Devotees appreciate the authentic *onsen* (Japanese-style baths)atmosphere of this health spa and small hotel a few miles northeast of town. Twelve light and airy hillside cottages are settled down a piñon-covered hill below the first-rate spa, which is tremendously popular with day visitors. The sleek, uncluttered accommodations have marble or stone wood-burning fireplaces, CD stereos, fine woodwork, low-slung beds or futons, and courtyards or patios; two come with full kitchens. There's also a cozy, vintage Airstream Bambi trailer available at much lower rates ($139 nightly)—with its ultramod interior, it's a kitschy, fun alternative to the much pricier cottages. The facility has private and communal indoor and outdoor hot tubs and spa treatments. Overnight guests can use the communal tubs for free. The snack bar serves sushi and other healthful treats. Ask about the Japanese movie nights. **Pros:** artful furnishings; peaceful setting; warm service. **Cons:** a bit remote, especially considering lack of a restaurant. ✉ *3451 Hyde Park Rd., 4 mi northeast of the Plaza* ⅅ *Box 10200, 87504* ☎ *505/982–9304* ⊕ *www.tenthousandwaves.com* ➯ *12 cottages, 1 trailer* ⅃ *In-room: no a/c, kitchen (some), refrigerator, no TV (some), Wi-Fi (some). In-hotel: spa, parking (free), some pets allowed* ☲ *D, MC, V* ✛ *H2.*

NIGHTLIFE AND THE ARTS

Few, if any, small cities in America can claim an arts scene as thriving as Santa Fe's—with opera, symphony, and theater in splendid abundance. The music acts here tend to be high-caliber, but rather sporadic. Nightlife, as in dance clubs, is considered fairly "bleak." When popular acts come to town the whole community shows up and dances like there's no tomorrow. A super, seven-week series of music on the Plaza bandstand runs through the summer with performances four nights a week. Gallery openings, poetry readings, plays, and dance concerts take place year-round, not to mention the famed opera and chamber-music festivals. Check the arts and entertainment listings in Santa Fe's daily newspaper, the *New Mexican* (⊕ *www.santafenewmexican.com*), particularly on Friday, when the arts and entertainment section, "Pasatiempo," is included, or check the weekly *Santa Fe Reporter* (⊕ *www. sfreporter.com*) for shows and events. As you suspect by now, activities peak in the summer.

NIGHTLIFE

Culturally endowed though it is, Santa Fe has a pretty mellow nightlife scene; its key strength is live music, which is presented at numerous bars, hotel lounges, and restaurants. Austin-based blues and country groups and other acts wander into town, and members of blockbuster bands have been known to perform unannounced at small clubs while vacationing in the area. But on most nights your best bet might be quiet cocktails beside the flickering embers of a piñon fire or under the stars out on the patio.

BARS AND LOUNGES

Corazón (⊠ *401 S. Guadalupe St., Railyard District* ☎ *505/983–4559* ⊕ *www.corazonsantafe.com*) has reinvented a well-known space in the Railyard District with great success. Depending on the night, it's hard to predict whether you'll be shaking your booty to hip-hop, poundin' blues, rock music, or sweet Americana. The local veterans of the music and bar scene who created Corazón book varied lineups in this often-packed space, which serves satisfying pub grub, too.

★ **The Cowgirl** (⊠ *319 S. Guadalupe St., Railyard District* ☎ *505/982–2565*) is one of the most popular spots in town for live blues, country, rock, folk, and even comedy, on occasion. The bar is friendly and the $3.50 happy hour margaritas provide a lot of bang for the buck. The pool hall is fun and can get wild as the night gets late.

Dragon Room (⊠ *406 Old Santa Fe Trail, Old Santa Fe Trail and South Capitol* ☎ *505/983–7712*), at the Pink Adobe restaurant *(⇨ Where to Eat, above)*, long a hot spot in town, has been tidied up and, consequently, it's no longer the fun, lively destination for colorful locals and curious tourists. Good drinks and bar food, though.

Eldorado Court and Lounge (⊠ *309 W. San Francisco St., The Plaza* ☎ *505/988–4455*), in the lobby of the classy Eldorado Hotel, is a gracious lounge where classical guitarists and pianists perform nightly. It has the largest wines-by-the-glass list in town.

★ **El Farol** (⊠ *808 Canyon Rd., East Side and Canyon Road* ☎ *505/983–9912*), with its big front porch, is a particularly choice spot to enjoy the afternoon and evenings of summer. The roomy, rustic bar has a true Old West atmosphere—there's been a bar on the premises since 1835—and you can order some fine Spanish brandies and sherries in addition to cold beers and tasty mixed drinks (particularly those margaritas locals are so fond of). It's a great place to see a variety of music; the dance floor fills up with a friendly crowd.

Evangelo's (⊠ *200 W. San Francisco St., The Plaza* ☎ *505/982–9014*) is an old-fashioned, street-side bar, with pool tables downstairs, 200 types of imported beer, and rock bands on many weekends.

Matador (⊠ *116 W. San Francisco St., Suite 113, enter downstairs on Galisteo St., The Plaza* ☎ *No phone*) is a dark, subterranean dive bar close to the Plaza. Owners Frank and César, both entertaining characters, have banished any notions of Southwest-style decor by painting the place black and covering the walls with old punk posters, and locals love it. You'll find a decent selection of beers, stiff mixed drinks, and some fine tequilas (this is Santa Fe, after all). The early crowd is older, and gets younger and hipper as the night goes on.

Milagro 139 (⊠ *139 W. San Francisco St., The Plaza* ☎ *505/995–0139* ⊕ *www.milagro139.com*) draws a friendly, mixed-age crowd thanks to great DJs on Friday and Saturday nights. It's one of the liveliest dance spots in town.

Fodor's Choice   **Secreto Lounge** (✉ *210 Don Gaspar Ave., The Plaza* ☎ *505/983–5700*
★   ⊕ *www.hotelstfrancis.com*) is the beautifully redesigned bar inside the
dramatically renovated Hotel St. Francis. Bar staff here make the best
and most interesting drinks in town, including a classic Manhattan with
clove tincture spritzed over the top. When the weather is good, try to
get a seat on the portal out front.

Santa Fe Brewing Company (✉ *35 Fire Pl., on NM 14, the Turquoise
Trail, South Side* ☎ *505/424–3333* ⊕ *www.santafebrewing.com*) hosts
all sorts of music and serves fine microbrews and food (and Taos's
Cow ice cream!) from its location about 15 minutes south of the Plaza.
Recent acts have included the BoDeans, Sierra Leone's Refugee All
Stars, Delbert McClinton, and local stars Hundred-Year Flood and
Goshen. Very kid-friendly, the venue has an indoor room for the cold
months, and a great outdoor stage where the performers, and the sun-
set, are on full view.

Second Street Brewery (✉ *1814 2nd St., South Side* ☎ *505/982–3030*
✉ *1607 Paseo de Peralta, beside farmers' market building, Railyard
District* ☎ *505/989–3278*) packs in an eclectic, easygoing bunch for its
own microbrewed ales, pub fare, live rock, folk, and some great local
DJs. There's an expansive patio at the original 2nd Street location, and
the staff is friendly. A newer branch opened in the Railyard District,
steps from the train station, in 2009.

Tin Star Saloon (✉ *411B W. Water St., near West of the Plaza* ☎ *505/984–
5050* ⊕ *www.tinstarsaloon.com*) is a welcome addition to Santa Fe's
nightlife, with a great bar in a cozy room and live music almost every
night. They book a wide range of music, from hard rock to R&B. The
crowd here likes to dance.

Tiny's (✉ *Cerrillos Rd. and St. Francis Dr., South Side* ☎ *505/983–9817*),
a retro-fabulous restaurant serving steaks and New Mexican fare, is a
legend in this town with politicos, reporters, and deal makers. The real
draw is the kitsch-filled '50s cocktail lounge.

THE ARTS

The performing arts scene in Santa Fe blossoms in summer when the
calendar is filled with classical or jazz concerts, Shakespeare on the
grounds of St. John's campus, experimental theater at Santa Fe Stages,
or flamenco. . . . "Too many choices!" is the biggest complaint. The
rest of the year is a bit quieter, but an increasing number of off-season
venues have developed in recent years. The "Pasatiempo" section of
the *Santa Fe New Mexican*'s Friday edition or the *Santa Fe Reporter*,
released on Wednesday, are great sources for current happenings.

The city's most interesting multiuse arts venue, the **Center for Contemporary Arts (CCA)** (✉ *1050 Old Pecos Trail, Old Santa Fe Trail and South
Capitol* ☎ *505/982–1338* ⊕ *www.ccasantafe.org*) presents indie and
foreign films, art exhibitions, provocative theater, and countless workshops and lectures.

CONCERT VENUES

Santa Fe's vintage Downtown movie house was fully restored and converted into the 850-seat **Lensic Performing Arts Center** (✉ *211 W. San Francisco St., The Plaza* ☎ *505/988–1234* ⊕ *www.lensic.com*) in 2001. The grand 1931 building, with Moorish and Spanish Renaissance influences, hosts the Santa Fe Symphony, theater, classic films, lectures and readings, noted world, pop, and jazz musicians, and many other noteworthy events.

The **St. Francis Auditorium** (✉ *Museum of Fine Arts,107 W. Palace Ave., northwest corner of the Plaza*) is the scene of cultural events such as theatrical productions and varied musical performances.

MUSIC

★ The acclaimed **Santa Fe Chamber Music Festival** (☎ *505/983–2075* ⊕ *www. sfcmf.org*) runs mid-July through late August, with performances nearly every night at the St. Francis Auditorium, or, occasionally, the Lensic Performing Arts Center. There are also free youth-oriented concerts given on several summer mornings. You can also attend many rehearsals for free; call for times.

Performances by the **Santa Fe Desert Chorale** (☎ *505/988–2282 or 800/244–4011* ⊕ *www.desertchorale.org*) take place throughout the summer at a variety of intriguing venues, from the Cathedral Basilica St. Francis to Loretto Chapel. This highly regarded singing group, which was started in 1982, also performs a series of concerts during the December holiday season.

Fodor's Choice **Santa Fe Opera** (☎ *505/986–5900 or 800/280–4654* ⊕ *www.santa-feopera.org*) performs in a strikingly modern structure—a 2,126-seat,
★ indoor-outdoor amphitheater with excellent acoustics and sight lines. Carved into the natural curves of a hillside 7 mi north of the city on U.S. 285/84, the opera overlooks mountains, mesas, and sky. Add some of the most acclaimed singers, directors, conductors, musicians, designers, and composers from Europe and the United States, and you begin to understand the excitement that builds every June. The company, which celebrated its 65th anniversary in 2011, presents five works in repertory each summer—a blend of seasoned classics, neglected masterpieces, and world premieres. Many evenings sell out far in advance, but inexpensive standing-room tickets are often available on the day of the performance. A favorite pre-opera pastime is tailgating in the parking lot before the evening performance—many guests set up elaborate picnics of their own, but you can also preorder picnic meals ($32 per meal) by calling (☎ *505/983–2433*) 24 hours in advance; pick up your meal up to two hours before the show, at the Angel Food Catering kiosk on the west side of the parking lot. Or you can dine at the Preview Buffet, set up 2½ hours before each performance by the Guilds of the Santa Fe Opera. These meals include a large spread of very good food along with wine, held on the opera grounds. During dessert, a prominent local expert on opera gives a talk about the evening's performance. The Preview Buffet is by reservation only, by calling the opera box office number listed above, and the cost is $50 per person.

The **Santa Fe Symphony** (☎ *505/983–1414 or 800/480–1319* ⊕ *www. sf-symphony.org*) performs seven concerts each season (October to April) in the Lensic Performing Arts Center.

THEATER

Santa Fe Performing Arts (☎ *505/984–1370* ⊕ *www.sfperformingarts. org*), running since 1986, has become a local favorite for its professional productions and adult resident company as well as its commitment to outreach education in the schools and for community youth in its after-school programs. The theater is committed to developing new works; call or check the Web site for the current schedule.

The oldest extant theater company west of the Mississippi, the **Santa Fe Playhouse** (✉ *142 E. De Vargas St., Old Santa Fe Trail and South Capitol* ☎ *505/988–4262* ⊕ *www.santafeplayhouse.org*) occupies a converted 19th-century adobe stable and has been presenting an adventurous mix of avant-garde pieces, classical drama, and musical comedy since 1922. The Fiesta Melodrama—a spoof of the Santa Fe scene—runs late August to mid-September.

SHOPPING

Santa Fe has been a trading post for eons. Nearly a thousand years ago the great pueblos of the Chacoan civilizations were strategically located between the buffalo-hunting tribes of the Great Plains and the Indians of Mexico. Native Americans in New Mexico traded turquoise and other valuables with Indians from Mexico for metals, shells, parrots, and other exotic items. After the arrival of the Spanish and the West's subsequent development, Santa Fe became the place to exchange silver from Mexico and natural resources from New Mexico for manufactured goods, whiskey, and greenbacks from the United States. With the building of the railroad in 1880, Santa Fe had access to all kinds of manufactured goods as well as those unique to the region via the old trade routes.

The trading legacy remains, but now Downtown Santa Fe caters to those looking for handcrafted goods. Sure, T-shirt outlets and a few major retail clothing shops have moved in, but shopping in Santa Fe consists mostly of one-of-a-kind independent stores. Canyon Road, packed with art galleries, is the perfect place to find unique gifts and collectibles. The Downtown district, around the Plaza, has unusual gift shops, clothing, and shoe stores that range from theatrical to conventional, curio shops, and art galleries. The funky, revitalized Railyard District, less touristy than the Plaza, is on Downtown's southwest perimeter and includes the Sanbusco Market Center and the Design Center, both hubs of unique and wonderful boutiques.

ART GALLERIES

The following are only a few of the nearly 200 galleries in greater Santa Fe—with the best of representational, nonobjective, Native American, Latin American, cutting-edge, photographic, and soulful works that defy categorization. The Santa Fe Convention and Visitors Bureau (⇨ *Visitor Information, in the Santa Fe Planner, above*) has a more extensive listing. *The Collectors Guide to Santa Fe, Taos, and Albuquerque* is a good resource and is available in hotels and at some galleries, as well as on the Web at ⊕ *www.collectorsguide.com*. Check the "Pasatiempo" pullout in the *Santa Fe New Mexican* on Friday for a preview of gallery openings.

Fodor's Choice ★ **Andrew Smith Gallery** (✉ *122 Grant Ave., The Plaza* ☎ *505/984–1234* ⊕ *www.andrewsmithgallery.com*) is a significant photo gallery dealing in works by Edward S. Curtis and other 19th-century chroniclers of the American West. Other major figures are Ansel Adams, Edward Weston, O. Winston Link, Henri Cartier-Bresson, Eliot Porter, Laura Gilpin, Dorothea Lange, Alfred Stieglitz, Annie Liebovitz, and regional artists like Barbara Van Cleve.

Bellas Artes (✉ *653 Canyon Rd., East side andCanyon Road* ☎ *505/983–2745* ⊕ *www.bellasartesgallery.com*), a sophisticated gallery and sculpture garden, has a captivating collection of ceramics, paintings, photography, and sculptural work, and represents internationally renowned artists like Judy Pfaff, Phoebe Adams, and Olga de Amaral. The vanguard modernist work of sculptor Ruth Duckworth is also well-represented.

Charlotte Jackson Fine Art (✉ *554 S. Guadalupe St., Railyard District* ☎ *505/989–8688* ⊕ *www.charlottejackson.com*) focuses primarily on monochromatic "radical" painting and sculpture and is set in a fantastic, open space in a renovated Railyard warehouse. Many of the pieces here are large scale, with "drama" the guiding force. Florence Pierce, Joe Barnes, William Metcalf, Anne Cooper, and Joseph Marioni are among the artists producing minimalist works dealing with light and space.

Fodor's Choice ★ **evo Gallery** (✉ *554 S. Guadalupe St., Railyard District* ☎ *505/982–4610* ⊕ *www.evogallery.org*) is another gallery that affirms Santa Fe's reputation as a leading center of contemporary art. Powerhouse artists like Jenny Holzer, Ed Ruscha, Donald Judd, Jasper Johns, and Agnes Martin, as well as emerging artists, are represented in this huge space in the Guadalupe District.

Fodor's Choice ★ **Gerald Peters Gallery** (✉ *1011 Paseo de Peralta, East Side and Canyon Road* ☎ *505/954–5700* ⊕ *www.gpgallery.com*) is Santa Fe's leading gallery of American and European art from the 19th century to the present. It has works by Max Weber, Albert Bierstadt, the Taos Society, the New Mexico modernists, and Georgia O'Keeffe, as well as contemporary artists.

Fodor's Choice ★ **James Kelly Contemporary** (✉ *1601 Paseo de Peralta, Railyard District* ☎ *505/989–1601* ⊕ *www.jameskelly.com*) mounts sophisticated, high-caliber shows by international and regional artists, such as Johnnie Winona Ross, Nic Nicosia, Peter Sarkisian, Tom Joyce, and Sherrie Levine in a renovated warehouse directly across from SITE Santa Fe. James Kelly has been instrumental in transforming the Railyard District into Santa Fe's hub for contemporary art.

LewAllen Contemporary (✉ *129 W. Palace Ave., The Plaza* ☎ *505/988–8997* ⊕ *www.lewallencontemporary.com*) is a leading center for a variety of contemporary arts by both Southwestern and other acclaimed artists, among them Judy Chicago and Janet Fish; sculpture, photography, ceramics, basketry, and painting are all shown in this dynamic space near the Plaza.

Fodor's Choice ★ **Linda Durham Contemporary Art** (✉ *1807 2nd St., No. 1107, South Side* ☎ *505/466–6600* ⊕ *www.lindadurham.com*) has showcased paintings, sculpture and photography of, primarily, New Mexico–based artists. This community-minded gallery has become well-regarded and its artists highly sought. The new space is bright and open, better suited to the myriad works held within.

Monroe Gallery (✉ *112 Don Gaspar Ave., The Plaza* ☎ *505/992–0800* ⊕ *www.monroegallery.com*) showcases works by the most celebrated black-and-white photographers of the 20th century, from Margaret Bourke-White to Alfred Eisenstaedt. The focus is on humanist and photojournalist style photography, and many iconic images are sold here.

Fodor's Choice ★ **Nedra Matteucci Galleries** (✉ *1075 Paseo de Peralta, East Side and Canyon Road* ☎ *505/982–4631* ✉ *555 Canyon Rd.* ⊕ *www.matteucci.com.* ☎ *505/983–2731*) exhibits works by California regionalists, members of the early Taos and Santa Fe schools, and masters of American impressionism and modernism. Spanish-colonial furniture, Indian antiquities, and a fantastic sculpture garden are other draws of this well-respected establishment. The old adobe building that the gallery is in is a beautifully preserved example of Santa Fe–style architecture.

Peyton Wright (✉ *237 E. Palace Ave., The Plaza* ☎ *505/989–9888* ⊕ *www.peytonwright.com*), tucked inside the historic Spiegelberg house, represents some of the most talented emerging and established contemporary artists in the country, such as Dorothy Brett and Jozef Bakós as well as antique and even ancient New Mexican, Russian, and Latin works.

Photo-eye Gallery (✉ *376–A Garcia St., East Side and Canyon Road* ☎ *505/988–5159* ⊕ *www.photoeye.com*) shows contemporary and historic photography in styles ranging from representational to ephemeral. This gallery and bookstore's dedication to the medium is staggering, with a stellar selection of new and out-of-print editions, and special auctions for especially rare editions or pieces.

Pushkin Gallery (✉ *550 Canyon Rd., East Side and Canyon Road* ☎ *505/982–1990* ⊕ *www.pushkingallery.com*) provides yet more evidence that Santa Fe's art scene is about so much more than regional work—here you can peruse works by some of Russia's leading 19th- and 20th-century talents, with an emphasis on impressionism.

Riva Yares Gallery (✉ *123 Grant St., The Plaza* ☎ *505/984–0330* ⊕ *www. rivayaresgallery.com*) specializes in contemporary artists of Latin American descent. There are sculptures by California artist Manuel Neri, color field paintings by Esteban Vicente, and works by Santa Feans Elias Rivera, Rico Eastman, and others—plus paintings by such international legends as Hans Hofmann, Milton Avery, and Helen Frankenthaler.

Santa Fe Art Institute (✉ *1600 St. Michael's Dr., South Side* ☎ *505/424– 5050*), a nonprofit educational art organization that sponsors several artists in residence and presents workshops, exhibitions, and lectures, has a respected gallery whose exhibits change regularly. The institute is set inside a dramatic contemporary building designed by Mexican modernist architect Ricardo Legorreta. Past artists in residence have included Richard Diebenkorn, Larry Bell, Moon Zappa, Henriette Wyeth Hurd, and Judy Pfaff.

Fodor's Choice ★   ☾ **Shidoni Foundry and Galleries** (✉ *B1508 Bishop's Lodge Rd., 5 mi north of Santa Fe, North of the Plaza, Tesuque* ☎ *505/988–8001* ⊕ *www. shidoni.com*) casts work for established and emerging artists from all over North America. On the grounds of an old chicken ranch, Shidoni has a rambling sculpture garden and a gallery. Self-guided foundry tours are permitted Saturday 9 to 5 and weekdays noon to 1, but the sculpture garden is open daily during daylight hours; you can watch bronze pourings most Saturday afternoons. This is a dream of a place to expose your kids to large-scale art and enjoy a lovely and, in this area, rare expanse of green grass at the same time.

Fodor's Choice ★   **Eight Modern** (✉ *231 Delgado St., East Side and Canyon Road* ☎ *505/995–0231* ⊕ *www.eightmodern.net*), in an unassuming building just off of Canyon Road, showcases modern and contemporary painting, photography, and sculpture by established artists from around the world. Eight Modern has staked a notable claim in Santa Fe's art world by bringing a number of internationally acclaimed artists here for the first time.

SPECIALTY STORES

ANTIQUES AND HOME FURNISHINGS

At **Asian Adobe** (✉ *310 Johnson St., The Plaza* ☎ *505/992–6846* ⊕ *www. asianadobe.com*) browse porcelain lamps, ornate antique baby hats and shoes, red-lacquer armoires, and similarly stunning Chinese and Southeast Asian artifacts and antiques. The jewelry selection often includes hard-to-find ethnic Chinese pieces as well as exceptional one-of-a-kind finds from the owner's travels.

Fodor's Choice ★   **Casa Nova** (✉ *530 S. Guadalupe St., The Railyard District* ☎ *505/983–8558* ⊕ *www.casanovagallery.com*) sells functional and decorative art from around the world, deftly mixing colors, textures, and cultural icons—old and new—from stylish pewter tableware from South Africa to vintage hand-carved ex-votos (votive offerings) from Brazil. There is a major emphasis here on goods produced by artists and cooperatives focused on sustainable economic development.

Fodor's Choice ★   The **Design Center** (✉ *418 Cerrillos Rd., Railyard District*), which occupies a former Chevy dealership in the Railyard District, contains some of the most distinctive antique and decorative-arts shops in town, plus a couple of small restaurants. Be sure to browse the precious Latin American antiques at **Claiborne Gallery** (☎ *505/982–8019*), along with the artful contemporary desks, tables, and chairs created by owner Omer Claiborne. **Gloria List Gallery** (☎ *505/982–5622*) specializes in rare 17th- and 18th-century devotional and folk art, chiefly from South America, Italy, Spain, and Mexico. At **Sparrow & Magpie Antiques**

(☎ 505/982–1446), look mostly for East Coast and Midwest folk art and textiles, although the shop carries some Southwestern pieces, too.

Design Warehouse (✉ 101 W. Marcy St., The Plaza ☎ 505/988–1555 ⊕ www.designwarehousesantafe.com), a welcome antidote to Santa Fe's preponderance of shops selling Native American and Spanish-colonial antiques, stocks hip, contemporary furniture, kitchenware, home accessories, and other sleek knickknacks, such as those made by the Italian firm Alessi. Note the select collection of amusing books for kids and adults.

Doodlet's (✉ 120 Don Gaspar Ave., The Plaza ☎ 505/983–3771) has an eclectic collection of stuff: pop-up books, silly postcards, tin art, hooked rugs, and stringed lights. Wonderment is in every display case, drawing the eye to the unusual. There's something for just about everyone at this delightfully quirky shop, and often it's affordable.

Jackalope (✉ 2820 Cerrillos Rd., South Side ☎ 505/471–8539 ⊕ www. jackalope.com), a legendary if somewhat overpriced bazaar, sprawls over 7 acres, incorporating several pottery barns, a furniture store, endless aisles of knickknacks from Latin America and Asia, and a huge greenhouse. There's also an area where craftspeople, artisans, and others sell their wares—sort of a mini flea market.

★ **La Mesa** (✉ 225 Canyon Rd., East Side and Canyon Road ☎ 505/984–1688 ⊕ www.lamesaofsantafe.com) has become well-known for showcasing contemporary handcrafted, mostly functional, works by more than 50, mostly local, artists including Kathy O'Neill, Gregory Lomayesva, and Melissa Haid. Collections include dinnerware, glassware, pottery, lighting, fine art, and accessories.

★ **Montez Gallery** (✉ Sena Plaza Courtyard, 125 E. Palace Ave., The Plaza ☎ 505/982–1828) sells Hispanic works of religious art and decoration, including *retablos* (holy images painted on wood or tin), *bultos* (carved wooden statues of saints), furniture, paintings, pottery, weavings, and jewelry. You'll find works by a number of award-winning local artists here.

Pachamama (✉ 223 Canyon Rd., East Side and Canyon Road ☎ 505/983–4020) carries a diverse and captivating collection of Latin American folk art, including small tin or silver *milagros,* the stamped metal images used as votive offerings, and gorgeous jewelry. The shop also carries weavings, Spanish-colonial antiques, and other delightful trinkets.

Sequoia (✉ 201 Galisteo St., The Plaza ☎ 505/982–7000) shows the sleek, imaginative, furniture creations of its owner, who was born in India. The natural glow of the materials in massive wood slab tables and chairs is remarkable. Curvaceous glass shelves, lamps, and candlesticks mix with paintings and fine linens.

BOOKS

More than a dozen shops in Santa Fe sell used books, and a handful of high-quality shops carry the latest releases from mainstream and small presses.

ALLÁ (✉ 102 W. San Francisco St., upstairs, The Plaza ☎ 505/988–5416) is one of Santa Fe's most delightful small bookstores. It focuses on hard-to-find Spanish-language books and records, including limited-edition handmade books from Central America. It also carries Native American books and music, as well as English translations.

Fodor'sChoice
★
Collected Works Book Store (✉ *202 Galisteo St., The Plaza* ☎ *505/988–4226* ⊕ *www.collectedworksbookstore.com*) carries art and travel books, including a generous selection of books on Southwestern art, architecture, and general history, as well as the latest in contemporary literature. In the new, expanded space still close to the Plaza, you can now enjoy organic coffees, snacks, and sandwiches. The patio invites long, leisurely reads. The proprietress, Dorothy Massey, and her staff are well-loved for their knowledge and helpfulness.

Garcia Street Books (✉ *376 Garcia St., East Side and Canyon Road* ☎ *505/986–0151* ⊕ *www.garciastreetbooks.com*) is an outstanding independent shop strong on art, architecture, cookbooks, literature, and regional Southwestern works—it's a block from the Canyon Road galleries. It hosts frequent talks by authors under its portal during the summer.

Nicholas Potter (✉ *211 E. Palace Ave., The Plaza* ☎ *505/983–5434*) specializes in used, rare, and out-of-print books with an extensive collection of Southwest art, culture, and history. Modern first editions and photography are other areas of focus. The quixotic shop also stocks used jazz and classical CDs. Potter is an amazing resource for those looking for a specific book or subject and his knowledge is encyclopedic.

Photo-eye Books (✉ *376 Garcia St., East Side and Canyon Road* ☎ *505/988–5152* ⊕ *www.photoeye.com*) has an almost unbelievable collection of new, rare, and out-of-print photography books and a staff of photographers who are excellent sources of information and advice on great spots to shoot in and around Santa Fe.

Travel Bug (✉ *839 Paseo de Peralta, The Plaza* ☎ *505/992–0418*) has a huge array of guidebooks and books about travel, and USGS and other maps. You'll also find all sorts of gadgets for hikers and backpackers. There's also a cozy coffeehouse (excellent java) with Wi-Fi.

CLOTHING AND ACCESSORIES

Many tourists arrive in clothing from mainstream department stores and leave bedecked in Western garb looking like they've stepped from a bygone era. If you simply cannot live without a getup Annie Oakley herself would envy, you will find shopping options beyond your wildest dreams. But take a look around at the striking and highly individualized styles of the locals and you'll see that Western gear is mixed with pieces from all over the globe to create what is the real Santa Fe style. There are few towns where you'll find more distinctive, sometimes downright eccentric, expressions of personal style on every age and every shape. Indians, cowboys, hipsters, students, artists, yogis, immigrants from all over the world, and world travelers all bring something to the style mix of this town and you'll find plenty of shops that will allow you to join in the fun.

It is worth asking specifically to see the work of locals during your wanderings. There are artists of every bent in this town and the surrounding areas, not only putting paint to canvas, but creating jewelry, clothing, accessories, and more. Informed by cultural traditions but as cutting-edge and innovative as anything you'll find in New York or San Francisco, the contemporary jewelry coming from Native American artists like Cody Sanderson and Pat Pruitt is incredible. The shops at IAIA Downtown and the Museum of Indian Arts and Culture on Museum Hill are good places to see these artists and many others.

Fodor'sChoice ★ **Back at the Ranch** (✉ *209 E. Marcy St., The Plaza* ☎ *505/989–8110 or 888/962–6687*) is the place for cowboy boots. The cozy space in an old, creaky-floored adobe is stocked with perhaps the finest handmade cowboy boots you will ever see—in every color, style, and embellishment imaginable. Other finds, like funky ranch-style furniture, 1950s blanket coats, jewelry, and belt buckles are also sold. The staff is top-notch and the boots are breathtaking.

Cupcake Clothing. (✉ *328 Montezuma Ave., Railyard District* ☎ *505/988–4744* ⊕ *www.cupcakeclothing.net*) is a hip store just off Guadalupe Street in the busy Railyard District. This cozy little shop has all sorts of stylish clothing, shoes, and accessories for women and a very friendly staff to boot. The clientele is pretty evenly split between tourists and locals.

Fodor'sChoice ★ **Double Take at the Ranch** (✉ *321 S. Guadalupe St., Railyard District* ☎ *505/820–7775*) ranks among the best consignment stores in the West, carrying elaborately embroidered vintage cowboy shirts, hundreds of pairs of boots, funky old prints, and amazing vintage Indian pawn and Mexican jewelry. The store adjoins its sister consignment store, also called Double Take, which carries a wide range of contemporary clothing and accessories for men and women; and Santa Fe Pottery, which carries the works of local artists.

Maya (✉ *108 Galisteo St., The Plaza* ☎ *505/989–7590*) is a groovy assemblage of unconventional and fun women's clothing, jewelry, accessories, select books, shoes, handbags, global folk art, hats, and a small selection of housewares. It's a funky shop with many lines from small design houses and local jewelers. Check out the selection of *relicario*-style (tiny images of saints in silver frames) jewelry from Wanda Lobito. The staff isn't always terribly helpful, but they aren't unfriendly.

Mirá (✉ *101 W. Marcy St., The Plaza* ☎ *505/988–3585*) clothing for women is hip, eclectic, and funky, combining the adventurous spirit of New Mexico with global contemporary fashion. The shop has jewelry, accessories, and collectibles from Latin America, the Flax line of natural-fiber clothing, and knockout dresses and separates not sold anywhere else in town.

Nathalie (✉ *503 Canyon Rd., East Side and Canyon Road* ☎ *505/982–1021* ⊕ *www.nathaliesantafe.com*) has long been the destination for those who've come to love Parisian-born owner Nathalie Kent's distinctive style and carefully curated collection of vintage and new pieces. Though Kent's passion clearly leans toward traditional Western wear, from cowboy boots to velvet skirts to exquisite Old Pawn jewelry, you'll also find gorgeous pieces from all over the globe—antique Moroccan treasures line up next to 100-year-old Navajo bracelets like long lost pals. Her home furnishings are stupendous, too.

Fodor's Choice
★

O'Farrell Hats (✉ *111 E. San Francisco St., The Plaza* ☎ *505/989–9666* ⊕ *www.ofarrellhatco.com*) is the domain of America's foremost hat-making family. Founder Kevin O'Farrell passed away in 2006, but the legacy continues with his son Scott and the highly trained staff. This quirky shop custom crafts one-of-a-kind beaver-felt cowboy hats that make the ultimate Santa Fe keepsake. This level of quality comes at a cost, but devoted customers—who have included everyone from cattle ranchers to U.S. presidents—swear by O'Farrell's artful creations.

Origins (✉ *135 W. San Francisco St., The Plaza* ☎ *505/988–2323*) borrows from many cultures, carrying pricey women's wear like antique kimonos and custom-dyed silk jackets, with the overall look of artsy elegance. One-of-a-kind accessories complete the spectacular look that Santa Fe inspires.

Fodor's Choice
★

For gear related to just about any outdoors activity you can think of, check out **Sangre de Cristo Mountain Works** (✉ *328 S. Guadalupe St., Railyard District* ☎ *505/984–8221* ⊕ *www.sdcmountainworks.com*), a well-stocked shop that both sells and rents hiking, climbing, camping, trekking, snowshoeing, and skiing equipment. There's a great selection of clothing and shoes for men and women. The superactive, knowledgeable staff here can also advise you on the best venues for local recreation.

FOOD AND COOKWARE

In the DeVargas shopping center, **Las Cosas Kitchen Shoppe** (✉ *De Vargas Mall, N. Guadalupe St. at Paseo de Peralta, North Side* ☎ *505/988–3394 or 877/229–7184* ⊕ *www.lascosascooking.com*) carries a fantastic selection of cookery, tableware, and kitchen gadgetry and gifts. The shop is also renowned for its cooking classes, which touch on everything from high-altitude baking to Asian-style grilling.

★

The Spanish Table (✉ *109 N. Guadalupe St., West of the Plaza* ☎ *505/986–0243* ⊕ *www.spanishtable.com*) stands out as a destination for all Spanish culinary needs. With its Spanish meats and cheeses, cookware and beautiful Majolica pottery, books, dry goods, and wonderful world-music selection, you will be challenged to leave empty-handed. The staff is always ready to help advise on a recipe or gift idea and will ship your purchases anywhere you like.

Fodor's Choice
★

Todos Santos (✉ *125 E. Palace Ave., The Plaza* ☎ *505/982–3855*) is a tiny candy shop in the 18th-century courtyard of Sena Plaza, carrying must-be-seen-to-be-believed works of edible art, including chocolate milagros and altar pieces gilded with 23-karat gold or silver leaf. Truffles come in exotic flavors, like tangerine chile, rose caramel, and lemon verbena. The buttery, spicy, handmade chipotle caramels melt in your mouth—buy several bags so you won't end up eating the gifts you intend to give. Amidst the taste sensations and quirky folk art are amazing and delightful customized Pez dispensers from Albuquerque folk artist Steve White and astonishing, intricate recycled paper creations from local phenom Rick Phelps.

JEWELRY

Eidos (✉ *500 Montezuma Ave., inside Sanbusco Center, Railyard District* ☎ *505/992–0020* ⊕ *www.eidosjewelry.com*) features "concept-led" minimalist contemporary jewelry from European designers and

Deborah Alexander and Gordon Lawrie, who own the store. It's a lovely, contemporary space with a fascinating array of materials, good range of prices, and helpful staff.

Golden Eye (⊠ *115 Don Gaspar St., The Plaza* ☎ *505/984–0040* ⊕ *www. goldeneyesantafe.com*) is a pint-size shop (even by Santa Fe standards) that features fine, handcrafted jewelry in high-karat gold, often paired with gemstones. Its experienced, helpful staff of artisans can help you pick out something beautiful and unusual.

Jett (⊠ *110 Old Santa Fe Trail, The Plaza* ☎ *505/988–1414*) showcases jewelers and artists, many local, who are remarkable for creative, original approaches to their work. Intriguing selection of surprisingly affordable silver and gold jewelry, modern artistic lighting, and delightful miniature objects like vintage trailers and circus tents made from recycled metal.

LewAllen & LewAllen Jewelry (⊠ *105 E. Palace Ave., The Plaza* ☎ *800/988–5112* ⊕ *www.lewallenjewelry.com*) is run by father-and-daughter silversmiths Ross and Laura LewAllen. Handmade jewelry ranges from whimsical to mystical inside their tiny shop just off the Plaza. There is something for absolutely everyone in here, including delightful charms for your pet's collar.

Fodor's Choice ★ **Patina** (⊠ *131 W. Palace Ave., The Plaza* ☎ *505/986–3432 or 877/877–0827* ⊕ *www.patina-gallery.com*) presents outstanding contemporary jewelry, textiles, and sculptural objects of metal, clay, and wood, in an airy, museum-like space. With a staff whose courtesy is matched by knowledge of the genre, artists-owners Ivan and Allison Barnett have used their fresh curatorial aesthetic to create a showplace for more than 110 American and European artists they represent—many of whom are in permanent collections of museums such as MoMA.

MARKETS

Pueblo of Tesuque Flea Market (⊠ *U.S. 285/84, 7 mi north of Santa Fe, Tesuque* ☎ *505/983–2667* ⊕ *www.pueblooftesuquefleamarket.com*) was once considered the best flea market in America by its loyal legion of bargain hunters. The Tesuque Pueblo took over the market in the late '90s and raised vendor fees, which increased the presence of predictable, often pricey goods brought in by professional flea-market dealers. In recent years, however, the pueblo has brought in a nice range of vendors, and this market may have hundreds of vendors showing their goods in peak season. The 12-acre market is next to the Santa Fe Opera and is open Friday to Sunday, mid-March to December.

Fodor's Choice ★ Browse through the vast selection of local produce, meat, flowers, honey, and cheese—much of it organic—at the thriving **Santa Fe Farmers' Market** (⊠ *1607 Paseo de Peralta, Railyard District* ☎ *505/983–4098* ⊕ *www.santafefarmersmarket.com*). The market is now housed in its new, permanent building in the Railyard and it's open year-round. It's a great people-watching event, with entertainment for kids as well as a snack bar selling terrific breakfast burritos and other goodies. With the growing awareness of the importance and necessity of eating locally grown and organic food, this market offers living testimony to the fact that farming can be done successfully, even in a high-desert region like this one.

NATIVE AMERICAN ARTS AND CRAFTS

Morning Star Gallery (✉ *513 Canyon Rd., East Side and Canyon Road* ☎ *505/982–8187* ⊕ *www.morningstargallery.com*) is a veritable museum of Native American art and artifacts. An adobe shaded by a huge cottonwood tree houses antique basketry, pre-1940 Navajo silver jewelry, Northwest Coast Native American carvings, Navajo weavings, and art of the Plains Indians. Prices and quality prohibit casual purchases, but the collection is magnificent.

Niman Fine Arts (✉ *125 Lincoln Ave., The Plaza* ☎ *505/988–5091* ⊕ *www.namingha.com*) focuses on the prolific work of contemporary Hopi artists Arlo, Dan, and Michael Namingha. Arlo is a sculptor working in bronze, wood, and stone; Dan paints and sculpts; and Michael works with digital imagery.

Packard's on the Plaza (✉ *61 Old Santa Fe Trail, The Plaza* ☎ *505/983–9241* ⊕ *www.packards-santafe.com*), the oldest Native American arts-and-crafts store on Santa Fe Plaza, also sells Zapotec Indian rugs from Mexico and original rug designs by Richard Enzer, old pottery, saddles, kachina dolls, and an excellent selection of coral and turquoise jewelry. Local favorite Lawrence Baca, whose iconic jewelry has made him a regular prizewinner at Spanish Market, is featured here. Prices are often high, but so are the standards. There's also an extensive clothing selection.

Fodor's Choice ★ The **Rainbow Man** (✉ *107 E. Palace Ave., The Plaza* ☎ *505/982–8706* ⊕ *www.therainbowman.com*), established in 1945, does business in an old, rambling adobe complex, part of which dates from before the 1680 Pueblo Revolt. The shop carries early Navajo, Mexican, and Chimayó textiles, along with photographs by Edward S. Curtis, a breathtaking collection of vintage pawn and Mexican jewelry, Day of the Dead figures, Oaxacan folk animals, New Mexican folk art, kachinas, and contemporary jewelry from local artists. The friendly staff possesses an encyclopedic knowledge of the art here.

Fodor's Choice ★ **Robert Nichols Gallery** (✉ *419 Canyon Rd., East Side and Canyon Road* ☎ *505/982–2145* ⊕ *www.robertnicholsgallery.com*) represents a remarkable group of Native American ceramics artists doing primarily nontraditional work. Diverse artists such as Glen Nipshank, whose organic, sensuous shapes would be right at home in MoMA, and Diego Romero, whose Cochiti-style vessels are detailed with graphic-novel-style characters and sharp social commentary, are right at home here. It is a treat to see cutting-edge work that is clearly informed by indigenous traditions.

Fodor's Choice ★ "Eclectic Modern Vintage" is **Shiprock Santa Fe**'s (✉ *53 Old Santa Fe Trail, The Plaza* ☎ *505/982–8478* ⊕ *www.shiprocksantafe.com*.) tagline, and it accurately sums up their incredible collection of pottery, textiles, painting, furniture, and sculpture. The gallery is notable for its dedication to showcasing exquisite vintage pieces alongside vanguard contemporary works.

Trade Roots Collection (✉ *411 Paseo de Peralta, The Plaza* ☎ *505/982–8168* ⊕ *www.traderoots.com*) sells Native American ritual objects, such as fetish jewelry and Hopi rattles, and magnificent strands of turquoise from famed American mines. Contemporary silver pieces using top-quality genuine stones are also popular. Open by appointment only, this store is an excellent source of fine ethnic crafts materials for artists.

Trader's Collection (✉ *218 Galisteo St., The Plaza* ☎ *505/992–0441*) was created by several key staff members when the venerable Shush Yaz gallery closed in August 2007. In this new showplace of American Indian arts and crafts, antique pieces commingle with contemporary works by artists such as Nocona Burgess and jeweler Kim Knifechief. The staff is friendly and knowledgeable.

SPORTS AND THE OUTDOORS

The Santa Fe National Forest is right in the city's backyard and includes the Dome Wilderness (5,200 acres in the volcanically formed Jémez Mountains) and the Pecos Wilderness (223,333 acres of high mountains, forests, and meadows at the southern end of the Rocky Mountains chain). The 12,500-foot Sangre de Cristo Mountains (the name translates as "Blood of Christ," for the red glow they radiate at sunset) fringe the city's east side, constant and gentle reminders of the mystery and power of the natural world. To the south and west, sweeping high desert is punctuated by several less formidable mountain ranges. The dramatic shifts in elevation and topography around Santa Fe make for a wealth of outdoor activities. Head to the mountains for fishing, camping, and skiing; to the nearby Rio Grande for kayaking and rafting; and almost anywhere in the area for bird-watching, hiking, and biking.

For a report on general conditions in the forest, contact the **Santa Fe National Forest Office** (✉ *11 Forest La., South Side* ☎ *505/438–5300* ⊕ *www.fs.fed.us/r3/sfe*). For a one-stop shop for information about recreation on public lands, which include national and state parks, contact the **New Mexico Public Lands Information Center** (✉ *301 Dinosaur Trail, South Side* ☎ *505/954–2002* ⊕ *www.publiclands.org*). It has maps, reference materials, licenses, permits—just about everything you need to plan an adventure in the New Mexican wilderness.

BICYCLING

You can pick up a map of bike trips—among them a 30-mi round-trip ride from Downtown Santa Fe to Ski Santa Fe at the end of NM 475—from the New Mexico Public Lands Information Center, or at the bike shops listed below. One excellent place to mountain bike is the Dale Ball Trail Network, which is accessed from several points.

Fodor's Choice ★ **Mellow Velo** (✉ *638 Old Santa Fe Trail, Old Santa Fe Trail and South Capitol* ☎ *505/995–8356* ⊕ *www.melovelo.com*) is a friendly, neighborhood bike shop offering group tours, privately guided rides, bicycle rentals ($35 per day—make reservations), and repairs. The helpful staff at this well-stocked shop offers a great way to spend a day—or seven!

New Mexico Bike N' Sport (✉ *524C W. Cordova Rd., Old Santa Fe Trail and South Capitol* ☎ *505/820–0809* ⊕ *www.nmbikensport.com*) is a big shop that provides rentals and a large selection of bikes, clothing, and all necessary gear.

Santa Fe Mountain Sports (✉ *1221 Flagman Way, Suite B1, South Side* ☎ *505/988–3337* ⊕ *www.santafemountainsports.com*) has a good selection of bikes for rent.

BIRD-WATCHING

☽ At the end of Upper Canyon Road, at the mouth of the canyon as
Fodor's Choice it wends into the foothills, the 135-acre **Randall Davey Audubon Center**
★ harbors diverse birds and other wildlife. Guided nature walks are given many weekends; there are also two major hiking trails that you can tackle on your own. The home and studio of Randall Davey, a prolific early Santa Fe artist, can be toured on Monday afternoons in summer. There's also a nature bookstore. ✉ *1800 Upper Canyon Rd., East Side and Canyon Road* ☎ *505/983–4609* ⊕ *http://nm.audubon.org/center/index.html* 🖼 *Center $2, house tour $5* ☽ *Weekdays 9–5, weekends 10–4; grounds daily dawn–dusk; house tours Mon. at 2.*

For a knowledgeable insider's perspective, take a tour with **WingsWest Birding Tours** (☎ *800/583–6928* ⊕ *www.wingswestnm.com*). Gregarious and knowledgeable guide Bill West leads four- to eight-hour early-morning or sunset tours that venture into some of the region's best bird-watching areas, including Santa Fe Ski Basin, Cochiti Lake, the Jémez Mountains, the Upper Pecos Valley, and Bosque del Apache National Wildlife Refuge. West also leads popular tours throughout Mexico.

GOLF

Marty Sanchez Links de Santa Fe (✉ *205 Caja del Rio Rd., off NM 599, the Santa Fe Relief Route, South Side* ☎ *505/955–4400* ⊕ *www.linksdesantafe.com*), an outstanding municipal facility with beautifully groomed 18- and 9-hole courses, sits on high prairie west of Santa Fe with fine mountain views. It has driving and putting ranges, a pro shop, and a snack bar. The greens fees are $35 for the 18-hole course, $25 on the par-3 9-holer.

HIKING

Hiking around Santa Fe can take you into high-altitude alpine country or into lunaresque high desert as you head south and west to lower elevations. For winter hiking, the gentler climates to the south are less likely to be snow packed, while the alpine areas will likely require snowshoes or cross-country skis. In summer, wildflowers bloom in the high country, and the temperature is generally at least 10 degrees cooler than in town. The mountain trails accessible at the base of the Ski Santa Fe area (end of NM 475) stay cool on even the hottest summer days. Weather can change with one gust of wind, so be prepared with extra clothing, rain gear, food, and lots of water. Keep in mind that the sun at 10,000 feet is very powerful, even with a hat and sunscreen. *See the Side Trips from Santa Fe section, below, for additional hiking areas near the city.*

For information about specific hiking areas, contact the New Mexico Public Lands Information Center. Any of the outdoor gear stores in town can also help with guides and recommendations. The **Sierra Club** (⊕ *www.riogrande.sierraclub.org*) organizes group hikes of all levels of difficulty; a schedule of hikes is posted on the Web site.

Fodor's Choice
★

Aspen Vista is a lovely hike along a south-facing mountainside. Take Hyde Park Road (NM 475) 13 mi, and the trail begins before the ski area. After walking a few miles through thick aspen groves you come to panoramic views of Santa Fe. The path is well marked and gently inclines toward Tesuque Peak. The trail becomes shadier with elevation—snow has been reported on the trail as late as July. In winter, after heavy snows, the trail is great for intermediate-advanced cross-country skiing. The round-trip is 12 mi and sees an elevation gain of 2,000 feet, but it's just 3½ mi to the spectacular overlook. The hillside is covered with golden aspen trees in late September.

Spurring off the Dale Ball trail system, the steep but rewarding (and dog-friendly) **Atalaya Trail** runs from the visitor parking lot of St. John's College (off Camino de Cruz Blanca, on the east side), up a winding, ponderosa pine–studded trail to the peak of Mt. Atalaya, which affords incredible 270-degree views of Santa Fe. The nearly 6-mi round-trip hike climbs nearly 2,000 feet (to an elevation of 9,121 feet), so pace yourself. The good news: the return to the parking area is nearly all downhill.

A favorite spot for a ramble, with a vast network of trails, is the **Dale Ball Foothills Trail Network** (⊕ *www.santafenm.gov/index.aspx?NID=1059*), a network of some 20 mi of paths that winds and wends up through the foothills east of town and can be accessed at a few points, including Hyde Park Road (en route to the ski valley) and the upper end of Canyon Road, at Cerro Gordo. There are trail maps and signs at these points, and the trails are very well marked.

HORSEBACK RIDING

New Mexico's rugged countryside has been the setting for many Hollywood Westerns. Whether you want to ride the range that Gregory Peck and Kevin Costner rode or just head out feeling tall in the saddle, you can do so year-round. Rates average about $20 an hour. *See the Side Trips from Santa Fe section for additional horseback listings in Galisteo and Española.*

Bishop's Lodge (⊠ *1297 Bishop's Lodge Rd., North Side* ☎ *505/983–6377*) provides rides and guides year-round. Call for reservations.

MULTIPURPOSE SPORTS CENTER

★
The huge **Genoveva Chavez Community Center** (⊠ *3221 Rodeo Rd., South Side* ☎ *505/955–4001* ⊕ *www.chavezcenter.com*) is a reasonably priced (adults $5 per day) facility with a regulation-size ice rink (you can rent ice skates for the whole family), an enormous gymnasium, indoor running track, 50-meter pool, leisure pool with waterslide and play structures, aerobics center, fitness room, two racquetball courts, and a child-care center.

RIVER RAFTING

If you want to watch birds and wildlife along the banks, try the laid-back Huck Finn floats along the Rio Chama or the Rio Grande's White Rock Canyon. The season is generally between April and September. Most outfitters have overnight package plans, and all offer half- and full-day trips. Be prepared to get wet, and wear secure water shoes. For a list of outfitters who guide trips on the Rio Grande and the Rio Chama, contact the **Bureau of Land Management (BLM), Taos Resource Area Office** (✉ *226 Cruz Alta Rd., Taos* ☎ *505/758–8851* ⊕ *www.nm.blm. gov*), or stop by the BLM visitor center along NM 68, 16 mi south of Taos in Pilar.

Kokopelli Rafting Adventures (✉ *551 W. Cordova Rd., #540, Old Santa Fe Trail and South Capitol* ☎ *505/983–3734 or 800/879–9035* ⊕ *www. kokopelliraft.com*) will take you on half-day to multiday river trips down the Rio Grande and Rio Chama. **New Wave Rafting** (✉ *Mile 21 Hwy. 68, Embudo* ☎ *800/984–1444* ⊕ *www.newwaverafting.com*) conducts full-day, half-day, and overnight river trips, as well as fly-fishing trips, from its new location in Embudo, 21 mi north of Española. **Santa Fe Rafting Company and Outfitters** (✉ *1000 Cerrillos Rd., South Side* ☎ *505/988–4914 or 888/988–4914* ⊕ *www.santaferafting.com*) leads day trips down the Rio Grande and the Chama River and customizes rafting tours. Tell them what you want—they'll figure out a way to do it.

SKIING

To save time during the busy holiday season you may want to rent skis or snowboards in town the night before hitting the slopes so you don't waste any time waiting during the morning rush. **Alpine Sports** (✉ *121 Sandoval St., South Side* ☎ *505/983–5155* ⊕ *www.alpinesports-santafe.com*) rents downhill and cross-country skis and snowboards. **Cottam's Ski Rentals** (✉ *3451 Hyde Park Rd., 7 mi northeast of Downtown, toward Ski Santa Fe* ☎ *505/982–0495 or 800/322–8267*) rents the works, including snowboards, sleds, and snowshoes.

★ **Santa Fe Mountain Sports** (✉ *1221 Flagman Way, Suite B1, South Side* ☎ *505/988–3337* ⊕ *www.santafemountainsports.com*) is a family-owned specialty mountain shop that rents boots, skis, and snowboards for the whole family in the winter, as well as bicycles in the summertime. The super-helpful staff is great to work with.

Ski Santa Fe (✉ *End of NM 475, 18 mi northeast of Downtown* ☎ *505/982–4429 general info, 505/983–9155 conditions* ⊕ *www.ski-santafe.com*), open roughly from late November through early April, is a fine, midsize operation that receives an average of 225 inches of snow a year and plenty of sunshine. It's one of America's highest ski areas—the 12,000-foot summit has a variety of terrain and seems bigger than its 1,700 feet of vertical rise and 660 acres. There are some great powder stashes, tough bump runs, and many wide, gentle cruising runs. The 44 trails are ranked 20% beginner, 40% intermediate, and 40% advanced; there are seven lifts. Snowboarders are welcome, and there's the Norquist Trail for cross-country skiers. Chipmunk Corner provides day care and supervised kids' skiing. The ski school is excellent. Rentals, a good restaurant, a ski shop, and Totemoff Bar and Grill round out the amenities.

SIDE TRIPS FROM SANTA FE

Take even a day or two to explore the areas around Santa Fe and you'll start to get a sense of just how ancient this region is and how deeply the modern culture has been shaped by the Pueblo and Spanish people who have been here for centuries. If you're a geology buff or just happy to wander through this dramatic environment, you'll see things you couldn't possibly expect. *Each of the excursions below can be accomplished in a day or less.* The High Road to Taos trip makes for a very full day, so start early or plan to spend the night near or in Taos.

SOUTH OF SANTA FE

The most prominent side trip south of the city is along the fabled Turquoise Trail, an excellent—and leisurely—alternative route to Albuquerque that's far more interesting than Interstate 25; *it's covered in the Side Trips from Albuquerque section, in chapter 2.* Although the drive down Interstate 25 offers some fantastic views of the Jémez and Sandia mountains, the most interesting sites south of town require hopping off the interstate. From here you can uncover the region's history at El Rancho de las Golondrinas and enjoy one of New Mexico's most dramatic day hikes at Tent Rocks canyon. Conversely, if you leave Santa Fe via Interstate 25 north and then cut down in a southerly direction along U.S. 285 and NM 41, you come to tiny Galisteo, a little hamlet steeped in Spanish colonial history.

PECOS NATIONAL HISTORIC PARK
★ *25 mi east of Santa Fe on I–25.*

Pecos was the last major encampment that travelers on the Santa Fe Trail reached before Santa Fe. Today the little village is mostly a starting point for exploring the Pecos National Historic Park, the centerpiece of which is the **ruins of Pecos,** once a major pueblo village with more than 1,100 rooms. Twenty-five hundred people are thought to have lived in this structure, as high as five stories in places. Pecos, in a fertile valley between the Great Plains and the Rio Grande Valley, was a trading center centuries before the Spanish conquistadors visited in about 1540. The Spanish later returned to build two missions.

The pueblo was abandoned in 1838, and its 17 surviving occupants moved to the Jémez Pueblo. Anglo travelers on the Santa Fe Trail observed the mission ruins with a great sense of fascination (and relief—for they knew it meant their journey was nearly over). A couple of miles from the ruins, **Andrew Kozlowski's Ranch** served as a stage depot, where a fresh spring quenched the thirsts of horses and weary passengers. The ranch now houses the park's law-enforcement corps and is not open to the public. You can view the mission ruins and the excavated pueblo on a ¼-mi self-guided tour in about two hours.

The pivotal Civil War battle of Glorieta Pass took place on an outly-ing parcel of parkland in late March 1862; a victory over Confederate forces firmly established the Union army's control over the New Mexico Territory. The Union troops maintained headquarters at Kozlowski's Ranch during the battle. Guided park tours ($2 per person, in summer only) to the battle site, Greer Garson's home (the late actress lived in the area for a time), and outlying ruins start at the park visitor center. ⊠ *NM 63, off I–25 at Exit 307, Pecos* ☎ *505/757–7200 park info, 505/757–7241 visitor center* ⊕ *www.nps.gov/peco* ⊡ *$3* ☉ *Late May–early Sept., daily 8–6; early Sept.–late May, daily 8–4:30.*

GALISTEO
25 mi south of Santa Fe via I–25 north to U.S. 285 to NM 41 south.

South of Santa Fe lie the immense open spaces and subtle colorings of the Galisteo Basin and the quintessential New Mexican village of Gali-steo—a blend of multigenerational New Mexicans and recent migrants who protect and treasure the bucolic solitude of their home. The drive from Santa Fe takes about 30 minutes and offers a panoramic view of the low, sculpted landscape of the Galisteo Basin, which is an austere contrast to the alpine country of the Sangre de Cristos. It's a good place to go for a leisurely lunch or a sunset drive to dinner, maybe with horseback riding. Aside from these options, there really isn't anything more to do here except enjoy the surroundings.

Founded as a Spanish outpost in 1614, with original buildings con-structed largely with stones from the large pueblo ruin nearby that had once housed 1,000 people, Galisteo has attracted a significant number of artists and equestrians (trail rides and rentals are available at local stables) to the otherwise very traditional community. Cottonwoods shade the low-lying Pueblo-style architecture, a premier example of vernacular use of adobe and stone. The small church is open only for Sunday services.

SPORTS AND THE OUTDOORS
Galarosa Stable (⊠ *NM 41, Galisteo* ☎ *505/466–4654 or 505/670–2467*) offers two-hour horseback rides starting at $70 per person, south of Santa Fe in the panoramic Galisteo Basin.

EL RANCHO DE LAS GOLONDRINAS
★ *15 mi south of Santa Fe off I–25 Exit 276 in La Cienega.*

The "Williamsburg of the Southwest," El Rancho de las Golondrinas ("Ranch of the Swallows") is a reconstruction of a small agricultural village with buildings from the 17th to 19th century. Travelers on El Camino Real would stop at the ranch before making the final leg of the journey north, a half-day ride from Santa Fe in horse-and-wagon time. By car, the ranch is only a 25-minute drive from the Plaza. From Inter-state 25, the village is tucked away from view, frozen in time. Owned and operated by the Paloheimo family, direct descendants of those who owned the ranch when it functioned as a *paraje*, or stopping place, the grounds maintain an authentic character without compromising history for commercial gain. Even the gift shop carries items that reflect ranch life and the cultural exchange that took place there.

Self-guided tours survey Spanish colonial lifestyles in New Mexico from 1660 to 1890: you can view a molasses mill, threshing grounds, and wheelwright and blacksmith shops, as well as a mountain village and a *morada* (meeting place) of the order of Penitentes (a religious fraternity known for its reenactment during Holy Week of the tortures suffered by Christ). Farm animals roam through the barnyards on the 200-acre complex. Wool from the sheep is spun into yarn and woven into traditional Rio Grande–style blankets, and the corn grown is used to feed the animals. During the spring and harvest festivals, on the first weekends of June and October, respectively, the village comes alive with Spanish-American folk music, dancing, and food and crafts demonstrations. The ranch hosts a wine festival over the weekend of July 4th, and the increasingly popular Viva Mexico! celebration in mid-July celebrates the two regions' interconnected relationship through demonstrations by Mexican master artisans, musicians, craftspeople, and the famed *voladores*—men who spin gracefully from ropes off 60-foot poles—perform a vibrant and daredevil show. There are ample picnic facilities, and a snack bar serves a limited number of items on weekends only. ⊠ *334 Los Pinos Rd.* ☎ *505/471–2261* ⊕ *www.golondrinas.org* ✉ *$5* ☉ *June–Sept., Wed.–Sun. 10–4; some additional weekends for special events.*

KASHA-KATUWE TENT ROCKS NATIONAL MONUMENT

☻ *40 mi south of Santa Fe via I–25 Exit 264.*

Fodor's Choice ★ This is a terrific hiking getaway, especially if you have time for only one hike. The sandstone rock formations look like stacked tents in a stark, water- and wind-eroded box canyon. Located 45 minutes south of Santa Fe, near Cochiti Pueblo, Tent Rocks offers excellent hiking year-round, although it can get hot in summer, when you should bring extra water. The drive to this magical landscape is equally awesome, as the road heads west toward Cochiti Dam and through the cottonwood groves around the pueblo. It's a good hike for kids. The round-trip hiking distance is only 2 mi, about 1½ leisurely hours, but it's the kind of place where you'll want to hang out for a while. Take a camera, but leave your pets at home—no dogs are allowed. There are no facilities here, just a small parking area with a posted trail map and a self-pay admission box; you can get gas and pick up picnic supplies and bottled water at Cochiti Lake Convenience Store. ⊠ *1405 Cochiti Hwy.* ⊹ *Take I–25 south to Cochiti Exit 264; follow NM 16 for 8 mi, turning right onto NM 22; continue approximately 3½ more mi past Cochiti Pueblo entrance; turn right onto BIA 92, which after 2 mi becomes Forest Service Rd. 266, a rough road of jarring, washboard gravel that leads 5 mi to well-marked parking area* ☎ *505/761–8700* ⊕ *www.nm.blm. gov* ✉ *$5 per vehicle* ☉ *Apr.–Oct., daily 7–7; Nov.–Mar., daily 8–5.*

SPORTS AND THE OUTDOORS

The 18-hole, par-72 **Pueblo de Cochiti Golf Course** (⊠ *5200 Cochiti Hwy., Cochiti Lake* ☎ *505/465–2239*), set against a backdrop of steep canyons and red-rock mesas, is a 45-minute drive southwest of Santa Fe. Cochiti was designed by Robert Trent Jones Jr. and offers one of the most challenging and visually stunning golfing experiences in the state. Greens fees are $62 (Friday) and include a cart. A number of special deals throughout the week make this course a good value.

PUEBLOS NEAR SANTA FE

For a pleasant side trip, visit several of the state's 19 pueblos, including San Ildefonso, one of the state's most picturesque, and Santa Clara, whose lands harbor a dramatic set of ancient cliff dwellings. Between the two reservations sits the striking landmark called Black Mesa, which you can see from NM 30 or NM 502. The solitary butte has inspired many painters, including Georgia O'Keeffe, and it is from this mesa that deer dancers descend at dawn during winter ceremonial dances. Both of these pueblos are home to outstanding potters and it is well worth visiting open studios to watch the process and see what is available. Plan on spending one to three hours at each pueblo, and leave the day open if you're there for a feast day, when dances are set to an organic rather than mechanical clock. Pueblo grounds and hiking areas do not permit pets.

POJOAQUE PUEBLO
17 mi north of Santa Fe on U.S. 285/84.

There's not much to see in the pueblo's plaza area, but the state visitor center and adjoining **Poeh Cultural Center and Museum** on U.S. 285/84 are well worth a visit. The latter is an impressive complex of traditional adobe buildings, including the three-story Sun Tower; the facility comprises a museum, a cultural center, and artists' studios. The museum holds some 8,000 photographs, including many by esteemed early-20th-century photographer Edward S. Curtis, as well as hundreds of works of both traditional and contemporary pottery, jewelry, textiles, and sculpture. There are frequent demonstrations by artists, exhibitions, and, on Saturday from May through September, traditional ceremonial dances. By the early 20th century the pueblo was virtually uninhabited, but the survivors eventually began to restore it. Pojoaque's feast day is celebrated with dancing on December 12. The visitor center is one of the friendliest and best stocked in northern New Mexico, with free maps and literature on hiking, fishing, and the area's history. The crafts shop in the visitor center is one of the most extensive among the state's pueblos; it carries weaving, pottery, jewelry, and other crafts by both Pojoaque and other indigenous New Mexicans. ⊠ *78 Cities of Gold Rd., off U.S. 285/84, 17 mi north of Santa Fe* ☎ *505/455–3460* ⊕ *www. poehmuseum.com* ▨ *Donations accepted.*

$

NEW MEXICAN

✗ **Gabriel's.** This restaurant has location (convenient for pre-opera and post-high-road tours), a gorgeous setting (the Spanish colonial–style art, the building, the flower-filled courtyard, and those mountain views!), and the made-to-order guacamole going for it. The margaritas aren't too shabby either. The caveat? The quality of the entrées tends to be wildly uneven. Service is generally friendly, but as uneven as the food. If you're content with a gorgeous setting and making the stellar guacamole and margaritas your mainstay, this is a fine place to go for sunset. Prices are reasonable and the views truly are spectacular. ⊠ *U.S. 285/84, Exit 176, just south of Buffalo Thunder Resort, 5 mi north of Santa Fe Opera* ☎ *505/455–7000* ▤ *AE, D, DC, MC, V.*

$$$

RESORT

🏨 **Buffalo Thunder Resort & Casino.** Managed by Hilton, this expansive, upscale gaming and golfing getaway is the closest full-service resort to

Santa Fe—it's just 15 mi north. The rooms are spacious and airy, all with large windows and some with full balconies taking in the surrounding vistas. The property offers plenty of leisure amenities: an extensive slate of treatments in the 16,000-square-foot Wo' P'in Spa, access to a pair of championship 18-hole layouts at the adjacent Towa Golf Resort, a concert venue, and good mix of upscale and casual restaurants and bars. There's also an enormous casino, but it's set well away from the lobby and public areas on a separate level, making it easy to ignore if gaming isn't your thing. Hilton also operates a less pricey but also quite nice Homewood Suites next door. **Pros:** Snazziest hotel between Santa Fe and Taos, convenient to opera and Los Alamos, panoramic mountain and mesa views. **Cons:** Just off of a busy highway, lobby is noisy and crowded with gamers on many evenings, nothing much within walking distance. ⊠ *30 Buffalo Thunder Rd.,off U.S. 285/84, Exit 177Pojoaque* ☎ *505/455–5555 or 877/455–7775* ⊕ *www. buffalothunderresort.com* ⇥ *290 rooms, 85 suites* ⚒ *In-room: a/c, safe, Wi-Fi. In-hotel: 5 restaurants, room service, bars, golf courses, tennis, pools, gym, spa, parking (free).* ⊟ *AE, D, DC, MC, V.*

NAMBÉ PUEBLO
4 mi east of Pojoaque on NM 503, 20 mi north of Santa Fe.

Nambé Pueblo (which means "People of the Round Earth") has no visitor center, so the best time to visit is during the October 4th feast day of St. Francis celebration or the very popular July 4th celebration. If you want to explore the landscape surrounding the pueblo, take the drive past the pueblo until you come to **Nambé Falls and Nambé Lake Recreation Area** (☎ *505/455–2304*). There's a shady picnic area and a large fishing lake that's open March to November (the cost is $15 for fishing, and $20 for boating—no gas motors are permitted). The waterfalls are about a 15-minute hike in from the parking and picnic area along a rocky, clearly marked path. The water pours over a rock precipice—a loud and dramatic sight given the river's modest size. Overnight RV ($35) and tent ($25) camping are also offered. The area is closed Monday. ⊠ *Nambé Pueblo Rd., off NM 503* ☎ *505/455–4444 info, 505/455–2304 ranger station* ⊕ *www.nambefalls.com* ⊠ *$10 per car.*

SAN ILDEFONSO PUEBLO
23 mi north of Santa Fe via U.S. 285/84 to NM 502 west.

Maria Martinez, one of the most renowned Pueblo potters, lived here. She first created her exquisite "black on black" pottery in 1919 and in doing so sparked a major revival of pueblo arts and crafts. She died in 1980, and the 26,000-acre San Ildefonso Pueblo remains a major center for pottery and other arts and crafts. Many artists sell from their homes, and there are trading posts, a visitor center, and a museum where some of Martinez's work can be seen on weekdays. San Ildefonso is also one of the more visually appealing pueblos, with a well-defined plaza core and a spectacular setting beneath the Pajarito Plateau and Black Mesa. The pueblo's feast day is January 23, when unforgettable buffalo, deer, and Comanche dances are performed from dawn to dusk. Cameras are not permitted at any of the ceremonial dances but may be used at other times with a permit. ⊠ *NM 502* ☎ *505/455–3549* ⊠ *$7 per vehicle,*

CLOSE UP

Pueblo Etiquette

When visiting pueblos and reservations, you're expected to follow a certain etiquette. Each pueblo has its own regulations for the use of still and video cameras and video and tape recorders, as well as for sketching and painting. Some pueblos, such as Santo Domingo, prohibit photography altogether. Others, such as Santa Clara, prohibit photography at certain times; for example, during ritual dances. Still others allow photography but require a permit, which usually costs from $10 to $20, depending on whether you use a still or video camera. The privilege of setting up an easel and painting all day will cost you as little as $35 or as much as $150 (at Taos Pueblo). Associated fees for using images also can vary widely, depending on what kind of reproduction rights you might require. **Be sure to ask permission before photographing anyone in the pueblos**; it's also customary to give the subject a dollar or two for agreeing to be photographed. Native American law prevails on the pueblos, and violations of photography regulations could result in confiscation of cameras.

Specific restrictions for the various pueblos are noted in the individual descriptions. Other rules are described below.

■ Possessing or using drugs and/or alcohol on Native American land is forbidden.

■ Ritual dances often have serious religious significance and should be respected as such. Silence is mandatory—that means no questions about ceremonies or dances while they're being performed. Don't walk across the dance plaza during a performance, and don't applaud afterward.

■ Kivas and ceremonial rooms are restricted to pueblo members only.

■ Cemeteries are sacred. They're off-limits to all visitors and should never be photographed.

■ Unless pueblo dwellings are clearly marked as shops, don't wander or peek inside. Remember, these are private homes.

■ Many of the pueblo buildings are hundreds of years old. Don't try to scale adobe walls or climb on top of buildings, or you may come tumbling down.

■ Don't litter. Nature is sacred on the pueblos, and defacing land can be a serious offense.

■ Don't bring your pet or feed stray dogs.

■ Even off reservation sites, state and federal laws prohibit picking up artifacts such as arrowheads or pottery from public lands.

---

still-camera permit $10, video-recorder permit $20, sketching permit $25 ⊙ *Apr.–Oct., daily 8–5; museum, weekdays, Apr.–Oct. 8–4:30.*

SANTA CLARA PUEBLO
27 mi northwest of Santa Fe, 10 mi north of San Ildefonso Pueblo via NM 30.

Santa Clara Pueblo, southwest of Española, is the home of a historic treasure—the awesome **Puyé Cliff Dwellings,** believed to have been built in the 13th to 14th centuries. They can be seen by driving 9 mi up a gravel road through a canyon, south of the village off NM 502. You can tour the cliff dwellings, topped by the ruins of a 740-room pueblo, on your own or with a guide—several special tours are available for additional fees. Pay your entrance fees and arrange for tours at the Puyé Cliffs Welcome Center, at the Valero gas station on the corner of NM 30 and Puyé Cliffs Road. ⊠ *NM 30, Santa Clara Pueblo, Española* ☏ *505/747–2455* ⊕ *www.puyecliffs.com* ✑ *$7* ☉ *Daily 8:30–6. Closed the week before Easter, June 13, Aug. 12, and Christmas day.*

The village's shops sell burnished red pottery, engraved blackware, paintings, and other arts and crafts. All pottery is made via the coil method, not with a pottery wheel. Santa Clara is known for its carved pieces, and Avanyu, a water serpent that guards the waters, is the pueblo's symbol. Other typical works include engagement baskets, wedding vessels, and seed pots. The pueblo's feast day of St. Claire is celebrated on August 12. The pueblo also contains four ponds, miles of stream fishing, and picnicking and camping facilities. Permits for the use of trails, camping, and picnic areas, as well as for fishing in trout ponds, are available at the sites. ⊠ *NM 30, off NM 502, Española* ☏ *505/753–7326* ✑ *Pueblo free, cliff dwellings $5, still-camera permits $5* ☉ *Daily 9–4:30.*

JÉMEZ COUNTRY

In the Jémez region, the 1,000-year-old Ancestral Puebloan ruins at Bandelier National Monument present a vivid contrast to Los Alamos National Laboratory, birthplace of the atomic bomb. You can easily take in part of Jémez Country in a day trip from Santa Fe.

On this tour you can see terrific views of the Rio Grande Valley, the Sangre de Cristos, the Galisteo Basin, and, in the distance, the Sandias. There are places to eat and shop for essentials in Los Alamos and a few roadside eateries along NM 4 in La Cueva and Jémez Springs. There are also numerous turnouts along NM 4, several that have paths leading down to the many excellent fishing spots along the Jémez River.

The 48,000-acre Cerro Grande fire of 2000 burned much of the pine forest in the lower Jémez Mountains, as well as more than 250 homes in Los Alamos. Parts of the drive are still scarred with charcoaled remains, but vegetation has returned, and many homes have been rebuilt in the residential areas.

LOS ALAMOS
35 mi from Santa Fe via U.S. 285/84 north to NM 502 west.

Look at old books on New Mexico and you rarely find a mention of Los Alamos, now a busy town of 19,000 that has the highest per capita income in the state. Like so many other Southwestern communities, Los Alamos was created expressly as a company town; only here the workers weren't mining iron, manning freight trains, or hauling lumber— they were busy toiling at America's foremost nuclear research facility, Los Alamos National Laboratory (LANL). The facility still employs some 8,000 full-time workers, most living in town but many others in the Española Valley and even Santa Fe. The lab has experienced some tough times over the years, from the infamous Wen Ho Lee espionage case in the late '90s to a slew of alleged security breaches in 2003 and 2004. The controversies have shed some doubt on the future of LANL.

A few miles from ancient cave dwellings, scientists led by J. Robert Oppenheimer built Fat Man and Little Boy, the atom bombs that in August 1945 decimated Hiroshima and Nagasaki, respectively. LANL was created in 1943 under the auspices of the intensely covert Manhattan Project, whose express purpose was to expedite an Allied victory during World War II. Indeed, Japan surrendered—but a full-blown cold war between Russia and the United States ensued for another four and a half decades.

LANL works hard today to promote its broader platforms, including "enhancing global nuclear security" but also finding new ways to detect radiation, fighting pollution and environmental risks associated with nuclear energy, and furthering studies of the solar system, biology, and computer sciences. Similarly, the town of Los Alamos strives to be more well-rounded, better understood, and tourist-friendly.

ⓒ The **Bradbury Science Museum** is Los Alamos National Laboratory's public showcase, and its exhibits offer a balanced and provocative examination of such topics as atomic weapons and nuclear power. You can experiment with lasers; witness research in solar, geothermal, fission, and fusion energy; learn about DNA fingerprinting; and view exhibits about World War II's Project Y (the Manhattan Project, whose participants developed the atomic bomb). ⊠ *Los Alamos National Laboratory, 15th St. and Central Ave.* ☎ *505/667–4444* ⊕ *www.lanl.gov/museum* ⌨ *Free* ☉ *Tues.–Fri. 9–5, Sat.–Mon. 1–5.*

New Mexican architect John Gaw Meem designed **Fuller Lodge**, a short drive up Central Avenue from the Bradbury Science Museum. The massive log building was erected in 1928 as a dining and recreation hall for a small private boys' school. In 1942 the federal government purchased the school and made it the base of operations for the Manhattan Project. Part of the lodge contains an art center that shows the works of northern New Mexican artists; there's a picturesque rose garden on the grounds. This is a bustling center with drop-in art classes, nine art shows per year, and a gallery gift shop featuring 70 local artisans. ⊠ *2132 Central Ave.* ☎ *505/662–9331* ⊕ *www.artfulnm.org* ⌨ *Free* ☉ *Mon.–Sat. 10–4.*

NEED A BREAK? Join the ranks of locals, Los Alamos National Laboratory employees, and tourists who line up each morning at **Chili Works** (⊠ *1743 Trinity Dr.* ☎ *505/662–7591*) to sample one of the state's best breakfast burritos. This inexpensive, simple takeout spot is also worth a stop to grab breakfast or lunch before heading off for a hike at Bandelier. The burritos are stellar and the chile is *hot*.

The **Los Alamos Historical Museum,** in a log building beside Fuller Lodge, displays exhibits on the once-volatile geological history of the volcanic Jémez Mountains, the 700-year history of human life in this area, and more on—you guessed it—the Manhattan Project. It's rather jarring to observe ancient Puebloan potsherds and arrowheads in one display and photos of an obliterated Nagasaki in the next. ✉ *1921 Juniper St.* ☎ *505/662–4493* ⊕ *www.losalamoshistory.org* 🎫 *Free* ⊗ *Mon.–Sat. 9:30–4:30, Sun. 1–4.*

WHERE TO EAT AND STAY

$ ✕ **Blue Window Bistro.** Despite its relative wealth, Los Alamos has never
ECLECTIC cultivated much of a dining scene, which makes this cheerful and elegant
★ restaurant all the more appreciated by foodies. The kitchen turns out a mix of New Mexican, American, and Continental dishes, from a first-rate Cobb salad to steak topped with Jack cheese and green chile to double-cut pork chops with mashed potatoes, applewood-smoked bacon, and red-onion marmalade. In addition to the softly lighted dining room with terra-cotta walls, there are several tables on a patio overlooking a lush garden. ✉ *813 Central Ave.* ☎ *505/662–6305* 🖃 *AE, D, DC, MC, V* ⊗ *Closed Sun.*

$ 🏨 **Best Western Hilltop House Hotel.** Minutes from the Los Alamos National
HOTEL Laboratory, this three-story hotel hosts both vacationers and scientists. It's standard chain-hotel decor here: rooms are done with contemporary, functional furniture and have microwaves, refrigerators, and coffee-makers; deluxe ones have kitchenettes. The La Vista Restaurant on the premises serves tasty, if predictable, American fare. The very good Blue Window Bistro is next door. **Pros:** great proximity to the restaurants and shops in town; friendly, easygoing staff. **Cons:** this isn't a property with much character; but it's sufficient for business travelers and those wanting to use Los Alamos as a jumping-off point for excursions beyond Santa Fe. ✉ *400 Trinity Dr.* ☎ *505/662–2441 or 800/462–0936* ⊕ *www.bwhilltop.com* 🛏 *73 rooms, 19 suites* ♿ *In-room: a/c, kitchen (some), refrigerator, Wi-Fi. In-hotel: restaurant, room service, bar, pool, gym, laundry facilities, some pets allowed* 🖃 *AE, D, DC, MC, V* 🍽 *CP.*

BANDELIER NATIONAL MONUMENT

☺ *10 mi south of Los Alamos via NM 501 south to NM 4 east; 40 mi*
Fodor's Choice *north of Santa Fe via U.S. 285/84 north to NM 502 west to NM 4 west.*
★ Seven centuries before the Declaration of Independence was signed, compact city-states existed in the Southwest. Remnants of one of the most impressive of them can be seen at **Frijoles Canyon in Bandelier National Monument**. At the canyon's base, near a gurgling stream, are the remains of cave dwellings, ancient ceremonial kivas, and other stone structures that stretch out for more than a mile beneath the sheer walls of the canyon's tree-fringed rim. For hundreds of years the ancestral Puebloan people, relatives of today's Rio Grande Pueblo Indians, thrived on wild game, corn, and beans. Suddenly, for reasons still undetermined, the settlements were abandoned.

Wander through the site on a paved, self-guided trail. Steep wooden ladders and narrow doorways lead you to the cave dwellings and cell-like rooms. There is one kiva in the cliff wall that is large, and tall enough to stand in. Don't forget to look up, sometimes way up, into the nooks and crevices of the canyon wall above the dwellings to view the remarkable, mysterious petroglyphs left behind by the Ancestral Puebloans.

Bandelier National Monument, named after author and ethnologist Adolph Bandelier (his novel *The Delight Makers* is set in Frijoles Canyon), contains 23,000 acres of backcountry wilderness, waterfalls, and wildlife. Sixty miles of trails traverse the park. A small museum in the visitor center focuses on the area's prehistoric and contemporary Native American cultures, with displays of artifacts from 1200 to modern times as well as displays on the forest fires that have devastated parts of the park in recent years. There is a small café in the wonderful, 1930s CCC-built stone visitors complex. It is worth getting up early to get here when there are still shadows on the cliff walls because the petroglyphs are fantastic and all but disappear in the bright light of the afternoon. If you are staying in the area, ask about the night walks at the visitor center, they're stellar! Pets are not allowed on any trails. ☎ *505/672–0343* ⊕ *www.nps.gov/band/index.htm* ☒ *$12 per vehicle, good for 7 days* ☉ *Late May–early Sept., daily 8–6; early Sept.–Oct. and Apr.–late May, daily 8–5:30; Nov.–Mar., daily 8–4:30.*

VALLES CALDERA NATIONAL PRESERVE
15 mi southwest of Los Alamos via NM 4.

ℭ
Fodor's Choice
★
A high-forest drive brings you to the awe-inspiring Valles Grande, which at 14 mi in diameter is one of the world's largest calderas and which became Valles (say *vah*-yes) Caldera National Preserve in 2000. The caldera resulted from the eruption and collapse of a 14,000-foot peak over 1 million years ago; the flow out the bottom created the Pajarito Plateau and the ash from the eruption spread as far east as Kansas. You can't imagine the volcanic crater's immensity until you spot what look like specks of dust on the lush meadow floor and realize they're elk. The Valles Caldera Trust manages this 89,000-acre multiuse preserve with the aim to "protect and preserve the scientific, scenic, geologic, watershed, fish, wildlife, historic, cultural, and recreational values of the Preserve, and to provide for multiple use and sustained yield of renewable resources within the Preserve."

The preserve is open to visitors for hiking, cross-country skiing, horseback riding, horse-drawn carriage rides, van wildlife photography tours, mountain-bike tours, bird-watching, and fly-fishing. Some of the activities require reservations and a fee, although there are two free, relatively short hikes signposted from the parking area along NM 4, and no reservations are needed for these. Drive into the Caldera to the check-in station to gain access to other short hikes, guided tours, and information about events. Their Web site is the best source to plan a visit to this breathtaking area. Fishing and hunting (elk and turkeys) permits are given out based on a lottery system; lottery "tickets" are sold for a nominal fee. ⊠ *18161 NM 4* ☎ *505/661–3333 or 866/382–5537* ⊕ *www.vallescaldera.gov.*

JÉMEZ SPRINGS
20 mi west of Valles Caldera on NM 4.

The funky mountain village of Jémez (say *hay*-mess) Springs draws outdoorsy types for hiking, cross-country skiing, and camping in the nearby U.S. Forest Service areas. The town's biggest tourist draws are

Jémez State Monument and Soda Dam, but many people come here for relaxation at the town's bathhouse.

The geological wonder known as **Soda Dam** was created over thousands of years by travertine deposits—minerals that precipitate out of geothermal springs. With its strange mushroom-shaped exterior and caves split by a roaring waterfall, it's no wonder the spot was considered sacred by Native Americans. In summer it's popular for swimming. ⊠ *NM 4, 1 mi north of Jémez State Monument.*

Jémez State Monument contains impressive Spanish and Native American ruins set throughout a 7-acre site and toured via an easy 1/3-mi loop trail. About 700 years ago ancestors of the people of Jémez Pueblo built several villages in and around the narrow mountain valley. One of the villages was Guisewa, or "Place of the Boiling Waters." The Spanish colonists built a mission church beside it, San José de los Jémez, which was abandoned by around 1640. ⊠ *NM 4* ☎ *575/829–3530* ⊕ *www. nmstatemonuments.org* ✉ *$3* ⊙ *Wed.–Mon. 8:30–5.*

★ Now owned and operated by the village of Jémez Springs, the original structure at the **Jémez Spring Bath House** was erected in the 1870s near a mineral hot spring. Many other buildings were added over the years, and the complex was completely renovated into an intimate Victorian-style hideaway in the mid-1990s. It's a funky, low-key spot that's far less formal and fancy than the several spa resorts near Santa Fe. You can soak in a mineral bath for $12 (30 minutes) or $17 (60 minutes). Massages cost between $42 (30 minutes) and $98 (90 minutes). An acupuncturist is available with advance notice. Beauty treatments include facials, manicures, and pedicures. The Jémez Package ($95) includes a half-hour bath, an herbal blanket wrap, and a one-hour massage. You can stroll down a short path behind the house to see where the steaming hot springs feed into the Jémez River. The tubs are not communal, but individual, and there are no outdoor tubs. Children under 14 are not allowed. ⊠ *062 Jémez Springs Plaza, off NM 4 Jémez Springs* ☎ *575/829–3303 or 866/204–8303* ⊕ *www.jemezsprings.org/ bathhouse.html* ✉ *Free* ⊙ *June–early Nov., daily 10–8; early Nov.–May, daily 10–6.*

Giggling Springs offers a large, outdoor, natural-mineral hot spring. Right across the street from the Laughing Lizard, this is a good option for the soakers who want hot water but don't want the individualized treatments at the Bath House. The staff is very accommodating. Children under 14 are not permitted. Pool capacity is limited to eight at a time; reservations are recommended. ⊠ *040 Abousleman Loop* ☎ *575/829–9175* ⊕ *www.gigglingsprings.com* ✉ *$15 per hour, $25 for two hours, $35 for the day* ⊙ *Closed Mon. and Tues.*

WHERE TO STAY

$ ⊡ **Cañon del Rio.** On 6 acres along the Jémez River beneath towering mesas, this light-filled, contemporary adobe inn has rooms with cove ceilings, tile floors, and Native American arts and crafts. All have French doors and open onto a courtyard with a natural-spring fountain. Wellness packages include massage, acupuncture, and aromatherapy. Breakfasts are a big deal here and they're delicious. **Pros:** property has an abundance of water—a real treat in New Mexico. **Cons:** though rooms are comfortable, the decor looks like that of a Southwestern chain hotel. ✉ *16445 NM 4* ☎ *575/829–4377* ⊕ *www.canondelrio.com* ↩ *6 rooms, 1 suite* ⚘ *In-room: a/c, kitchen (some), no TV. In-hotel: Wi-Fi hotspot* ▤ *AE, D, MC, V* ⦿ *CP.*

¢ ▦ **Laughing Lizard Inn and Cafe.** Consisting of a simple four-room motel-style inn and a cute adobe-and-stone café with a corrugated-metal roof, the Laughing Lizard makes for a sweet and cheerful diversion—it's right in the center of the village. Rooms are cozy and simple with white linens, dressers, books, and porches that look out over the rugged mesa beyond the river valley. Tasty, eclectic fare—great salads, freshly ground burgers, super calzones and pizzas, and a lineup of New Mexican favorites—is served in the homey café, which has a Saltillo-tile screened porch and an open-air wooden deck. This hub of friendly energy is owned and operated by the Lagan family, and their care and attention shows. **Pros:** great staff; beautiful location. **Cons:** rooms are fairly small; no a/c. ✉ *NM 4* ☎ *575/829–3108* ⊕ *www.thelaughinglizard.com* ↩ *4 rooms* ⚘ *In-room: no a/c. In-hotel: restaurant, some pets allowed* ▤ *D, MC, V.*

JÉMEZ PUEBLO
12 mi south of Jémez Springs via NM 4; 85 mi west of Santa Fe via U.S. 285/84 and NM 4; 50 mi north of Albuquerque via I–25, U.S. 550, and NM 4.

As you continue southwest along NM 4, the terrain changes from a wooded river valley with high mesas on either side to an open red-rock valley, the home of the Jémez Pueblo, which is set along the Jémez River. After the pueblo at Pecos (⇨ *Pecos National Historic Park, above*) was abandoned in 1838, Jémez was the state's only pueblo with residents who spoke Towa (different from Tiwa and Tewa). The Jémez Reservation encompasses 89,000 acres, with two lakes, Holy Ghost Springs and Dragonfly Lake (off NM 4), open for fishing by permit only, April to October on weekends and holidays. The only part of the pueblo open to the public is the **Walatowa Visitor Center,** a fancy Pueblo Revival building that contains a small museum, an extensive pottery and crafts shop, and rotating art and photography exhibits; there's a short nature walk outside. The pueblo is sometimes open to the public for special events, demonstrations, and ceremonial dances—call for details. The pueblo is noted for its polychrome pottery. The Walatowa gas and convenience store, on NM 4 next to the visitor center, is one of the few such establishments between Los Alamos and Bernalillo. Photographing, sketching, and video recording are prohibited. ✉ *7413 NM 4* ☎ *575/834–7235* ⊕ *www.jemezpueblo.org* ▥ *Free* ☾ *Daily 8–5.*

GEORGIA O'KEEFFE COUNTRY

It's a 20-minute drive north of Santa Fe to reach the Española Valley, where you head west to the striking mesas, cliffs, and valleys that so inspired the artist Georgia O'Keeffe—she lived in this area for the final 50 years of her life. You first come to the small, workaday city of Española, a major crossroads from which roads lead to Taos, Chama, and

Abiquiu. The other notable community in this area is tiny Ojo Caliente, famous for its hot-springs spa retreat.

ESPAÑOLA
20 mi north of Santa Fe via U.S. 285/84.

This small but growing city midway along the Low Road from Santa Fe to Taos is a business hub for the many villages and pueblos scattered throughout the region north of Santa Fe. The area at the confluence of the Rio Grande and Rio Chama was declared the capital for Spain by Don Juan de Oñate in 1598, but wasn't more than a collection of small settlements until the town was founded in 1880s as a stop on the Denver & Rio Grande Railroad. Lacking the colonial charm of either Santa Fe or Taos, Española is known for being pretty rough-and-tumble. There are many cheap burger joints, New Mexican restaurants, and a few chain motels, but few reasons to stick around for more than a quick meal. The city has become known as the "lowrider capital of the world" because of the mostly classic cars that have been retrofitted with lowered chassis and hydraulics that allow the cars to bump and grind as they cruise the streets on perpetual parade. The cars are often painted with religious murals, homages to dead relatives, and other spectacular scenes.

You may see a number of people wearing white (and sometimes orange or blue) turbans; they are members of the large American Sikh community that settled on the south end of town in the late 60s. Initially viewed with suspicion by the provincial Hispanics of the area, the Sikhs have become integral members of the community, teaching Kundalini yoga, establishing businesses and medical practices, and influencing many local restaurants to add vegetarian versions of New Mexican dishes to their menus.

All the main arteries converge in the heart of town amidst a series of drab shopping centers, so watch the signs on the town's south side. Traffic moves slowly, especially on weekend nights when cruisers bring car culture alive.

NEED A BREAK? **Lovin' Oven** serves delicious homemade donuts, apple fritters, biscochito cookies, turnovers, and hot coffee amidst all the latest news and gossip shared amongst the hordes of locals who pour through the doors at this sweet little shop on Española's south end. Get there early—once the goodies are gone they're gone. ⊠ 🖷 *107 N. Riverside Dr.* ☎ *505/753-5461.*

The region is known for its longstanding weaving traditions, and one place you can learn about this heritage is the **Española Valley Fiber Arts Center** (⊠ *325 Paseo de Oñate* ☎ *505/747-3577* ⊕ *www.evfac.org* 🖷 *Free* ☉ *Mon. 9–8, Tues.–Sat. 9–5, Sun. noon–5*), a nonprofit, teaching facility set inside an adobe building in the city's historic section. Here you can watch local weavers working with traditional materials and looms and admire (and purchase) their works in a small gallery. There are also classes offered on spinning, weaving, and knitting, which are open to the public and range from one day to several weeks. Emphasis here is placed on the styles of weaving that have been practiced here in the northern Rio Grande Valley since the Spaniards brought sheep and treadle looms here in the late 16th century. The center also celebrates the ancient traditions of New Mexico's Navajo and Pueblo weavers.

WHERE TO EAT AND STAY

$$

MEXICAN

Fodor's Choice

★

✕ **El Paragua Restaurant.** With a dark, intimate atmosphere of wood and stone, this historic place started out as a lemonade-cum-taco stand in the late 1950s but is now known for some of the state's most authentic New Mexican and regional Mexican cuisine. Steaks and fish are grilled over a mesquite-wood fire; other specialties include chorizo enchiladas, panfried breaded trout amandine, and menudo. This restaurant is still a family affair; service is gracious and the food is worth the drive. If you don't have time to sit down for a meal, stop at El Parasol taco stand (¢) in the parking lot next door for excellent, cheap Mexican–New Mexican fare. Vegetarians rejoice! Ask for the Khalsa special, a superdelicious veggie quesadilla created for the local Sikhs (the many folks you may see around the area wearing white turbans), or try the veggie tacos. You'll also find El Parasol restaurants on the 84/285 frontage road in Pojoaque, and at 1833 Cerrillos Road in Santa Fe. ⊠ *603 Santa Cruz Rd., NM 76 just east of NM 68* ☎ *505/753–3211 or 800/929–8226* ⊕ *www.elparagua.com* ⊟ *AE, DC, MC, V.*

$$$$

INN AND VILLAS

Fodor's Choice

★

▦ **Rancho de San Juan.** This secluded 225-acre compound hugs Black Mesa's base. Many of the inn's rooms are self-contained suites, some set around a courtyard and others amid the wilderness. All rooms have Southwestern furnishings, Frette robes, Aveda bath products, and CD stereos; nearly all have kiva fireplaces. The top units have such cushy touches as two bedrooms, 12-foot ceilings, Mexican marble showers, kitchens, Jacuzzis, and private patios. The à la carte menu in the Three Forks restaurant (dinner Tuesday through Saturday, by reservation only) features inventive contemporary cuisine, changes weekly. Past fare has included Texas quail stuffed with corn bread, green chiles, and linguica sausage, and Alaskan halibut with tomatillo-lime salsa, caramelized butternut squash, and creamed spinach. Hike to a beautiful hand-carved sandstone shrine on a bluff above the property. In-suite spa and massage services are available. **Pros:** an ideal secluded getaway close to Ojo Caliente and out of the bustle of Santa Fe. **Cons:** property is a virtual island in rural New Mexico and you must drive to sights and restaurants; service not always as attentive to guests' needs considering the rates. ⊠ *U.S. 285, 3½ mi north of U.S. 84* ⌂ *Box 4140, 87533* ☎ *505/753–6818* ⊕ *www.ranchodesanjuan.com* ⇲ *4 suites, 9 casitas* ⚒ *In-room: no a/c (some), kitchen (some), no TV. In-hotel: restaurant, Wi-Fi hotspot, no kids under 8* ⊟ *AE, D, DC, MC, V* ⅏ *MAP.*

HORSEBACK RIDING

Santa Fe Stables (⊠ *115 NM 399, Espanola* ☎ *505/231–7113* ⊕ *www. santaferidingcompany.com*) clearly treats its horses well, and the staff of wranglers are good with people, too. Private rides ensure you're a personal experience as you explore the gorgeous scenery on Santa Clara Pueblo's Black Mesa. Rides are generally two hours; special trips can be arranged in advance.

ABIQUIU
24 mi northwest of Española via U.S. 84.

This tiny, very traditional Hispanic village was originally home to freed *genizaros,* indigenous and mixed-blood slaves who served as house servants, shepherds, and other key roles in Spanish, Mexican, and American households well into the 1880s. Genizaros now make up a significant population of the state. Many descendants of original families still live in the area, although since the late 1980s Abiquiu and its surrounding countryside have become a nesting ground for those fleeing big-city life, among them actresses Marsha Mason and Shirley MacLaine. Abiquiu—along with parts of the nearby Española Valley— is also a hotbed of organic farming, with many of the operations here selling their goods at the Santa Fe Farmers' Market and to restaurants throughout the Rio Grande Valley. Newcomers or visitors may find themselves shut out by locals; it's best to observe one very important local custom: no photography is allowed in and around the village.

A number of artists live in Abiquiu, and several studios showing traditional Hispanic art as well as contemporary works and pottery, are open regularly to the public; many others open each year over Columbus Day weekend (second weekend of October) for the **Annual Abiquiu Studio Tour** (☎ *505/685–4454* ⊕ *www.abiquiustudiotour.org*).

Fodor's Choice You can visit **Georgia O'Keeffe's home** through advance reservation (about
★ four months is recommended if you come during high season) with the **Georgia O'Keeffe Museum** (☎ *505/685–4539* ⊕ *www.okeeffemuseum. org*), which conducts one-hour tours Tuesday, Thursday, and Friday, mid-March through November for $30, with additional tours on Wednesday in July and August, for $40. In 1945 Georgia O'Keeffe bought a large, dilapidated late-18th-century Spanish-colonial adobe compound just off the plaza. Upon the 1946 death of her husband, photographer Alfred Stieglitz, she left New York City and began dividing her time permanently between this home, which figured prominently in many of her works, and the one in nearby Ghost Ranch. She wrote about the house, "When I first saw the Abiquiu house it was a ruin. As I climbed and walked about in the ruin I found a patio with a very pretty well house and a bucket to draw up water. It was a good-sized patio with a long wall with a door on one side. That wall with a door in it was something I had to have. It took me 10 years to get it—three more years to fix the house up so I could live in it—and after that the wall with the door was painted many times." The patio is featured in *Black Patio Door* (1955) and *Patio with Cloud* (1956). O'Keeffe died in 1986 at the age of 98 and left provisions in her will to ensure that the property's houses would never be public monuments.

WHERE TO STAY

$$ ⊡ **Abiquiu Inn and Cafe Abiquiu.** Deep in the Chama Valley, the inn has
INN   a secluded, exotic feel—almost like an oasis—with brightly decorated rooms, including several four-person casitas, with woodstoves or fireplaces and tiled baths; some units have verandas with hammocks and open views of O'Keeffe Country. The café ($$) serves commendable New Mexican, Italian, and American fare, from blue-corn tacos stuffed

with grilled trout to lamb-and-poblano stew; it's also known for its seasonal fresh-fruit cobblers. The inn is the departure point for O'Keeffe-home tours, where the O'Keeffe Museum has a small office. It has an art gallery featuring local work, crafts shop, and gardens. Two basic but very comfortable rooms are available for $80. The RV park on the property offers full hookups and a dump station for $35 per night. **Pros:** good base for exploring O'Keeffe Country; gorgeous, lush setting **Cons:** service is friendly but fairly hands-off; rooms at the front of the inn get noise from the road. ⊠ *21120 U.S. 84* ⊕ *Box 120, 87510* ☎ *505/685–4378 or 888/735–2902* ⊕ *www.abiquiuinn.com* ⥅ *25 rooms, 6 suites, 5 casitas* ⌂ *In-room: a/c, kitchen (some). In-hotel: restaurant, Wi-Fi hotspot* ⊟ *AE, D, DC, MC, V.*

SHOPPING

Bode's (⊠ *U.S. 84, look for Phillips 66 gas station sign* ☎ *505/685–4422* ⊕ *www.bodes.com*), pronounced *boh*-dees, across from the Abiqui post office, is much more than a gas station. It's a popular stop for newspapers, quirky gifts, locally made arts and crafts, cold drinks, supplies, fishing gear (including licenses), amazing breakfast burritos, hearty green-chile stew, sandwiches, and other short-order fare. The friendly, busy station serves as general store and exchange post for news and gossip.

GHOST RANCH

10 mi northwest of Abiquiu on U.S. 84.

For art historians, the name Ghost Ranch brings to mind Georgia O'Keeffe, who lived on a small parcel of this 20,000-acre dude and cattle ranch. The ranch's owner in the 1930s—conservationist and publisher of *Nature Magazine*, Arthur Pack—first invited O'Keeffe here to visit in 1934; Pack soon sold the artist the 7-acre plot on which she lived summer through fall for most of the rest of her life.

In 1955 Pack donated the rest of the ranch to the Presbyterian Church, which continues to use Pack's original structures and about 55 acres of land as a conference center.

Ⓢ **Fodor's Choice** ★ The **Ghost Ranch Education and Retreat Center,** open to the public year-round, is busiest in summer, when the majority of workshops take place. Subjects range from poetry and literary arts to photography, horseback riding, and every conceivable traditional craft of northern New Mexico. These courses are open to the public, and guests camp or stay in semirustic cottages or casitas. If you're here for a day trip, after registering at the main office, you may come in and hike high among the wind-hewn rocks so beloved by O'Keeffe. The **Florence Hawley Ellis Museum of Anthropology** contains Native American tools, pottery, and other artifacts excavated from the Ghost Ranch Gallina digs. Pioneer anthropologist Florence Hawley Ellis conducted excavations at Chaco Canyon and at other sites in New Mexico. Adjacent to the Ellis Museum, the **Ruth Hall Museum of Paleontology** exhibits the New Mexico state fossil, the *Coelophysis,* also known as the littlest dinosaur (it was about 7 to 9 feet long), originally excavated near Ghost Ranch. For the art lover, or the lover of the New Mexican landscape, Ghost Ranch offers guided O'Keeffe & Ghost Ranch Landscape Tours of the specific sites on the ranch that O'Keeffe painted during the five decades that she summered here. Her original house is not part of the tour and is closed to the public. These one-hour tours are available mid-March through mid-October, on Tuesday, Wednesday, Friday, and Saturday at 1:30 and 3; the cost is $25, and you must call first to make a reservation. The landscape tours are timed to coincide with the tours given at her house in Abiquiu, although they have nothing to do with the O'Keeffe studio tours offered there. Here's a little-known tidbit: limited camping is available on Ghost Ranch for both RVs and tents ($16–$26) and full hookups are available for RVs.

The **Ghost Ranch Piedra Lumbre Education and Visitor Center** (⊠ *U.S. 84, just north of main Ghost Ranch entrance* ☎ *505/685–4312*), which is part of the Ghost Ranch organization has a gallery with rotating art presentations, exhibits on New Mexico's natural history, a gift shop, and two museums. ⊠ *U.S. 84, between mileposts 224 and 225, about 13 mi north of Abiquiu* ☎ *505/685–4333* ⊕ *www.ghostranch.org* ☜ *$3 minimum suggested donation* ⊠ *U.S. 84, just north of main Ghost Ranch entrance* ☎ *505/685–4312* ⊕ *www.ghostranch.org* ☜ *Donations accepted* ☉ *Visitor center Mar.–Oct., daily 9–5. Florence Hawley Ellis Museum of Anthropology and Ruth Hall Museum of Paleantology late May–early Sept., Tues.–Sat. 9–5, Sun. and Mon. 1–5; early Sept.–late May, Tues.–Sat. 9–5.*

OFF THE BEATEN PATH

Monastery of Christ in the Desert. Designed by renowned Japanese-American architect and wood carver George Nakashima, this remote rock-and-adobe church—with one of the state's most spectacular natural settings—can be visited for daily prayer or silent overnight retreats (if requested in advance by mail or e-mail); there are basic accommodations for up to 16 guests (10 single and 3 double rooms), and there's a two-night minimum, with most visitors staying for several days. A suggested per-night donation of $50 to $125 is requested, depending on the room, and none have electricity. Day visitors can come anytime and stroll the grounds, visit the gift shop, and participate in different prayer services throughout the day, but are asked to respect the silence practiced at the monastery. The road is rutted in places and becomes impassable during rainy weather—you can definitely get stuck here for a day, or even a few days, during particularly wet periods, such as summer monsoon season. Check weather forecasts carefully if you're only intending to visit for the day. ⊹ *Pass Ghost Ranch visitor center and turn left on Forest Service Rd. 151; follow dirt road 13 mi to monastery* ⊡ *Box 270, Abiquiu 87510* ☎ *801/545–8567 messages only* ⊕ *www. christdesert.org.*

CHAMA
95 mi northwest of Taos on U.S. 64, 59 mi north of Abiquiu on U.S. 84.

A railroad town nestled at the base of 10,000-foot Cumbre Pass, lush and densely wooded Chama offers year-round outdoor activities, as well as a scenic railroad. From here, U.S. 84 hugs the Rio Chama and leads southward through monumental red rocks and golden sandstone spires that inspired Georgia O'Keeffe's vivid paintings of creased mountains, stark crosses, bleached animal skulls, and adobe architecture.

The booms and busts of Chama have largely coincided with the popularity of train transportation. The town's earliest boom, which precipitated its founding, occurred in the 1880s when workers piled into town to construct the Denver & Rio Grande Railroad. In those days, narrow-gauge trains chugged over the high mountain tracks carrying gold and silver out from the mines of the San Juan Mountains, which straddle the nearby Colorado–New Mexico border. Gambling halls, moonshine stills, speakeasies, and brothels were a fixture along the main drag, Terrace Avenue. The lumber industry also thrived during the early years, and the town still has quite a few houses and buildings fashioned out of spare hand-hewn railroad ties.

Chama's outdoor recreation opportunities are hard to beat. Vast meadows of wildflowers and aspen and ponderosa pines blanket the entire region. Hunters are drawn here by the abundant wildlife. There's cross-country skiing and snowmobiling in winter; camping, rafting, hiking, and fishing in summer, all in a pristine, green, high-mountain setting that feels like the top of the world. The temperate mountain air means that most lodgings in the area neither have nor need air-conditioning.

The big attraction in Chama is the historic **Cumbres & Toltec Scenic Railroad,** the narrow-gauge coal-driven steam engine that runs through the San Juan Mountains and over the Cumbres Pass. You chug over ancient trestles, around breathtaking bends, and high above the Los Pinos River—if the terrain looks at all familiar, you may have seen this railroad's "performance" in *Indiana Jones and the Last Crusade.* Midway through the trip you break for lunch and can switch to a waiting Colorado-based train to complete the 64 mi to Antonito, Colorado (from which you'll be shuttled back by bus), or return from this point on the same train. ⊠ *15 Terrace Ave.* ☎ *575/756–2151 or 888/286–2737* ⊕ *www.cumbrestoltec.com* ⊠ *$65–$134* ☼ *Late May–mid.-Oct., daily departures at 10* am.

LOS OJOS

13 mi south of Chama on U.S. 64/84.

Los Ojos, midway between Tierra Amarilla and Chama, could well serve as a model for rural economic development worldwide. The little town has experienced an economic revival of sorts by returning to its ancient roots—the raising of Churro sheep (the original breed brought over by the Spanish, prized for its wool) and weaving. Ganados del Valle, the community-based, nonprofit economic development corporation headquartered here, has created jobs and increased prosperity by returning to the old ways, with improved marketing. You can also find a smattering of artists' studios, most of them in rustic buildings with corrugated metal roofs.

The cooperative **Tierra Wools** produces some of the finest original weavings in the Southwest. Designs are based on the old Rio Grande styles, and weavers make rugs and capes of superb craftsmanship entirely by hand, using old-style looms. Weaving workshops are offered. ⊠ *91 Main St.* ☎ *575/588–7231 or 888/709–0979* ⊕ *www.handweavers.com* ☼ *June–Oct., Mon.–Sat. 10–6, Sun. 11–4; Nov.–May, Mon.–Sat. 10–5.*

OJO CALIENTE

28 mi northeast of Abiquiu by way of El Rito via NM 554 to NM 111 to U.S. 285, 50 mi north of Santa Fe on U.S. 285.

Ojo Caliente is the only place in North America where five different types of hot springs—iron, lithium, arsenic, salt, and soda—are found side by side. The town was named by Spanish explorer Cabeza de Vaca, who visited in 1535 and believed he had stumbled upon the Fountain of Youth. Modern-day visitors draw a similar conclusion about the restorative powers of the springs. The spa itself, originally built in the 1920s, comprises a hotel and cottages, a restaurant, a gift shop, massage rooms, men's and women's bathhouses, a chlorine-free swimming pool, and indoor and outdoor mineral-water tubs. The hotel, one of the original bathhouses, and the springs are all on the National Register of Historic Places, as is the adjacent and recently restored Round Barn, from which visitors can take horseback tours and guided hikes to ancient Pueblo dwellings and petroglyph-etched rocks. Spa services include wraps, massage, facials, and acupuncture. The setting at the foot of sandstone cliffs topped by the ruins of ancient Native American pueblos is nothing short of inspiring and is heavily frequented by locals as well as tourists.

WHERE TO STAY

$$
RESORT COT-
TAGES

🏨 **Ojo Caliente Mineral Springs Spa and Resort.** Accommodations run the gamut from spartan in the unfussy 1916 hotel (no TVs, simple furnishings) to rather upscale in the elegant suites, which were added in recent years. Rooms in the hotel have bathrooms but no showers or tubs—bathing takes place in the mineral springs (it's an arrangement that pleases most longtime devotees but doesn't sit well with others). The cottages are quite comfy, with refrigerators and TVs; some have kitchenettes, with tile showers in the bathrooms. The 12 spacious suites have such luxury touches as kiva fireplaces and patios; half have private, double soaking tubs outside, which are filled with Ojo mineral waters. All lodgers have complimentary access to the mineral pools and *milagro* (miracle) wraps, and the bathhouse has showers. Horseback tours can be prearranged. The Artesian Restaurant ($$) serves world-beat fare in a charming dining room. Four-day and overnight packages are available. There's also camping on-site, beside the cottonwood-shaded Rio Ojo Caliente—double-occupancy camping rates are $20 for tents, $20 for RVs. **Pros:** can feel like a real getaway for fairly reasonable rates. **Cons:** service and treatments can be lackluster. ⊠ *50 Los Baños Dr., off U.S. 285, 30 mi north of Española* ☎ *Box 68, 87549* ☏ *505/583–2233 or 800/222–9162* ⊕ *www.ojocalientesprings.com* ➶ *19 rooms, 19 cottages, 12 suites, 3 3-bedroom houses* ⚐ *In-room: no a/c, no phone, kitchen (some), refrigerator (some), no TV (some), Wi-Fi. In-hotel: restaurant, spa* ☐ *AE, D, DC, MC, V.*

LOW ROAD TO TAOS

Widely considered the efficient route to Taos, the Low Road actually offers plenty of dazzling scenery once you get through traffic-clogged Española and into the Rio Grande Gorge. As you emerge from the gorge roughly 25 minutes later, NM 68 cuts up over a plateau that affords utterly stupendous views of Taos, the Rio Grande gorge, and the surrounding mountains. Note that whether you take the Low Road or the High Road (⇨ *below*), you first follow U.S. 285/84 north from Santa Fe for about 20 mi, where it's a wide, limited-access freeway. Whereas you exit the highway just north of Pojoaque in order to travel the High Road, you remain on U.S. 285/84 all the way to Española to follow the Low Road; once there, you pick up NM 68 north. Just before you enter into the Rio Grande Gorge, where you parallel the river for several scenic miles, you pass through the tiny but lavishly fertile Velarde, which has a number of fruit and vegetable stands worth stopping for. Without stops, it takes 80 to 90 minutes to make it from Santa Fe to Taos via the Low Road, whereas the High Road takes 2 to 2½ hours.

DIXON

45 mi north of Santa Fe via U.S. 285/84 and NM 68, 20 mi south of Taos via NM 68.

The small village of Dixon and its surrounding country lanes are home to a surprising number of artists. Artistic sensitivity, as well as generations of dedicated farmers, account for the community's well-tended fields, pretty gardens, and fruit trees—a source of produce for restaurants and farmers' markets such as the one in Santa Fe. It's simple to find your way around; there's only one main road.

At the enormously popular **Dixon Studio Tour** (⊕ *www.dixonarts.org*), the first full weekend in November, when area artists open up their home studios to the public. The Web site suggests several nearby guesthouse accommodations and provides a detailed map of the village and its participating artists. The Dixon Arts Association has some four dozen members, many represented in a cooperative gallery attached to **Métier Weaving & Gallery** (✉ *NM 75* ☎ *505/579–4111*), which also has a showroom that sells the textiles and weavings of artists and owners Irene Smith and Lezlie King.

WHERE TO STAY

$ 🏨 **Rock Pool Gardens.** This private guesthouse has two warmly furnished
INN two-bedroom suites, one with a kitchenette and a bathroom connecting the bedrooms, the other with a full kitchen. Each has its own access and patio. The rustic walls, Mexican tile work, and country furnishings lend a cozy air to these otherwise contemporary suites, and lush gardens surround the building. There's a Jacuzzi under the trees and an indoor heated pool set in natural rock. Both suites can be rented for a group for $160 per night. **Pros:** one of the few accommodations between Española and Taos, and it's also a good value. **Cons:** no restaurants or sights within walking distance. ✉ *NM 75* ☎ *505/579–4602* ⇆ *2 suites* ⚒ *In-room: a/c, kitchen, refrigerator, Wi-Fi. In-hotel: pool, some pets allowed* ▭ *No credit cards* ○| *CP.*

THE HIGH ROAD TO TAOS

The main highway to Taos (NM 68) is a good, even scenic, route if you've got limited time, but by far the most spectacular route is what is known as the High Road. Towering peaks, lush hillsides, orchards, and meadows surround tiny, ancient Hispanic villages that are as picturesque as they are historically fascinating. The High Road follows U.S. 285/84 north to NM 503 (a right turn just past Pojoaque), to County Road 98 (a left toward Chimayó), to NM 76 northeast to NM 75 east, to NM 518 north. The drive takes you through the badlands of stark, weathered rock—where numerous Westerns have been filmed—quickly into rolling foothills, lush canyons, and finally into pine forests. Although most of these insular, traditional Hispanic communities offer little in the way of shopping and dining, the region has become a haven for artists.

From Chimayó to Peñasco, you can find mostly low-key but often high-quality art galleries, many of them run out of the owners' homes. During the final two weekends in September each year, more than 100 artists show their work in the **High Road Art Tour** (☎ *866/343–5381* ⊕ *www.highroadnewmexico.com*) ; call or visit the Web site for a studio map.

Depending on when you make this drive, you're in for some of the state's most radiant scenery. In mid-April the orchards are in blossom; summer turns the valleys into lush green oases; and in fall the smell of piñon adds to the sensual overload of golden leaves and red-chile ristras hanging from the houses. In winter the fields are covered with quilts of snow, and the lines of homes, fences, and trees stand out like bold pen-and-ink drawings against the sky. But the roads can be icy and treacherous—if in doubt, stick with the Low Road to Taos. If you decide to take the High Road just one way between Santa Fe and Taos, you might want to save it for the return journey—the scenery is even more stunning when traveling north to south.

CHIMAYÓ

28 mi north of Santa Fe, 10 mi east of Española on NM 76.

From U.S. 285/84 north of Pojoaque, scenic NM 503 winds past horse paddocks and orchards in the narrow Nambé Valley, then ascends into the red-sandstone canyons with a view of Truchas Peaks to the northeast before dropping into the bucolic village of Chimayó. Nestled into hillsides where gnarled piñons seem to grow from bare bedrock, Chimayó is famed for its weaving, its red chiles, and its two chapels.

Fodor'sChoice **El Santuario de Chimayó,** a small, frontier, adobe church, has a fantasti-
★ cally carved and painted reredos (altar screen) and is built on the site where, believers say, a mysterious light came from the ground on Good Friday in 1810 and where a large wooden crucifix was found beneath the earth. The chapel sits above a sacred *pozito* (a small hole), the dirt from which is believed to have miraculous healing properties. Dozens of abandoned crutches and braces placed in the anteroom—along with many notes, letters, and photos—testify to this. The Santuario draws a steady stream of worshippers year-round—Chimayó is considered the Lourdes of the Southwest. During Holy Week as many as 50,000 pilgrims come here. The shrine is a National Historic Landmark. It's surrounded by small adobe shops selling every kind of religious curio imaginable and some very fine traditional Hispanic work from local

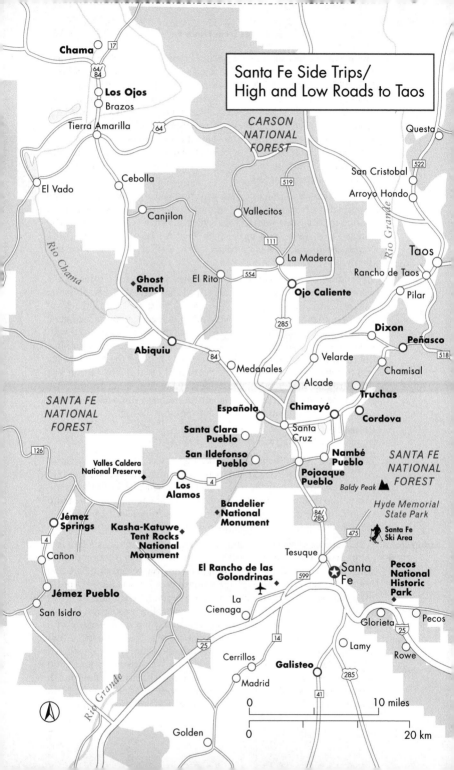

Santa Fe Side Trips/
High and Low Roads to Taos

Chama
17
64/84
Los Ojos
Brazos
Tierra Amarilla
64
CARSON
NATIONAL
FOREST
Questa
522
San Cristobal
Arroyo Hondo
519
Vallecitos
Cebolla
El Vado
Canjilon
Rio Chama
111
La Madera
Taos
Ghost
Ranch
El Rito
554
Rancho de Taos
Ojo Caliente
Pilar
285
Dixon
Peñasco
Abiquiu
84
Medanales
Velarde
518
Chamisal
Alcade
Truchas
SANTA FE
NATIONAL
FOREST
Española
Chimayó
Cordova
126
Santa Clara
Pueblo
Santa
Cruz
San Ildefonso
Pueblo
Nambé
Pueblo
SANTA FE
NATIONAL
FOREST
Valles Caldera
National Preserve
4
Pojoaque
Pueblo
Baldy Peak
Los
Alamos
Hyde Memorial
State Park
Jémez
Springs
Kasha-Katuwe
Tent Rocks
National
Monument
Bandelier
National
Monument
84/
285
475
Santa Fe
Ski Area
4
Cañon
Tesuque
599
Pecos
National
Historic
Park
Jémez Pueblo
El Rancho de las
Golondrinas
Santa
Fe
San Isidro
La
Cienaga
Glorieta
25
Pecos
14
Lamy
Rowe
25
Cerrillos
Galisteo
285
Madrid
41
0   10 miles

0   20 km

Golden

artists. ⊠ *Signed lane off CR 98* ☎ *505/351–4889* ⊕ *www.holychimayo. us* ☞ *Free* ☉ *June–Sept., daily 9–5; Oct.–May, daily 9–4.*

A smaller chapel 200 yards from El Santuario was built in 1857 and dedicated to **Santo Niño de Atocha.** As at the more famous Santuario, the dirt at Santo Niño de Atocha's chapel is said to have healing properties in the place where the *Santo Niño* was first placed. The little boy saint was brought here from Mexico by Severiano Medina, who claimed Santo Niño de Atocha had healed him of rheumatism. San Ildefonso pottery master Maria Martinez came here for healing as a child. Tales of the boy saint's losing one of his shoes as he wandered through the countryside helping those in trouble endeared him to the people of northern New Mexico. It became a tradition to place shoes at the foot of the statue as an offering. Many soldiers who survived the Bataan Death March during World War II credit Santo Niño for saving them, adding to his beloved status in this state where the percentage of young people who enlist in the military remains quite high. ⊠ *Signed lane off CR 98* ☞ *Free* ☉ *June–Sept., daily 9–5; Oct.–May, daily 9–4.*

WHERE TO EAT AND STAY

$ ✕ **Rancho de Chimayó.** In a century-old adobe hacienda tucked into the
SOUTHWESTERN mountains, with whitewashed walls, hand-stripped vigas, and cozy din-
★ ing rooms, the Rancho de Chimayó is still owned and operated by the family that first occupied the house. There's a fireplace in winter and, in summer, a terraced patio shaded by catalpa trees. Serviceable New Mexican fare is served, and it's hard to deny the ambience of the place. Try the signature Chimayó Cocktail with apple cider, premium tequila, and crème de cassis. You can take an after-dinner stroll on the grounds' paths. Lunch entrées are reasonable, about half the price of dinner. The owners also operate the seven-room **Hacienda de Chimayó B&B** (☎ *505/351–2222*) just across the road. ⊠ *CR 98* ☎ *505/351– 4444* ⊕ *www.ranchodechimayo.com* ☐ *AE, D, DC, MC, V* ☉ *Closed Mon. Nov.–May.*

¢ ✕ **Leona's Restaurante.** This fast-food-style burrito and chile stand under
SOUTHWESTERN a massive catalpa tree at one end of the Santuario de Chimayó parking
★ lot has only a few tables, and in summer it's crowded—with good reason. Delicious dishes from the kitchen include homemade posole stew, carne adovada, and green-chile-and-cheese tamales. The specialty is flavored tortillas—everything from jalapeño to butterscotch. The tortillas have become so legendary that owner Léona Medina-Tiede opened a tortilla factory in Chimayó's Manzana Center and now does a thriving mail-order business. ⊠ *Off CR 98, behind Santuario de Chimayó* ☎ *505/351–4569 or 888/561–5569* ⊕ *www.leonasrestaurante.com* ☐ *AE, D, DC, MC, V* ☉ *Closed Tues. and Wed. No dinner.*

$ ⌂ **Casa Escondida.** Intimate and peaceful, this adobe inn has sweeping
BED AND views of the Sangre de Cristo range. The setting makes it a great base
BREAKFAST for mountain bikers. The scent of fresh-baked strudel wafts through
★ the rooms, which are decorated with antiques and Native American and other regional arts and crafts. Ask for the Sun Room, in the main house, which has a private patio, viga ceilings, and a brick floor. The separate one-bedroom Casita Escondida has a kiva-style fireplace, tile floors, kitchenette, and a sitting area. A large hot tub is hidden in a

grove behind wild berry bushes, there are several covered porches, and a massive bird-feeding station that draws dozens and dozens of birds. In-room massage is available by appointment, and special packages—romance or birthday, for example—are also available. **Pros:** very good value, with gracious hosts and in beautiful surroundings; there's not a TV on the entire property. **Cons:** remote setting means you must drive to sights. ⊠ *CR 0100, off NM 76* ⌂ *Box 142, 85722* ☎ *505/351–4805 or 800/643–7201* ⊕ *www.casaescondida.com* ♿ *In-room: no phone, kitchen (some), no TV, Wi-Fi. In-hotel: Wi-Fi hotspot, some pets allowed (paid)* ➹ *7 rooms, 1 suite* ⊟ *MC, V* ⦿ *BP.*

$ ▣ **Rancho Manzana Bed & Breakfast.** Facing Plaza del Cerro, one of the
INN state's best-preserved Spanish-colonial plazas, this eco-conscious, dis-
Fodor'sChoice tinctive retreat affords guests the opportunity to stay in a traditional
★ New Mexico village. Rooms are in private casitas and have natural mud walls, high ceilings, and comfortable, homey furnishings. Each has a private deck. Hearty, organic breakfasts are served. Lush gardens, apple orchards, and massive-walled adobe buildings surround a scenic communal garden and acequia. A fire pit and outdoor hot tub invite stargazing; the proprietors offer cooking classes and can provide excellent advice on touring the area. **Pros:** totally secluded yet convenient to Chimayó attractions; beautiful setting. **Cons:** credit cards aren't accepted. ⊠ *26 Camino de Mision* ☎ *505/351–2227 or 888/505–2227* ⊕ *www.ranchomanzana.com* ➹ *4 rooms* ♿ *In-room: no a/c, Wi-Fi. In-hotel: no kids under 12* ⊟ *No credit cards.*

SHOPPING

Centinela Traditional Arts (⊠ *NM 76, 1 mi east of junction with CR 98* ☎ *505/351–2180 or 877/351–2180* ⊕ *www.chimayoweavers.com*) continues the Trujillo family weaving tradition, which started in northern New Mexico more than seven generations ago. Irvin Trujillo and his wife, Lisa, are both gifted, award-winning master weavers, creating Rio Grande–style tapestry blankets and rugs, many of them with natural dyes that authentically replicate early weavings. Most designs are historically based, but the Trujillos are never shy about innovating and their original works are as breathtaking as the traditional ones. The shop and gallery carry these heirloom-quality textiles, with a knowledgeable and very friendly staff on hand to demonstrate or answer questions about the weaving techniques.

Ortega's Weaving Shop (⊠ *NM 76 at CR 98* ☎ *505/351–2288 or 877/351–4215* ⊕ *www.ortegasweaving.com*) sells Rio Grande– and Chimayó-style textiles made by the family whose Spanish ancestors brought the craft to New Mexico in the 1600s. The Galeria Ortega, next door, sells traditional New Mexican and Hispanic and contemporary Native American arts and crafts. In winter the shop is closed on Sunday.

In the plaza just outside the Santuario, **Highroad Marketplace** (⊠ *CR 98* ☎ *505/351–1078 or 866/343–5381*) stocks a variety of arts and crafts created all along the High Road, from Chimayó to Peñasco. Be sure to stop into **El Potrero**, a treasure trove of trinkets as well as high-quality arts and crafts from local artists. Don't be surprised if you're helped by one of the acclaimed Spanish Market artists who moonlight here.

CORDOVA

4 mi east of Chimayó via NM 76.

You'll have to turn south off NM 76 to get down into the narrow, steep valley that this lovely village sits it in, but you'll be happy you did. A picturesque mountain village with a small central plaza, a school, a post office, and a church, Cordova is the center of the centuries-old regional wood-carving industry. The town supports more than 30 full-time and part-time carvers. Many of them are descendants of José Dolores López, who in the 1920s created the village's signature unpainted "Cordova style" of carving. Most of the *santeros* (makers of religious images) have signs outside their homes indicating that santos are for sale. Many pieces are fairly expensive, a reflection of the hard work and fine crafts-manship involved—ranging from several hundred dollars for small ones to several thousand for larger figures—but there are also affordable and delightful small carvings of animals and birds. The St. Anthony of Padua Chapel, which is filled with handcrafted retablos (wood tablets painted with saints) and other religious art, is worth a visit.

TRUCHAS

4 mi northeast of Cordova via NM 76.

Truchas (Spanish for "trout") is where Robert Redford shot the movie *The Milagro Beanfield War* (based on the novel written by Taos author John Nichols). This pastoral village is perched dramatically on the rim of a deep canyon beneath the towering Truchas Peaks, mountains high enough to be almost perpetually capped with snow. The tallest of the Truchas Peaks is 13,102 feet, the second-highest point in New Mexico. This is an insular town, and locals aren't oriented toward selling their specialness to outsiders: be friendly, be discreet when taking pictures, and remember you're treading in someone else's paradise. Truchas has been gaining appeal with artsy, independent-minded transplants from Santa Fe and Taos, who have come for the cheaper real estate and the breathtaking setting. There are several galleries in town, most open by chance, as well as a small general store that sells snacks and a few gifts.

Continue 7 mi north on NM 76, toward Peñasco, and you come to the marvelous San José de Gracia Church in the village of Trampas. It dates from circa 1760.

SHOPPING

In the heart of Truchas, **Cordova's Handweaving Workshop** (✉ *Country Rd. 75* ☎ *505/689–2437*) produces vibrant and colorful contemporary and traditional rugs.

PEÑASCO

15 mi north of Truchas on NM 76.

Although still a modest-size community, Peñasco is one of the "larger" villages along the High Road and a good bet if you need to fill your tank with gas or pick up a snack at a convenience store.

WHERE TO EAT

$ ✕ **Sugar Nymphs Bistro.** It's taken a little time for people to learn about,
CONTEMPORARY   let alone find, this delightful little place set inside a vintage theater in
Fodor's Choice   sleepy Peñasco. You can't miss the vivid murals on the building, it's right
★

on the High Road, and it is hands down the best restaurant along this entire route. If you get an early start from Santa Fe and get through Chimayó in the morning, you'll get here right in time for a fabulous lunch, or an early dinner if you've meandered. Chef-owner Kai Harper Leah earned her stripes at San Francisco's famed vegetarian restaurant, Greens, and presents an eclectic menu of reasonably priced, inspired food: creatively topped pizzas, bountiful salads, juicy bacon cheeseburgers, butternut-squash ravioli. Try the fantastic green-chile bison stew, with meat from neighboring Picuris Pueblo's bison herd; it comes with perfectly moist but crumbly corn bread to soak up all the goodness. Desserts are memorable—consider the chocolate pecan pie. You can dine on the patio in warm weather. The Sunday brunch is excellent. ⊠ *15046 NM 75* ☎ *505/587–0311* ▭ *MC, V* ☉ *Closed Mon. and Tues.*

Taos

WORD OF MOUTH

"Just returned from a visit to Taos. There is a visitor's center on the main drag at the south end of town, where you can get maps, info on places to go, river runner outfitters, etc. Definitely go to the Pueblo for a fascinating glimpse at a culture that has inhabited those lands for centuries."

—donnawho

Updated
by Andrew
Collins

Taos casts a lingering spell. Set on a rolling mesa at the base of the Sangre de Cristo Mountains, it's a place of piercing light and spectacular views, where the desert palette changes almost hourly as the sun moves across the sky. Adobe buildings—some of them centuries old—lie nestled amid pine trees and scrub, some in the shadow of majestic Wheeler Peak, the town's (and state's) highest point, at just over 13,000 feet. The smell of piñon-wood smoke rises from the valley from early autumn through late spring; during the warmer months, the air smells of fragrant sage.

The earliest residents, members of the Taos-Tiwa tribe, have inhabited this breathtaking valley for more than a millennium; their descendants still live and maintain a traditional way of life at Taos Pueblo, a 95,000-acre reserve 3 mi northeast of Taos Plaza. Spanish settlers arrived in the 1500s, bringing both farming and Catholicism to the area; their influence remains most pronounced in the diminutive village of Ranchos de Taos, 4 mi south of town, where the massive adobe walls and *camposanto* (graveyard) of San Francisco de Asís Church have been attracting photographers for generations.

In the early 20th century, another population—artists—discovered Taos and began making the pilgrimage here to write, paint, and take photographs. The early adopters of this movement, painters Bert Phillips and Ernest Blumenschein stopped here in 1898 quite by chance to repair a wagon wheel while en route from Denver to Mexico in 1898. Enthralled with the earthy beauty of the region, they abandoned their intended plan, settled near the plaza, and in 1915 formed the Taos Society of Artists. In later years, many illustrious artists—including Georgia O'Keeffe, Ansel Adams, and D. H. Lawrence—frequented the area, helping cement a vaunted arts tradition that thrives to this day. The steadily emerging bohemian spirit has continued to attract hippies, counterculturalists, New Agers, gays and lesbians, and free spirits. Downtown—along with some outlying villages to the south and north, such as Ranchos de Taos and Arroyo Seco—now support a rich abundance of galleries and design-driven shops. Whereas Santa Fe, Aspen, Scottsdale, and other gallery hubs in the West tend toward pricey work, much of it by artists living elsewhere, Taos remains very much an ardent hub of local arts and crafts production and sales. A half-dozen excellent museums here also document the town's esteemed artistic history.

About 5,000 people live year-round within Taos town limits, but another 25,000 reside in the surrounding county, much of which is unincorporated, and quite a few others live here seasonally. This means that in summer and, to a lesser extent, during the winter ski season, the town can feel much larger than you might expect. It also supports a retail, restaurants, and hotel infrastructure that's typical of what you'd find in a much larger town. Still, overall, the valley and soaring mountains of Taos enjoy relative isolation, low population-density, and magnificent scenery, making this an ideal retreat for those aiming to escape, slow down, and embrace a distinct regional blend of art, cuisine, outdoor recreation, and natural beauty.

ORIENTATION AND PLANNING

GETTING ORIENTED

Taos is small and resolutely rustic, but for the prosaic stretch of chain motels and strip malls that greet you as you approach from the south. Persevere to the central plaza, and you'll find several highly walkable blocks of galleries, shops, restaurants, and art museums. Easygoing Taoseños are a welcoming lot, and if you ever lose your orientation, you'll find locals happy to point you where you need to go. It's difficult to reach Taos without a car, and you'll need one to reach those attractions outside the village center (the Rio Grande Gorge, Millicent Rogers Museum, and the area's best skiing and hiking), as well as to many accommodations and restaurants. The narrow, historic streets near the plaza can be choked with traffic in the peak summer and winter seasons, especially on Fridays and Sundays—ask locals about the several shortcuts for avoiding traffic jams, and try walking when exploring the blocks around the plaza.

TAOS NEIGHBORHOODS

Plaza and Vicinity. More than four centuries after it was laid out, the Taos Plaza and adjacent streets remain the community's hub commercial and social activity. Dozens of upscale shops and galleries, along with several notable restaurants, hotels, and museums, thrive in this pedestrian-friendly area. The plaza itself is a bit overrun with mediocre souvenir shops, but you only need to walk a block in any direction—especially north and east—to find worthy offerings.

South Side. The first Spanish settlers were agrarian, and many families continue to till the fertile land south of Taos. Ranchos de Taos, a small village a few miles south of the plaza, is home to the iconic San Francisco de Asís Church, memorialized by Georgia O'Keeffe and photographer Ansel Adams. The main approach road into Taos from the south, NM 68, is low on curb appeal but nonetheless contains plenty of handy services, like gas stations, convenience stores, and chain motels.

Taos Pueblo. The Pueblo is the ancient beating heart of the entire valley, the historic and architectural basis for everything that Taos has become. A small, bland casino aside, this area a short drive northeast of the plaza has been spared commercial development and remains a neighborhood of modest homes and farms. The Pueblo itself is the sole draw for visitors and well worth a visit.

El Prado. As you drive north from Taos toward Arroyo Seco and points north or west, you'll first take the main thoroughfare, Paseo del Pueblo Norte (U.S. 64) through the small village of El Prado, a mostly agrarian

TOP REASONS TO GO

Small-town sophistication. For a tiny, remote community, Taos supports a richly urbane culinary scene, a fantastic bounty of galleries and design shops, and plenty of stylish B&Bs and inns.

Indigenous roots. The Taos Pueblo and its inhabitants have lived in this region for centuries and continue to play a vital role in local art, culture, and civic life.

Desert solitaire. Few panoramas in the Southwest can compare with that of the 13,000-foot Sangre de Cristo Mountains soaring over the adobe homes of Taos, and beyond that, the endless high-desert mesa that extends for miles to the west.

area that's notable for having several of the area's best restaurants, B&Bs, and shops.

West Side. Taos is hemmed in by the Sangre de Cristo mountains on the east, but to the west, extending from Downtown clear across the precipitously deep Rio Grande Gorge (and the famous bridge that crosses it), the landscape is dominated by sweeping, high-desert scrub and wide-open spaces. The west side is mostly residential and makes for a scenic shortcut around the sometimes traffic-clogged plaza (from Ranchos de Taos, just follow NM 240 to Blueberry Hill Road to complete this bypass).

Arroyo Seco. Set on a high mesa north of Taos, this funky yet hip village and arts center is an ideal spot to browse galleries, grab a meal at one of a handful of excellent restaurants, or simply pause to admire the dramatic views before driving on to the Enchanted Circle or Taos Ski Valley. You'll find a few excellent B&Bs here as well.

Taos Ski Valley. Home to New Mexico's most acclaimed ski area, Taos Ski Valley is a fully separate community from Taos proper—it's 20 mi north, via Arroyo Seco, and nestled in a lush, pine-studded valley with a base elevation of 9,200 feet (meaning it can be chilly here even in July). Many businesses here are open only in winter, but a handful of inns and restaurants serve visitors year-round, as this is also the setting off point for some amazing hikes, including the strenuous but popular trek to the state's highest point, Wheeler Peak.

TAOS PLANNER

WHEN TO GO

With more than 300 days of sunshine annually, Taos typically yields good—if often chilly—weather year-round. The summer high season brings warm days (80s) and cool nights (50s), as well as frequent afternoon thunderstorms. A packed arts and festival schedule in summer means hotels and B&Bs sometimes book well in advance, lodging rates are high, restaurants are jammed, and traffic anywhere near the plaza can slow to a standstill. Spring and fall are stunning and favor mild days and cool nights, fewer visitors, and reasonable hotel prices. In winter, especially during big years for snowfall, skiers arrive en masse but tend to stay close to the slopes and only venture into town for an occasional meal or shopping raid.

GETTING HERE AND AROUND
AIRPORTS AND TRANSFERS
Albuquerque International Sunport (*ABQ* ☎ *505/244–7700* ⊕ *www.cabq. gov/airport*), **about 130 mi away** and a 2½-hour drive, is the nearest major airport to Taos. The small **Santa Fe Municipal Airport** (*SAF* ☎ *505/955–2900*), a 90-minute drive, also has daily service on American Airlines from Dallas and Los Angeles.

Alternatively, as Taos is one of the gateway towns to New Mexico if coming from Colorado, some visitors fly into Denver (five-hour drive) or Colorado Springs (four hours) as part of a trip to both states. Taos Municipal Airport, 12 mi west of town, serves only charters and private planes.

By appointment only, Faust's Transportation, Twin Hearts Express, and Taos Shuttle provide shuttle service from Taos, Taos Ski Valley, and nearby towns to Albuquerque and Santa Fe. The cost is about $50 to $60 per person for Albuquerque, and $25 to $35 for Santa Fe. Some companies have a three-person minimum, and it's always a good idea to book your rides at least 48 hours in advance. Given the high cost of shuttle service and relatively reasonable rates for rental cars at Albuquerque's airport, it's more economical and typically more convenient to rent a car. However, if you're coming solely to ski, staying for a week or more, or planning to stick mostly around the plaza, the shuttle option can make more sense (and you can always rent a car at one of the two agencies in Taos if you're planning an occasional trip farther afield).

Shuttle Contacts: **Faust's Transportation** (☎ *575/758–3410* or *888/231–2222* ⊕ *www.newmexiconet.com/trans/faust/faust.html*). Taos Shuttle (☎ *575/779– 5641*). **Twin Hearts Express** (☎ *575/751–1201* or *800/654–9456*).

CAR TRAVEL
A car is your most practical means both for reaching and getting around Taos. The main route from Santa Fe is via U.S. 285 north to NM 68 north, also known as the Low Road, which winds between the Rio Grande and red-rock cliffs before rising to a spectacular view of the plain and river gorge. You can also take the wooded High Road to Taos, which takes longer but offers a wonderfully scenic ride—many visitors come to Taos via the Low Road, which is more dramatic when driven south to north, and then return to Santa Fe via the High Road (⇨ *High Road to Taos, in Side Trips from Santa Fe, chapter 3*), which has better views as you drive south. From Denver, it's a five-hour drive south via I–25, U.S. 160 west (at Walsenburg), and CO 159 to NM 522; from points east or west, take U.S. 64 (keeping in mind that U.S. 64 west of Taos, between Tres Piedras and Tierra Amarilla, is often closed because of snow in winter).

Cottam Walker Ford and Enterprise are the two local car-rental agencies in Taos; rates typically start around $200 per week but vary greatly depending on the season.

Festivals of Tradition

Several yearly festivals celebrate the Native American and Hispanic roots of Taos. During the last weekend in September, La Hacienda de los Martínez hosts the **Old Taos Trade Fair,** a reenactment of autumn gatherings of the 1820s, when Plains Indians and trappers came to Taos to trade with the Spanish and the Pueblo Indians. The two-day event includes demonstrations of blacksmithing, weaving, and other crafts, a chile cook-off, native foods, music, and dancing.

The **Wool Festival** (⊕ www. taoswoolfestival.org), held in early October in Kit Carson Park, commemorates the long tradition of wool growing and weaving begun in the 16th century, when Spanish settlers brought the tough little Churro sheep to northern New Mexico. Every aspect of the craft "from sheep to shawl" is demonstrated, including shearing, spinning, and weaving. Handmade woolen items are for sale, and you can taste favorite lamb dishes.

During the second weekend of July, the **Taos Pueblo Powwow** (⊕ www. taospueblopowwow.com) attracts Native Americans from many Indian nations. Visitors are welcome to watch the traditional drumming and dancing, shop at the arts-and-crafts market, and partake of fry bread, mutton, green-chile sauce, and other local delicacies.

Car Rental Contacts: Cottam Walker Ford (⊠ 1320 Paseo del Pueblo Sur ☎ 575/751–3200 ⊕ www.forddetaos.com). **Enterprise** (⊠ 1354 Paseo del Pueblo Sur ☎ 575/758–5553 ⊕ www.enterprise.com).

TAXI TRAVEL

Taxi service in Taos is sparse, but Faust's Transportation and Taos Shuttle both serve the area. Rates are $5 at pick up, $2.50 per each additional person, and $1 per mile.

Taxi Contacts: Faust's Transportation (☎ 575/758–3410 or 888/231–2222 ⊕ www.newmexiconet.com/trans/faust/faust.html). Taos Shuttle (☎ 575/779–5641).

GUIDED TOURS

Taos Art Tours (☎ 575/737–5595 ⊕ www.taosarttours.com), run by knowledgeable guide Marian Bradley Jackson, offers art walks around Taos that cover key museums, and customized tours of several different studios. Tours cost $40.

VISITOR INFORMATION

Taos Visitors Center (⊠ 1139 Paseo del Pueblo Sur ⌂ Drawer I, Taos 87571 ☎ 505/758–3873 or 877/587–9007 ⊕ www.taosvisitor.com). **Taos Ski Valley Chamber of Commerce** (☎ 575/776–1413 or 800/517–9816 ⊕ www.taosskivalley.com).

PLANNING YOUR TIME

Whether you've got an afternoon or a week in the area, begin by strolling around Taos Plaza and along Bent Street, taking in the galleries, Native American crafts shops, and eclectic clothing stores. Take Ledoux Street south from the west side of the plaza and walk two blocks to the

Harwood Museum, then walk back to the plaza and cross over to Kit Carson Road, where you can find more shops and galleries as well as the Kit Carson Home and Museum. Return to Paseo del Pueblo and walk north to the Taos Art Museum and Fechin House to complete a tour that takes in the best of the town center's shopping and museums. However, a few of the must-see attractions in the area are a bit farther afield, and you need at least two days and ideally three or four to take in everything. Among the top outlying attractions, it's possible to visit Taos Pueblo, the magnificent Millicent Rogers Museum, the village of Arroyo Seco, and the Rio Grande Gorge Bridge all in one day—you can connect them to make one loop to the north and west of the city. If you're headed south, stop at La Hacienda de los Martínez to gain an appreciation of early Spanish life in Taos and then to Ranchos de Taos to see the stunning San Francisco de Asís Church. If you approach Taos from the south, as most visitors do, you could also visit both these attractions on your way into town, assuming you arrive by early afternoon.

EXPLORING TAOS

The Museum Association of Taos includes five properties: the Harwood Museum, Taos Art Museum, Millicent Rogers Museum, E. L. Blumenschein Home and Museum, and La Hacienda de los Martínez. Each of the museums charges $8 for admission, but you can buy a combination ticket—$25 for all five, valid for one year.

PLAZA AND VICINITY

E. L. Blumenschein Home and Museum. For an introduction to the history of the Taos art scene, start with Ernest L. Blumenschein's residence, which provides a glimpse into the cosmopolitan lives led by the members of the Taos Society of Artists, of which Blumenschein was a founding member. One of the rooms in the adobe-style structure dates from 1797. On display are the art, antiques, and other personal possessions of Blumenschein and his wife, Mary Greene Blumenschein, who also painted, as did their daughter Helen. Several of Ernest Blumenschein's vivid oil paintings hang in his former studio, and works by other early Taos artists are also on display. ⊠ *222 Ledoux St.* ☏ *575/758–0505* ⊕ *www.taoshistoricmuseums.org* ⊠ *$8, 5-museum Museum Association of Taos combination ticket $25* ⊙ *Apr.–Oct., Mon.–Sat. 10–5, Sun. noon–5; Nov.–Mar., Mon.–Tues. and Thurs.–Sat. 10–4, Sun. noon–4.*

☪ **Firehouse Collection.** More than 100 works by well-known Taos artists like Joseph Sharp, Ernest L. Blumenschein, and Bert Phillips hang in the Taos Volunteer Fire Department building. The exhibition space adjoins the station house, where five fire engines are maintained at the ready and an antique fire engine is on display. ⊠ *323 Camino de la Placita* ☏ *575/758–3386* ⊠ *Free* ⊙ *Weekdays 9–4:30.*

☪ **Governor Bent Museum.** In 1846, when New Mexico became a U.S. possession as a result of the Mexican War, Charles Bent, a trader, trapper, and mountain man, was appointed governor. Less than a year later he was killed in his house by an angry mob protesting New Mexico's

IF YOU LIKE

ARTS AND CRAFTS

If your idea of fun is museum going and gallery hopping, Taos has much to offer you. The creative spirit is strong here, and it's contagious. Even if you begin by just browsing, you might find that you can't go home without a certain painting or pot that captures the region's unmistakable enchantment. At galleries, you can often meet the artists themselves, or join in the flow of creative energy by participating in one of the town's many art workshops. It's easy to visit a lot of galleries in a short time; many are side by side on a few streets around Taos Plaza. Southwestern landscapes and Native American themes are ubiquitous subjects, but many galleries also show abstract and less regionalized work. Look for outstanding weaving, jewelry, tinwork, and other crafts, too.

NEW MEXICAN CUISINE

For a small town, Taos excels when it comes to authentic New Mexican fare, prepared with local chiles and homemade tortillas, but the town also draws raves for outstanding contemporary restaurants with impressive wine lists. The generally eco-conscious, progressive local population has created a demand for fresh, organic cuisine, including plenty of vegetarian options. Pan-Asian, Middle Eastern, and Mediterranean flavors also greatly influence Taos menus.

OUTDOOR ACTIVITIES

The glorious landscape around Taos draws serious athletes as well as those simply up for an adventure beneath northern New Mexico's mesmerizing skies and towering mountain peaks. Cycling is popular, with rallies and races held in summer. The vast Carson National Forest encompasses thousands of acres of prime hiking and camping terrain, from strenuous alpine climbs to simpler scrambles into rocky gorges or pine-shaded glens. A good variety of rivers and lakes yield excellent trout fishing; you can arrange for outings with local expert guides. The waters also invite rafters, especially when spring runoff fills the rivers with white water. If you're really after a thrill or something different, try a hot-air balloon ride into the Rio Grande Gorge or llama trekking in the wilderness. And of course winter brings skiers from all over to the world-class slopes of Taos Ski Valley, Angel Fire, and Red River. Wherever you play outdoors, just remember the region's high altitude and sometimes extreme day-to-night temperature differences can tax and exhaust you—go easy in the beginning, and talk with local experts before setting out on any ambitious endeavors.

annexation by the United States. Governor Bent was married to María Ignacia, the older sister of Josefa Jaramillo, the wife of mountain man Kit Carson. A collection of Native American artifacts, Western Americana, and family possessions is squeezed into five small rooms of the adobe building where Bent and his family lived. ⊠ *117 Bent St.* ☎ *575/758–2376* ⊒ *$3* ⊘ *Daily 10–5.*

Fodor's Choice **Harwood Museum.** The Pueblo Revival former home of Burritt Elihu ★ "Burt" Harwood, a dedicated painter who studied in France before moving to Taos in 1916, is adjacent to a museum dedicated to the

A GOOD WALK: TAOS PLAZA

Begin at the gazebo in the middle of **Taos Plaza**. After exploring the plaza, head south from its western edge down the small, unmarked alley (its name is West Plaza Drive), crossing Camino de la Placita, to where West Plaza Drive becomes Ledoux Street. Continue south to the **E. L. Blumenschein Home and Museum** and, a few doors farther south, the **Harwood Museum**. (Parking for the Harwood Foundation is at Ledoux and Ranchitos Road.)

From the Harwood Foundation, walk back north on Ranchitos Road a few blocks, make a left on Camino de la Placita, and go right onto Don Fernando Road. Follow it east, crossing the north side of the plaza and then Paseo del Pueblo Norte (NM 68), to where Don Fernando Road becomes Kit Carson Road. You'll soon come to the **Kit Carson Home and Museum**. Then head back to Paseo del Pueblo Norte, turn right (north) and go past the Taos Inn, turning left (west) to browse Bent Street's shops, boutiques, and galleries.

In a tiny plaza is the **Governor Bent Museum**, the modest home of the first Anglo governor of the state. Across the street is the John Dunn House. Once the homestead of a colorful and well-respected Taos gambling and transportation entrepreneur, the Dunn House is now a small shopping plaza. At the western end of Bent Street, head north on Camino de la Placita. In about 2½ blocks you'll come to the Taos Volunteer Fire Department building, which doubles as a fire station and the **Firehouse Collection** exhibition space.

Head east on Civic Plaza and cross Paseo del Pueblo Norte, turning left to reach **Kit Carson Park** and the **Taos Art Museum and Fechin House**, named for the iconoclastic artist Nicolai Fechin.

TIMING
The entire walk can be done in five hours, but allow about eight hours if you stop for lunch along the way and browse in the shops and galleries. You can tour each of the museums in less than an hour.

works of local artists. Traditional Hispanic northern New Mexican artists, early art-colony painters, post–World War II modernists, and contemporary artists such as Larry Bell, Agnes Martin, Ken Price, and Earl Stroh are represented. Mabel Dodge Luhan, a major arts patron, bequeathed many of the 19th- and early-20th-century works in the Harwoods' collection, including *retablos* (painted wood representations of Catholic saints) and *bultos* (three-dimensional carvings of the saints). In the Hispanic Traditions Gallery upstairs are 19th-century tinwork, furniture, and sculpture. Downstairs, among early-20th-century art-colony holdings, look for E. Martin Hennings's *Chamisa in Bloom,* which captures the Taos landscape particularly beautifully. A tour of the ground-floor galleries shows that Taos painters of the era, notably Oscar Berninghaus, Ernest Blumenschein, Victor Higgins, Walter Ufer, Marsden Hartley, and John Marin, were fascinated by the land and the people linked to it. An octagonal gallery exhibits works by Agnes Martin. Martin's seven large canvas panels (each 5 feet square) are studies in

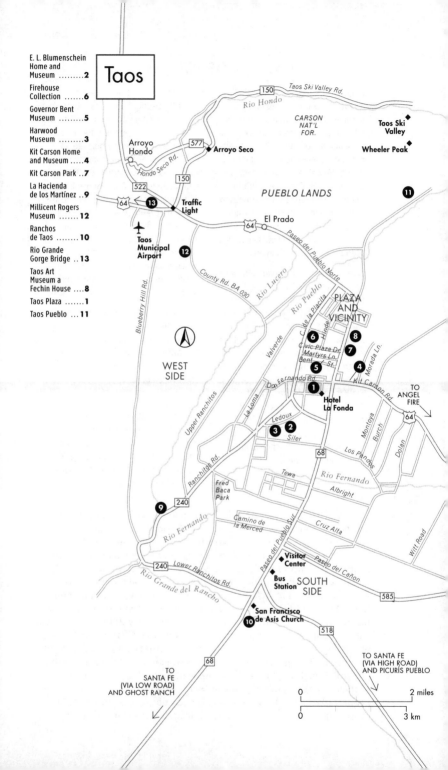

Taos

Taos Ski Valley Rd.

150

Rio Hondo

CARSON NAT'L FOR.

Taos Ski Valley

Wheeler Peak

Arroyo Hondo

577

Arroyo Seco

Hondo Seco Rd.

150

522

64

13

Traffic Light

El Prado

64

Paseo del Pueblo Norte

PUEBLO LANDS

11

Taos Municipal Airport

12

County Rd. BA 030

Rio Lucero

Rio Pueblo

Blueberry Hill Rd.

Calle de la Placita

Linda

PLAZA AND VICINITY

Valverde

6

Civic Plaza Dr.

8

7

WEST SIDE

Martyrs Ln.

Bent

F. St.

5

4

Morada Ln.

La Loma

Don Fernando Rd.

1

Kit Carson Rd.

TO ANGEL FIRE

Upper Ranchitos

Hotel La Fonda

Ledoux

3

2

Siler

Montoya

Burch

Dolan

64

Ranchitos Rd.

68

Los Pandos

Fred Baca Park

Tewa

Rio Fernando

Albright

9

240

Rio Fernando

Camino de la Merced

Cruz Alta

240

Lower Ranchitos Rd.

Paseo del Pueblo Sur

Visitor Center

Paseo del Cañon

Witt Road

Rio Grande del Rancho

Bus Station

SOUTH SIDE

585

San Francisco de Asis Church

10

518

68

TO SANTA FE (VIA LOW ROAD) AND GHOST RANCH

TO SANTA FE (VIA HIGH ROAD) AND PICURÍS PUEBLO

0   2 miles

0   3 km

white, their precise lines and blocks forming textured grids. Operated by the University of New Mexico since 1936, the Harwood is the second-oldest art museum in the state. ✉ *238 Ledoux St.* ☎ *575/758–9826* ⊕ *www.harwoodmuseum.org* 🖃 *$8, 5-museum Museum Association of Taos combination ticket $25* ⊘ *Tues.–Sat. 10–5, Sun. noon–5.*

Kit Carson Home and Museum. Kit Carson bought this low-slung 12-room adobe home in 1843 for his wife, Josefa Jaramillo, the daughter of a powerful, politically influential Spanish family. Three of the museum's rooms are furnished, as they were when the Carson family lived here. The rest of the museum is devoted to gun and mountain-man exhibits, such as rugged leather clothing and Kit's own Spencer carbine rifle with its beaded leather carrying case, and early Taos antiques, artifacts, and manuscripts. ✉ *113 Kit Carson Rd.* ☎ *575/758–0505* 🖃 *$8* ⊘ *Tues.–Sat. 10–4, Sun. noon–4.*

4

NEED A BREAK? Let the aroma of fresh-ground coffee draw you into the tiny **World Cup** (✉ *102-A Paseo del Pueblo Norte* ☎ 575/737–5299), where you can sit at the counter or wander outside to a bench on the porch. Locals engage in political rhetoric here, often slanted toward the left, so be prepared for a rousing debate if you dare to dissent.

Kit Carson Park. The noted pioneer is buried in the park that bears his name. His grave is marked with a *cerquita* (a spiked, wrought-iron, rectangular fence), traditionally used to outline and protect burial sites. Also interred here is Mabel Dodge Luhan, the pioneering patron of the early Taos art scene. The 32-acre park has swings and slides for recreational breaks. It's well marked with big stone pillars and a gate. ✉ *211 Paseo del Pueblo Norte* ☎ *575/758–8234* 🖃 *Free* ⊘ *Late May–early Sept., daily 8–8; early Sept.–late May, daily 8–5.*

Fodor's Choice ★ **Taos Art Museum and Fechin House.** The interior of this extraordinary adobe house, built between 1927 and 1933 by Russian émigré and artist Nicolai Fechin, is a marvel of carved Russian-style woodwork and furniture. Fechin constructed it to showcase his daringly colorful paintings. The house became host to the Taos Art Museum in 2003, with a collection of paintings from more than 50 Taos artists, including founders of the original Taos Society of Artists, among them Joseph Sharp, Ernest Blumenschein, Bert Phillips, E. I. Couse, and Oscar Berninghaus. ✉ *227 Paseo del Pueblo Norte* ☎ *575/758–2690* ⊕ *www.taosartmuseum.org* 🖃 *$8, 5-museum Museum Association of Taos combination ticket $25* ⊘ *Tues.–Sun. 10–5.*

Taos Plaza. The first European explorers of the Taos Valley came here with Captain Hernando de Alvarado, a member of Francisco Vásquez de Coronado's expedition of 1540. Basque explorer Don Juan de Oñate arrived in Taos in July 1598 and established a mission and trading arrangements with residents of Taos Pueblo. The settlement developed into two plazas: the plaza at the heart of the town became a thriving business district for the early colony, and a walled residential plaza was constructed a few hundred yards behind. It remains active today, home to a throng of mostly shlocky gift shops. The covered gazebo was donated by heiress and longtime Taos resident Mabel Dodge Luhan. On

A GOOD DRIVE

From Taos Plaza, head southwest 2½ mi on NM 240 (also known as Ranchitos Road) to **La Hacienda de los Martínez**. As you pass by the adobe cottages and modest homes dotting the landscape, you get a sense of the area's rural roots. From the hacienda continue along NM 240, which winds in the shape of a C for another 4 mi to NM 68 and the small farming village of **Ranchos**
de Taos. Watch for signs for **San Francisco de Asís Church,** which is on the east side of NM 68. The small plaza here contains several galleries and gift shops worth checking out.

TIMING
Set aside about two hours to tour the hacienda, a bit of Ranchos de Taos, and San Francisco de Asís Church.

the southeastern corner of Taos Plaza is the **Hotel La Fonda de Taos.** Some infamous erotic paintings by D. H. Lawrence that were naughty in his day but are quite tame by present standards can be viewed ($3 entry fee for nonguests) in the former barroom beyond the lobby.

SOUTH SIDE

La Hacienda de los Martínez. Spare and fortlike, this adobe structure built between 1804 and 1827 on the bank of the Rio Pueblo served as a community refuge during Comanche and Apache raids. Its thick walls, which have few windows, surround two central courtyards. Don Antonio Severino Martínez was a farmer and trader; the hacienda was the final stop along El Camino Real (the Royal Road), the trade route the Spanish established between Mexico City and New Mexico. The restored period rooms here contain textiles, foods, and crafts of the early 19th century. There's a working blacksmith's shop, usually open to visitors on Saturday, and weavers create beautiful textiles on reconstructed period looms. ⊠ *708 Hacienda Rd., off Ranchitos Rd. (NM 240)* ☎ *575/758–1000* ⊕ *www.taoshistoricmuseums.org* ⊠ *$8, 5-museum Museum Association of Taos combination ticket $25* ☉ *Apr.–Oct., Mon.–Sat. 10–5, Sun. noon–5; Nov.–Mar., Mon.–Tues. and Thurs.–Sat. 10–4, Sun. noon–4.*

Ranchos de Taos. A few minutes' drive south of the center of Taos, this village still retains some of its rural atmosphere despite the highway traffic passing through. Huddled around its famous adobe church and dusty plaza are cheerful, remodeled shops and galleries standing shoulder to shoulder with crumbling adobe shells. This ranching, farming, and budding small-business community was an early home to Taos Native Americans before being settled by Spaniards in 1716. Although many of the adobe dwellings have seen better days, the shops, modest galleries, taco stands, and two fine restaurants point to an ongoing revival.

The massive bulk of **San Francisco de Asís Church** (⊠ *NM 68, 500 yards south of NM 518, Ranchos de Taos* ☎ *575/758–2754* ⊕ *www. nps.gov/nr/travel/amsw/sw44.htm*) is an enduring attraction. The Spanish mission–style church was erected in 1815 as a spiritual and physical refuge from raiding Apaches, Utes, and Comanches. In 1979 the deteriorated church was rebuilt with traditional adobe bricks by community volunteers. Every spring a group gathers to re-mud the facade. The earthy, clean lines of the exterior walls and supporting bulwarks have inspired generations of painters and photographers. The late-afternoon light provides the best exposure of the heavily buttressed rear of the church—though today's image takers face the challenge of framing the architecturally pure lines through rows of parked cars and a large, white sign put up by church officials; morning light is best for the front. Bells in the twin belfries call Taoseños to services on Sunday and holidays. Monday through Saturday from 9 to 4 you can step inside. In the parish hall just north of the church (and for a $3 fee) you can view a 15-minute video presentation every half hour that describes the history and restoration of the church and explains the mysterious painting *Shadow of the Cross,* on which each evening the shadow of a cross appears over Christ's shoulder (scientific studies made on the canvas and the paint pigments cannot explain the phenomenon). The fee also allows you to view the painting.

NEED A BREAK? Join the locals at the north or south location of the Bean (⌂ *900 Paseo del Pueblo Norte, El Prado* ☎ *No phone* ⌂ *1033 Paseo del Pueblo Sur, South Side* ☎ *575/758–5123*). The Bean roasts its own coffee, and the South Side location—where you can dine on an outside patio—offers good breakfast and lunch fare. The north location, in an adobe building, displays local artwork and is the more atmospheric of the two.

TAOS PUEBLO

☺ **Taos Pueblo.** For nearly 1,000 years the mud-and-straw adobe walls of
Fodor's Choice Taos Pueblo have sheltered Tiwa-speaking Native Americans. A United
★ Nations World Heritage Site, this is the largest collection of multistory pueblo dwellings in the United States. The pueblo's main buildings, Hlauuma (north house) and Hlaukwima (south house), are separated by a creek. These structures are believed to be of a similar age, probably built between 1000 and 1450. The dwellings have common walls but no connecting doorways—the Tiwas gained access only from the top, via ladders that were retrieved after entering. Small buildings and corrals are scattered about.

The pueblo today appears much as it did when the first Spanish explorers arrived in New Mexico in 1540. The adobe walls glistening with mica caused the conquistadors to believe they had discovered one of the fabled Seven Cities of Gold. The outside surfaces are continuously maintained by replastering with thin layers of mud, and the interior walls are frequently coated with thin washes of white clay. Some walls are several feet thick in places. The roofs of each of the five-story structures are supported by large timbers, or vigas, hauled down from the mountain forests. Pine or aspen *latillas* (smaller pieces of wood) are placed side by side between the vigas; the entire roof is then packed with dirt.

A GOOD DRIVE

Drive 2 mi north on Paseo del Pueblo Norte (NM 68), and keep your eyes peeled for the signs on the right, beyond the post office, directing you to **Taos Pueblo**. To reach the **Millicent Rogers Museum** next, return to NM 68 to head north about 4½ mi and make a left onto County Road BA030. If you find yourself at the intersection with U.S. 64 and NM 150, you've gone too far. Continue down the county road to the big adobe wall; the sign for the museum is on the right. After exploring the museum, return to NM 68 north; then make a left on U.S. 64 and drive 8 mi west to the **Rio Grande Gorge Bridge**, a stunning marriage of natural wonder and human engineering. If you're up for it, bring along sturdy hiking shoes and plenty of water and snacks for an invigorating walk down into the gorge. But remember, what goes down must come up, and it's an arduous path.

TIMING

Plan on spending 1½ hours at the pueblo. Taos can get hot in summer, but if you visit the pueblo in the morning, you'll avoid the heat and the crowds. If your visit coincides with a ceremonial observance, set aside several hours, because the ceremonies, though they are worth the wait, never start on time. Two hours should be enough time to take in the museum and the grandeur of the Rio Grande Gorge Bridge, but allow another hour or two if you hike down into the gorge.

Even after 400 years of Spanish and Anglo presence in Taos, inside the pueblo the traditional Native American way of life has endured. Tribal custom allows no electricity or running water in Hlauuma and Hlaukwima, where varying numbers (usually fewer than 150) of Taos Native Americans live full-time. About 1,900 others live in conventional homes on the pueblo's 95,000 acres. The crystal-clear Rio Pueblo de Taos, originating high above in the mountains at the sacred Blue Lake, is the primary source of water for drinking and irrigating. Bread is still baked in *hornos* (outdoor domed ovens). Artisans of the Taos Pueblo produce and sell (tax-free) traditionally handcrafted wares, such as mica-flecked pottery and silver jewelry. Great hunters, the Taos Native Americans are also known for their work with animal skins and their excellent moccasins, boots, and drums.

Although the population is about 80% Catholic, the people of Taos Pueblo, like most Pueblo Native Americans, also maintain their native religious traditions. At Christmas and other sacred holidays, for instance, immediately after Mass, dancers dressed in seasonal sacred garb proceed down the aisle of St. Jerome Chapel, drums beating and rattles shaking, to begin other religious rites.

The pueblo **Church of San Geronimo**, or St. Jerome, the patron saint of Taos Pueblo, was completed in 1850 to replace the one destroyed by the U.S. Army in 1847 during the Mexican War. With its smooth symmetry, stepped portal, and twin bell towers, the church is a popular subject for photographers and artists (though the taking of photographs inside is discouraged).

The public is invited to certain ceremonial dances held throughout the year (a full list of these is posted on the pueblo Web site): highlights include the Feast of Santa Cruz Foot Race and Corn Dance (May 3); Taos Pueblo Pow Wow (July 8–10); Feast of San Geronimo Sunset Dance (July 25 and 26, Septem-

> **DID YOU KNOW?**
>
> The privilege of setting up an easel and painting all day at a pueblo will cost you as little as $35 or as much as $150 (at Taos Pueblo).

ber 29 and 30); Vespers and Bonfire Procession (December 24); and Deer Dance or Matachines Dance (December 25). While you're at the pueblo, respect the restricted area signs that protect the privacy of residents and native religious sites; do not enter private homes or open any doors not clearly labeled as curio shops; do not photograph tribal members without asking permission; do not enter the cemetery grounds; and do not wade in the Rio Pueblo de Taos, which is considered sacred and is the community's sole source of drinking water.

The small, rather prosaic, and smoke-free Taos Mountain Casino (open daily) is just off Camino del Pueblo after you turn right off Paseo del Pueblo on your way to the main pueblo. ⊠ *Head to right off Paseo del Pueblo Norte just past Best Western Kachina Lodge* ☎ *575/758–1028* ⊕ *www.taospueblo.com* ⊠ *Tourist fees $10; guided tours; photography and video permits $6 per camera, cell phone (if you're using it to take pictures), or video-recording device; commercial photography, sketching, or painting only by prior permission from governor's office* (☎ *575/758–1028); fees vary; apply at least 10 days in advance* ☉ *Daily 8–4:30, tours by appointment. Closed for funerals, religious ceremonies, and for 10-week quiet time in late winter or early spring, and last part of Aug.; call ahead before visiting at these times.*

NEED A BREAK?

Look for signs that read fry bread on dwellings in the pueblo: you can enter the kitchen and buy a piece of fresh bread dough that's flattened and deep-fried until puffy and golden brown and then topped with honey or powdered sugar. You also can buy delicious bread that's baked daily in the clay *hornos* (outdoor adobe ovens) that are scattered throughout the pueblo.

WEST SIDE

Fodor's Choice ★ **Millicent Rogers Museum.** More than 5,000 pieces of spectacular Native American and Hispanic art, many of them from the private collection of the late Standard Oil heiress Millicent Rogers, are on display here. Among the pieces are baskets, blankets, rugs, kachina dolls, carvings, paintings, rare religious artifacts, and, most significantly, jewelry (Rogers, a fashion icon in her day, was one of the first Americans to appreciate the turquoise-and-silver artistry of Native American jewelers). Other important works include the pottery and ceramics of Maria Martinez and other potters from San Ildefonso Pueblo (23 mi north of Santa Fe). Docents conduct guided tours by appointment, and the museum hosts lectures, films, workshops, and demonstrations. The two-room gift shop has exceptional jewelry, rugs, books, and pottery. ⊠ *1504 Millicent*

Rogers Rd.; from Taos Plaza head north on Paseo del Pueblo Norte and left at sign for CR BA030 (Millicent Rogers Rd.) ☎ 575/758–2462 ⊕ www.millicentrogers.com ⌑ $8, 5-museum Museum Association of Taos combination ticket $25 ⊙ Daily 10–5; closed Mon. in Nov.

🔆 **Rio Grande Gorge Bridge.** It's a dizzying experience to see the Rio Grande 650 feet underfoot, where it flows at the bottom of an immense, steep rock canyon. In summer the reddish rocks dotted with green scrub contrast brilliantly with the blue sky, where you might see a hawk lazily floating in circles. The bridge is the second-highest suspension bridge in the country. Hold on to your camera and eyeglasses when looking down. Shortly after daybreak, hot-air balloons fly above and even inside the gorge. There's a campground with picnic shelters and basic restrooms on the west side of the bridge. ⊠ U.S. 64, 12 mi west of town.

ARROYO SECO

Fodor's Choice
★

Arroyo Seco. Established in 1834 by local Spanish farmers and ranchers, this charming village has today become a secluded, artsy escape from the sometimes daunting summer crowds and commercialism of the Taos Plaza—famous residents include actress Julia Roberts and former U.S. Defense Secretary Donald Rumsfeld, who own ranches adjacent to one another. You reach the tiny commercial district along NM 150, about 5 mi north of the intersection with U.S. 64 and NM 522 (it's about 9 mi north of the plaza). The drive is part of the joy of visiting, as NM 150 rises steadily above the Taos Valley, offering panoramic views of the Sangre de Cristos—you pass through Arroyo Seco en route to the Taos Ski Valley.

Arroyo Seco is without any formal attractions or museums, and that's partly its charm. The main reasons for making the trip here are to behold the dramatic scenery, grab a bite at one of the handful of excellent restaurants (ice cream from **Taos Cow Cafe** and tamales from **Abe's Cantina** are both revered by locals), and browse the several galleries and boutiques, whose wares tend to be a little more idiosyncratic but no less accomplished than those sold in Taos proper.

TAOS SKI VALLEY

Taos Ski Valley. Skiers and snowboarders from around the world return to the slopes and hospitality of Taos Ski Valley every year. This world-class area is known for its Alpine-village atmosphere, one of the finest ski schools in the country, and the variety of its 72 runs—it's also slowly but surely becoming more of a year-round destination, as the valley attracts outdoors enthusiasts with spectacular, and often challenging, hiking in summer and fall. There aren't many hotels in the valley but most have been converted to ski-in ski-out condos since the early 2000s, further evidence that the once-funky ski area is becoming more of a Colorado-style full-scale resort town. Some of the best trails in Carson National Forest begin at the Village of Taos Ski Valley and traverse dense woodland up to alpine tundra. There are relatively few summer visitors, so you can have the trails up to Bull-of-the-Woods, Gold Hill, Williams

Lake, Italianos, and Wheeler Peak nearly all to yourself. Special events like barn dances and wine tastings occur occasionally throughout the nonskiing seasons.

Taos Ski Valley lies about 10 mi beyond Arroyo Seco—just continue up NM 150, which crosses a high plain, then plunges into the Rio Hondo Canyon to follow the cascading brook upstream through the forest and up into the mountains where NM 150 ends. (The road does not continue to Red River, as some disappointed motorists discover.)

WHERE TO EAT

For a relatively small town many miles from any big city, Taos has a sophisticated and eclectic dining scene. It's as fine a destination for authentic New Mexican fare as any town its size in the state, but you'll also find several upscale spots serving creative fare utilizing mostly local ingredients, a smattering of excellent Asian and Middle Eastern spots, and several very good cafés and coffeehouses perfect for light but bountiful breakfast and lunch fare.

WHAT IT COSTS					
	¢	$	$$	$$$	$$$$
AT DINNER	under $10	$10–$17	$18–$24	$25–$30	over $30

Prices are for a main course, excluding 8.25% sales tax.

Use the coordinate ✛ B2 at the end of each listing to locate a site on the corresponding map.

PLAZA AND VICINITY

$ ✗ **Antonio's.** Chef Antonio Matus has been delighting discerning diners
MEXICAN in the Taos area for many years. This rambling, art-filled adobe compound with a delightful redbrick courtyard is the flagship of his three local eateries (the other two are Rellenos Cafe *(⇨ below)* and Sabor, which opened inside La Fonda de Taos hotel inside the old Joseph's Table space in summer 2010). Matus focuses on regional Mexican, as opposed to local New Mexican, specialties, such as *chile en nogada* (poblano peppers stuffed with pork, pears, and raisins and topped with a walnut-cream sauce) and *huachinango a la Veracruzana* (red snapper topped with a tomato-jalapeño-olive sauce), plus a fantastic *tres leches* (three milks) cake and a rich chipotle-chocolate cake. Less conventional options include burgers of locally raised yak and mahimahi ceviche. The Sunday brunch is one of the best in town. ✉ *122 Dona Luz St.* ☎ *575/751–4800* ⊕ *www.antoniosoftaos.com* ▭ *MC, V* ⊗ *No dinner Sun.* ✛ *C4.*

$ ✗ **Bent Street Café & Deli.** Try for a seat on the cheery, covered out-
AMERICAN door patio next to giant sunflowers, as the interior of this often-packed spot can feel a bit cramped, although service is friendly and helpful wherever you sit. Enjoy breakfast burritos, eggs Benedict, homemade granola, fresh-baked goods, dozens of deli sandwiches, tortilla soup,

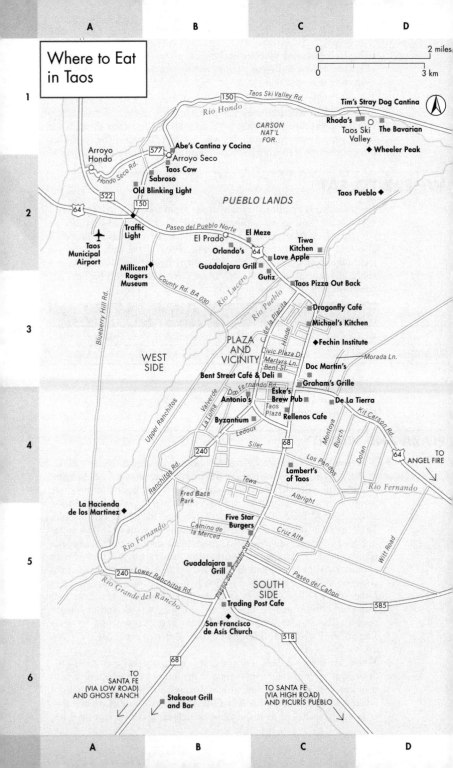

Where to Eat in Taos

0 ... 2 miles
0 ... 3 km

Rio Hondo

Taos Ski Valley Rd.

150

CARSON NAT'L FOR.

Tim's Stray Dog Cantina

Rhoda's

Taos Ski Valley

The Bavarian

Arroyo Hondo

577

Abe's Cantina y Cocina

Arroyo Seco

Hondo Seco Rd.

Taos Cow

Sabroso

Old Blinking Light

◆ Wheeler Peak

522

64

150

PUEBLO LANDS

Taos Pueblo ◆

Traffic Light

Paseo del Pueblo Norte

Taos Municipal Airport

El Prado

El Meze

Orlando's

64

Tiwa Kitchen

Love Apple

Millicent Rogers Museum

County Rd. BA 030

Guadalajara Grill

Gutiz

Taos Pizza Out Back

Rio Lucero

Rio Pueblo

Dragonfly Café

Michael's Kitchen

Blueberry Hill Rd.

Calle de la Placita

Placita

PLAZA AND VICINITY

◆ Fechin Institute

Morada Ln.

WEST SIDE

Civic Plaza Dr.

Martyrs Ln.

Bent St.

Doc Martin's

Bent Street Café & Deli

Don Fernando Rd.

Graham's Grille

Upper Ranchitos

Valverde

La Loma

Antonio's

Eske's Brew Pub

Taos Plaza

De La Tierra

Ledoux

Byzantium

Rellenos Cafe

Siler

240

68

Kit Carson Rd.

Montoya

Burch

Dolan

64

TO ANGEL FIRE

Ranchitos Rd.

Los Pandos

Rio Fernando

Lambert's of Taos

Fred Baca Park

Tewa

Albright

La Hacienda de los Martinez ◆

Rio Fernando

Five Star Burgers

Camino de la Merced

Cruz Alta

Witt Road

Guadalajara Grill

240

Lower Ranchitos Rd.

Paseo del Pueblo Sur

SOUTH SIDE

Paseo del Cañón

585

Rio Grande del Rancho

Trading Post Cafe

San Francisco de Asís Church

518

68

TO SANTA FE (VIA LOW ROAD) AND GHOST RANCH

Stakeout Grill and Bar

TO SANTA FE (VIA HIGH ROAD) AND PICURÍS PUEBLO

and homemade soups and stews. You might finish your meal with a chocolate-nut brownie. Beer, wine, and gourmet coffees are also served. ✉ *120-M Bent St.* ☎ *575/758–5787* ⊕ *http://johndunnshops.com/ BentStreetDeli.html* ▭ *MC, V* ☻ *No dinner* ✛ *C3.*

$$ ✕ **Byzantium.** Off a grassy courtyard near the Blumenschein and Har-
ECLECTIC wood museums, this quirky locals' favorite defies its traditional-look-
ing adobe exterior to present an eclectic menu with American, Asian, Mediterranean, and Middle Eastern influences. You might start with sesame-steamed ginger-and-chicken dumplings, before moving on to simple but fresh fire-roasted tomatoes and Parmesan over angel-hair pasta, or a hearty mixed grill of strip steak, pork loin, chicken, ribs, and bacon with smoky house-made barbecue sauce. Service is friendly, and the vibe is low-key—this is a spot relatively few tourists discover. ✉ *11–C La Placita* ☎ *575/751–0805* ▭ *AE, MC, V* ☻ *Closed Tues. and Wed. No lunch* ✛ *C4.*

$$$ ✕ **De La Tierra.** A dashing, dramatic, high-ceiling restaurant inside the
ECLECTIC fancifully plush El Monte Sagrado resort, this chic spot presents dar-
ing, globally influenced cuisine. Top starters include steamed Thai mus-
sels with lemongrass, coconut milk, and kaffir lime and organic greens with Granny Smith apples, candied walnuts, and blue cheese. Among the mains, you can't go wrong with the chile- and chocolate-rubbed Muscovy duck breast over roasted corn–lima bean–mango succotash—
there's also a wide selection of hefty steaks. It's dressy by Taos stan-
dards, but you'll still fit in wearing smartly casual threads, and the management has dropped prices considerably in recent years to compete with the town's other comparable restaurants. ✉ *El Monte Sagrado, 317 Kit Carson Rd.* ☎ *575/758–3502* ⊕ *www.elmontesagrado.com* ▭ *AE, D, DC, MC, V* ✛ *C4.*

$$ ✕ **Doc Martin's.** The stylish restaurant of the Historic Taos Inn takes
SOUTHWESTERN its name from the building's original owner, a local physician who
saw patients in the rooms that are now the dining areas. The creative menu hews toward innovative takes on comforting classics, with an emphasis on sustainable ingredients—try the curious but quite tasty rattlesnake-rabbit sausage with ancho chile–cherry sauce among the starters. Entrées of note include grilled pork loin with green chile–cheese polenta and bacon-fennel salsa, and a juicy elk burger with crisp fries. There's an extensive wine list, and the adjoining Adobe Bar serves up some of the best margaritas in town. In winter ask for a table near the cozy kiva fireplace. ✉ *Historic Taos Inn, 125 Paseo del Pueblo Norte* ☎ *575/758–1977* ⊕ *www.taosinn.com* ▭ *AE, D, MC, V* ✛ *C3.*

$ ✕ **Dragonfly Café and Bakery.** This charming café bakes its own bread
ECLECTIC and serves a variety of ethnic specialties including organic Asian salads,
Middle Eastern lamb with a Greek salad, hummus and pita bread, cur-
ried chicken salad, bison burgers, and Vietnamese chicken salad. You can sit out front on a shaded outdoor patio with a fountain when it's warm and watch the tourists go by. Dragonfly also does a brisk mail-
order business with its red-chile–infused truffles, delicious granola, and many other tasty products. Wine and beer are served. ✉ *402 Paseo del Pueblo Norte* ☎ *575/737–5859* ⊕ *www.dragonflytaos.com* ▭ *MC, V* ☻ *No dinner Sun. Closed Tues.* ✛ *C3.*

¢　✗**Eske's Brew Pub.** This casual, dining-and-quaffing pub is favored by
AMERICAN　off-duty ski patrollers and river guides. The menu mostly covers hearty
sandwiches (try the grilled bratwurst and sauerkraut sandwich), soups,
and salads. The microbrewery downstairs produces everything from
nutty, dark stout to light ales, but you shouldn't leave without sam-
pling the house specialty—Taos green-chile beer. There's live music on
weekends, and in good weather you can relax on the patio. ⊠ *106 Des
Georges La.* ☎ *575/758–1517* ⊕ *www.eskesbrewpub.com* ▭ *MC, V*
⊹ *C4.*

$$　✗**Graham's Grille.** The folks who frequent this upscale bar and eatery
ECLECTIC　tend to be hip and sophisticated—just like the artful, Southwestern-
Fodor's Choice　based but cross-cultural food served in this minimalist environment.
★　Local, seasonal produce, cage-free chickens, and homemade stocks are
key to the fresh flavors and creative combinations prepared by chef
Leslie Fay, a long-time Taos restaurateur. Small plates worth sampling
include mac-and-cheese with mild green chiles and hickory-smoked
bacon, duck-breast flatbread with orange-*charmoula* sauce, and black
bean soup with a touch of cumin. The buffalo-brisket sandwich is a
winner at lunch. Main courses range from blue corn–crusted red trout
with cilantro-lime butter to hearty tamale pies. Worthy desserts include
a coconut cake with mango cream and a lemon-and-piñon pound cake
with blueberry coulis. There's a memorable Sunday brunch. ⊠ *106
Paseo del Pueblo Norte* ☎ *575/751–1350* ⊕ *www.thefayway.com/
dining* ▭ *AE, MC, V* ⊹ *C3.*

$　✗**Guadalajara Grill.** Some of the tastiest Mexican food this side of the
MEXICAN　border makes the well-priced menu of this relaxed and friendly estab-
lishment so popular that there's a location on both the north and south
ends of town. It's ultracasual here (you select your own beer from a
cooler, and order from the counter). The extensive menu includes grilled
fish tacos served in soft homemade tortillas, shrimp with garlic sauce,
bulging burritos smothered in red or green chiles, and for the adventur-
ous, shark enchiladas. ⊠ *822 Paseo del Pueblo Norte* ☎ *575/737–0816*
⊠ *1384 Paseo del Pueblo Sur, South Side* ☎ *575/751–0063* ▭ *MC, V*
⊹ *C2, B5.*

$　✗**Gutiz.** This ambitious and consistently terrific favorite for lunch and
ECLECTIC　breakfast blends French, Spanish, and South American culinary influ-
ences. Best bets in the morning include cinnamon French toast made
with thick homemade bread and a baked omelet topped with a green
tapenade. Lunch specialties include a warm salad Niçoise and *chicharon
de pollo*—fried chicken tenders topped with hot *aji* Amarillo sauce.
Meals are served on a gravel patio or inside the small lilac-hued din-
ing room with views of the open kitchen. ⊠ *812B Paseo del Pueblo
Norte* ☎ *575/758–1226* ⊘ *Reservations not accepted* ▭ *No credit cards*
☺ *Closed Mon. No dinner* ⊹ *C3.*

$$$　✗**Lambert's of Taos.** Superb service and creative cuisine define this Taos
AMERICAN　landmark located 2½ blocks south of the plaza. Among starters, don't
miss the marinated roasted-beet salad with warm goat cheese and
pumpkin seeds, sautéed lobster and shallots with a vanilla-champagne
sauce, and corn-and-applewood-smoked-bacon chowder. Or have all
three and call it a night. The signature entrées include pepper-crusted

lamb with a red-wine demi-glace and roasted duck with an apricot-chipotle glaze. Memorable desserts are a warm-apple-and-almond crisp topped with white-chocolate ice cream and a dark-chocolate mousse with raspberry sauce. A small-plate bistro menu is available in the cozy bar or in the spacious dining rooms. The lengthy wine list includes some of California's finest vintages. The owners also operate the Old Blinking Light up near Arroyo Seco (⇨ *below*). ⊠ *309 Paseo del Pueblo Sur* ☎ *575/758–1009* ⊕ *www.lambertsoftaos.com* ▭ *AE, DC, MC, V* ☾ *No lunch* ✛ *C4.*

$ ✕ **Michael's Kitchen.** This casual, homey restaurant serves up a bit of
AMERICAN everything—you can have a hamburger while your friend who can't get enough chile sauce can order up vegetarian cheese enchiladas garnished with lettuce and tomatoes. Brunch is popular with the locals (dig into a plate of strawberry-banana-pecan pancakes), and amusing asides to the waitstaff over the intercom contribute to the energetic buzz. Breakfast and lunch are served daily, with dinner available up until 8 on Friday, Saturday, and Sunday. ⊠ *304 Paseo del Pueblo Norte* ☎ *575/758–4178* ⊕ *www.michaelskitchen.com* ⌖ *Reservations not accepted* ▭ *AE, D, MC, V* ✛ *C3.*

$ ✕ **Rellenos Cafe.** Touted as the only organic New Mexican restaurant in
NEW MEXICAN town, this casual eatery from the talented team behind Antonio's and Sabor also offers wheat-free, gluten-free, and vegan menu options. Popular specialties include killer chiles rellenos topped with a brandy-cream sauce, grilled garlic shrimp, and seafood paella. Service is friendly—don't be put off by the bland exterior on a busy stretch of Paseo del Pueblo Sur (there's a nice patio in back). The house drink, a fruity sangria, is served in gargantuan Mexican glasses. ⊠ *135 Paseo del Pueblo Sur* ☎ *575/758–7001* ⌖ *Reservations not accepted* ▭ *MC, V* ☾ *Closed Sun.* ✛ *C4.*

SOUTH SIDE

$ ✕ **Five Star Burgers.** A standout amid the strip of mostly unmemorable
AMERICAN fast-food restaurants along Paseo del Pueblo on the south side of town, this airy, high-ceiling contemporary space serves stellar burgers using hormone-free Angus beef from respected Harris Ranch; turkey, veggie, Colorado lamb, bison, and salmon burgers are also available, and you can choose from an assortment of novel toppings, including fried eggs, wild mushrooms, caramelized onions, and applewood-smoked bacon. Beer and wine are also served. ⊠ *1032 Paseo del Pueblo Sur* ☎ *575/758–8484* ⊕ *www.5starburgers.com* ▭ *AE, D, MC, V* ✛ *C5.*

$$$$ ✕ **Stakeout Grill and Bar.** On Outlaw Hill in the foothills of the Sangre
STEAK de Cristo Mountains, this old adobe homestead has 100-mi-long views
Fodor's Choice and sunsets that dazzle. The outdoor patio encircled by a piñon forest
★ has kiva fireplaces to warm you during cooler months. The decadent fare is well prepared, fully living up to the view it accompanies—try filet mignon with béarnaise sauce, buffalo rib eye with chipotle-cilantro butter, almond-crusted wild sockeye salmon with shaved fennel, or fall-off-the-bone braised Colorado lamb shank with orange and port-wine jus. Don't miss the tasty Kentucky bourbon pecan pie and crème brûlée with toasted coconut for dessert. ⊠ *Stakeout Dr.; 8 mi south of Taos*

4

Plaza, east of NM 68, look for cowboy sign ☎ *575/758–2042* ⊕ *www. stakeoutrestaurant.com* ☰ *AE, D, DC, MC, V* ☉ *No lunch* ✛ *B6.*

$$ ✕ **Trading Post Cafe.** Local hipsters outnumber tourists at this casual spot
ITALIAN   serving mostly modern Italian fare with regional accents. Intelligent and
attentive service along with well-presented contemporary Southwestern
art make any meal a pleasure. For starters try the signature noodle soup
or minestrone with smoked ham before moving on to an oven-roasted
duck with seasonal vegetables and creamy mashed potatoes or any of
the traditional pasta dishes. Superb desserts include a coconut-cream
pie and rich strawberry shortcake. Parking is just around the back, off
NM 518. ✉ *4179 Paseo del Pueblo Sur, Ranchos de Taos* ☎ *575/758–
5089* ⊕ *http://tradingpostcafe.com* ☰ *AE, D, MC, V* ☉ *Closed Mon.
No lunch Sun.* ✛ *B5.*

TAOS PUEBLO

¢   ✕ **Tiwa Kitchen.** This one-of-a-kind restaurant, even for Taos, serves
NATIVE   authentic Native American food in a casual setting. Ben White Buf-
AMERICAN falo and his wife Debbie Moonlight Flowers organically grow many
of the restaurant's ingredients themselves and use traditional beehive
wood-fired ovens just outside the back door for baking corn and roast-
ing peppers. Try the blue-corn taco made with blue-corn fry bread or
grilled buffalo sausage served with red or green chile. ✉ *328 Veterans
Hwy. (Taos Pueblo Rd.)* ☎ *575/751–1020* ☰ *No credit cards* ☉ *Closed
Tues. and 10 wks in spring during the Pueblo's traditional "quiet time."*
✛ *C2.*

EL PRADO

$$ ✕ **El Meze.** Set back from NM 68 in tiny El Prado, this adobe house
SPANISH   with an expansive back patio that affords unobstructed views of the
Sangre de Cristo Mountains reopened in December 2010 following a
fire. Tightly spaced tables, polished-wood floors, and bright red adobe
walls make it easy to imagine you're tucked away inside a small cafe in
the southern Spain countryside, and indeed, El Meze specializes in the
flavorful cuisine and wine of this region (along with some more regionally inspired fare). Andalusian-style *chicharrones* (fried pork rinds) and
buffalo short ribs *adovada* (marinated in red chile) make terrific starters, while grilled whole trout with preserved lemon, mint, cilantro, and
garlic is perfectly prepared. The well-chosen wine list includes Torron-
tes, Albarino, and fine Rioja blends from throughout Spain. ✉ *1017
Paseo del Pueblo Norte* ☎ *575/751–3337* ⊕ *www.elmeze.com* ☰ *MC,
V* ☉ *Closed Sun. No lunch* ✛ *C2.*

¢   ✕ **Orlando's.** This family-run local favorite is likely to be packed during
NEW MEXICAN   peak hours, while guests wait patiently to devour perfectly seasoned
Fodor's Choice favorites such as *carne adovada* (red chile–marinated pork), blue-
★   corn enchiladas, and scrumptious shrimp burritos. You can eat in the
cozy dining room, outside on the umbrella-shaded front patio, or call
ahead for takeout if you'd rather avoid the crowds. Margaritas here
are potent. ✉ *114 Don Juan Valdez La., off Paseo del Pueblo Norte*
☎ *575/751–1450* ⊕ *www.orlandostaos.com* ☰ *MC, V* ✛ *B2.*

$ ✕**Love Apple.** It's easy to drive by the small adobe former chapel that
ECLECTIC houses this delightful restaurant a short drive north of Taos Plaza, just
Fodor's Choice beyond the driveway for Hacienda del Sol B&B. But slow down—you
★ don't want to miss the culinary magic inside. Chef Andrea Meyer uses
organic, mostly local ingredients in the preparation of simple yet sophisticated farm-to-table creations like homemade sweet-corn tamales with
red-chile mole, a fried egg, and crème fraîche, and robustly seasoned
posole stew with grilled lamb sausage, pancetta, caramelized onion, and
radish-lime relish. The price is right, too—just remember it's cash-only.
⊠ *803 Paseo del Pueblo Norte* ☎ *575/751–0050* ⊕ *www.theloveapple.
net* ⊟ *No credit cards.* ☾ *Closed Mon. No lunch* ✛ *C2.*

$ ✕**Taos Pizza Out Back.** Set in a funky timber-frame shack of a building
PIZZA with a large tree-shaded patio hemmed in with coyote fencing, this venerable pizza joint has cultivated a loyal following over the years for its
thick-crust, creatively topped pies (plus very good pastas and salads).
Distinctive pizza combos include the Ranchero, with Italian sausage,
sundried tomatoes, smoked cheddar, and green onions; and the classic
white pizza with fresh tomato, basil, ricotta, Parmesan, and mozzarella.
Everything is available by the slice (they're massive), or in several pie
sizes. Organic ingredients are favored, and there's a good list of beers
and wines. ⊠ *712 Paseo del Pueblo Norte* ☎ *575/758–3112* ⊕ *www.
taospizzaoutback.com* ⊟ *AE, D, MC, V* ✛ *C3.*

ARROYO SECO

¢ ✕**Abe's Cantina y Cocina.** Family-owned and -operated since the 1940s,
CAFÉ no-frills Abe's is both a convenience store (nothing special, but okay for
candy or chips) and restaurant—that's the special part. You can have
your breakfast burrito, rolled tacos, or homemade tamales at one of the
small tables crowded next to the canned goods, or take it on a picnic.
⊠ *489 NM 150 (Taos Ski Valley Rd.)* ☎ *575/776–8643* ⊟ *AE, D, MC,
V* ☾ *Closed Sun. No dinner* ✛ *B1.*

$ ✕**Old Blinking Light.** About a mile up NM 150 toward the ski valley from
NEW MEXICAN the landmark "old blinking light" (now a regular stoplight, where U.S.
64, NM 522, and NM 150 meet), this rambling adobe is known for
its steaks, ribs, and enormous (and potent) margaritas. There's also a
long list of tasty appetizers, such as posole stew and chipotle-shrimp
quesadillas. Several huge burgers are available, plus first-rate chicken
mole. In summer you can sit out in the walled garden and take in the
spectacular mountain view. There's a wine shop on the premises, and
the restaurant is owned by the same talented team behind Lambert's
of Taos. ⊠ *Mile Marker 1, Taos Ski Valley Rd., between El Prado and
Arroyo Seco* ☎ *575/776–8787* ⊕ *www.oldblinkinglight.com* ⊟ *AE,
MC, V* ☾ *No lunch* ✛ *A2.*

$$$ ✕**Sabroso.** Reasonably priced, innovative cuisine and outstanding
MEDITERRANEAN wines are served in this 150-year-old adobe hacienda, where you can
Fodor's Choice also relax in lounge chairs near the bar, or on a delightful patio sur-
★ rounded by plum trees. The Mediterranean-influenced contemporary
menu changes regularly, but an evening's entrée might be pan-seared
sea scallops, risotto cakes, and ratatouille, or rib-eye steak topped with
a slice of Stilton cheese. There's live jazz and cabaret in the piano bar

several nights a week. Order from the simpler bar menu if you're seeking something light—the antipasto plate and white-truffle-oil fries are both delicious. ⊠ *470 NM 150 (Taos Ski Valley Rd.)* ☎ *575/776–3333* ⊕ *www.sabrosotaos.com* ⊟ *AE, MC, V* ⊘ *No lunch* ✛ *B2.*

¢ ✕ **Taos Cow.** Locals, hikers, and skiers headed up to Taos Ski Valley, and
CAFÉ visitors to funky Arroyo Seco flock to this cozy storefront café operated by the famed Taos Cow ice-cream company. This isn't merely a place to sample amazing homemade ice cream (including such innovative flavors as piñon-caramel, lavender, and Chocolate Rio Grande—chocolate ice cream packed with cinnamon-chocolate chunks). You can also nosh on French toast, omelets, turkey-and-Brie sandwiches, black-bean-and-brown-rice bowls, organic teas and coffees, natural sodas, homemade granola, and more. ⊠ *485 NM 150* ☎ *575/776–5640* ⊕ *www.taoscow. com* ⊟ *MC, V* ⊘ *No dinner* ✛ *B2.*

TAOS SKI VALLEY

$$$ ✕ **The Bavarian.** The restaurant inside the romantic, magically situated
GERMAN alpine lodge, which also offers Taos Ski Valley's most luxurious accom-
Fodor's Choice modations, serves outstanding contemporary Bavarian-inspired cuisine,
★ such as baked artichokes and Gruyère, and braised pork loin with garlic-mashed potatoes and red cabbage. Lunch is more casual and less expensive, with burgers and salads available—in summer this is an excellent spot to fuel up before attempting an ambitious hike, as the restaurant is steps from the trailhead for Wheeler Peak and other popular mountains. There's an extensive wine list, plus a nice range of beers imported from Spaten Brewery in Munich. ⊠ *100 Kachina Rd.* ⌂ *Box 653, Taos Ski Valley 87525* ☎ *575/776–8020* ⊕ *www.thebavarian.net* ⊟ *AE, MC, V* ⊘ *Closed early Apr.–late May and mid-Oct.–late Nov.; closed Mon.–Wed. in summer.* ✛ *D1.*

$ ✕ **Rhoda's Restaurant.** Rhoda Blake founded Taos Ski Valley with her
AMERICAN husband, Ernie. Her slope-side restaurant serves pasta, burgers, and sandwiches for lunch. Dinner fare is a bit more substantive, such as veal medallions with pancetta and seafood chiles rellenos with ancho chile sauce. ⊠ *Resort Center, on the slope* ☎ *575/776–2291* ⊕ *http:// taoswebb.com/menu/rhodas.html* ⊟ *AE, MC, V* ⊘ *Closed June–Sept.* ✛ *D1.*

$ ✕ **Tim's Stray Dog Cantina.** This wildly popular spot occupies a chalet-
SOUTHWESTERN style building in the heart of the Taos ski area, and it's a favorite spot for breakfast (try the eggs Benedict topped with red chile sauce), lunch, dinner, and après-ski cocktails, including highly refreshing margaritas. Favorites include steak tacos, pork mole enchiladas, huevos rancheros, barbecue-pulled pork sandwiches, and green-chile burgers (both beef and veggie). Hours vary and are more limited outside of ski season—call ahead. ⊠ *105 Sutton Pl.* ☎ *575/776–2894* ⊕ *www.straydogtsv.com* ⊟ *MC, V.* ✛ *D1.*

WHERE TO STAY

The hotels and motels along NM 68 (Paseo del Pueblo), most of them on the south side of town, suit every need and budget; rates vary little between big-name chains and smaller establishments—Comfort Suites is the best maintained of the chains. Make advance reservations and expect higher rates during ski season (usually from late December to early April, and especially for lodgings on the north side of town, closer to the ski area) and in the summer. Skiers have many lodging choices, from in town to spots nestled beneath the slopes, although several of the hotels up at Taos Ski Valley have been converted to condos in recent years, diminishing the supply of overnight accommodations. Arroyo Seco is a good alternative if you can't find a room right up in the Ski Valley. The area's many B&Bs offer some of the best values, when you factor in typically hearty full breakfasts, personal service, and often roomy casitas with private entrances.

4

WHAT IT COSTS					
	¢	$	$$	$$$	$$$$
FOR TWO PEOPLE	under $70	$70–$130	$131–$190	$191–$260	over $260

Prices are for a standard double room in high season, excluding 10%–12% tax.

Use the coordinate ✛ B2 at the end of each listing to locate a site on the corresponding map.

PLAZA AND VICINITY

$$
BED & BREAKFAST

⊡ Adobe & Pines Inn. Native American and Mexican artifacts decorate the main house of this B&B, which has expansive mountain views. Part of the main adobe building dates from 1830. The rooms and suites contain Mexican-tile baths, kiva fireplaces, and fluffy goose-down pillows and comforters, plus such modern touches as flat-screen TVs, DVD players, Wi-Fi, and CD players. Separate casitas and suites are more spacious and offer plenty of seclusion, with private entrances and courtyard access. The owners serve gourmet breakfasts in a sunny, glass-enclosed patio. **Pros:** quiet rural location; fantastic views; beautiful gardens. **Cons:** a bit of a drive south of town; some bedrooms are small. ⊠ *4107 NM 68* ⌂ *Box 837, Ranchos de Taos 87557* ☎ *575/751–0947 or 800/723–8267* ⊕ *www.adobepines.com* ⤶ *4 rooms, 2 suites, 2 casitas* ⚿ *In-room: a/c, kitchen (some), refrigerator (some), DVD, Wi-Fi. In-hotel: some pets allowed* ⊟ *MC, V* ❘⊘❘ *BP* ✛ *B6.*

$$$
BED & BREAKFAST

⊡ Casa de las Chimeneas. Tile hearths, French doors, and traditional viga ceilings grace the "House of Chimneys" B&B, two-and-a-half blocks from the plaza and secluded behind thick walls. Each room in the 1912 structure has a private entrance, a fireplace, handmade New Mexican furniture, bathrooms with Talavera tiles, and a bar stocked with complimentary beverages. All rooms overlook the gardens, and facilities include a small but excellent spa offering a wide range of treatments. The three-course breakfasts are impressive, and full evening suppers are

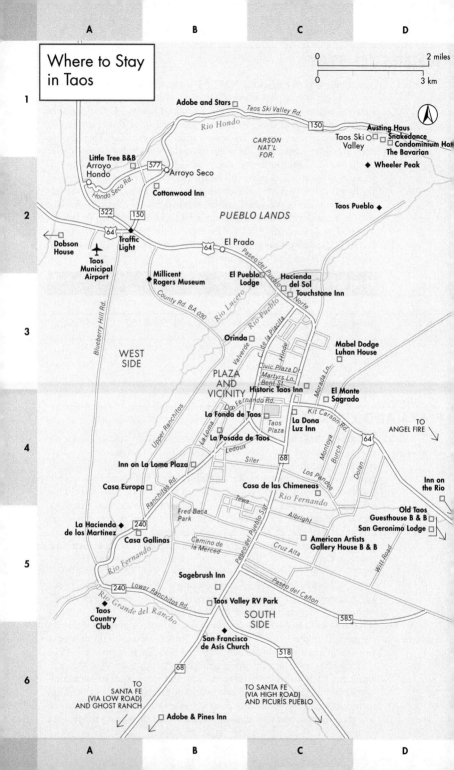

Where to Stay in Taos

	A	B	C	D
1		Adobe and Stars	Taos Ski Valley Rd.	Austing Haus / Snakedance / Condominium Hotel / The Bavarian
			Rio Hondo	150
			CARSON NAT'L FOR.	Taos Ski Valley
				Wheeler Peak
	Little Tree B&B / Arroyo Hondo	577 / Arroyo Seco		
	Hondo Seco Rd.	Cottonwood Inn	PUEBLO LANDS	Taos Pueblo
2	522 / 150			
	64 / Traffic Light	El Prado	64	
	Dobson House	Taos Municipal Airport	Paseo del Pueblo	
	Blueberry Hill Rd.	Millicent Rogers Museum	El Pueblo Lodge	Hacienda del Sol / Touchstone Inn
3	WEST SIDE	County Rd. BA 030 / Rio Lucero	Norte	
		Orinda	Rio Pueblo / Calle la Placita / Valverde / Hinde	Mabel Dodge Luhan House
		PLAZA AND VICINITY	Civic Plaza Dr. / Martyrs Ln. / Bent St.	Morada Ln.
			Historic Taos Inn	El Monte Sagrado
4		La Fonda de Taos	Don Fernando Rd. / Taos Plaza	La Dona Luz Inn / Kit Carson Rd.
		La Loma	La Posada de Taos	Montoya / Burch / 64 / TO ANGEL FIRE / Dolan
		Inn on La Loma Plaza	Ledoux / Siler / 68	
			Los Pandos	Inn on the Rio
		Casa Europa	Tewa / Rio Fernando	Old Taos Guesthouse B & B / San Geronimo Lodge
5	La Hacienda de los Martinez	240 / Casa Gallinas	Fred Baca Park / Camino de la Merced	Albright
		Rio Fernando	Paseo del Pueblo Sur / Cruz Alta	American Artists Gallery House B & B
		Sagebrush Inn		Paseo del Cañon
		240 / Lower Ranchitos Rd.	Taos Valley RV Park	585
		Rio Grande del Rancho	SOUTH SIDE	518
		Taos Country Club	San Francisco de Asis Church	
6		68 / TO SANTA FE (VIA LOW ROAD) AND GHOST RANCH	TO SANTA FE (VIA HIGH ROAD) AND PICURÍS PUEBLO	
		Adobe & Pines Inn		

0 — 2 miles
0 — 3 km

included in the rates. **Pros:** private setting; on-site spa; walking distance from plaza. **Cons:** 30-day cancellation policy; expensive (rates include dinner, but in a town with so many great restaurants, many guests prefer to eat out). ⊠ *405 Cordoba Rd.* ☎ *575/758–4777 or 877/758–4777* ⊕ *www.visittaos.com* ↝ *6 rooms, 2 suites* ⟁ *In-room: a/c, refrigerator, Wi-Fi. In-hotel: gym, spa, laundry facilities* ▤ *AE, D, DC, MC, V* ⦿ *MAP* ✛ *C4.*

$

BED & BREAKFAST

Fodor'sChoice

★

Casa Europa. The main part of this exquisite 18th-century adobe estate has been tastefully expanded to create an unforgettable B&B with old-world romance. Each room has a fireplace and is furnished with handpicked European antiques accented with Southwestern accessories. The two main common areas are light and airy, with comfortable chairs to relax in while the fireplace crackles. Breakfasts are elaborate, and complimentary homemade afternoon baked treats are served. Although the property is less than 2 mi from the plaza, its pastoral setting makes it feel a world away. Innkeepers Lisa and Joe McCutcheon take personal pride in offering their guests every courtesy and assistance. **Pros:** attentive service; memorable setting and sophisticated style; smallest rooms are very affordable. **Cons:** short drive to town. ⊠ *840 Upper Ranchitos Rd.* ☎ *575/758–9798* ⊕ *www.casaeuropanm.com* ↝ *5 rooms, 2 suites* ⟁ *In-room: a/c, refrigerators, Wi-Fi. In-hotel: some pets allowed* ▤ *MC, V* ⦿ *BP* ✛ *B4.*

$$$

RESORT

El Monte Sagrado. Although rates have been lowered considerably in recent years, this posh, eco-sensitive, and decidedly quirky small resort—part of Marriott's distinctive, high-end Autograph Collection brand—is still among the priciest properties in the state. Suites and casitas are accented with exotic themes, ranging from Native American designs to foreign flourishes from faraway lands including Japan or Tibet—some have their own outdoor soaking tubs and private courtyards. All units come with flat-screen TVs, iPod docks, and top-of-the-line bath amenities. A popular outdoor area dubbed the Sacred Circle is a patch of grassy land encircled by cottonwoods—this leads to the impressive on-site spa and fitness center, where you might book a lemon-verbena body polish or hot-stone massage. The on-site restaurant, De la Tierra, serves inventive cuisine, and the Anaconda Bar makes a warm and inviting spot to sip and socialize. **Pros:** eco-friendly; imaginative and whimsical decor; terrific spa. **Cons:** unusual decor isn't to everybody's taste; service doesn't always measure up to premium rates. ⊠ *317 Kit Carson Rd.* ☎ *575/758–3502 or 888/213–4419* ⊕ *www. elmontesagrado.com* ↝ *48 rooms, 6 casitas, 30 suites* ⟁ *In-room: a/c, safe, refrigerator, Wi-Fi. In-hotel: 2 restaurants, room service, bar, pool, gym, spa, bicycles, laundry service, some pets allowed* ▤ *AE, D, DC, MC, V* ✛ *C4.*

$

HOTEL

El Pueblo Lodge. Among the budget-minded properties in town, this well-maintained adobe-style hotel with a fun retro sign out front and the vibe of an old-school motel comprises several buildings on a peaceful 3-acre spread several blocks north of the plaza. Rooms in the West Building, constructed in the '80s, are a bit more spacious, and some have kiva-style fireplaces. But the original building, a vintage 1940s motor lodge, has more character, with its thick adobe walls and viga ceilings. **Pros:** terrific value; short walk north of the plaza. **Cons:** nothing fancy about the decor. ⊠ *412 Paseo del Pueblo Norte* ☎ *575/758–8700 or 800/433–9612* ⊕ *www.elpueblolodge.com* ↪ *50 rooms* ⚿ *In-room: a/c, refrigerator, Wi-Fi. In-hotel: pool, some pets allowed* ⊟ *AE, D, MC, V* ⏺ *CP* ✛ *C3.*

$$ ⊡ **Historic Taos Inn.** A 10-minute walk north of Taos Plaza, this celebrated
INN property is a local landmark, with some devotees having been regulars here for decades. Spanish-colonial architecture, including decorative alcoves in rooms, lends a warm, distinctive aesthetic to the four buildings, including the upscale Helen's House, which contains some of the fanciest rooms. Older units have thick adobe walls, viga ceilings, and other elements typical of vintage Taos architecture. In summer there's dining alfresco on the patio. The lobby, which also serves as seating for the Adobe Bar, is built around a former town well from which a fountain bubbles forth. Many shops and eateries are within walking distance, and the restaurant, Doc Martin's, is great for people-watching. **Pros:** a short walk from the plaza; lushly furnished rooms, exudes character and history. **Cons:** noise from street traffic and the bar; some rooms are very small. ⊠ *125 Paseo del Pueblo Norte* ☎ *575/758–2233 or 888/518–8267* ⊕ *www.taosinn.com* ↪ *40 rooms, 3 suites* ⚿ *In-room: a/c (some), Internet. In-hotel: restaurant, bar, Wi-Fi hotspot* ⊟ *AE, DC, MC, V* ✛ *C3.*

$$$ ⊡ **Inn on La Loma Plaza.** Surrounded by thick walls, this early-1800s
INN Pueblo Revival building—and the surrounding gardens—capture the spirit and style of Spanish-colonial Taos. The rooms, which are appointed with fresh-cut flowers, have kiva fireplaces, CD stereos, coffeemakers, and Mexican-tile bathrooms, and many have private patios or decks. The living room has a well-stocked library with books on Taos and art. Owners Jerry and Peggy Davis provide helpful advice about the area and serve a generous breakfast, afternoon snacks, and evening coffee. Guests have privileges at the nearby health club (and the inn has its own hot tub). **Pros:** towering trees and lush gardens; inspiring views; extremely comfy rooms and beds. **Cons:** lots of stairs; on a busy street. ⊠ *315 Ranchitos Rd., Box 4159* ☎ *575/758–1717 or 800/530–3040* ⊕ *www.vacationtaos.com* ↪ *5 rooms, 1 suite, 2 studios* ⚿ *In-room: a/c (some), kitchen (some), DVD, Wi-Fi* ⊟ *AE, D, MC, V* ⏺ *BP* ✛ *B4.*

$ ⊡ **Inn on the Rio.** This property started as a strip motel, but over the
INN years it's been transformed with adobe-style decorative touches and hand-painted murals into a charming B&B. If you look hard enough, you can still discern the motel roots of these tastefully furnished rooms with Southwestern art and linens and hand-painted bathrooms, but the rates are very fair. A well-tended garden overflowing with wildflowers and herbs surrounds the pool and hot tub area. Innkeepers Robert and Jules Cahalane prepare homemade bread, green-chile-and-egg casseroles, and cinnamon-infused coffee for breakfast. **Pros:** one of the few outdoor heated pools in town; private entrance to each room. **Cons:** traffic noise; small bathrooms. ⊠ *910 E. Kit Carson Rd.* ☎ *575/758–7199 or 800/737–7199* ⊕ *www.innontherio.com* ↪ *12 rooms* ⚿ *In-room: no a/c, Wi-Fi. In-hotel: pool, some pets allowed* ⊟ *AE, D, MC, V* ⏺ *BP* ✛ *D4.*

$ ⊞ **La Dona Luz Inn.** Paul "Paco" Castillo, who hails from a long line of
BED & BREAKFAST   local Taos artists and curio-shop owners, runs this festive and friendly
B&B just a block off of Kit Carson Road and a few minutes' stroll
from the plaza. It's one of the best bargains in the neighborhood, and
rooms in this 19th-century adobe structure with latilla-and-viga ceilings are decorated with art and antiques from New Mexico, Mexico,
and Spain—many have Jacuzzi tubs. The quirkiest and coziest room
is also the least expensive room—it's hidden up a spiral staircase and
has low ceilings, but there's a nice view of Wheeler Peak to the east.
Pros: affordable rooms; a short walk from the plaza. **Cons:** in a slightly
busy and noisy area (especially in summer). ⊠ *206 Des Georges La.*
☎ *575/758–9000 or 888/758–9060* ⊕ *www.ladonaluz.com* ➪ *6 rooms,
2 suites* ⟁ *In-room: a/c, no phone, kitchen (some), refrigerator (some),
DVD, Wi-Fi. In-hotel: some pets allowed* ▤ *D, MC, V* ⎮○⎮ *CP* ✛ *C4.*

$$ ⊞ **La Fonda de Taos.** This handsomely updated and elegant historic prop-
HOTEL   erty (there's been a hotel on this location since 1840) is ideal if you wish
to be in the heart of the action—it's directly on the plaza. The warm
decor, easy proximity to nightlife and dining, and no-children-under-
eight policy make this a great choice for a romantic getaway. The rooms
are rustic yet elegant and are furnished in neutral colors with luxury
linens and hand-tiled bathrooms. A luxury penthouse on the top floor
can be joined with other suites into a super-posh four-bedroom retreat.
La Fonda also houses the Sabor restaurant, which opened in summer
2010. **Pros:** the most central location of any hotel in town; the build-
ing has a great history. **Cons:** less than ideal if you're seeking peace
and quiet. ⊠ *108 S. Plaza* ☎ *575/758–2211 or 800/833–2211* ⊕ *www.
lafondataos.com* ➪ *19 rooms, 5 suites, 1 penthouse* ⟁ *In-room: a/c,
kitchen (some), refrigerator, Wi-Fi. In-hotel: 2 restaurants, bar, no kids
under 8* ▤ *AE, D, MC, V* ✛ *C4.*

$$ ⊞ **La Posada de Taos.** A couple of blocks from Taos Plaza, this fam-
INN   ily-friendly 100-year-old inn has beam ceilings, a decorative arched
doorway, and the intimacy of a private hacienda. Five guest rooms
are in the main house; the sixth unit is a separate cottage with a king-
size bed, sitting room, and fireplace. The rooms all have mountain or
courtyard garden views, and some open onto private patios. Almost
all have kiva-style fireplaces. Breakfasts are hearty. **Pros:** a few blocks
from the plaza; historic building. **Cons:** small rooms; not much privacy
in the main house. ⊠ *309 Juanita La., Box 1118* ☎ *575/758–8164 or
800/645–4803* ⊕ *www.laposadadetaos.com* ➪ *5 rooms, 1 cottage* ⟁ *In-
room: no a/c, no phone, Wi-Fi.* ▤ *AE, MC, V* ⎮○⎮ *BP* ✛ *B4.*

$$ ⊞ **Mabel Dodge Luhan House.** Quirky and offbeat—much like Taos—this
INN   National Historic Landmark was once home to the heiress who drew
illustrious writers and artists—including D. H. Lawrence, Willa Cather,
Georgia O'Keeffe, Ansel Adams, Martha Graham, and Carl Jung—to
Taos. The main house, which has kept its simple, rustic feel, has nine
cozy guest rooms; there are eight more in a modern building, as well
as two two-bedroom cottages. The house exudes early-20th-century
elegance, and the grounds offer numerous quiet corners for private
conversations or solo meditation. Guests can stay in what was Mabel's
room, in her hand-carved double bed to be precise; or in the solarium,

an airy room at the top of the house that is completely surrounded by glass (and accessible by a ladder). For art groupies, nothing can quite compare with sleeping in the elegant room Georgia O'Keeffe stayed in while visiting. The inn is frequently used for artistic, cultural, and educational workshops—hence the tiny, but exceptional, bookstore in the lobby specializing in local authors and artists. **Pros:** historically relevant; rural setting, yet just blocks from the plaza. **Cons:** lots of stairs and uneven paths. ⊠ *240 Morada La.* ☎ *575/751–9686 or 800/846–2235* ⊕ *www.mabeldodgeluhan.com* ↪ *16 rooms, 1 suite, 2 casitas* ⚐ *In-room: a/c, no phone, no TV, Wi-Fi.* ▤ *AE, MC, V* ⦶ *BP* ⊹ *C3.*

$$ 🖼 **Orinda.** Built in 1947, this adobe estate has spectacular views and
BED & BREAKFAST country privacy. The rustic rooms have separate entrances, kiva-style fireplaces, traditional viga ceilings, and Mexican-tile baths. Some of the rooms can be combined with a shared living area into a large suite. One has a two-person Jacuzzi. The hearty breakfast is served family-style in the soaring two-story sun atrium amid a gallery of artworks, all for sale. **Pros:** most rooms are spacious; gorgeous views of Taos Mountain. **Cons:** rooms are a little bland; a bit pricey for what is offered. ⊠ *461 Valverde* ☎ *575/758–8581 or 800/847–1837* ⊕ *www.orindabb. com* ↪ *5 rooms* ⚐ *In-room: no a/c (some), refrigerator. In-hotel: Wi-Fi hotspot, some pets allowed* ▤ *AE, MC, V* ⦶ *BP* ⊹ *C3.*

SOUTH SIDE

$ 🖼 **American Artists Gallery House Bed & Breakfast.** Each of the immaculate
BED & BREAKFAST adobe-style rooms and suites here is called a "gallery," and owners LeAn and Charles Clamurro have taken care to decorate them with local arts and crafts. Some have Jacuzzis and all have kiva fireplaces; one family-friendly suite has a full kitchen; and all have private entrances, wood-burning fireplaces, and front porches where you can admire the view of Taos Mountain. Sumptuous hot breakfasts—along with conversation and suggestions about local attractions—are served up at a community table in the main house each morning, where you can often see the resident peacock, George, preening outside the windows (keep in mind that George can make a little noise from time to time). **Pros:** private entrances; true gourmet breakfast; reasonable rates. **Cons:** some rooms have small bathrooms; limited common spaces. ⊠ *132 Frontier La., Box 584* ☎ *575/758–4446 or 800/532–2041* ⊕ *www. taosbedandbreakfast.com* ↪ *7 rooms, 3 suites* ⚐ *In-room: a/c, kitchen (some), refrigerator, Wi-Fi. In-hotel: some pets allowed* ▤ *AE, D, DC, MC, V* ⦶ *BP* ⊹ *C5.*

$$ 🖼 **Casa Gallinas.** This peaceful compound of three stylishly appointed
INN casitas is out in a rural area near the Hacienda de los Martinez
Fodor's Choice museum—a spot where you can hear the birds sing and enjoy relative
★ isolation, but you're still just a five-minute drive from the restaurants and shopping on the plaza. Each casita is filled with tasteful artwork, painted with vibrant colors, and decorated with one-of-a-kind hand-crafted furnishings and fine textiles—one has two bedrooms, and they all have fully equipped kitchens, making them ideal for longer stays. The Bantam Roost has a large deck off the second-floor bedroom. Host Richard Spera is a massage therapist with a studio on the property—he's

happy to help guests plan their days, or to leave them to their own devices. This is really the perfect balance between a vacation rental and an upscale country inn. **Pros:** gorgeous furnishings; pastoral setting; significant discount for stays of a week or more. **Cons:** you're on your own for breakfast, but each unit has a kitchen; not within walking distance of town. ⊠ *613 Callejon* ☎ *575/758–2306* ⊕ *www.casagallina.net* ↪ *3 casitas* ⟁ *In-room: no a/c kitchen, DVD, Wi-Fi* ⊟ *No credit cards* ⊹ *A5.*

$
BED & BREAKFAST

▣ **Old Taos Guesthouse B&B.** Once a ramshackle 180-year-old adobe hacienda, this homey B&B on 7½ verdant acres has been completely and lovingly outfitted with the owners' hand-carved doors and furniture, Western artifacts, and antiques—all have private entrances, and some have fireplaces. There are 80-mi views from the outdoor hot tub, and a shady veranda surrounds the courtyard. The owners welcome families. Breakfasts are healthy and hearty. **Pros:** beautifully appointed; private entrance to each room; serene setting. **Cons:** small bathrooms; some rooms are dark; a short drive from town. ⊠ *1028 Witt Rd., Box 6552* ☎ *575/758–5448 or 800/758–5448* ⊕ *www.oldtaos.com* ↪ *7 rooms, 2 suites* ⟁ *In-room: a/c, no phone (some), kitchen (some). In-hotel: Wi-Fi hotspot, some pets allowed* ⊟ *D, MC, V* ⦿ *BP* ⊹ *D5.*

$
HOTEL

▣ **Sagebrush Inn.** Georgia O'Keeffe once lived and painted in a third-story room of the original inn. These days it's not as upscale—or expensive—as many other lodging options in Taos, and most rooms are in a newer building, but it has a shaded patio with large trees, a serviceable restaurant, and a collection of antique Navajo rugs. Many of the guest rooms have kiva-style fireplaces; some have balconies. There's country-western music nightly. **Pros:** good value; nightly music. **Cons:** very spread out; many of the rooms are dark; traffic noise. ⊠ *1508 Paseo del Pueblo Sur* ☎ *575/758–2254 or 800/428–3626* ⊕ *www.sagebrushinn. com* ↪ *68 rooms, 32 suites* ⟁ *In-room: a/c, Wi-Fi. In-hotel: 2 restaurants, bar, pool, some pets allowed* ⊟ *AE, D, DC, MC, V* ⦿ *BP* ⊹ *B5.*

$$
HOTEL

▣ **San Geronimo Lodge.** Built in 1925, this property was one of the earliest hotels in Taos and sits on 2½ acres that front majestic Taos Mountain and adjoin the Carson National Forest. Owners Charles and Pam Montgomery have worked hard to modernize and brighten rooms while preserving the property's historical charm and appeal. An extensive library, attractive grounds, rooms with gas or wood fireplaces and private decks, and five rooms for guests with pets are among the draws. Hanging Navajo rugs, Talavera-tile bathrooms, and high viga ceilings provide an authentic Southwestern experience. **Pros:** serene inside and out; extensive common rooms. **Cons:** some rooms have small bathrooms; a short drive from town. ⊠ *1101 Witt Rd.* ☎ *575/751–3776 or 800/894–4119* ⊕ *www.sangeronimolodge.com* ↪ *18 rooms* ⟁ *In-room: a/c, DVD, Wi-Fi. In-hotel: pool, some pets allowed* ⊟ *AE, D, MC, V* ⦿ *BP* ⊹ *D5.*

EL PRADO

$$
Fodor'sChoice
★

▣ **Hacienda del Sol.** Art patron Mabel Dodge Luhan bought this house about a mile north of Taos Plaza in the 1920s and lived here with her husband, Tony Luhan, while building their main house. It was also their private retreat and guesthouse for visiting notables; Frank

Waters wrote *People of the Valley* here—other guests have included Willa Cather and D. H. Lawrence. Most of the rooms contain kiva fireplaces, Southwestern handcrafted furniture, and original artwork, and all have CD players—a few have Jacuzzi tubs. Certain adjoining rooms can be combined into suites. Breakfast is a gourmet affair that might include huevos rancheros or Belgian waffles. Perhaps above all else, the "backyards" of the rooms and the secluded outdoor hot tub have a view of Taos Mountain. **Pros:** cozy public rooms; private setting; some excellent restaurants within walking distance. **Cons:** traffic noise; some rooms are less private than others. ⊠ *109 Mabel Dodge La.* ☎ *575/758–0287 or 866/333–4459* ⊕ *www.taoshaciendadelsol. com* ⊲⊐ *11 rooms* ᗺ *In-room: a/c, refrigerator (some), no TV, Wi-Fi* ⊟ *AE, D, MC, V* ⏐◯⏐ *BP* ⊹ *C3.*

$$

BED & BREAKFAST

🖳 **Touchstone Inn.** D. H. Lawrence visited this house in 1929; accordingly, the inn's owner, Taos artist Bren Price, has named many of the antique-filled rooms after famous Taos literary figures. The grounds overlook part of the Taos Pueblo lands, about a mile north of Taos Plaza. Some rooms have fireplaces. The enormous Royale Suite has a second-story private deck and large bathroom with Jacuzzi, walk-in shower, and skylight. Early-morning coffee is available in the living room, and breakfasts with inventive vegetarian presentations (such as blueberry pancakes with lemon sauce) are served in the glassed-in patio. The adjacent spa offers a wide range of beauty and skin treatments. **Pros:** extensive common rooms; impeccably furnished rooms; within walking distance of a few excellent restaurants. **Cons:** some highway noise; lots of stairs; a short drive from the plaza. ⊠ *110 Mabel Dodge La.* ☎ *575/758–0192 or 800/758–0192* ⊕ *www.touchstoneinn.com* ⊲⊐ *6 rooms, 3 suites* ᗺ *In-room: a/c, refrigerator, DVD, Wi-Fi. In-hotel: spa* ⊟ *MC, V* ⏐◯⏐ *BP* ⊹ *C3.*

WEST SIDE

$

BED & BREAKFAST

🖳 **Dobson House.** Guests who book one of the two private suites at this ecotourist destination can help preserve the environment in style. This eclectic B&B relies primarily on passive heating and cooling and electricity is provided by solar panels. In addition, the 6,000-square-foot residence, within walking distance of the Rio Grande gorge, was built by hand by innkeepers Joan and John Dobson using 2,000 old tires, 20,000 recycled aluminum cans, and 28,000 pounds of dry cement and packed earth. Even so, guests live luxuriously with Ralph Lauren linens, and Joan's full breakfasts of Texas pecan biscuits, chicken-apple sausage, and Mexican baked eggs, plus extensive afternoon snacks and refreshments. The couples' sophisticated art collection adorns the home's authentic adobe walls. **Pros:** environmentally friendly; serene and private; each suite can accommodate up to four. **Cons:** a long drive to town. ⊠ *475 Tune Dr., West Side* ☎ *575/776–5738* ⊕ *www.new-mexico-bed-and-breakfast.com* ⊲⊐ *2 suites* ᗺ *In-room: no a/c, no phone, no TV. In-hotel: no kids under 14* ⊟ *No credit cards* ⏐◯⏐ *BP* ⊹ *A2.*

ARROYO SECO

$$
BED & BREAKFAST

⚏ **Adobe and Stars.** This light-filled adobe-style contemporary inn was built in 1996 on a plateau in Arroyo Seco with panoramic views in all directions—it's directly in the shadows of the Sangre de Cristos, a quick drive to the ski valley. The eight rooms have beam ceilings and traditional Southwestern art and furnishings. Those on the upper floors have the best views, some with private decks. While more affordable downstairs rooms open to a charming courtyard. All have kiva fireplaces and robes, and guests are treated to a substantial hot breakfast each morning. **Pros:** big windows in the rooms let in lots of light; short drive or leisurely stroll from shops and eateries, stunning views. **Cons:** a 20-minute drive from the plaza. ✉ *584 NM 150, 1 mi north of Arroyo Seco village center* ☎ *575/776–2776 or 800/211–7076* ⊕ *www. taosadobe.com* ➴ *8 rooms* ⚒ *In-room: a/c, no phone, no TV (some), Wi-Fi (some). In-hotel: some pets allowed* ⊟ *D, MC, V* ⚓ *B1.*

$$
BED & BREAKFAST
Fodor's Choice
★

⚏ **Cottonwood Inn.** This rambling, two-story adobe house with 11 fireplaces and such classic regional architectural details as *bancos, nichos,* and high latilla-and-viga ceilings is right along the road to the ski valley, just a couple of miles south of Arroyo Seco's quaint village center. Rooms are consistently plush and elegant, with 450-thread-count linens, hand-carved wood furniture, and regional folk art, but they offer plenty of variety in size and price. The largest have huge bathrooms with steam shower-baths or Jacuzzi tubs, and the highly popular Mesa Vista Room has both of these features as well as its own private entrance. Organic, local ingredients are used in the hearty breakfasts, which include plenty of fresh-baked pastries, cookies, and scones. **Pros:** closer to Taos than most accommodations in Arroyo Seco; some of the largest and fanciest bathrooms of any B&Bs in Taos; great views of mesa and mountains. **Cons:** not within walking distance of any restaurants. ✉ *NM 230, just beyond junction with NM 150* ☎ *575/776–5826 or 800/324–7120* ⊕ *www.taos-cottonwood.com* ➴ *8 rooms* ⚒ *In-room: no a/c, no phone, refrigerator, DVD, Wi-Fi. In-hotel: some pets allowed* ⊟ *AE, MC, V* ⚓ *B2.*

$$
BED & BREAKFAST

⚏ **Little Tree B&B.** In an authentic adobe house in the open country between Taos and the ski valley, Little Tree's rooms are built around a garden courtyard and have magnificent views of Taos Mountain and the high desert that spans for nearly 100 mi to the west. Some have kiva fireplaces and Jacuzzis, and all are decorated in true Southwestern style. **Pros:** rare opportunity to stay in a real adobe (not stucco) home; spotless and beautifully maintained; incredible views. **Cons:** 15-minute drive to Taos; isolated. ✉ *226 Hondo Seco Rd., Arroyo Hondo* ⏏ *Box 509, 87571* ☎ *575/776–8467 or 800/334–8467* ⊕ *www.littletreebandb. com* ➴ *4 rooms* ⚒ *In-room: no a/c, Wi-Fi* ⊟ *MC, V* ⦿ *BP* ⚓ *A2.*

TAOS SKI VALLEY

$$
HOTEL

⚏ **Austing Haus.** Owner Paul Austing constructed much of this handsome, glass-sheathed building, 1½ mi from Taos Ski Valley, along with many of its furnishings. The breakfast room has large picture windows, stained-glass paneling, and an impressive fireplace. Aromas of fresh-baked goods, such as Paul's apple strudel, come from the kitchen. Guest rooms are pretty and quiet with harmonious, peaceful colors; some have four-poster beds and fireplaces. In winter the inn offers ski packages. **Pros:** cozy Alpine ambience; close to skiing but slightly removed from crowds of ski area; excellent breakfasts. **Cons:** not directly located at ski slopes. ⊠ *NM 150, Village of Taos Ski Valley* ☎ *575/776–2649 or 800/748–2932* ⊕ *www.austinghaus.net* ⇆ *22 rooms, 3 chalets* ♿ *In-room: Wi-Fi. In-hotel: restaurant* ▤ *AE, DC, MC, V* †⦿†*BP.* ⊹ *D1.*

$$$$
VACATION LODGE

🏠 **The Bavarian.** This luxurious, secluded re-creation of a Bavarian lodge has the only midmountain accommodations in the Taos Ski Valley. The King Ludwig suite has a dining room, kitchen, marble bathroom, and two bedrooms with canopied beds. Three suites have whirlpool tubs. Summer activities include hiking, touring with the resident botanist, horseback riding, rafting, and fishing. Seven-night ski packages are offered. The restaurant on-site is one of the most atmospheric in the Taos region. **Pros:** Stunningly plush rooms, only ski-in; ski-out property at midmountain, exceptional onsite dining. **Cons:** Steep rates; difficult driveway to negotiate in winter weather. ⊠ *100 Kachina Rd., Taos Ski Valley* ☎ *575/776–8020* ⊕ *www.thebavarian.net* ⇆ *4 suites* ♿ *In-room: no a/c, kitchen, Wi-Fi. In-hotel: restaurant* ▤ *AE, MC, V* ⊗ *Closed early Apr.–late May and mid-Oct.–late Nov.* †⦿†*BP.* ⊹ *D1.*

$$$$
VACATION
CONDOS

🏠 **Snakedance Condominiums Hotel.** This modern condominium resort is right on the slopes and contains a handsome library where guests can enjoy an après-ski coffee or after-dinner drink next to a fieldstone fireplace. Some units—which range from studios to three-bedroom apartments—have fireplaces. A small spa provides a slew of services, from facials to deep-tissue massages, as well as bodywork aimed specifically to work muscles tested on the ski slopes and hiking trails. In winter, guests can take advantage of the helpful ski valet and ski storage with boot dryers. And in summer the hotel offers weeklong vacation packages, including a cooking school and fitness adventure courses, and rates are a fraction of what they are during ski season. Hondo Restaurant ($$) turns out very good contemporary American fare. **Pros:** Ski-in, ski-out accommodations; handy to have a spa on-site; some great deals in summer. **Cons:** Unless you're a skier, there's little reason to stay here in winter; a good distance from Taos proper, as is true for all hotels in the area. ⊠ *110 Sutton Place Rd., Village of Taos Ski Valley 87525* ☎ *575/776–2277 or 800/322–9815* ⇆ *33 condo units* ♿ *In-room: a/c, kitchen, Wi-Fi. In-hotel: restaurant, bar, gym, spa* ▤ *AE, D, DC, MC, V* ⊗ *Closed mid-Apr.–Memorial Day* †⦿†*CP.* ⊹ *D1.*

NIGHTLIFE AND THE ARTS

Evening entertainment is modest in Taos. Some motels and hotels present solo musicians or small combos in their bars and lounges. Everything from down-home blues bands to Texas two-step dancing blossoms on Saturday and Sunday nights in winter. In summer things heat up during the week as well. For information about what's going on around town pick up *Taos Magazine*. The weekly *Taos News*, published on

The Taos Hum

Investigations into what causes a mysterious low-frequency sound dubbed the "Taos Hum" are ongoing, although the topic was more popular during a worldwide news media frenzy in the 1990s. Taos isn't the only place where the mysterious hum has been heard, but it's probably the best-known locale for the phenomenon. (The Taos Hum, for example, now has been officially documented in *Encyclopaedia Britannica*.)

Scientists visited Taos during the 1990s in unsuccessful good-faith efforts to trace the sound, which surveys indicated were heard by about 2% of the town's population. Described as a frequency similar to the low, throbbing engine of a diesel truck, the Taos Hum has reportedly created disturbances among its few hearers from mildly irritating to profoundly disturbing. In the extreme, hearers say they experience constant problems, including interrupted sleep and physical effects such as dizziness and nosebleeds.

Speculation about the Taos Hum abounds. Conspiracy theorists believe the sound originates from ominous, secret, government testing, possibly emanating from the federal defense establishment of Los Alamos National Laboratory 55 mi southwest of Taos. The theory correlates with reports of some hearers that the sound began suddenly, as though something had been switched on.

Some investigators say the hearers may have extraordinary sensitivity to low-frequency sound waves, which could originate from all manner of human devices (cell phones, for one) creating constant sources of electromagnetic energy. Still other theorists postulate that low-frequency sound waves may originate in the Earth's lower atmosphere. One intriguing theory says that the hum could be explained by vibrations deep within the Earth, as a sort of precursor to earthquakes (although earthquakes are extremely rare in New Mexico).

Although many believe there's something to the mysterious Taos Hum, less kindly skeptics have dismissed the phenomenon as New Age nonsense linked to mass hysteria. But while you're here, you may as well give it a try (no one need know what you're up to). Find yourself a peaceful spot. Sit quietly. And listen.

Thursday, carries arts and entertainment information in the "Tempo" section. The arts scene is much more lively, with festivals every season for nearly every taste.

NIGHTLIFE

Fodor'sChoice ★ The **Adobe Bar** (✉ *Taos Inn, 125 Paseo del Pueblo Norte, Plaza and Vicinity* ☎ *575/758–2233*), a local meet-and-greet spot often dubbed "Taos's living room," books talented acts, from solo guitarists to small folk groups and, two or three nights a week, jazz musicians.

Fodor'sChoice ★ **Alley Cantina** (✉ *121 Teresina La., Plaza and Vicinity* ☎ *575/758–2121*) has jazz, folk, and blues—as well as shuffleboard, pool, and board games for those not moved to dance. It's housed in the oldest structure in Downtown Taos.

Caffe Tazza (⊠ *122 Kit Carson Rd., Plaza and Vicinity* ☏ *575/758–8706*) presents free evening performances throughout the week—folk-singing, jazz, belly dancing, blues, poetry, and fiction readings.

The **Kachina Lodge Cabaret** (⊠ *Best Western Kachina Lodge, 413 Paseo del Pueblo Norte, Plaza and Vicinity* ☏ *575/758–2275*) usually brings in an area radio DJ to liven up various forms of music and dancing.

The piano bar at **Sabroso** (⊠ *470 CR 150, Arroyo Seco* ☏ *575/776–3333*) often presents jazz and old standards—the patio out front is a stunning spot to watch sunsets.

The **Sagebrush Inn** (⊠ *1508 Paseo del Pueblo Sur, South Side* ☏ *575/758–2254*) hosts musicians and dancing in its lobby lounge. There's usually no cover charge for country-western dancing.

THE ARTS

Long a beacon for visual artists, Taos is also becoming a magnet for touring musicians, especially in summer, when performers and audiences are drawn to the heady high-desert atmosphere. Festivals celebrate the visual arts, music, poetry, and film.

The **Taos Center for the Arts** (⊠ *133 Paseo del Pueblo Norte, Plaza and Vicinity* ☏ *575/758–2052* ⊕ *http://tcataos.org*), which encompasses the Taos Community Auditorium, presents films, plays, concerts, and dance performances.

The **Taos Fall Arts Festival** (☏ *575/758–21063 or 800/732–8267* ⊕ *www. taosfallarts.com*), from late September to early October, is the area's major arts gathering, when buyers are in town and many other events, such as a Taos Pueblo feast, take place.

The **Taos Spring Arts Celebration** (☏ *575/758–3873 or 800/732–8267*), held throughout May, is a showcase for the visual, performing, and literary arts of the community and allows you to rub elbows with the many artists who call Taos home. The Mother's Day Arts and Crafts weekend during the festival always draws an especially large crowd.

MUSIC

Fodor's Choice
★
From mid-June to early August the Taos School of Music fills the evenings with the sounds of chamber music at the **Taos School of Music Program and Festival** (☏ *575/776–2388* ⊕ *www.taosschoolofmusic.com*). Running strong since 1963, this is America's oldest chamber music summer program and possibly the largest assembly of top string quartets in the country. Concerts are presented a couple of times a week from mid-June through early August, at the Taos Community Auditorium and at Taos Ski Valley. Tickets cost $10 to $20. The events at Taos Ski Valley are free.

Fodor's Choice
★
Solar energy was pioneered in this land of sunshine, and each year in late June the flag of sustainability is raised at the three-day **Taos Solar Music Festival** (⊕ *www.solarmusicfest.com*). Top-name acts appear, and booths promote alternative energy, permaculture, and other eco-friendly technologies.

SHOPPING

Retail options on Taos Plaza consist mostly of T-shirt emporiums and souvenir shops that are easily bypassed, though a few stores carry quality Native American artifacts and jewelry. The more upscale galleries and boutiques are two short blocks north on Bent Street, including the John Dunn House Shops. Kit Carson Road (U.S. 64), has a mix of the old and the new. There's metered municipal parking Downtown, though the traffic can be daunting. Some shops worth checking out are in St. Francis Plaza in Ranchos de Taos, 4 mi south of the plaza near the San Francisco de Asís Church. Just north of Taos off NM 522 you can find Overland Ranch (including Overland Sheepskin Co.), which has gorgeous sheepskin and leather clothing, along with a few other shops and galleries (plus a restaurant), and an outdoor path winding through displays of wind sculptures. You'll find another notable cluster of galleries and shops, along with a few good restaurants, in the village of Arroyo Seco, a 15-minute drive north of Taos toward the ski valley.

ART GALLERIES

For at least a century, artists have been drawn to Taos's natural grandeur. The result is a vigorous art community with some 80 galleries, a lively market, and an estimated 1,000 residents producing art full- or part-time. Many artists explore themes of the Western landscape, Native Americans, and adobe architecture; others create abstract forms and mixed-media works that may or may not reflect the Southwest. Some local artists grew up in Taos, but many—Anglo, Hispanic, and Native Americans—are adopted Taoseños.

Envision Gallery (✉ *Overland Ranch, NM 522, north of Taos, El Prado* ☎ *505/751–1344* ⊕ *www.envisiongallery.net*) is roughly split between painters—most of them working in contemporary, abstract styles—and sculptors. Many of the latter produce large, outdoor works that are displayed on the open grounds at this impressive gallery that's part of the scenic Overland Ranch complex, in El Prado. About two-dozen artists are represented.

Farnsworth Gallery Taos (✉ *133 Paseo del Pueblo Norte, Plaza and Vicinity* ☎ *575/758–0776* ⊕ *www.johnfarnsworth.com*) contains the work of artist John Farnsworth, best known for his finely detailed paintings of horses, and also includes colorful local landscapes, large-scale still-lifes, and scenes of Native American kiva dancers.

Inger Jirby Gallery (✉ *207 Ledoux St., Plaza and Vicinity* ☎ *575/758–7333,* ⊕ *www.jirby.com*) displays Jirby's whimsical, brightly colored landscape paintings. Be sure to stroll through the lovely sculpture garden.

J. D. Challenger Gallery (✉ *221 Paseo del Pueblo Norte, Plaza and Vicinity* ☎ *575/751–6773 or 800/511–6773*) is the home base of personable painter J. D. Challenger, who has become famous for his dramatically rendered portraits of Native Americans from tribes throughout North America.

Lumina Fine Art & Sculpture Gardens (✉ *11 NM 230, Arroyo Seco* ☎ *575/776–0123 or 877/558–6462* ⊕ *www.luminagallery.com*) exhibits paintings by worldwide artists and has 3 acres of sculpture gardens, including works of Japanese stone carvers. The setting is beautiful, a short distance off of NM 150 in Arroyo Seco.

Michael McCormick Gallery (✉ *106-C Paseo del Pueblo Norte, Plaza and Vicinity* ☎ *575/758–1372 or 800/279–0879* ⊕ *www.mccormickgallery. com*) is home to the sensual, stylized female portraits of Miguel Martinez and the iconic portraits of Malcolm Furlow. The gallery also has an extensive collection of Rembrandt etchings.

Mission Gallery (✉ *138 E. Kit Carson Rd., Plaza and Vicinity* ☎ *575/758– 2861*) carries the works of early Taos artists, early New Mexico modernists, and important contemporary artists. The gallery is in the former home of painter Joseph H. Sharp.

Navajo Gallery (✉ *210 Ledoux St., Plaza and Vicinity* ☎ *575/758–3250*) shows the works of the internationally renowned Navajo painter and sculptor R. C. Gorman, who died in 2005 and who was known for his ethereal imagery—especially his portraits of Native American women.

Nichols Taos Fine Art Gallery (✉ *403 Paseo del Pueblo Norte, Plaza and Vicinity* ☎ *575/758–2475*) has exhibits of oils, watercolors, pastels, charcoal, and pencils from artists representing many prestigious national art organizations.

Parks Gallery (✉ *127-A Bent St., Plaza and Vicinity* ☎ *575/751–0343,* ⊕ *www.parksgallery.com*) specializes in contemporary paintings, sculptures, and prints. The late and critically acclaimed mixed-media artist Melissa Zink shows here, as does painter Jim Wagner.

R. B. Ravens Gallery (✉ *4146 NM 68, South Side* ☎ *575/758–7322 or 866/758–7322* ⊕ *www.rbravens.com*) exhibits paintings by the founding artists of Taos, pre-1930s Native American weavings, and ceramics in a spare museumlike setting. Be sure to admire the beautiful collection of Navajo saddle blankets.

Fodor's Choice ★ **Robert L. Parsons Fine Art** (✉ *131 Bent St., Plaza and Vicinity* ☎ *575/751– 0159 or 800/613–5091* ⊕ *www.parsonsart.com*) is one of the best sources of early Taos art-colony paintings, antiques, and authentic antique Navajo blankets. Inside you'll find originals by such luminaries as Ernest Blumenschein, Bert Geer Phillips, Oscar Berninghaus, Joseph Bakos, and Nicolai Fechin.

Stray Arts Gallery (✉ *120 Camino de la Placita, Plaza and Vicinity* ☎ *575/758–9780* ⊕ *www.strayhearts.org/stray_arts.php*) sells donated, bargain-priced art to raise funds for the Stray Hearts Animal Shelter. Of course, in a town like Taos, you can find works here by prominent artists (Ouray Meyers, Harriet Green, R. C. Gorman, and many others), making this something of an unexpected find as well as a great cause.

Studio de Colores Gallery (✉ *119 Quesnel, El Prado* ☎ *575/751–3502 or 888/751–3502* ⊕ *www.decoloresgallery.com*) is home to the work of two artists, Ann Huston and Ed Sandoval, who are married to one another but have extremely distinctive styles. Sandoval is known for his trademark *Viejito* (Old Man) images and swirling, vibrantly colored landscapes; Ann specializes in soft-hue still lifes and scenes of incredible stillness.

Total Arts Gallery (✉ *122-A Kit Carson Rd., Plaza and Vicinity* ☎ *575/758–4667* ⊕ *www.totalartsgallery.com*) comprises several rooms displaying works by some of the area's most celebrated artists, including Barbara Zaring, David Hettinger, Doug Dawson, and Ken Elliott. Themes vary greatly from contemporary paintings and sculptures to more traditional landscapes and regional works.

Fodor's Choice ★ At **Two Graces Gallery** (✉ *San Francisco Plaza, South Side* ☎ *575/758–4639*) owner and artist Robert Cafazzo displays an astonishing assortment of traditional Indian pottery and kachinas, contemporary art by local artists, old postcards, and rare books on area artists.

SPECIALTY STORES

BOOKS

Brodsky Bookshop (✉ *226-A Paseo del Pueblo Norte, Plaza and Vicinity* ☎ *575/758–9468* ⊕ *www.taosbooks.com*) has new and used books—contemporary literature, Southwestern classics, children's titles—piled here and there, but amiable proprietor Rick Smith will help you find what you need.

G. Robinson Old Prints and Maps (✉ *John Dunn House, 124-D Bent St., Plaza and Vicinity* ☎ *575/758–2278*) stocks rare books, maps, and prints—some of these priceless and fascinating maps date as far back as the 14th century.

Moby Dickens (✉ *John Dunn House, 124-A Bent St., Plaza and Vicinity* ☎ *575/758–3050* ⊕ *www.mobydickens.com*), a full-service bookstore, specializes in rare and out-of-print books and carries a wide selection of contemporary fiction and nonfiction. It's one of the finest independent bookshops in the state.

CLOTHING

Andean Softwear (✉ *118 Sutton Pl., Taos Ski Valley* ☎ *575/776–2508* ⊕ *www.andeansoftware.com*), which was begun at the Ski Valley in 1984 but has a second location close to the plaza, carries warm, sturdy, but beautifully designed clothing and textiles, as well as jewelry. Much of the wares here come from Peru, Bolivia, and Ecuador, as the name of the store implies, but owner Andrea Heckman also imports from Bali, Mexico, Turkey, and plenty of other far-flung locales with distinct arts traditions. Note the deliciously soft alpaca sweaters from Peru.

Artemisia (✉ *115 Bent St., Plaza and Vicinity* ☎ *575/737–9800* ⊕ *www. artemisiataos.com*) has a wide selection of one-of-a-kind wearable art by local artist Annette Randell. Many of her creations incorporate Native American designs. The store also carries jewelry, bags, and accessories by several local artists.

Francesca's (✉ *492 NM 150, Arroyo Seco* ☎ *575/776–8776*) has long been a fixture among the cluster of hip boutiques and galleries in Arroyo Seco—the boutique is inside the former post office. She specializes in reasonably priced, fanciful, and stylish threads with materials and design inspirations from India, Nepal, and Southeast Asia.

Mariposa Boutique Inc. (⊠ *120-F Bent St., Plaza and Vicinity* ☎ *575/758–9028*) sells fanciful handmade women's and children's specialty clothing, including two original lines made in-house.

Fodor'sChoice ★ **Overland Sheepskin Company** (⊠ *Overland Ranch, NM 522, 4 mi north of Taos, El Prado* ☎ *575/758–8820 or 888/754–8352*) carries high-quality sheepskin coats, hats, mittens, and slippers, many with Taos beadwork. This is the original location of what has become a network of about a dozen stores, mostly in the West, and the setting—in the shadows of the Sangre de Cristos, amid a complex of several other shops, is itself a reason for a visit.

Steppin' Out (⊠ *120-K Bent St. Plaza and Vicinity* ☎ *575/758–4487*) carries European footwear, distinctive clothing (including the popular Eileen Fisher brand), handmade handbags, and unique accessories.

COLLECTIBLES AND GIFTS

Fodor'sChoice ★ **Arroyo Seco Mercantile** (⊠ *488 State Rd. 15, Arroyo Seco* ☎ *575/776–8806* ⊕ *www.secomerc.com*) carries a varied assortment of 1930s linens, handmade quilts, candles, organic soaps, vintage cookware, hand-thrown pottery, decorated crosses, and souvenirs.

Coyote Moon (⊠ *120-C Bent St., Plaza and Vicinity* ☎ *575/758–4437*) has a great selection of south-of-the-border folk art, painted crosses, jewelry, and Day of the Dead figurines, some featuring American rock stars.

Horse Feathers (⊠ *109-B Kit Carson Rd., Plaza and Vicinity* ☎ *575/758–7457* ⊕ *www.cowboythings.com*) is a fun collection of cowboy antiques and vintage Western wear—boots, hats, buckles, jewelry, and all manner of paraphernalia.

Letherwerks (⊠ *124-B Bent St.,Plaza and Vicinity* ☎ *575/758–2778* ⊕ *www.letherwerks.com*) has been making and selling deftly crafted leather belts, bags, wallets, and backpacks since 1969—they also carry quite a few pieces made by other talented local artists around Taos.

Taos Drums (⊠ *NM 68, 5 mi south of Plaza, South Side* ☎ *575/758–9844 or 800/424–3786*) is the factory outlet for the Taos Drum Factory. The store, 5 mi south of Taos Plaza (look for the large tepee), stocks handmade Pueblo log drums, leather lamp shades, and wrought-iron and Southwestern furniture.

HOME FURNISHINGS

Fodor'sChoice ★ **Alhambra** (⊠ *124 Paseo del Pueblo Sur, Plaza and Vicinity* ☎ *575/758–4161*) carries exquisite, high-end antique furniture, rugs, and textiles from India, Tibet, Nepal, Thailand, and China.

At **Antiquarius Imports** (⊠ *487 State Road 150, Arroyo Seco* ☎ *575/776–8381* ⊕ *www.antiquariusimports.com*), Ivelisse Brooks's eclectic shop, you'll find rare Indian, Afghan, and African antiques and furniture along with contemporary, naturally dyed carpets made in Pakistan.

Casa Cristal Pottery (⊠ *1306 Paseo del Pueblo Norte, El Prado* ☎ *575/758–1530*), 2½ mi north of the Taos Plaza, has a huge stock of stoneware, serapes, clay pots, Native American ironwood carvings, fountains, sweaters, ponchos, clay fireplaces, Mexican blankets, tiles, piñatas, and blue glassware from Guadalajara.

Country Furnishings of Taos (⌂ *534 Paseo del Pueblo Norte, Plaza and Vicinity* ☎ *575/758–4633* ⊕ *www. cftaos.com*), which occupies a

rambling, picturesque adobe house, sells folk art from northern New Mexico, handmade furniture, metalwork lamps and beds, and colorful accessories.

Starr Interiors (⌂ *117 Paseo del Pueblo Norte, Plaza and Vicinity* ☎ *575/758–3065*) has a striking collection of Zapotec Indian rugs and hangings.

Taos Blue (⌂ *101-A Bent St., Plaza and Vicinity* ☎ *575/758–3561* ⊕ *www.taosblue.com*) carries jewelry, pottery, and contemporary works by Native Americans (masks, rattles, sculpture), as well as Hispanic santos.

Taos Tin Works (⌂ *1204-D Paseo del Pueblo Norte, El Prado* ☎ *575/758– 9724* ⊕ *www.taostinworks.com*) sells handcrafted tinwork such as wall sconces, mirrors, lamps, and table ornaments by Marion Moore.

Weaving Southwest (⌂ *106A Paseo del Pueblo North, Plaza and Vicinity* ☎ *575/758–0433* ⊕ *www.weavingsouthwest.com*) represents 20 tapestry artists who make beautiful rugs and blankets. The store also sells supplies for weavers, including hand-dyed yarn.

NATIVE AMERICAN ARTS AND CRAFTS

Buffalo Dancer (⌂ *103-A E. Plaza, Plaza and Vicinity* ☎ *575/758–8718* ⊕ *www.buffalodancer.com*) buys, sells, and trades Native American arts and crafts, including pottery, belts, kachina dolls, hides, and silver-coin jewelry.

El Rincón Trading Post (⌂ *114 E. Kit Carson Rd., Plaza and Vicinity* ☎ *575/758–9188*) is housed in a large, dark, cluttered century-old adobe. Native American items of all kinds are bought and sold here: drums, feathered headdresses, Navajo rugs, beads, bowls, baskets, shields, beaded moccasins, jewelry, arrows, and spearheads. The packed back room contains Native American, Hispanic, and Anglo Wild West artifacts.

SPORTING GOODS

Fodor's Choice ★ **Cottam's Ski & Outdoor** (⌂ *207-A Paseo del Pueblo Sur, Plaza and Vicinity* ☎ *575/758–2822,* ⊕ *www.cottamsskishops.com*) carries hiking and backpacking gear, maps, fishing licenses and supplies, and ski and snowboard equipment and rentals, along with related clothing and accessories. There are also shops near the ski lifts at Taos Ski Valley and Angel Fire.

Mudd–n–Flood Mountain Shop (⊠ *134 Bent St., Plaza and Vicinity* ☎ *575/751–9100*) has gear and clothing for rock climbers, backpackers, campers, and backcountry skiers.

Taos Mountain Outfitters (⊠ *114 S. Plaza, Plaza and Vicinity* ☎ *575/758–9292* ⊕ *www.taosmountainoutfitters.com*) has supplies for kayakers, skiers, climbers, and backpackers, as well as maps, books, and handy advice.

SPORTS AND THE OUTDOORS

Whether you plan to cycle around town, jog along Paseo del Pueblo Norte, or play a few rounds of golf, keep in mind that the altitude in Taos is higher than 7,000 feet. It's best to keep physical exertion to a minimum until your body becomes acclimated to the altitude—a full day to a few days, depending on your constitution.

BALLOONING

Hot-air ballooning has become nearly as popular in Taos as in Albuquerque, with a handful of outfitters offering rides, most starting at about $225 per person. **Paradise Balloons** (☎ *575/751–6098* ⊕ *www. taosballooning.com*) will thrill you with a "splash and dash" in the Rio Grande River as part of a silent journey through the 600-foot canyon walls of Rio Grande Gorge. **Pueblo Balloon Company** (☎ *575/751–9877* ⊕ *www.puebloballoon.com*) conducts balloon rides over and into the Rio Grande Gorge.

BICYCLING

Taos-area roads are steep and hilly, and none have marked bicycle lanes, so be careful while cycling. The West Rim Trail offers a fairly flat but view-studded 9-mi ride that follows the Rio Grande canyon's west rim from the Rio Grande Gorge Bridge to near the Taos Junction Bridge.

Gearing Up Bicycle Shop (⊠ *129 Paseo del Pueblo Sur, Plaza and Vicinity* ☎ *575/751–0365* ⊕ *www.gearingupbikes.com*) is a full-service bike shop that can supply advice on best routes and organized group rides. **Native Sons Adventures** (⊠ *1033-A Paseo del Pueblo Sur, South Side* ☎ *575/758–9342 or 800/753–7559,* ⊕ *www.nativesonsadventures. com*) offers guided mountain-biking tours.

FISHING

Carson National Forest has some of the best trout fishing in New Mexico. Its streams and lakes are home to rainbow, brown, and native Rio Grande cutthroat trout.

Reasonably priced and with very knowledgeable guides, **Blue Yonder Fly Fishing** (☎ *575/779–9002* ⊕ *www.blueyonderflyfishing.com*) can customize anything from a casual half-day outing for beginners to an extensive all-day adventure for experienced anglers—gear, instruction, and meals are included. Just south of Taos Plaza, **Cottam's Ski & Outdoor** (⊠ *207-A Paseo del Pueblo Sur, Plaza and Vicinity* ☎ *575/758–2822 or 800/322–8267* ⊕ *www.cottamsoutdoor.com*) provides fishing and bike trips and ski and snowboard rentals. **Solitary Angler** (☎ *575/758–5653 or 866/502–1700* ⊕ *www.thesolitaryangler.com*) guides fly-fishing expeditions that search out uncrowded habitats. Well-known area fishing guide Taylor Streit of **Taos Fly Shop & Streit Fly Fishing** (✉ *308-C Paseo del Pueblo Sur, Plaza and Vicinity* ☎ *575/751–1312* ⊕ *www.taosflyshop.com*) takes individuals or small groups out for fishing and lessons.

> **DID YOU KNOW?**
>
> Anyone over the age of 12 who wishes to fish must buy a New Mexico fishing license. Many sporting goods stores in the state sell them.

GOLF

Views from the course at the **Taos Country Club** (✉ *54 Golf Course Dr., South Side* ☎ *575/758–7300* ⊕ *www.taoscountryclub.com*) are some of the most dazzling in northern New Mexico. The layout is stunning and quite hilly, and water hazards are few. Greens fees at the 18-hole, par-72 championship course are $62 to $72.

HIKING

Fodor's Choice
★

Wheeler Peak is a designated wilderness area of Carson National Forest (⇨ *The Enchanted Circle tour, below*), where travel is restricted to hiking or horseback. Part of the Sangre de Cristo Mountains, this 13,161-foot peak is New Mexico's highest. The most popular and accessible trail to the peak is the Williams Lake Trail, which is about 8-mi round-trip and begins in Taos Ski Valley just east of the Bavarian lodge and restaurant. Only experienced hikers should tackle this strenuous trail all the way to the top, as the 4,000-foot elevation gain is taxing, and the final mile or so to the peak is a steep scramble over loose scree. However, for a moderately challenging and still very rewarding hike, you take the trail to the halfway point, overlooking the shores of rippling Williams Lake. Numerous other rewarding hikes of varying degrees of ease and length climb up the many slopes that rise from the village of Taos Ski Valley—check with rangers or consult the Carson National Forest Web site for details. Trailheads are usually well-signed. Dress warmly even in summer, take plenty of water and food, and pay attention to *all* warnings and instructions distributed by rangers. ✉ *Parking area for Williams Lake Trail is along Kachina Rd. by the Bavarian lodge and restaurant* ☎ *575/758–6200* ⊕ *www.fs.fed.us/r3/carson*.

LLAMA TREKKING

One of the most offbeat outdoor recreational activities in the Taos area, llama trekking is offered by **Wild Earth Llama Adventures** (☎ *575/586–0174 or 800/758–5262* ⊕ *www.llamaadventures.com*) in a variety of packages, from one-day tours to excursions lasting several days in wilderness areas of the nearby Sangre de Cristo Mountains. Llamas, relatives of the camel, are used as pack animals on trips that begin at $99 for a day hike. Gourmet lunches eaten on the trail are part of the package, along with overnight camping and meals for longer trips.

RIVER RAFTING

Fodor's Choice
★

The Taos Box, at the bottom of the steep-walled canyon far below the Rio Grande Gorge Bridge, is the granddaddy of thrilling white water in New Mexico and is best attempted by experts only—or on a guided trip—but the river also offers more placid sections such as through the Orilla Verde Recreation Area, just south of Taos in the village of Pilar (here you'll also find a small shop and cafe called the Pilar Yacht Club, which caters heavily to rafters and fishing enthusiasts). Spring runoff is the busy season, from mid-April through June, but rafting companies conduct tours March to November. Shorter two-hour options usually cover the fairly tame section of the river. The **Bureau of Land Management, Taos Resource Area Office** (⊠ *226 Cruz Alta* ☎ *575/758–8851* ⊕ *www. blm.gov/nm/st/en.html*) has a list of registered river guides and information about running the river on your own.

Big River Raft Trips (☎ *575/758–9711 or 800/748–3760* ⊕ *www. bigriverrafts.com*) offers dinner float trips and rapids runs. **Far Flung Adventures** (☎ *575/758–2628 or 800/359–2627* ⊕ *www.farflung.com*) operates half-day, full-day, and overnight rafting trips along the Rio Grande and the Rio Chama. **Los Rios River Runners** (☎ *575/776–8854 or 800/544–1181* ⊕ *www.losriosriverrunners.com*) will take you to your choice of spots—the Rio Chama, the Lower Gorge, or the Taos Box. **Native Sons Adventures** (⊠ *1335 Paseo del Pueblo Sur* ☎ *575/758–9342 or 800/753–7559* ⊕ *www.nativesonsadventures.com*) offers several trip options on the Rio Grande.

SKIING

Fodor's Choice ★ With 72 runs—more than half of them for experts—and an average of more than 300 inches of annual snowfall, **Taos Ski Valley** ranks among the country's most respected—and challenging—resorts. The slopes, which cover a 2,600-foot vertical gain of lift-served terrain and another 600 feet of hike-in skiing, tend to be narrow and demanding (note the ridge chutes, Al's Run, Inferno), but 25% (e.g., Honeysuckle) are for intermediate skiers, and 24% (e.g., Bambi, Porcupine) for beginners. Until 2008 it was one of the nation's few resorts that banned snowboarding, but this activity is welcome—and very popular—now. Taos Ski Valley is justly famous for its outstanding ski schools, some of the best in the country. If you're new to the sport, this is a terrific resort to give a try. ⊠ *Village of Taos Ski Valley* ☎ *575/776–2291* ⊕ *www.skitaos. org* ⊠ *Lift tickets $71* ⊙ *Late Nov.–early Apr.*

SIDE TRIPS FROM TAOS

Surrounded by thousands of acres of pristine Carson National Forest and undeveloped high desert, Taos makes an ideal base for road-tripping. Most of the nearby adventures involve the outdoors, from skiing to hiking to mountain biking, and there are several noteworthy campgrounds in this part of the state. Although these side trips can be done in a day, the ski-resort communities mentioned in this section have a decent selection of overnight accommodations.

THE ENCHANTED CIRCLE

Fodor's Choice ★ The Enchanted Circle, an 84-mi loop north from Taos and back, rings Wheeler Peak, New Mexico's highest mountain, and takes you through glorious panoramas of alpine valleys and the towering mountains of the lush Carson National Forest. You can see all the major sights as an ambitious one-day side trip, or take a more leisurely tour and stay overnight.

From Taos, head north about 15 mi via U.S. 64 to NM 522, keeping your eye out for the sign on the right that points to the D.H. Lawrence Ranch and Memorial. You can visit the memorial, which is well-marked from the road, but the other buildings on the ranch are closed to the public. Continue north a short way

> **DID YOU KNOW?**
>
> Your best guarantee of authenticity, particularly involving Navajo blankets, is to purchase directly from a reputable reservation outlet.

to reach Red River Hatchery, and then go another 5 mi to the village of Questa. Here you have the option of continuing north on NM 522 and detouring for some hiking at Wild Rivers Recreation Area, or turning east from Questa on NM 38 and driving for about 12 mi to the unpretentious, family-friendly town of Red River, a noteworthy ski town in winter and an increasingly popular summer-recreation hub during the warmer months.

From here, continue 16 mi east along NM 38 and head over dramatic Bobcat Pass, which rises to just under 10,000 feet. You'll come to the sleepy, old-fashioned village of Eagle Nest, comprising a few shops and down-home restaurants and motels. From here, U.S. 64 joins with NM 38 and runs southeast about 15 mi to one of the state's fastest-growing communities, Angel Fire, an upscale ski resort that's popular for hiking, golfing, and mountain biking in summer. *(See also Northeastern New Mexico, chapter 6, for information on exploring Eagle Nest and Angel Fire by approaching from the east, via Cimarron, or the south, via Mora.)* It's about a 25-mi drive west over 9,000-foot Palo Flechado Pass and down through winding Taos Canyon to return to Taos.

Leave early in the morning and plan to spend the entire day on this trip. Especially during ski season, which runs from late November to early April, but in summer as well you may want to spend a night or more in Red River, which has a number of mostly rustic lodges and vacation rentals, or in Angel Fire, which is becoming increasingly respected as a year-round resort. Watch for snow and ice on the roads from late fall through early spring. A sunny winter day can yield some lovely scenery.

Carson National Forest surrounds Taos and spans almost 200 mi across northern New Mexico, encompassing mountains, lakes, streams, villages, and much of the Enchanted Circle. Hiking *(⇨ Wheeler Peak, in Hiking, above)*, cross-country skiing, horseback riding, mountain biking, backpacking, trout fishing, boating, and wildflower viewing are among the popular activities here. The forest is home to big-game animals and many species of smaller animals and songbirds. For canyon climbing, head into the rocky Rio Grande Gorge. The best entry point into the gorge is at the Wild Rivers Recreation Area, north of Questa. You can drive into the forestland at various points along the Enchanted Circle via NM 522, NM 150, NM 38, and NM 578. Carson National Forest also has some of the best trout fishing in New Mexico, with several lakes rife with rainbow, brown, and native Rio Grande cutthroat trout.

The forest provides a wealth of camping opportunities, from organized campgrounds with restrooms and limited facilities to informal roadside campsites and sites that require backpacking in. If mountains, pines, and streams are your goal, stake out sites in Carson National Forest along the Rio Hondo or Red River; if you prefer high-desert country along the banks of the Rio Grande, consider Orilla Verde or Wild Rivers Recreation Area. Backcountry sites are free; others cost up to $7 per night.

If you're coming from a lower altitude, you should take time to acclimatize, and all hikers should follow basic safety procedures. Wind, cold, and wetness can occur any time of year, and the mountain climate produces sudden storms. Dress in layers and wear sturdy footwear; carry water, food, sunscreen, hat, sunglasses, and a first-aid kit. Contact the Carson National Forest's visitor center for maps, safety guidelines, camping information, and conditions (it's open weekdays 8 to 4:30). ⊠ *Forest Service Bldg., 208 Cruz Alta Rd., Taos* ☎ *575/758–6200* ⊕ *www.fs.fed.us/r3/carson.*

The Enchanted Circle Bike Tour takes place in mid-September. The rally loops through the entire 84-mi Enchanted Circle, revealing a brilliant blaze of fall color. In summer you can head up the mountainside via ski lifts in Red River and Angel Fire.

QUESTA
25 mi north of Taos via U.S. 64 to NM 522.

Literally a *questa* (hill) in the heart of the Sangre de Cristo Mountains, Questa is a quiet village nestled against the Red River and amid some of New Mexico's most striking mountain country. **St. Anthony's Church,** built of adobe with 5-foot-thick walls and viga ceilings, is on the main street. Questa's **Cabresto Lake,** in Carson National Forest, is about 8 mi from town. Follow NM 563 northeast to Forest Route 134, then 2 mi of a primitive road (134A)—you'll need a four-wheel-drive vehicle. You can trout fish and boat here from about June to October.

Although it's only a few miles west of Questa as the crow flies, you have to drive about 15 mi north of Questa via NM 522 to NM 378 to reach **Wild Rivers Recreation Area,** which offers hiking access to the dramatic confluence of two national wild and scenic rivers, the Rio Grande and Red River. There are some fairly easy and flat trails along the gorge's rim, including a ½-mi interpretive loop from the visitor center out to La Junta Point, which offers a nice view of the river. But the compelling reason to visit is a chance to hike down into the gorge and study the rivers up close, which entails hiking one of a couple of well-marked but steep trails down into the gorge, a descent of about 650 feet. It's not an especially strenuous trek, but many visitors come without sufficient water and stamina, have an easy time descending into the gorge, and then find it difficult to make it back up. There are also about 30 basic campsites, some along the rim and others along the river. ⊠ *NM 522, follow signed dirt road from hwy., Cerro* ☎ *575/586–1150 visitor center, 575/758–8851 BLM regional field office* ⊕ *www.blm.gov/nm/st/en.html* ▧ *$3 per vehicle; camping $7 per vehicle* ☉ *Daily 6 am–10 pm; visitor center late May–early Sept., daily 9–6.*

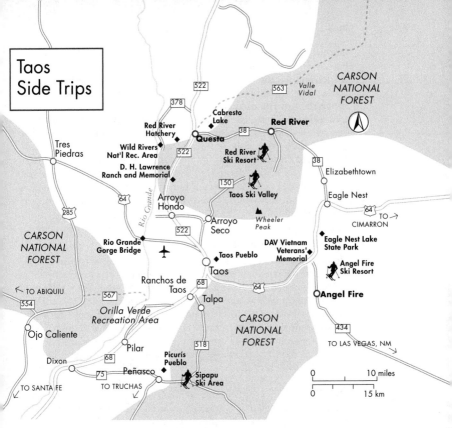

Taos
Side Trips

CARSON
NATIONAL
FOREST

522   563   Valle
                               Vidal

378
        Cabresto
        Lake
Red River   38   Red River
Hatchery
Tres   Questa
Piedras   Wild Rivers   522   Red River
          Nat'l Rec. Area   Ski Resort
          D. H. Lawrence   38   Elizabethtown
          Ranch and Memorial
                  150
64   Arroyo   Taos Ski Valley   Eagle Nest
     Hondo
285   Wheeler   64   TO →
          Arroyo   Peak   CIMARRON
          Seco
CARSON   DAV Vietnam   Eagle Nest Lake
NATIONAL Rio Grande   Veterans'   State Park
FOREST   Gorge Bridge   Memorial
                    Taos Pueblo   Angel Fire
                                            Ski Resort
← TO ABIQUIU Ranchos de   68   Taos
554   Taos   567   64   Angel Fire
              Orilla Verde   Talpa
              Recreation Area
Ojo Caliente   CARSON
                              NATIONAL   434
          Pilar   518   FOREST   TO LAS VEGAS, NM
Dixon
          68   Picuris
                Pueblo
          75   Peñasco   Sipapu   0   10 miles
TO SANTA FE TO TRUCHAS   Ski Area
                                           0   15 km

NEED A BREAK? Good snacking options are a rarity on the first section of the Enchanted Circle, but the funky **Front Porch Cafe & Ice Cream Shop** (✉ *2322 S. NM 522* ☎ *575/586–1344*) is a refreshing stop for coffee, sandwiches, ice cream, and other light treats. It's the perfect place to stock up on food before hiking at Wild Rivers Recreation Area.

At the **Red River Hatchery,** freshwater trout are raised to stock waters in Questa, Red River, Taos, Raton, and Las Vegas. You can feed them and learn how they're hatched, reared, stocked, and controlled. The visitor center has displays and exhibits, a fishing pond, and a machine that dispenses fish food. The self-guided tour can last anywhere from 20 minutes to more than an hour, depending on how enraptured you become. There's a picnic area and camping on the grounds. ✉ *NM 522, 5 mi south of town* ☎ *575/586-0222* ✉ *Free* ◷ *Daily 8–5.*

The influential and controversial English writer David Herbert Lawrence and his wife, Frieda, arrived in Taos at the invitation of Mabel Dodge Luhan, who collected famous writers and artists the way some people collect butterflies. Luhan provided them a place to live, Kiowa Ranch, on 160 acres in the mountains. Rustic and remote, it's now known as the **D. H. Lawrence Ranch and Memorial,** though Lawrence never actually owned it. Lawrence lived in Taos on and off for about 22 months during a three-year period between 1922 and 1925. He wrote his novel *The Plumed Serpent* (1926), as well as some of his finest short stories and poetry, while in Taos and on excursions to Mexico. The houses here, owned by the University of New Mexico, are not open to the public, but you can enter the small cabin where Dorothy Brett, the Lawrences' traveling companion, stayed. You can also visit the D.H. Lawrence Memorial, a short walk up Lobo Mountain. A white shed-like structure, it's simple and unimposing. The writer fell ill while in France and died in a sanatorium there in 1930. Five years later Frieda had Lawrence's body disinterred and cremated and brought his ashes back to Taos. Frieda Lawrence is buried, as was her wish, in front of the memorial. ⊠ *NM 522, follow signed dirt road from highway, San Cristobal* ☎ *575/776-2245* ⌑ *Free* ☉ *Daily dawn-dusk.*

RED RIVER
12 mi east of Questa via NM 38.

Home of a major ski resort that has a particularly strong following with visitors from Oklahoma and the Texas panhandle, Red River (elevation 8,750 feet) came into being as a miners' boomtown in 1895, taking its name from the river whose mineral content gives it a rosy color. When the gold petered out, Red River died, only to be rediscovered in the 1920s by migrants escaping the dust storms in the Great Plains. An Old West flavor remains: Main Street shoot-outs, an authentic melodrama, and square dancing and two-stepping are among the diversions. Because of its many country dances and festivals, Red River is affectionately called "The New Mexico Home of the Texas Two-Step." The bustling little Downtown area contains souvenir shops and sportswear boutiques, casual steak and barbecue joints, and about 40 mostly family-oriented, midpriced to economical motels, lodges, and condos. There's good fishing to be had in the Red River itself, and excellent Alpine and Nordic skiing in the surrounding forest.

About 16 mi southeast of Red River, NM 38 leads to the small village of Eagle Nest, the home of **Eagle Nest Lake State Park** (⊠ *42 Marina Way, south of town* ☎ *575/377-1594* ⊕ *www.emnrd.state.nm.us* ⌑ *$5* ☉ *Daily 6 am–9 pm*). This 2,400-acre lake is one of the state's top spots for kokanee salmon and rainbow trout fishing as well as a favorite venue for boating; there are two boat ramps on the lake's northwest side. You may also spy elk, bears, mule deer, and even reclusive mountain lions around this rippling body of water, which in winter is popular for snowmobiling and ice fishing. Camping is not permitted.

Thousands of acres of national forest surround rustic Eagle Nest, population 189, elevation 8,090 feet. The shops and other buildings here evoke New Mexico's mining heritage, while a 1950s-style diner, Kaw-Lija's, serves a memorable burger; you can also grab some takeout food in town and bring it to Eagle Nest Lake for a picnic.

WHERE TO EAT
$ ✕ **Sundance.** Always packed with skiers and winter-sports enthusiasts
MEXICAN   during the cooler months, Sundance is a worthy year-round option for huge portions of stick-to-your-ribs Tex-Mex and New Mexican cooking. You won't find any big surprises here, but the pork tamales

and chiles rellenos are both very good, as is the honey-chipotle-glazed barbecue pork tenderloin. If you like your chiles with heat, specify as much—seasoning is generally milder here than in Taos. There's a good beer list, and margaritas are made with agave wine. ⊠ *401 High St.* ☎ *575/754–2971* ▤ *MC, V.*

$ ✕ **Timbers Steakhouse.** This Wild West-inspired two-story restaurant on
AMERICAN Red River's main drag has a fanciful timber facade and serves best and most varied food in town—it's still tried-and-true American fare, but with high-quality ingredients and occasionally novel preparations. Beyond the excellent chicken-fried and bourbon-glazed steaks, consider breaded catfish with roasted-corn salsa, a first-rate meatloaf with a rich red wine–wild mushroom reduction, and a steak salad over mixed greens with marinated tomatoes and blue cheese. ⊠ *402 W. Main St.,* ☎ *575/754–6242* ▤ *AE, D, MC, V* ☉ *No lunch.*

WHERE TO STAY

$ ▦ **Best Western Rivers Edge.** This reliable property in the center of
HOTEL Red River has ski-in, ski-out access and rooms equipped with sturdy lodge-inspired furnishings, flat-screen TVs, microwaves and refrigerators. Substantial renovations in 2010 greatly improved the lobby and common areas. As the name indicates, it's set right on the Red River. **Pros:** well-maintained; central location. **Cons:** it's pretty easy to hear noise from adjoining rooms. ⊠ *301 W. River St.* ☎ *575/754–1766 or 877/600–9990* ⊕ *www.bestwesternnewmexico.com* ⇲ *30 rooms* ₾ *In-room: a/c, kitchen (some), refrigerator, DVD (some), Wi-Fi. In-hotel: some pets allowed* ▤ *AE, D, DC, MC, V* ⑉ *CP.*

¢ ⚠ **Roadrunner RV Resort.** The Red River runs right through this woodsy mountain campground set on 25 rugged acres. There are two tennis courts and a video-game room. ⊠ *1371 E. Main St., Box 588* ☎ *575/754–2286 or 800/243–2286* ⊕ *www.redrivernm.com/roadrunnerrv* ₾ *Flush toilets, full hookups, drinking water, guest laundry, showers, picnic tables, electricity, public telephone, general store, play area, swimming (river)* ⇲ *141 RV sites, 2 cabins* ▤ *No credit cards* ☉ *Closed mid-Sept.–Apr.*

SPORTS AND THE OUTDOORS

At the **Enchanted Forest Cross-Country Ski Area,** 24 mi of groomed trails loop from the warming hut, stocked with snacks and hot cocoa, through 600 acres of meadows and pines in Carson National Forest, 3 mi east of Red River. ⊠ *417 W. Main St.* ☎ *575/754–6112* ⊕ *www. enchantedforestxc.com* ▧ *$15* ☉ *Late Nov.–Easter, weather permitting.*

The **Red River Ski Area** is in the middle of the historic gold-mining town of Red River, with lifts within walking distance of restaurants and hotels. Slopes for all levels of skiers make the area popular with families, and there's an extensive snowboarding park. There are 57 trails served by seven lifts, and the vertical drop is about 1,600 feet, with annual snowfall averaging about 215 inches. Red River has plenty of rental shops, plus quite a few accommodations and vacation rentals at the base of the slopes or nearby. The resort also books snowmobile tours, and has tubing ($12 per tube). In summer, tubing remains a popular activity on the slopes, along with mountain biking, hiking, disc golf, and chair rides to the top of the mountain. ⊠ *400 Pioneer Rd., off NM*

38 ☎ *575/754–2223* ⊕ *www.redriverskiarea.com* ✉ *Lift tickets $63* ☉ *Late Nov.–late Mar.*

ANGEL FIRE

30 mi south of Red River and 13 mi south of Eagle Nest via NM 38 and U.S. 64.

Named for its blazing sunrise and sunset colors by the Ute Indians who gathered here each autumn, Angel Fire is known these days primarily as a ski resort, generally rated the second best in the state after Taos. In summer there are arts and music events as well as hiking, river rafting, and ballooning. A prominent landmark along U.S. 64, just northeast of town, is the **DAV Vietnam Veterans Memorial** (⊕ *www.angelfirememorial. com*), a 50-foot-high wing-shaped monument built in 1971 by D. Victor Westphall, whose son David was killed in Vietnam.

WHERE TO STAY

$ 🏨 **Angel Fire Resort.** The centerpiece of New Mexico's fastest growing and most highly acclaimed four-season sports resort, this mid-range hotel is set at the mountain's base, a stone's throw from the chairlift. Indeed, winter is the busiest season here, but during the warmer months it's a popular retreat with hikers, golfers, and other outdoorsy types who appreciate retiring each evening to spacious digs. Even the standard rooms are 500 square feet, and the larger deluxe units have feather pillows, ski-boot warmers, and fireplaces. The resort also manages a variety of privately owned and somewhat more upscale condo units, from studios to three-bedrooms, which are available nightly or long-term. There are several decent restaurants at the resort, none worth a drive to Angel Fire solely on the merit of their cuisine, but the Roasted Clove is quite good. **Pros:** slope-side location; fantastic views. **Cons:** rooms and public areas need updating. ✉ *10 Miller La., Box Drawer B* ☎ *575/377–6401 or 800/633–7463* ⊕ *www.angelfireresort.com* ⇗ *139 rooms* ⌂ *In-room: refrigerator, Wi-Fi. In-hotel: 4 restaurants, bars, golf course, tennis courts, bicycles* ▭ *AE, D, MC, V.*

CAMPING

¢   🏕 **Enchanted Moon Campground.** In Valle Escondido, off U.S. 64 near Angel Fire, this wooded area with a trout pond has views of the Sangre de Cristos. Features include horse stalls, a chuckwagon, and an indoor recreation area with video games. ✉ *7 Valle Escondido Rd., Valle Escondido* ☎ *575/758–3338* ⊕ *www.emooncampground.com* ⌂ *Flush toilets, full hookups, drinking water, showers, grills, picnic tables, electricity, play area, Wi-Fi* ⇗ *27 RV sites, 22 tent sites* ▭ *No credit cards* ☉ *Closed mid-Oct.–Apr.*

NIGHTLIFE AND THE ARTS

Music from Angel Fire (☎ *575/377–3233 or 888/377–3300* ⊕ *www. musicfromangelfire.org*) is a nightly series of classical (and occasional jazz) concerts presented at venues around Angel Fire and Taos for about three weeks from late August to early September. Tickets cost $20 to $30 per concert, and the festival—begun in 1983—continues to grow in popularity and esteem each year.

SPORTS AND THE OUTDOORS

The 18-hole golf course at the **Angel Fire Country Club** (✉ *Country Club Dr. off NM 434* ☎ *575/377–3055* ⊕ *www.angelfireresort.com*), one of the highest in the nation, is open May to mid-October, weather permitting. The challenging front 9 runs a bit longer than the back and takes in great views of aspen- and pine-shaded canyons; the shorter back 9 has more water play and somewhat tighter fairways. Greens fees are $65 to $85.

The beautifully maintained **Angel Fire Resort** is a popular ski destination that's not as acclaimed as Taos Ski Valley but has steadily developed cachet as one of the state's better venues. There are 74 runs (about half are intermediate, and a quarter each expert and beginner), five lifts, 16 mi of cross-country trails, and four terrain parks; the vertical drop is about 2,100 feet. Other amenities include a 1,000-foot snow-tubing hill, a ski and snowboard school, snow biking (also taught at the school), ice fishing, a children's ski-and-snowboard center, and superb snow-making capacity (annual snowfall averages about 215 inches). ✉ *N. Angel Fire Rd., off NM 434* ☎ *575/377–6401 resort, 575/377–4222 snow conditions* ⊕ *www.angelfireresort.com* ✉ *Lift tickets $64* ⊗ *Mid-Dec.–late Mar.*

Travel Smart Santa Fe, Taos & Albuquerque

WORD OF MOUTH

"Anything even remotely outside the Plaza area of [Santa Fe] will require a car. Do you want to see any outdoorsy things? Visit a Pueblo, see Taos, go hiking? All of these will require a car. If you want to shop, eat, go to galleries, go to museums, you can do that without a car."

—DebitNM

GETTING HERE AND AROUND

A car is the best way to take in the entire state. Public transportation options do exist in some metropolitan areas, but they are not very convenient for visitors. City buses and taxi service are available only in a few larger communities such as Albuquerque and Santa Fe. Don't expect to find easy transportation for rural excursions.

▌ AIR TRAVEL

To reach north-central New Mexico by air, it's best to fly into Albuquerque. Visitors to Taos may also want to consider flying into Denver, which is an hour or two farther than Albuquerque but receives a high number of direct domestic and international flights. Santa Fe receives very limited commercial flights from Dallas and Los Angeles. From Albuquerque airport, ground transportation is available to both Santa Fe and Taos. Although Albuquerque has a small, clean, and user-friendly airport, it also has relatively few direct flights compared with larger cities around the country. With a few exceptions, travelers coming from the East Coast and to a certain extent the West Coast have to connect through other airports to fly here.

Flying time between Albuquerque and Los Angeles is 2 hours for direct flights (available only on Southwest Airlines and United Airlines) and 3½ to 4 when connecting through another airport; Chicago, 2 hours and 45 minutes; New York, 5½ to 6½ hours (there are no direct flights, so this factors in time for connections); Dallas, 1 hour and 45 minutes.

AIRPORTS

The major gateway to North-Central New Mexico is Albuquerque International Sunport (ABQ), which is 65 mi southwest of Santa Fe and 130 mi south of Taos. Some travelers to Taos prefer to fly into Denver (four to five hours' drive), which has far more direct flights to the rest of the country than Albuquerque—it's a scenic drive, too.

▌TIP→ **Long layovers don't have to be only about sitting around or shopping. These days they can be about burning off vacation calories. Check out ⊕ www.airportgyms. com for lists of health clubs that are in or near many U.S. and Canadian airports.**

Airport Information Albuquerque International Sunport (☎ 505/244–7700 ⊕ www. cabq.gov/airport). Denver International Airport (☎ 303/342–2000 or 800/247-2336 ⊕ www.flydenver.com). El Paso International Airport (☎ 915/780–4749 ⊕ www. elpasointernationalairport.com).

MUNICIPAL AIRPORTS

Cavern City Air Terminal (CNM), Carlsbad (☎ 575/887–3060). Clovis Municipal Airport (CVN), Carlsbad (☎ 575/389–1056). Four Corners Regional Airport (FMN), Farmington (☎ 505/599–1395). Grant County Airport (SVC), Silver City area (☎ 575/388–4554). Roswell Municipal Airport (ROW) (☎ 575/624–6700). Santa Fe Municipal Airport (SAF) (☎ 505/955–2900).

FLIGHTS

Most major domestic airlines provide service to Albuquerque. Mesa Airlines offers shuttle flights between Albuquerque and Farmington, Colorado Springs, Roswell, Hobbs, and Carlsbad. Great Lakes Airlines flies from Denver to Santa Fe and from Albuquerque to Silver City and Clovis (and then from Clovis on to Amarillo, Texas). Frontier Airlines flies daily from Denver to Albuquerque. Skywest Airlines, a subsidiary of Delta, flies between Albuquerque and Salt Lake City.

Ask the local tourist board about hotel and local transportation packages that include tickets to major museum exhibits or other special events.

GROUND TRANSPORTATION

From the terminal at Albuquerque Airport, it's 5 to 20 minutes by car to get anywhere in town. Taxis, available at clearly marked stands, charge about $10 to $25 for most trips from the airport to around Albuquerque. Sun Tran Buses stop at the sunburst signs every 30 minutes; the fare is $1. Some hotels provide shuttle service to and from the airport. Airport Shuttle and Sunport Shuttle both cost less than $10 to most Downtown locations.

Shuttle buses between the Albuquerque International Sunport and Santa Fe take about 1 hour and 20 minutes and cost about $20 to $25 each way. Shuttle service runs from Albuquerque to Taos and nearby ski areas; the ride takes 2¾ to 3 hours and costs $40 to $50.

There's also Greyhound bus service between Albuquerque International Sunport and many New Mexico towns and cities; times are much more limited but fares are considerably less than those charged by the shuttle services listed here.

TRANSFERS BETWEEN AIRPORTS

Around Albuquerque Airport Shuttle (☎ 505/765–1234). ABQ Ride (☎ 505/843–9200 ⊕ www.cabq.gov/transit). Sunport Shuttle (☎ 505/883–4966 or 866/505–4966 ⊕ www.sunportshuttle.com)

Between Albuquerque & Santa Fe Faust's Transportation (☎ 575/758–3410 or 888/830–3410 ⊕ www.newmexiconet. com/trans/faust/faust.html). Sandia Shuttle Express (☎ 505/474–5696 or 888/775–5696 ⊕ www.sandiashuttle.com).

Between Albuquerque & Taos Faust's Transportation (☎ 575/758–3410 or 888/830–3410 ⊕ www.newmexiconet.com/ trans/faust/faust.html).

▮ BUS TRAVEL

Bus service on Texas, New Mexico & Oklahoma Coaches, affiliated with Greyhound Lines, connects Albuquerque, with many towns and cities elsewhere in the state and throughout the Southwest and Rocky Mountain regions.

Greyhound offers the **North America Discovery Pass,** which allows unlimited travel in the United States (and certain parts of Canada and Mexico) within any 7-, 15-, 30-, or 60-day period ($239–$539, depending on length of the pass). You can also buy similar passes covering different areas (America and Canada, the West Coast of North America, the East Coast of North America, Canada exclusively), and international travelers can purchase international versions of these same passes, which offer a greater variety of travel periods and cost considerably less. Greyhound also has senior-citizen, military, children's, and student discounts, which apply to individual fares and to the Discovery Pass.

BUS INFORMATION

Greyhound/Texas, New Mexico & Oklahoma Coaches (☎ 800/231–2222 ⊕ www. greyhound.com).

▮ CAR TRAVEL

A car is a basic necessity in New Mexico, as even the few cities are challenging to get around strictly using public transportation. Distances are considerable, but you can make excellent time on long stretches of interstate and other four-lane highways with speed limits of up to 75 mph. If you wander off major thoroughfares, slow down. Speed limits here generally are only 55 mph, and for good reason. Many such roadways have no shoulders; on many twisting and turning mountain roads speed limits dip to 25 mph. For the most part, the scenery you'll take in while driving makes the drive a form of sightseeing in itself.

Interstate 25 runs north from the state line at El Paso through Albuquerque and Santa Fe, then angles northeast to the Colorado line through Raton.

U.S. highways connect all major cities and towns in the state with a good network of paved roads—many of the state's U.S. highways, including large stretches of U.S. 285 and U.S. 550, have four lanes and high speed limits. You can make nearly as good time on these roads as you can on interstates. State roads are mostly paved two-lane thoroughfares, but some are well-graded gravel. Roads on Native American lands are designated by wooden, arrow-shaped signs and you'd best adhere to the speed limit; some roads on reservation or forest land aren't paved. Even in cities, you're likely to find a few surface streets are unpaved and often bumpy and narrow—Santa Fe, for instance, has a higher percentage of dirt roads than any other state capital in the nation.

Morning and evening rush-hour traffic is light in most of New Mexico, although it can get a bit heavy in Albuquerque. Keep in mind also that from most cities in New Mexico, there are only one or two main routes to Albuquerque, so if you encounter an accident or some other delay on a major thoroughfare into Albuquerque (or even Santa Fe), you can expect significant delays. It's a big reason to leave early and give yourself extra time when attempting to drive to Albuquerque to catch a plane.

Parking is plentiful and either free or inexpensive in most New Mexico towns, even Albuquerque and Santa Fe. During busy times, however, such as summer weekends, parking in Santa Fe, Taos, and parts of Albuquerque can be tougher to find.

Here are some common distances and approximate travel times between Albuquerque and several popular destinations, assuming no lengthy stops and averaging the 65 to 75 mph speed limits: Santa Fe is 65 mi and about an hour; Taos is 135 mi and about 2½ hours; Farmington is 185 mi and 3 hours; Gallup is 140 mi and 2 hours; Denver is 450 mi and 6 to 7 hours; Phoenix is 465 mi and 6½ to 7½ hours; Silver City is 230 mi and 3½ to 4 hours; Las Cruces is 225 mi and 3½ hours; Carlsbad is 280 mi and 4½ to 5 hours; El Paso is 270 mi and 4 hours; Dallas is 650 mi and 10 to 11 hours

GASOLINE

There's a lot of high, dry, lonesome country in New Mexico—it's possible to go 50 or 60 mi in some of the less-populated areas between gas stations. For a safe trip **keep your gas tank full.** Self-service gas stations are the norm in New Mexico, though in some of the less-populated regions you can find stations with full service. The cost of unleaded gas at self-service stations in New Mexico is close to the U.S. average, but it's usually 15¢ to 30¢ more per gallon in Santa Fe, Taos, and certain spots off the beaten path.

RENTAL CARS

All the major car-rental agencies are represented at Albuquerque's airport, and you can also find a limited number of car-rental agencies in other communities throughout the state.

Rates at Albuquerque's airport begin at around $25 a day and $150 a week for an economy car with air-conditioning, automatic transmission, and unlimited mileage; although you should expect to pay more during busier times.

If you want to explore the backcountry, consider renting an SUV, which will cost you about $40 to $60 per day and $200 to $400 per week, depending on the size of the SUV and the time of year. Dollar in Albuquerque has a fleet of smaller SUVs, still good on dirt roads and with much better mileage than larger ones, and they often run extremely reasonable deals, as low as $160 a week. You can save money by renting at a nonairport location, as you then are able to avoid the hefty (roughly) 10% in extra taxes charged at airports. Check the different agencies' websites as there are often excellent "web-only" car rental offers.

ROAD CONDITIONS

Arroyos (dry washes or gullies) are bridged on major roads, but lesser roads often dip down through them. These can be a hazard during the rainy season, late

June to early September. Even if it looks shallow, **don't try to cross an arroyo filled with water**—it may have an axle-breaking hole in the middle. Wait a little while, and it will drain off almost as quickly as it filled. If you stall in a flooded arroyo, get out of the car and onto high ground if possible. In the backcountry, never drive (or walk) in a dry arroyo bed if the sky is dark anywhere upstream. A sudden thunderstorm 15 mi away could send a raging flash flood down a wash in a matter of minutes.

Unless they are well graded and graveled, **avoid unpaved roads in New Mexico when they are wet.** The soil contains a lot of caliche, or clay, which gets slick when mixed with water. During winter storms roads may be shut down entirely; call the State Highway Department for road conditions.

At certain times in fall, winter and spring, New Mexico winds can be vicious for large vehicles like RVs. Driving conditions can be particularly treacherous in passages through foothills or mountains where wind gusts and ice are concentrated.

New Mexico has a high incidence of drunk driving and uninsured motorists. Factor in the state's high speed limits, many winding and steep roads, and eye-popping scenery, and you can see how important it is to drive as alertly and defensively as possible. On the plus side, major traffic jams are a rarity even in cities—and recent improvements to the state's busiest intersection, the I–40/I–25 interchange in Albuquerque, has helped to reduce rush-hour backups there. Additionally, a major highway widening and improvement along U.S. 285/84, north of Santa Fe, has also greatly smoothed the flow and speed of traffic up toward Taos.

State Highway Department (☎ 800/432-4269 ⊕ www.nmshtd.state.nm.us).

ROADSIDE EMERGENCIES

In the event of a roadside emergency, call 911. Depending on the location, either the New Mexico State Police or the county sheriff's department will respond. Call the city or village police department if you encounter trouble within the limits of a municipality. Native American reservations have tribal police headquarters, and rangers assist travelers within U.S. Forest Service boundaries.

▌ TRAIN TRAVEL

Amtrak's *Southwest Chief,* from Chicago to Los Angeles via Kansas City, stops in Raton, Las Vegas, Lamy (near Santa Fe), Albuquerque, and Gallup daily.

The state's commuter train line, the *New Mexico Rail Runner Express* runs from Santa Fe south through Bernalillo and into the city of Albuquerque, continuing south through Los Lunas to the suburb of Belén, covering a distance of about 100 mi. The Rail Runner offers a very inexpensive alternative to getting to and from the Albuquerque airport to Santa Fe.

Amtrak offers a **North America rail pass** that gives you unlimited travel within the United States and Canada within any 30-day period ($389-$749), and several kinds of **USA Rail passes** (for non-U.S. residents only) offering unlimited travel for 15 to 45 days. Amtrak also has senior-citizen, children's, disability, and student discounts, as well as occasional deals that allow a second or third accompanying passenger to travel for half price or even free. The **Amtrak Vacations** program customizes entire vacations, including hotels, car rentals, and tours.

Sample one-way fares on the *Southwest Chief* are $120 from Chicago to Lamy; $50 to $70 Denver to Las Vegas; and $65 Albuquerque to Los Angeles.

The *New Mexico Rail Runner Express* runs daily. Tickets cost $1 to $4 one-way, depending on the distance traveled; passes are available.

Contact Amtrak (☎ 800/872-7245 ⊕ www. amtrak.com). **New Mexico Rail Runner Express** (☎ 866/795-7245 ⊕ www. nmrailrunner.com).

ESSENTIALS

■ ACCOMMODATIONS

With the exceptions of Santa Fe and Taos, two rather upscale tourist-driven destinations with some of the higher lodging rates in the Southwest, New Mexico has fairly low hotel prices. Albuquerque is loaded with chain hotels, and four or five new ones seem to open each year, further saturating the market and driving down prices. During busy times or certain festivals (the Balloon Fiesta in Albuquerque, some of the art markets and events in Taos and Santa Fe), it can be extremely difficult to find a hotel room, and prices can be steep. Check to make sure there's not a major event planned for the time you're headed to New Mexico, and book well ahead if so. You'll find bigger big selection and some very good deals by checking the usual major travel sites, such as⊕ *www.expedia.com.* You'll be charged a hotel tax, which varies among towns and counties, throughout New Mexico.

Most hotels and other lodgings require you to give your credit-card details before they will confirm your reservation. If you don't feel comfortable e-mailing this information, ask if you can fax it (some places even prefer faxes). However you book, get confirmation in writing and have a copy of it handy when you check in.

If you book through an online travel agent, discounter, or wholesaler, you might even want to confirm your reservation with the hotel before leaving home—just to be sure everything was processed correctly.

Be sure you understand the hotel's cancellation policy. Some places allow you to cancel without any kind of penalty—even if you prepaid to secure a discounted rate—if you cancel at least 24 hours in advance. Others require you to cancel a week in advance or penalize you the cost of one night. Small inns and B&Bs are most likely to require you to cancel far in advance. Most hotels allow children under a certain age to stay in their parents' room at no extra charge, but others charge for them as extra adults; find out the cutoff age for discounts.

■TIP➜ Assume that hotels operate on the European Plan (EP, no meals) unless we specify that they use the Breakfast Plan (BP, with full breakfast), Continental Plan (CP, Continental breakfast), Full American Plan (FAP, all meals), Modified American Plan (MAP, breakfast and dinner) or are all-inclusive (AI, all meals and most activities).

APARTMENT AND HOUSE RENTALS

Some parts of New Mexico are popular for short- and long-term vacation rentals, such as Santa Fe, Taos, and Ruidoso. See the book's individual regional chapters for rental agency listings in these locations.

BED AND BREAKFASTS

B&Bs in New Mexico run the gamut from rooms in locals' homes to grandly restored adobe or Victorian homes. Rates in Santa Fe and Taos can be high, but there are several properties that offer excellent value for very comparable prices; they're a little lower in Albuquerque and rival those of chain motels in the outlying areas.

See the book's individual chapters for names of local reservation agencies.

Reservations Bed & Breakfast.com (☎ 512/322–2710 or 800/462–2632 ⊕ www. bedandbreakfast.com) also sends out an online newsletter. **Bed & Breakfast Inns Online** (☎ 800/215–7365 ⊕ www.bbonline.com). **BnB Finder.com** (☎ 888/469-6663 ⊕ www. bnbfinder.com). **New Mexico Bed and Breakfast Association** (☎ 800/661-6649 ⊕ www. nmbba.org).

HOME EXCHANGES

With a direct home exchange you stay in someone else's home while they stay in yours. Some outfits also deal with vacation homes, so you're not actually staying in someone's full-time residence, just their vacant weekend place.

Exchange Clubs Home Exchange.com (☎ 800/877–8723 ⊕ www.homeexchange. com); $9.95 per month for a membership. **HomeLink International** (☎ 800/638–3841 ⊕ www.homelink.org); $119 yearly for Web access and listing in the catalog. **Intervac U.S** (☎ 800/756–4663 ⊕ www.intervac-homeexchange.com).; $99.99 for membership (includes Web access and a catalog).

HOSTELS

Hostels offer bare-bones lodging at low, low prices—often in shared dorm rooms with shared baths—to people of all ages, though the primary market is young travelers, especially students. Most hostels serve breakfast; dinner and/or shared cooking facilities may also be available. In some hostels you aren't allowed to be in your room during the day, and there may be a curfew at night. Nevertheless, hostels provide a sense of community, with public rooms where travelers often gather to share stories. Many hostels are affiliated with Hostelling International (HI), an umbrella group of hostel associations with some 4,500 member properties in more than 70 countries. Other hostels are completely independent and may be nothing more than a really cheap hotel.

Membership in any HI association, open to travelers of all ages, allows you to stay in HI-affiliated hostels at member rates. One-year membership is about $28 for adults; hostels charge about $10 to $30 per night. Members have priority if the hostel is full; they're also eligible for discounts around the world, even on rail and bus travel in some countries.

Several New Mexico communities have hostels, including Albuquerque, Cedar Crest (on the Turquoise Trail, near Albuquerque), Santa Fe, and Taos.

Information Hostelling International—USA (☎ 301/495–1240 ⊕ www.hiusa.org).

▮ EATING OUT

New Mexico is justly famous for its distinctive cuisine, which utilizes ingredients and recipes common to Mexico, the Rockies, the Southwest, and the West's Native American communities. Most longtime residents like their chile sauces and salsas with some fire—throughout North-central New Mexico chile is sometimes celebrated for its ability to set off smoke alarms. Most restaurants offer a choice of red or green chile with one type typically being milder than the other. If you want both kinds with your meal, when your server asks you if you'd like "red or green," reply "Christmas." If you're not used to spicy foods, you may find even the average chile served with chips to be quite a lot hotter than back home—so proceed with caution (you can always request it be served on the side). Excellent barbecue and steaks also can be found throughout New Mexico, with other specialties being local game (especially elk and bison) and trout. The restaurants we list are the cream of the crop in each price category.

MEALS AND MEALTIMES

Statewide, many kitchens stop serving around 8 pm, so **don't arrive too late** if you're looking forward to a leisurely dinner.

Unless otherwise noted, the restaurants listed in this guide are open daily for lunch and dinner.

PAYING

Credit cards are widely accepted at restaurants in major towns and cities and even most smaller communities, but in the latter places, you may occasionally encounter smaller, independent restaurants that are cash only.

For guidelines on tipping see Tipping below.

RESERVATIONS AND DRESS

Regardless of where you are, it's a good idea to make a reservation if you can. In some places (the top restaurants in Santa Fe, for example), it's expected. We only mention them specifically when reservations are essential (there's no other way you'll ever get a table) or when they are not accepted. For popular restaurants in Santa Fe, book as far ahead as you can, and reconfirm as soon as you arrive. (Large parties should always call ahead to check the reservations policy.) We mention dress only when men are required to wear a jacket or a jacket and tie—which is a rarity, indeed.

Online reservation services make it easy to book a table before you even leave home. OpenTable covers most states, including 20 major cities, and has limited listings in Canada, Mexico, the United Kingdom, and elsewhere. DinnerBroker has restaurants throughout the United States as well as a few in Canada.

Contacts OpenTable (⊕ *www.opentable.com*).

WINES, BEER AND SPIRITS

Like many other states, New Mexico has some fine microbreweries; Sierra Blanca Brewing Co. and Santa Fe Brewing Co. are two of the best known. New Mexico also has a growing number of wineries, some of them producing first-rate vintages. Franciscan monks first planted their vines here before moving more successfully to northern California, and the state's winemaking industry has really taken off since the late '90s. The New Mexico Wine Growers Association provides extensive information on the many fine wineries around the state as well as details on several prominent wine festivals (⊕ *www.nmwine.com*).

▌ EMERGENCIES

In an emergency dial 911.

ALBUQUERQUE

Hospitals **Presbyterian Hospital** (⊠ *1100 Central Ave. SE, Downtown* ☎ *505/841–1234*). **University Hospital** (⊠ *2211 Lomas Blvd. NE, University of New Mexico* ☎ *505/272-2111*).

SANTA FE

Christus St. Vincent Hospital (⊠ *455 St. Michael's Dr.* ☎ *505/983-3361*).

TAOS

Holy Cross Hospital (⊠ *1397 Weimer Rd.* ☎ *505/758-8883* ⊕ *www.taoshospital.org*).

▌ HOURS OF OPERATION

Although hours differ little in New Mexico from other parts of the United States, some businesses do keep shorter hours here than in more densely populated parts of the country. In particular, outside of the larger towns in New Mexico, it can be hard to find shops open past 6pm and restaurants open past 8 or 9 in the evening. Within the state, businesses tend to keep later hours in Albuquerque and Santa Fe than in rural areas.

Most major museums and attractions are open daily or six days a week (with Monday or Tuesday being the most likely day of closing). Hours are often shorter on Saturday and especially Sunday, and a handful of museums in larger cities stay open late one nights a week, usually Friday. New Mexico's less populated areas also have quite a few smaller museums—historical societies, small art galleries, highly specialized collections—that open only a few days a week, and sometimes only by appointment during slow times. It's always a good idea to call ahead if you're planning to go out of your way to visit a smaller museum.

Banks are usually open weekdays from 9 to 44:30or a bit later and some Saturday mornings, the post office from 8 to 5 or 6 weekdays and often on Saturday mornings. Shops in urban and touristy areas, particularly in indoor and strip malls, typically open at 9 or 10 daily and stay open until anywhere from 6 pm to 9 pm on weekdays and Saturday, and until 5 or 6 on Sunday. Hours vary greatly, so call ahead when in doubt.

On major highways and in densely populated areas you can usually find at least one or two supermarkets, drugstores, and gas stations open 24 hours, and in Albuquerque, you can find a smattering of all-night fast-food restaurants, diners, and coffeehouses. Bars and discos stay open until 1 or 2 am.

▌ MONEY

In North-Central New Mexico, Santa Fe is by far the priciest city: meals, gasoline, and motel rates are all significantly higher in the state's capital. Overall travel costs in Santa Fe, including dining and lodging, typically run 30% to 50% higher than in Albuquerque and other communities in the state. Taos, too, can be a little expensive because it's such a popular tourist destination, but you have more choices for economizing there than in Santa Fe. As the state's largest metropolitan area, Albuquerque has a full range of price choices.

CREDIT CARDS

Throughout this guide, the following abbreviations are used: **AE**, American Express; **D**, Discover; **DC**, Diners Club; **MC**, MasterCard; and **V**, Visa.

It's a good idea to inform your credit-card company before you travel, especially if you're going abroad and don't travel internationally very often. Otherwise, the credit-card company might put a hold on your card owing to unusual activity—not a good thing halfway through your trip. Record all your credit-card numbers—as well as the phone numbers to call if your cards are lost or stolen—in a safe place, so you're prepared should something go wrong. Both MasterCard and Visa have general numbers you can call (collect if you're abroad) if your card is lost, but you're better off calling the number of your issuing bank, since Master-Card and Visa usually just transfer you to your bank; your bank's number is usually printed on your card.

Reporting Lost Cards American Express (☎ 800/992-3404 in U.S.; 336/393-1111 collect from abroad ⊕ www.americanexpress. com). **Diners Club** (☎ 800/234-6377 in U.S.; 303/799-1504 collect from abroad ⊕ www. dinersclub.com). **Discover** (☎ 800/347-2683 in U.S.; 801/902-3100 collect from abroad ⊕ www.discovercard.com). **MasterCard** (☎ 800/622-7747 in U.S.; 636/722-7111 collect from abroad ⊕ www.mastercard.com). **Visa** (☎ 800/847-2911 in U.S.; 410/581-9994 collect from abroad ⊕ www.visa.com).

▌ PACKING

Typical of the Southwest and southern Rockies, temperatures can vary considerably in North-Central New Mexico from sunup to sundown. Generally, you should **pack for warm days and chilly nights** from late spring through early fall, and for genuinely cold days and freezing nights in winter if you're headed to Taos and Santa Fe (Albuquerque runs about 10 to 15 degrees warmer). Because temperatures vary greatly even within this relatively compact area, it's important to check local weather conditions before you leave home and pack accordingly. In April for instance, you may need to pack for night-time lows in the 20s and daytime highs in the 60s in Taos, but daytime highs in the low 80s and nighttime lows in the 40s in Albuquerque. Any time of year pack at least a few warm outfits, gloves, a hat and a jacket; in winter pack very warm clothes—coats, parkas, and whatever else your body's thermostat and your ultimate destination dictate. Sweaters and jackets are also needed in summer at higher elevations, because though days are warm, nights can dip well below 50°F. And **bring comfortable shoes**; you're likely to be doing a lot of walking.

New Mexico is one of the most informal and laid-back areas of the country, which for many is part of its appeal. Probably no more than three or four restaurants in the entire state enforce a dress code, even for dinner, though men are likely to feel more comfortable wearing a jacket in the major hotel dining rooms. If you need a rule, stick to business casual and you'll feel comfortable wherever you go.

The Western look has, of course, never lost its hold on the West, though Western-style clothes now get mixed with styles from all over the globe. You can wear your boots and big belt buckles anywhere in the state, even Albuquerque, but if you come strolling through the lobby of the Eldorado Hotel looking like Hopalong Cassidy, you'll get some funny looks.

Bring skin moisturizer; even people who rarely need this elsewhere in the country can suffer from dry and itchy skin in New Mexico. Sunscreen is a necessity. And **bring sunglasses** to protect your eyes from the glare of lakes or ski slopes, not to mention the brightness present everywhere. High altitude can cause headaches and dizziness, so at a minimum drink at least half your body weight in ounces in water (150lb person=75 oz water), and eat plenty of juicy fruit. When planning even a short day trip, especially if there's hiking or exercise involved, always pack a bottle or two of water—it's very easy to become dehydrated in New Mexico. Check with your doctor about medication to alleviate symptoms.

▌ RESOURCES

ONLINE TRAVEL TOOLS
Check out the New Mexico Home page (⊕ *www.state.nm.us*) for information on state government, and for links to state agencies on doing business, working, learning, living, and visiting in the Land of Enchantment. A terrific general resource for just about every kind of recreational activity is⊕ *www.gorp.com*; just click on the New Mexico link under "Destinations," and you'll be flooded with links to myriad topics, from wildlife refuges to ski trips to backpacking advice. Also excellent for information on the state's recreation pursuits is the New Mexico Outdoor Sports Guide (⊕ *www.nmosg.com*). Check the site of the New Mexico Film Office (⊕ *www.nmfilm.com*) for a list of movies shot in New Mexico as well as links to downloadable clips of upcoming made–in–New Mexico movies. A wide range of reviews and links to dining, culture, and services

in Albuquerque and Santa Fe is available at⊕ *www.citysearch.com* and⊕ *www.yelp.com*, and⊕ *www.999dine.com* is a site that sells steeply discounted meal certificates to dozens of top restaurants in Albuquerque, Santa Fe, and Taos. Visit⊕ *www.farmersmarketsnm.org* for information on the dozens of great farmers' markets around the state, and see⊕ *www.nmwine.com* for tours and details related to the region's burgeoning wine-making industry.

ALL ABOUT NEW MEXICO
Safety **Transportation Security Administration** (*TSA* ⊕ *www.tsa.gov*)

Other Resources **CIA World Factbook** (⊕ *www.odci.gov/cia/publications/factbook/index.html*) has profiles of every country in the world. It's a good source if you need some quick facts and figures.

Timeanddate.com (⊕ *www.timeanddate.com/worldclock*) can help you figure out the correct time anywhere.

Weather.com (⊕ *www.weather.com*) is the Web site for the Weather Channel.

VISITOR INFORMATION
The New Mexico Department of Tourism can provide general information on the state, but you'll find more specific and useful information by consulting the local chambers of commerce, tourism offices, and convention and visitors bureaus in individual communities throughout the state (⇨ *See individual chapter Essentials*).

Contacts **New Mexico Department of Tourism** (☎ 505/827–7400 ⊕ *www.newmexico.org*). **Indian Pueblo Cultural Center** (☎ 505/843–7270 or 866/855–7902 ⊕ *www.indianpueblo.org*). **USDA Forest Service, Southwestern Region** (☎ 505/842–3292; 877/864–6985 *for fire restrictions and closures* ⊕ *www.fs.fed.us/r3*).

PASSPORTS AND VISAS
PASSPORTS
We're always surprised at how few Americans have passports—only 25% at this writing. This number is expected to grow

in coming years, when it becomes impossible to reenter the United States from trips to neighboring Canada or Mexico without one. Remember this: a passport verifies both your identity and nationality—a great reason to have one.

U.S. passports are valid for 10 years. You must apply in person if you're getting a passport for the first time; if your previous passport was lost, stolen, or damaged; or if your previous passport has expired and was issued more than 15 years ago or when you were under 16. All children under 16 must appear in person to apply for or renew a passport. Both parents must accompany any child under 14 (or send a notarized statement with their permission) and provide proof of their relationship to the child.

There are 13 regional passport offices, as well as 7,000 passport acceptance facilities in post offices, public libraries, and other governmental offices. If you're renewing a passport, you can do so by mail. Forms are available at passport acceptance facilities and online.

The cost to apply for a new passport is $140 for adults, $120 for children under 16; renewals are $$120-140. Allow six weeks for processing, both for first-time passports and renewals. For an expediting fee of $60 you can reduce this time to about two weeks. If your trip is less than two weeks away, you can get a passport even more rapidly by going to a passport office with the necessary documentation. Private expediters can get things done in as little as 48 hours, but charge hefty fees for their services.

■TIP➔ Before your trip, make two copies of your passport's data page (one for someone at home and another for you to carry separately). Or scan the page and e-mail it to someone at home and/or yourself.

U.S. Passport Information U.S. Department of State (☎ 877/487–2778 ⊕ travel.state.gov/passport).

U.S. Passport & Visa Expediters A. Briggs Passport & Visa Expeditors (☎ 800/806–0581 or 202/338–0111⊕ www.abriggs.com). American Passport Express (☎ 800/455–5166 or ⊕ www.americanpassport.com). Passport Express (☎ 800/362–8196 ⊕ www.passportexpress.com). Travel Document Systems (☎ 800/874–5100 or 202/638–3800 ⊕ www.traveldocs.com). Travel the World Visas (☎ 866/886–8472 202/223-8822⊕ www.world-visa.com).

▌TAXES

The standard state gross receipts tax rate is 5%, but municipalities and counties enact additional charges at varying rates. Sales tax in Santa Fe is just under 8%. If you're on a budget and plan on renting a car and/or staying in hotels, be sure to ask for the exact amount of your lodgers and rental car taxes, as they can be quite steep and can make a big dent in a tight budget.

▌TIME

New Mexico observes mountain standard time, switching over with most of the rest of the country to daylight saving time in the spring through fall. In New Mexico, you'll be two hours behind New York and one hour ahead of Arizona (except during daylight saving time, which Arizona does not observe) and California.

▌TIPPING

The customary tipping rate for taxi drivers is 15% to 20%, with a minimum of $2; bellhops are usually given $2 per bag in luxury hotels, $1 per bag elsewhere. Hotel maids should be tipped $2 per day of your stay. A doorman who hails or helps you into a cab can be tipped $1 to $2. You should also tip your hotel concierge for services rendered; the size of the tip depends on the difficulty of your request, as well as the quality of the concierge's work. For an ordinary dinner reservation or tour arrangements, $3 to $5 should do; if the concierge scores seats at a popular restaurant or show or performs unusual services (getting your laptop repaired, finding a good pet-sitter, etc.), $10 or more is appropriate.

Waiters should be tipped 15% to 20%, though at higher-end restaurants, a solid 20% is more the norm. Many restaurants add a gratuity to the bill for parties of six or more. Ask what the percentage is if the menu or bill doesn't state it. Tip $1 per drink you order at the bar, though if at an upscale establishment, those $15 martinis might warrant a $2 tip.

INDEX

PHOTO CREDITS

NOTES

NOTES

NOTES

NOTES

NOTES

NOTES

NOTES

ABOUT OUR WRITERS

Former Fodor's staff editor **Andrew Collins** lives in Portland Oregon, but resided in New Mexico for many years and still visits often (usually stuffing his carry-on bag with fresh green chiles). A long-time contributor to this guide, he's also the author of Fodor's *Gay Guide to the USA* and has written or contributed to dozens of other guidebooks. He's the expert "guide" on gay travel for About.com, and he writes for a variety of publications (including *Travel + Leisure, New Mexico Journey, Sunset, Out Traveler,* and *New Mexico Magazine*).

Georgia de Katona, who updated the Santa Fe chapter, is a freelance writer and Kundalini yoga instructor. A born-and-bred Westerner, she has spent her life exploring the nooks and crannies of the West by foot, car, bicycle, and motorcyle. Exploring Latin America has occupied much of her travel for the past few years, but it's the beauty of the high desert and the quirky individuality of Western people that always makes coming home to Santa Fe a pleasure.